THE POLITICAL ECONOMY OF MODERN IRAN

THE POLITICAL ECONOMY OF MODERN IRAN

Despotism and Pseudo-Modernism, 1926–1979

Homa Katouzian

M

First published 1981 by
THE MACMILLAN PRESS LTD
London and Basingstoke
Companies and representatives throughout the world

ISBN 0 333 26961 6

Printed in Hong Kong

TO THE MEMORY OF DR MUHAMMAD MUṢADDIQ

for his development of a genuinely *Iranian* concept of democracy, and his lifelong struggle for its realisation

Muslim Persia must be Muslim and Iranian

Sayyed Ḥasan Mudarris, 1921

The people could read about . . . human rights in the Constitution, but if the state was not willing, they could not enjoy them, or put them to use. . . . I am an Iranian and a Muslim, and, as long as I am alive, I will fight against anything that would threaten the Iranian and Islamic way of life.

Dr Muhammad Muṣaddiq, 1945

We must help [*the other left- and right-wing political forces*] *to have faith in . . . the power of their own* [*Iranian*] *people. . . . The preacher . . . the speaker . . . the white-collar worker . . . the peasant and worker . . . the student . . . who speak about social justice. . . . In principle, the only standard available for determining the aims of a party is the means that that party employs: if the means and methods used by a party contradict its declared aims, then we should conclude that that party lacks the objectives which it claims to have, and that its real aims are those which are found at the end of the road that it follows.*

Khalīl Malekī, 1951

Sleep happily, Cyrus, because we are awake!

The Shah, 1971

Contents

Preface

I am an Iranian economist, and since my childhood I have been reading liberally both in the 'non-economic' social sciences and in humanities. During those marvellous formative years I developed a sense of social consciousness and commitment, and began to participate in political activity. This book is a synthetic product of such a cultural, intellectual and personal history; and it draws on the development of my knowledge and experience of the subject over twenty years and more. I began to clarify its main theoretical tenets, methods and approach more than a decade ago, and I gradually developed them in some of my (published and unpublished) Persian and English writings, including the draft of an unpublished book on the Iranian economy, written (in English) in 1972, and the draft of a social and literary biography of the modern Iranian writer Ṣādiq Hedayat, written (also in English) in 1976, and which I hope to rewrite and publish sometime in the future. Therefore, neither has the book itself, nor have its approach and arguments, been a product of recent events in Iran. I began the final draft during the recent revolution, and this is reflected in occasional references to current events, as they were unfolding while various chapters were being written. As a rule, I decided not to bring these references up to date afterwards; for example, my reference in Chapter 6 to the Shah and Queen of Iran was made at a time when they were still in power, and I have let the reference stand. However, after the collapse of the *ancien régime*, a number of important documents and memoirs appeared in the Iranian press, and where appropriate I have cited such new evidence in the notes.

The contents of this book, with the multiplicity of its various aspects, the period of time it covers, and so on, could have been presented in a number of volumes. The reason why I have condensed them into a single volume is that my purpose was not to produce a lifetime's *magnum opus*, but to offer a framework for the solution of past, present and future problems. If this approach and framework are found to be of any value, then perhaps others will be prepared to expand on my ideas, and fill in the many details which I have omitted from the discussion. However, a consequence of the economy with which I have presented my argument is that some of the chapters tend to reflect the intensity of a journal article. Yet, I have done my best to present the material as clearly as possible, and I very much hope that it can be read and understood by any intelligent reader. To this end, I have also avoided any demonstration of technical cleverness, or theoretical mystification, which, in any case, I regard as an unnecessary burden on the advancement and spread of social knowledge. Finally, with regard to the relevance of my ideas and methods, I can only repeat with Marx (without, however, pretending to any comparison with him and his works) that 'I welcome every opinion based on scientific criticism. As to the prejudices of so-called public opinion, to which I have never made concessions, now, as ever, my maxim is that of the great Florentine: "Sequi il tuo corso, e lascia dir le genti" ["Follow your own path, and let the people say what they will"]' (from K. Marx, *Capital*, vol. I, Preface).

I wish to acknowledge my great debt to John Gurney, whose thorough readings of the manuscript, and scholarly suggestions for the improvement of both form and content, were characteristically generous, and extremely helpful. A part of the manuscript was typed and prepared by Muriel Waring, Freda Vincent and (occasionally) other members of the secretarial staff in Rutherford College, University of Kent, to all of whom I am grateful for their care and concern. I am also indebted to Farkhundeh Zarjam for typing some of the remaining chapters with sympathy as well as efficiency. The task could not have been accomplished without the sacrifices which I often demanded of my wife and children. But my debt to my wife cannot be fully acknowledged, for, apart from her moral support and understanding, she made a substantial contribution to the typing of the rest of the manuscript, and to the final preparation of the whole work.

In a profoundly philosophical verse, Ḥāfiẓ once wrote that 'Tomorrow when the Realm of Reality appears, embarrassed will be the Seeker who acted on Appearance.' This is not only a most appropriate epitaph for the past events, ideas and personages of the political economy of modern Iran, but also an excellent lesson for those that will be making its future.

September 1979 H. K.

1 Introduction

This book's title raises two questions, about the meaning and significance of the words 'modern' and 'political economy'. The word 'modern' limits the scope of the study to the twentieth century, with a greater emphasis on the more recent decades. The purpose of the study is to analyse social and economic change in Iran, to emphasise the role of those human and material forces, their relations, and their interactions, which – though not entirely unique to Iran – together give rise to the distinctly Iranian features of politiconomic development. It has been presented in a historical setting because those forces and relations – the techniques, values and institutions – are difficult to identify, and impossible to understand, unless their roots are discovered in their true locations. It is not an economic and political history of modern Iran, nor a historical study of the Iranian political economy; it is a study of Iranian politiconomic development with the same 'practical' and 'operational' claims as the orthodox studies of economic development.

The term 'political economy' (or 'politiconomy') refers to the method, spirit and approach of the study. Briefly, this involves an interdisciplinary – although not imprecise or unrigorous – approach; it implies an orientation towards solving real problems, as opposed to abstract or imaginary puzzles; it combines the use of theory, history, and statistical data in its arguments and expositions; it merges analysis and description, and uses qualitative as well as quantitative evidence in its evaluations. Some historians may be dissatisfied with the relative lack of emphasis on the use of documents, even though we have utilised many sources of historical evidence (for example, literature) which are not normally used in any single historical study. Some sociologists may note that some of the more rarefied sociological concepts and terms are absent – although not through ignorance – from the discussion. Some political scientists might prefer a greater emphasis on institutional details, in spite of my use of political theory and analysis when appropriate. But perhaps economists will be even less satisfied with my approach than the other professional disciplinarians: some may regard it as no less than a betrayal of the economist's professional purity, and sense of superiority, in its entire conception; others may not be impressed because it does not demonstrate a knowledge of elementary mathematics; still others may be disappointed with the absence of sophisticated statistical and econometric games; and so on. However, the absence in this book of games which all of us can play is because (a) they would not have been helpful in solving the *problem* in hand; and

(b) they have already been played by others in books and articles, the scientific value of whose results may now be assessed against the present knowledge of the Iranian economy. Apart from that, while the use of any technique is admissible in economic (and other) studies, the uncritical, imitative application of any given set of techniques to each and every problem adds very little to our knowledge. I have discussed this issue in my *Ideology and Method in Economics* (London: Macmillan, 1980), to which interested readers are referred. Finally, my occasional usage of the term 'politiconomy' instead of 'political economy', and invariable application of its adjective, 'politiconomic', for 'politico-economic', requires a note of explanation. The term 'economy' is of Greek origin, meaning 'principles of housekeeping' (from the Greek words *oikos* and *nomos*); the term 'political economy' was coined in the sixteenth and seventeenth centuries to mean principles of statecraft or social management. Yet, etymological consistency would have required the term to be 'politiconomy' (from the Greek words *polis* or *politikos*, and *nomos*). However, my reason for proposing this new form is simply that its adjective, 'politiconomic', is easier to apply, and that it opens the way to the use of such terms as 'politiconomics' and its derivatives to denote a new approach to economic science.

The book is divided into four distinct parts. Part I, consisting of Chapters 2, 3 and 4, provides the broader historical as well as theoretical perspectives for the main topic of the study, and thus is essential to a full understanding of the rest of the book. In Chapter 2, the controversy over the nature and logic of Iran's historical development is briefly discussed, because it makes a great deal of difference to our understanding of modern Iranian politiconomy whether or not it can be described as having been a basically feudal political economy until the land reform of the 1960s. Chapter 3 is an analytical assessment of the economic history of Iran in the last century, within the existing – limited, as well as unreliable – numerical data, and Chapter 4 is a theoretical evaluation of the causes, nature and consequences of the Persian Revolution (1905–9) in the light of previous developments.

Part II covers the period 1921–41, which began with the rise of Reżā Khān, and ended with the abdication of Reżā Shah. These twenty years make up the first phase of a long cycle of despotic restoration, combined with pseudo-modernist and pseudo-nationalist methods and aspirations, which was completed with the collapse of Muhammad Reżā Shah's régime early in 1979. It describes the full cycle of the Pahlavi rule, but its analytical significance is in the discontinuous rise and the final collapse of pseudo-modernist despotism, which is now being replaced with a pseudo-traditionalist 'system' of political economy. Chapter 5 discusses the various events, forces and tendencies which led to the eventual triumph of Reżā Shah, the restoration of despotism, and the ideological supremacy of pseudo-modernism. Chapters 6 and 7 analyse the form and content of this new phenomenon, in the two successive phases of Reżā Shah's consolidation of absolute and arbitrary power (1926–33 and

1933–41). They provide an essential basis for an understanding of his son's Development Strategy in the past fifteen years.

Part III develops the stages through which the pseudo-modernist hold over the political economy was first interrupted (1941–51), then put on the defensive (1951–3), until, in an alliance with the conservative–traditionalist forces, it gradually began to reassert itself (1953–61). Chapter 8 covers the war period and its aftermath, when the economy was depressed, the country threatened with disintegration, and various domestic and foreign political forces were engaged in a fierce competition to gain control. Chapter 9, covering the period of Dr Muṣaddiq's government (1951–3), discusses the emergence and failure of the first genuinely Iranian democratic movement, within the context of the nationalisation of Iranian oil, and Chapter 10 analyses the nature as well as the politiconomic implications of the dictatorial (though not despotic) régime which replaced it (1953–61).

Part IV of the book contains a description, analysis and evaluation of contemporary political and economic developments, in which the combination of ancient Iranian despotism, the modern phenomenon of pseudo-modernism in the Third World, and the ahistorical agency of oil revenues have led to a unique system of political economy. Chapter 11 analyses the power struggle which resulted (though not inevitably) in the triumph of *petrolic* pseudo-modernist despotism, and Chapter 17 analyses the ways in which this petrolic despotism developed the seeds of its own destruction, culminating in the People's Revolution of 1977–9.

Chapters 12 to 16, inclusive, contain a study of the country's economic development in all its aspects, within the context of a broader theoretical framework for the study of petrolic political economies. These five chapters form the most important part of this study for a knowledge of the logic and strategy of Iran's recent economic development, as well as the prediction of the outcome of alternative strategies which may be pursued in the future. The latter issues could have been more extensively discussed, but the main purpose was not to produce a large technological blueprint of little practical value, but to suggest a framework on the basis of which even technological blueprints may have a better chance of standing the test of the time. In this respect, some of the related arguments and observations may be of some use in the studies of other petrolic societies, and even of non-petrolic underdeveloped countries. Chapter 18 concludes the whole work by offering a preliminary analysis of the present situation, and suggesting a general approach to the long-term progress and prosperity of the country and its people.

The names of people and places, as well as other Persian words and sentences, have been transliterated on the basis of the standard rules used by *The International Journal of Middle Eastern Studies*, except in the few cases when the transliterated form of a name has already been established by practice. Apart from that, in cases where, in the Persian language, words of Arabic origin are pronounced differently – for example, the Perso-Arabic *dawleh*, for the Arabic *daula* – they have been transliterated in accordance with their Persian, not Arabic, pronunciations. Finally, whereas the words 'Persia' and 'Iran' (and their related adjectives) are interchangeable, 'Iran' and its derivatives are preferred except in certain historical contexts and with reference to the country's language and literature.

We may never know the beginning and the end, but we can try to be *consciously* a part of the process that links them together; and our genuine attempts at understanding the world about us form, despite mistakes, an indispensable part of that consciousness. This book is a product of such an attitude towards human life and labour, and, if it is so received by its public, it will have accomplished its main objective; for, in that case, the mistakes and shortcomings that remain may be explained by the vicissitudes of the learning process itself.

Part I

The State and Revolution: Historical Perspectives

2 On the Mode of Production: Feudalism or Despotism?

When, in 1961, the issue of a land reform was being publicly debated, no Iranian political party or tendency doubted the claim that productive relations in Iranian agriculture were characteristically feudal. In fact, both the Marxist and the non-Marxist Iranian intellectuals and educated elite had for a long time discussed the country's history – and its recent history in particular – with reference to such familiar Western terms and concepts as 'feudalism', 'capitalism', 'bourgeois', 'liberal', 'proletarian' and so on. The same is also true of many modern – i.e. 'analytical' – works on Iran written by Western (including Russian) academics and journalists.[1] Both groups have suffered from the fact that their analytical concepts and models have been borrowed, and applied, directly from the European context; and that they have begun, and usually ended, their analyses with a greater understanding of European, rather than Iranian, history. This does not mean that European history and social science are of no use in a serious analysis of Iran's history, sociology or political economy; it simply means that here – *as in every other analytical context* – we should dispense with the pragmatic benefits of intellectual complacency, and take the trouble of looking for models and theories which may result in genuine additions to our knowledge of the world.

At any rate, it is only since the land reform that some Iranian and other intellectuals and writers have begun to wonder whether Iranian history can be fruitfully discussed within the traditional European analytical frameworks. The question has been generally limited to the relevance or irrelevance of the concept of feudalism to Iranian history; and, unfortunately, even this has degenerated into a debate on 'feudalism *versus* oriental despotism', which betrays the same old attitude. Indeed, having claimed that neither the one nor the other is strictly validated by our knowledge of Iranian history, one has had to suffer the recurrent question, *what* was it then? Clearly, although we are now beginning to become more flexible in our approach to socio-economic problems, we still tend to resort to ready-made and well-worn concepts and theories. The attitude is somewhat analogous to that of the medieval scholars – described in a tale by Francis Bacon – who, upon failing to discover from sacred and classical books how many teeth a horse possesses, declared the problem to be an everlasting mystery; they disregarded the advice of a youthful farrier who had told them to 'go to the horse's mouth'.

This subject is important in its own right. But, more significantly, a brief discussion of it here will serve to provide the background, set the scene, and expose the approach with which we shall conduct the whole of this inquiry.

The Problem

The concepts of 'mode of production' and its counterpart, 'social formation', refer to hypothetical models constructed for the analysis of real political, social, economic and technological structures – including their spatial interconnections, and their temporal transformations. In general, such broader theoretical frameworks or visions are helpful – sometimes indispensable – to social and economic analysis. And they exist, even though beneath the surface, in nearly all approaches to political economy, including orthodox economic theory: here, the basic framework is that of an abstract society – based on private property, wage contracts and modern technology – in which what unites *and* divides men is the motive to increase (or 'maximise') their individual material gains. In spite of its well-known limitations, even this framework has served its purpose (both for and against capitalism) in its relevant time and place. Yet capitalism – its abstraction *and* its reality – is neither universal nor immutable: it is a comparatively recent phenomenon in the history of a few societies; therefore, many of the theories and facts based on this particular system of political economy are not readily applicable to pre-capitalist societies, past and present.

The founding fathers of classical political economy and liberal social philosophy were themselves aware of the multiplicity of social formations, and the significance of time as history. Furthermore, some of them even made scattered (and sometimes analytically acute) remarks on life and labour in different 'civilisations': for example, they observed some basic differences between European and Asiatic societies in the role and function of the state – hence, the network of freedoms, rights and obligations.

Prejudice apart, classical Greek (and, later, Roman) philosophers and historians had already drawn attention to some anomalies between their own social and institutional arrangements and those of their 'oriental' – especially Iranian – neighbours.[2] The revival of classicism – the Renaissance – in Europe coincided with the fall of Byzantium and the foundation of the Ottoman Empire. Therefore, past ideas and immediate realities led some modern European thinkers, such as Machiavelli, to compare Eastern and Western social systems. This was reinforced by the tales and travelogues of contemporary European travellers, such as Marco Polo. By the time Marx and Engels began their discussions of the Asiatic Mode of Production, many European thinkers – notably Montesquieu, Adam Smith, James and J. S. Mill, Hegel and Richard Jones – had taken up the subject. In this connection, Marx greatly benefited from the historico-analytical observations of Richard

Jones, whom he generally held in a high esteem as a political economist.[3]

However, neither Marx nor Engels developed his own concept of the Asiatic Mode of Production with the theoretical rigour and empirical thoroughness which is characteristic, particularly, of Marx's application. Marx sometimes emphasised the role of 'communal property' and the associated 'system' of scattered and 'self-sufficient' villages; and, sometimes, the despotic, centralised and 'egalitarian' nature of the state, with its fundamental economic functions drawn from, and/or resulting in, its monopoly of land-ownership.[4] Many of the earlier theorists had already stressed the relevance of geographical and environmental factors – the climatic aridity, the vastness of land mass, the sparseness of population, and so forth – which he used as basic data.

Like so many other theoretical frameworks, the concept of the Asiatic Mode of Production has had a turbulent career in the science, dogmas and politics of Marxism. For a long time, the application, perhaps even mention of it was forbidden in the Soviet Union, even to social scientists.[5] More recently, it has crept back into academic discourse in that country, probably with some degree of official blessing.[6] It is likely, judging from current political events, that the similar ban hitherto enforced by China, and pro-Chinese communists everywhere, will soon be also lifted. Post-war studies of the subject in the West have particularly involved a number of American historians of China, such as Owen Lattimore, and have been crowned by Karl Wittfogel's gigantic generalisation in his celebrated book *Oriental Despotism*. This is a scholarly piece of work, but it suffers from the great methodological weakness from which, in the name of 'science', so much Western social science has suffered in the past century and a half – that is, the *universalisation* of abstract and general theories. In the controversy which has followed, critics have seldom pointed to the bizarre *methodological* similarities between the protagonists of 'feudalism' and those of 'oriental despotism'. Instead, we have witnessed arguments ranging from the sublime to the ridiculous, including one by two authors who – though they betray little knowledge of oriental societies and their history – reject the notion of the Asiatic Mode of Production *because*, they tell us, it is 'conceptually incorrect'![7]

The following section presents a brief but broad theoretico-historical discussion of feudalism, as a preface to our observations on the development of the Iranian political economy.

Feudalism in Theory and Practice: A Brief Discussion

A NOTE ON METHOD

Feudalism is an abstract and general model of a society with distinct socio-economic, technological and institutional characteristics. Like all abstract models, it emphasises the most significant uniformities of life and labour in some real and historical societies by abstracting from their many individual differences. Such simplifications for the sake of generalisation do not usually cause serious disagreements between natural scientists in their attempts to apply models and theories to real physical phenomena: if the *basic* assumptions and predictions of a theory are consistent with a given case, then it is upheld; if not, then that case is excluded by the theory. They do not demand *perfect* correspondence between theory and reality, but neither do they try to fit the model to each and every situation by all – legitimate and illegitimate – means. There may be weaker or stronger electromagnetic fields, or none at all. But one seldom hears of 'semi-electromagnetic' fields or 'quasi-liver diseases'. One of the greatest barriers to progress in the social sciences is this state of methodological confusion where many abstract models are *identified* with the world of reality as if they were an *empirical description* of their concrete counterparts.

Therefore, in our present assessment of the nature and scope of feudalism, we shall first outline those basic properties which, taken together, define a feudal society; and, secondly, make some very brief references to the *variety* of concrete historical experiences in *European* societies, for which the model was originally intended. The case of Iranian society will be discussed in the next section against this general background of feudalism in theory and practice.

FEUDALISM IN THEORY

For the sake of clarity and economy it would be best to present a list of the most significant features of the abstract model of feudalism, leaving it largely to the reader to observe the equally important connections between them.

1. European feudalism was founded upon the breakdown, and break-up, of the Roman Empire, which was accompanied by the disappearance of its slave-based economic system.
2. It took a number of centuries for 'the' feudal system everywhere in Europe to develop some or all of the following socio-economic features.
3. Private property in land, and its concentration both in space *and* through time, by such 'laws' and rigidly observed customs as entail and primogeniture.
4. Serfdom or bondage, in a variety of forms, tying the peasant to the land and obliging him to pass on the surplus of production – over and above 'the' subsistence level – in rents, tithes, taxes, and so on.
5. A variety of other peasant obligations, such as the provision of direct and indirect services to the landlord, payment of fees for obtaining leave to marry, etc.
6. The manorial system, involving the landlord's presence on his estate.

7. Rigid class structure, and the existence of a numerically small class of aristocratic peers. The private monopoly of land-ownership in space and time leads to an oligarchy of aristocratic peerage through birth, yet these two interrelated economic and social frameworks are perpetuated through time only by 'legal' and customary sanctions against the resale of land, and the rigid rules governing inheritance and succession. (It follows from the above points that, in a feudal society, social, occupational and geographical mobility are highly restricted.)
8. Concentration of economic and political power in the rural sector, where nearly all manufacturing as well as agricultural production is carried out; dominance of the local markets, relative weakness of financial wealth, insignificant domestic trade, and virtual non-existence – and, later, relative insignificance – of boroughs and 'towns'.
9. Contractual rights and obligations of the various classes, and of the 'state' and its feudal–aristocratic base, in relation to each other. Therefore, while political power is in the hands of the 'state' (which includes the feudal aristocracy), its exercise is regulated by contract: 'laws', traditions, customs, and so forth. Hence, there is no generalised exercise of *arbitrary* power; the 'law' may permit the execution of a poacher on conviction, but it does not permit the killing, or the amputation of the bodily organs, of a peasant (let alone a peer) at the landlord's or the king's pleasure; it may permit, or even sanction, the landlord's right to cohabit with the brides of his serfs for a limited period, but it disallows an arbitrary extension of this period, or the rape of peasant women on an *ad hoc* basis.
10. A church that is likewise hierarchical, stratified and led by its own princely peerage. Through doctrine (and sometimes even dogma) it sanctions the whole social system and justifies its existence. The Roman Catholic Church was a perfect replica of the secular state, which it both served and balanced.

A few more remarks on some of these points will be helpful to our discussion of the case of Iran. It is commonly agreed that, in a feudal society, private property in land is strong and powerful, both in economic and in political terms. This is certainly true in so far as it refers to the *income*, and political power, enjoyed by the landlords, each according to his rank. Yet, as we have seen, it is generally incorrect in relation to the freedom of bequeathing, inheriting or disposing of such property. Indeed, this was one of the greatest evils of the feudal system in the eyes of the early liberal thinkers, for example Adam Smith who devoted several pages of his *magnum opus* to the condemnation of such restrictions. More recently, C. B. Macpherson has drawn attention to this obvious yet long-forgotten truth by contrasting the more restricted feudal concept of property with the liberal, *possessive*, concept which replaced it: whereas in a feudal society the concept of private property implied a *title* to ownership and a *right* to enjoy its fruit, in the early capitalist system it meant sole possession, with perfect *freedom* of transfer and alienation, for the owner.[8] In a word, feudalism itself could not survive without *restraining* the proprietor from the destruction of the monopolistic basis of land-ownership; capitalism could not begin to flourish without the *freedom* (that is, the *absence of restraint*) of ownership for financial capital.

The diffusion of political power among members of the aristocracy is marked by the absence of a centralised state, bureaucracy and army. There is no state property apart from the personal estates of the prince or king, the feudal-in-chief. Insignificant domestic (and international) trade, and the contractual security against generalised arbitrary extortion and plunder further limit public revenues, and expenditures. The state enjoys few rights, and suffers few obligations independently of the aristocracy, which can judge its own members as well as those of the lower classes. Each man must, theoretically, keep to his 'station'; but each man is also entitled to the rights and bound by the obligations defined for his station.

All laws, customs, traditions, rules and regulations are (for good or evil) occasionally, and sometimes frequently, violated; but *erratic violations of the law* are fundamentally distinct from *systematic and generalised lawlessness.*

FEUDALISM IN PRACTICE

The above basic elements make up an *abstract and general* picture, which, if applied with scientific caution and modesty, is useful for social and historical analysis. European feudalism has, in part or *in toto*, been present for nearly fourteen centuries in one or another corner of Europe; and some of its deep-rooted aspects still partially survive in some mature capitalist countries, particularly Britain: for example, the relative rigidity of class structure. Apart from that, the feudal societies of Europe each had their own peculiarities, influenced by location, general environment, types of international and intercontinental contact, and all other factors which contribute to the formation of a unique culture. For this reason, the rise and fall of feudalism in different European countries occurred in (sometimes significantly) different periods, and took a variety of forms: for example, when it had already begun to decline in England, it was about to emerge in the Russian principalities of Novgorod and Muscovy.

The decline of feudalism in England was accompanied by the rise of free towns or boroughs, the increase in (mainly international) trade, the accumulation of financial capital in the hands of the bourgeois class, and the temporary alliance of this class with the king and state against the aristocracy and the Roman church. This marks the beginning of the brief period of 'despotism' (in fact, absolutism) in England. In France, where the state was already more powerful than in England, the rise of despotism was better disguised as a confrontation not between church and state, but between the followers of Protestantism and Roman Catholicism. Hence, it finally established itself as a result of a protracted civil war, ending with the accession of Henry of Navarre (Henry IV of France) at the end of the sixteenth century; in consequence, the conflict between the rival religious sects lost all *internal political* significance. In Russia, feudalism and despotism emerged at the same time, almost as a synthetic and inseparable social fabric. Yet, the nature of European – including, to a lesser extent, Russian – despotism was significantly different from despotism in the East; it also survived for a much shorter period. We shall return to some of these issues in discussing the Iranian case.

The Case of Iran

WAS THERE A SLAVE ECONOMY?

If a variation of the feudal society is to be identified for a stage of development in Iranian history, then consistent universalism – an attitude which is *mistaken* for scientific generalisation – must also identify a slave-based system of political economy as its preceding stage. After all, according to the universalist outlook, everything must be at least essentially the same everywhere: liberals would hold this view for all times and places; Marxists would subscribe to it only for the relevant 'stage of development' across the globe. And, as the Persian expression has it, 'seekers are finders': once we are convinced, *a priori*, that there simply must be a stage of slavery followed by the stage of feudalism, we may seize upon any and every piece of 'evidence' as 'proof' of our *a priori* conviction. We need not (and, because of the limitations of space, *cannot*) take up the arguments and evidence which have been concocted to identify a stage of slavery – comparable to the Graeco-Roman experience – in Iranian history. The fact is that all such 'evidence' is based on wild speculations, fanciful 'interpretations', incorrect translations, and limitless stretches of imagination. There simply is no *positive* evidence put forward that could be taken seriously by anyone who knows both the Graeco-Roman experience and the full implications of the model of a slave-based political economy. Therefore, as in all cases, the onus is on the advocates to prove their claims, not on their opponents to disprove them.[9]

Yet, there is at least a great deal of negative evidence from ancient Persia which is somehow conveniently glossed over. There was, we know, no concept or status of citizenship – with its significant social implications – in the ancient, pre-Islamic society, though this is central to the slave-based political economies of Greece and Rome: there was, therefore, no notion of democracy (in its classical sense) or of dictatorship which did *not* mean despotism but signified the concentration of *political* power by delegation or usurpation.

Clearly, there was slavery in the empirical sense of this term, and it survived until the beginnings of this century. But the nature of the relationship between the state and the 'freeman' was not so fundamentally different from that of the 'freeman', the master, and the slave. We have evidence of great public works – for example, the monumental imperial highway stretching from Susa to Sardis – which are indicative not only of social wealth but also, particularly, of the economic power of the state.[10] The system of state administration was rigidly hierarchical : the *shatradar* (satrap), and the *marzaban* were, respectively, the civilian and military governors appointed by the king–emperor to each and every province; they were each directly responsible to the king–emperor himself; and they usually were watched by undercover agents from within or outside their own departments. This system has survived virtually to the present day.[11] There were no city-states nor a Roman-type imperial (let alone republican) system of government. The Shah was not a king – nor the Shah-in-Shah an emperor – in any of the European senses of these terms. He was a despot whose authority, and therefore legitimacy, was founded largely, if not entirely, on personal success rather than on legitimate succession. The myth of the divine right of 'kings' was indeed functional, because it did not so much legitimise dynastic succession as legitimise personal success: it was the divine right of personal might, rather than of ancestral privilege. All catastrophes may have been divinely ordained, but this does not mean that every catastrophe has to be legitimated by its predecessor.

Finally, there is yet another important issue which the inventors of a stage of slave economy have to face: if there has been such a stage in Iranian history, then there must have been a cut-off period in which some powerful socio-economic forces resulted in a fairly rapid transformation of the slave economy into a feudal system. Yet, there is no evidence for such an event, and no period in Iranian history has been – or can be – identified which would fit the requirement.

WAS THERE A FEUDAL SOCIETY?

However, the problem of immediate interest is whether or not Iran has had a feudal system over a long stretch of its history. In this case, there have been relatively more serious arguments and evidence put forward by the claimants. Nevertheless, this view is incorrect, for it cannot withstand a serious study of social and historical experience in Iran. To prove the case, let us compare the main features of Iranian society with the basic characteristics of a feudal system, as outlined in the preceding section.

1. The origin of so-called Iranian feudalism is unknown. There was no slave economy which, because of internal and/or external forces, gave way to a feudal society.
2. There is no evidence for the existence of any form of serfdom or bondage in

Iranian history. The peasant may have been 'fair game', permanently at the mercy of the landlord; but this itself is a negation of a well-defined network of productive relations which characterises the manorial system. The term *ra'īyat*, which, in the past few centuries has been commonly applied to all classes of the Iranian peasantry, simply means 'subject', though it has a different social significance from the word 'subject' in Europe: *ra'īyat* is a subject of a ruler (*hākim*) or overlord (*arbāb*); he is subject to a given power, not the law or even a sovereign body. That is why, until the Persian Revolution (1905–9), the term was generally applied to every single member of the community except the Shah himself.[12]

The peasant was of course obliged to pass on the surplus of production, in the form of dues, taxes and so forth, to some agent of exploitation: the state, the overlord, the tax farmer or whoever. But this is no evidence, much less proof, of feudal relations.

3. There existed no manorial system, and the overlord was characteristically based in the urban centres. That is why the usage of the term 'absentee landlord' by Western students of Iran is a total misapplication. Historically, the term refers to the small minority of European landlords who neglected their duties and responsibilities by their absence from their estate. But the 'obligations' (as, also, the 'rights') of Iranian landlords were entirely different, and they did not generally include residential supervision of life and labour in the village.
4. The class structure was anything but rigid; there was no peerage, no aristocracy, and no oligarchical distribution of power. On the contrary, the laws of inheritance, both before and after Islam, inhibited the concentration of private wealth, and the perpetuation of social station. At any rate, there was no guarantee that a man's fortune, of whatever form, would be passed on to any or all of his descendants: it could be easily confiscated or usurped by public bodies or 'private' persons. All classes of the society, irrespective of significant differences in wealth and position, were ultimately subjects in the sense described above. Therefore, there was much greater social mobility, both upwards and downwards, on the social 'ladder'. From this point of view, the Iranian 'ladder' was – and, to some extent, still is – more of a triangle (or, to add another dimension to it, pyramid) with a very wide base, and a relatively low distance between the base and the vertex (imagine a triangle with an obtuse angle at its vertex).
5. There was no relationship of lasting (i.e. constitutional) contractual rights and obligations between the various classes, and between the state and the people. Clearly, there were functions which, if the state systematically failed to perform them, would eventually lead to its downfall. Yet, precisely for this reason, these functions were not fulfilled in accordance with any contractual (or constitutional) obligations: they were carried out in order to maintain the state itself in power. It is one thing to *pay a person* for his services, and quite another to *pay him off* for his support or complicity.

There was a great insight in Marx's reference to the 'egalitarian' nature of oriental society, which has offended the 'revolutionary' sensibilities of some of his own latter-day adherents – even though he did not, perhaps could not, develop it further. For the Iranian people, at any rate, were ultimately *all equal before naked power*: the Grand Vazīr's person and property were just as easily subject to violation by the Shah as were those of the lesser magnates to violation by the Grand Vazīr, and those of the common people to violation by the lesser magnates; furthermore, the lives and possessions of them all were vulnerable to the will of the one single arbiter at the top. Putting aside appearances, things have not even yet radically changed in this respect. A well-known Persian expression summarises the position: 'equal injustice is just'.

Down to the present day, the clearest line of social demarcation (even stratification) has been that which divides the state (*dawlat*) from the people (*mellat*). The Perso-Arabic term *mellat* does not mean 'the nation', as is invariably believed: it means *the people* as opposed to *dawlat, the state*. The people themselves obviously are classified into different ethnic, linguistic, professional and income groups and classes; yet the most persistent Iranian equivalent to European class conflict or antagonism has been manifested between the people as a whole and the state: a wealthy merchant without links with the state is regarded as *mellī*, 'of the people', while a much less wealthy state official is categorised as *dawlatī*, 'of the state'.[13] Until a few decades ago, members of the 'civil service' were universally described as *nawkarān-i dawlat*, or 'lackeys of the state'; this was later *officially* replaced by the terms 'state official' and, subsequently, 'state employee'. Yet the older, and much more meaningful, term persists in informal usage. Likewise, it is only in recent decades that – in a conscious emulation of European practice – the term *mellī* has been treated as meaning 'national' and has been officially applied to state monopolies and corporations; but even now the common usage of the term *mellī* (as opposed to *dawlatī*) in economics and politics corresponds to the European term 'private' (as opposed to 'public'), though it means 'of, or for, the people' (as against 'of, or for, the state'). The term *mellat*, meaning the public, not the nation, is counterposed to the state; in Iran, 'the public', both as a term and as a concept, is not interchangeably used for the state and the people, as it certainly is in English-speaking countries.

It follows that, contrary to the European feudal system, economic and political power was concentracted in the urban, not rural, sector: it was not 'the country' *versus* 'the town' ; it was 'the country' (*shatr*, later *shahr*) *versus* 'the village' (*dih*). In other words, the original Persian word for 'country' – i.e. *shahr* – has been extended to describe urban (not rural) centres, which in the system of Persian Despotism have always formed the seat of politiconomic power. As a result domestic, and (especially) international trade was quite extensive, and 'towns' and 'cities' (although these terms have certain socio-historical connotations which make them imperfect equivalents for their Persian counterparts) were comparatively numerous and populated. There was a large merchant community in each 'town', communally organised and concentrated around the main *bāzār* (or 'market place'). The terms *bāzār* and *bāzargān* ('merchant'), still in vogue, are pre-Islamic. There has existed since at least ten centuries ago an extensive network of credit transfer between distant cities through bills of exchange.

6. There was no religious organisation before or after Islam with features which were even remotely comparable to the role and significance of the Roman Catholic Church in feudal Europe. The Zoroastrian spiritual leadership was perhaps somewhat more ordinal than the Islamic. The absence of a rigid religious hierarchy in Islam is well known. As for the Shī'a sect, which has played a very important role in post-Islamic Iranian society, it was an entirely communal institution which drew its legitimacy and power from its membership. Shī'ism has been, always in theory, and often in practice, in opposition to the state.[14]

WHAT ABOUT THE NATURE OF PROPERTY OWNERSHIP?

This is the question with which the tireless debaters begin and, unfortunately, usually end, as if all that they associate with feudalism is a narrow *mechanistic* type of property relations. At present, the most impressive study of the variety of land-ownership, and its evolution, in Iran is A. K. S. Lambton's classic work of scholarship *Landlord and Peasant in Persia*. Indeed, this is the main source of such information for many of the protoganists of 'feudalism in Iran', as well as of their opponents.[15] All that is added is usually no more than personal interpretations of her facts and data, by the standard method of 'semi-this' and 'quasi-that' analysis. Here, for considerations both of space and of originality, we shall not provide yet another summary of her work, but assert that the invaluable information provided by her, as well as the wealth of classical Persian literature, both historical and literary, leads us to the following conclusions.

1. The *direct* state ownership of land, in recent centuries known as *khāṣṣeh*, and, later, *khāliṣeh*, was – even though varying in proportion – always quite extensive.
2. Uncultivable and uncultivated land were all state property, at least in principle.
3. Most of the remaining cultivable land was *assigned* by the state to individuals, normally members of the royal household and state functionaries. There was no contractual security of title to ownership, and there was no automatic right of bequest.[16]
4. Otherwise various systems of tax-farming were in use. It is interesting to

note that a class of tax-farmers in Moghul India was known as *zamindar*s – a Persian word meaning 'landlord' or, better, 'landholder'.

5. There were scattered smallholdings held by local cultivators; but even in their case there was no security of ownership.
6. There were both public and private endowments in land. The former – enjoying greater security – were a source of income and scholarship grants for religious dignitaries and colleges; the latter were a source of income for the descendants of the rich – landlords as well as merchants. Neither was nearly as inviolable as private ownership in Europe, let alone European endowments.

Even if we put aside all that has been said earlier about the general characteristics of the history of the Iranian political economy, these simple observations about the institution of land-ownership leave us with a clear conclusion: Iran has not been a feudal society; and – in the absence of serious arguments and evidence to the contrary – those who disagree are no doubt entitled to their private opinions.

WAS THERE NO SOCIAL AND ECONOMIC DEVELOPMENT?

This is a curious, though sadly understandable, source of worry for some of the advocates of the feudal view of the Iranian society. Armed (or disarmed) with a mechanistic and universalist approach, they believe that, in the absence of a European-style class structure, class conflict, and so forth, there could have been no technological change and social transformation. Yet, we know that there *has* been; therefore, even though they do it unconsciously, they try to fit the reality to their model, rather than change the model itself.

The subject can be discussed extensively and in detail, but the limitations of space and scope forbid this. For present purposes, the following notes must suffice.

1. Social change everywhere must have a certain, though not absolutely deterministic and impersonal, mechanism; it does not follow that specific modes of social change (say those of European history) must be equally applicable everywhere.
2. Although Marxist and other models of social development put the greatest emphasis on internal, domestic forces of social transformations, even these models do not wholly disregard the influence of external, foreign forces. For example, according to the Marxist model, changes in the 'forces of production' must have played the most significant role in the basic destabilisation of the Roman slave economy; yet, even in this case, the fall of that system would have taken a different form without the persistent onslaught of the northern 'barbarians' who founded the feudal system afterwards. Or, to take another example, capitalism would not have

emerged without technical progress and the accumulation of *physical* capital; but Marx was well aware of the significance of the preceding accumulation of *commercial* capital and the role of *international* trade (even official piracy) in the drive for financial accumulation.

3. Iran has always been, willy nilly, an open country. It both has and has been conquered and subjected many a time; and international trading has been one of its permanent features. It is unthinkable that such violent and peaceful contacts with foreign peoples have had little or no impact on basic changes – technological as well as institutional – in Iranian society. Even in recent times, the Persian Revolution of 1905–9 owed a great deal – both directly and indirectly – to the rise of industry and empire in Europe (see Chs 3 and 4). And the subsequent drive for modernism in this century – which is the principal topic of our present discourse – was predominantly influenced by ill-adapted European ideas and techniques.
4. Apart from that, internal forces have also played their part. This is a country which has already witnessed the rise and fall of science and technology, the growth of urbanisation and public welfare at levels which would have been unimaginable in medieval Europe, followed, though gradually, by depopulation, poverty and destitution. Eurocentric analysts of all nationalities would do well to take a leaf from the much larger book of the history of human experience, even for their studies of the prospects of European society and its offshoots: the history of Iran alone suffices to teach us that, in any given society, technological progress and material development are neither inevitable *nor* – and this is the more important lesson – irreversible.
5. Clearly, Iranian history has witnessed no private accumulation of physical capital, similar to the modern European experience, which might have led to an industrial revolution. The question of the 'obstacles to the development of an Iranian bourgeoisie' (at least until the nineteenth century) has tended to worry both sides in the debate on feudalism *versus* oriental despotism, some of the contributors to which have shed light on certain aspects of the problem.[17] Yet they have all managed to miss the most important 'obstacle': the weakness and discontinuity of *all forms* of private wealth and property.

We have seen that the private monopoly of land-ownership in feudal Europe automatically implied restrictions on the freedom of ownership – restrictions which did not apply to capital in capitalist Europe until earlier in the present century, when reformist state interventions (through progressive taxation, death duties, and so forth) began to apply some restrictions even in this case. Yet, even though the European feudal landlord did not enjoy perfect *freedom* to alienate, transfer or dispose of his property at his own will, his *title* to ownership and his *right* of enjoying its fruits were inviolable, both for him and for his descendants. The Iranian 'landlord', be he a land assignee, a tax-farmer, an endowment beneficiary, or even a local smallholder, enjoyed no such right to his title, or security of his income. If European capitalist property involved an inviolable ('natural') *freedom*, and feudal property an inalienable ('natural') *right*, Iranian landed income and wealth were an alienable (arbitrary) *privilege*. The Iranian 'landlord' was certainly in a higher stratum of the society than, say, the merchant. But this was not because of his ownership of land: on the contrary, it was because of his relation to the state, from which he derived his landed privileges.

The same state of insecurity of income and wealth applied to merchant capital – both in the merchant's lifetime and after. The difference was that (a) merchant capital was more obviously earned, rather than granted by privilege, though even here good relations with the state were very helpful; and (b) merchant capital could be more easily realised in money form, moved from place to place, or even buried. Capital accumulation requires postponement of present consumption, i.e. saving; and saving necessitates a minimum degree of security and certainty concerning the future. In a country in which money itself – let alone financial and physical assets – has been under the threat of confiscation and expropriation, even by a local magnate, on the slightest pretext, it is impressive that financial capital *was* accumulated and trade *was* carried out to the extent that they were. The Iranian merchant was not 'naturally' charitable or spendthrift; and it was certainly not merely the teachings of Islam which encouraged him to spend rather than accumulate: the socio-political environment simply left him with no rational alternative.[18] All this is not to mention the question of inheritance laws, which, together with both the pre-Islamic and the post-Islamic *urban* practice of polygamy, would have militated against the concentration of wealth, even in the best of circumstances.

In general, the absence of a legal code of conduct – that is, the *arbitrary* nature of power at all levels – leaves little room for *personal*, let alone political, economic or financial, security and predictability. The entire course of Iranian history, and the existing chronicles of its events, are crowded with examples of this state of insecurity and unpredictability, too numerous, and somewhat embarrassing, to cite.[19] And Persian literature abounds with subtle and indirect social and ontological evidence for it.[20]

WAS IT 'ORIENTAL DESPOTISM'?

The system was certainly despotic; and the country, by the wider definition of this term, oriental. The question, though, is whether or not Iranian society answers to the analytical models variously described as the Asiatic mode of production, or oriental despotism.

It should by now be clear that many, though not all, of the features of life and labour that Marx, Engels and their precursors described as present in Asiatic society have indeed been present in the economic and social relations of the country. It is true, too, that the general aridity of the country, which has made water scarce and artificial irrigation widespread, has been an important factor. But Wittfogel's basic concept of the existence of a centralised and extensive functional bureaucracy (generalised from Chinese history) is not entirely relevant to the Iranian case. Besides, his gigantic generalisation of the 'hydraulic society' is too simple, too mechanistic, too deterministic, and too exclusive to be accepted in its entirety; and in particular, there is little evidence of the direct provision and allocation of water supplies as a major function of the Iranian state. This is not to overlook the merits of his contribution, especially for its time; but simply to point out the defects of his model, both in general and in the case of Iran. Finally, Wittfogel's emphasis on the *totality* of state power has unwittingly diverted attention from its more important feature: that is, its *arbitrary* nature, which has infected the exercise of power at all levels, and not merely at the top of the social pyramid. Apart from that, it has encouraged the development of alternative theories – such as those of royal absolutism and absolutist states – which tend to underemphasise the distinctiveness of Eastern despotism by focusing attention on *degrees* of absolutism from western Europe to eastern Asia.[21] The distinctive characteristic of the Iranian state is that it monopolised not just power, but *arbitrary* power – not the absolute power of laying down the law, but the absolute power of exercising lawlessness (see further Ch. 4).

It is not so vital to look for a Newtonian first cause, for an analytical model by which to understand a country's past and present, and broadly predict its future.[22] In any case, in the development of human societies basic social and institutional features tend to have a long life, much beyond the first cause or causes, whatever they might have been, which were initially responsible for their emergence: witness the numerous feudal habits, institutions and relations which still survive beneath the surface of British society after at least two centuries of industrial capitalism and social reformism.

Whatever the first cause, Iranian society has been run by a functional despotism for two and a half millennia.

NOTES

1. The Tūdeh (Communist) Party of Iran has had the largest share among Iranian political parties and the like in an imprecise as well as uncritical application of these terms, concepts and theories to Iranian history and society. Many European and American writers have also applied this universalist vision of historical development to Iranian society, and Soviet writers have had the greatest single influence in shaping the views of educated Iranians on the subject. For more specific references, see the following notes, especially note 9 below.
2. For example, Herodotus, Aristotle and Plutarch.
3. Richard Jones was a classical political economist of the early nineteenth century who placed much emphasis on comparative social and economic history as an instrument of politiconomic analysis. He was openly critical of Ricardo's abstract

and universalist methods, and his own studies of Indian history led him to the development of ideas which he may have originally taken from Adam Smith's general remarks on Asiatic societies; see further H. Katouzian, *Ideology and Method in Economics* (London: Macmillan, 1980) ch. 2; and Guy Routh, *The Origin of Economic Ideas* (London: Macmillan, 1975) ch. 1.

4. The more important primary references are to be found in Marx's contributions to the American newspaper *Daily Tribune* in the 1850s, and his brief analytical classification in the Preface to his *Contributions to a Critique of Political Economy* (1859). For detailed bibliographical references, see Perry Anderson, *Lineages of the Absolutist State* (London: New Left Books, 1974); and Karl A. Wittfogel, *Oriental Despotism* (New Haven, Conn.: Yale University Press, 1957). For a laborious application of the views of Marx and Engels to a study of Iranian history, see Ervand Abrahamian, 'Oriental Despotism: The Case of Qajar Iran', *International Journal of Middle Eastern Studies*, no. 5 (1974) pp. 3–31. Although a painstaking piece of research, Abrahamian's argument suffers from three main weaknesses:

   (a) in its rather too emphatic division of the views of Marx and Engels on this subject it gives the impression that each of them had produced a consistent and well-defined concept of the Asiatic mode of production;
   (b) it largely ignores the economic aspects of Iranian society in the nineteenth century; and
   (c) in comparing 'the' theories of Marx and Engels with the Iranian socio-political situation *in the nineteenth century alone*, it leaves the reader wondering whether (and according to which of 'the two concepts') Iran had been an Asiatic society, a feudal society, or something else, before the Qajar period.

5. See Wittfogel, *Oriental Despotism*, for a considerable amount of evidence concerning this issue. But a good deal of (less direct) evidence may also be found in the works of Soviet and Soviet-inspired writers and pamphleteers themselves.
6. The following is a quotation by Ernest Gellner from L. V. Danielova, (ed.), *Problems of the History of Pre-Capitalist Societies*, a collection of esseys published in Moscow (1968):

   > Mankind faces many new problems which did not face the founders of Marxist theory and for which, naturally, one cannot seek solutions in their work. . . . The scale and vigour of current discussions is largely explained by the fact that for a long time, concrete research was limited by the five-term scheme (primitive society, slave society, feudalism, capitalism communism) . . . *this scheme . . . arises from the historical experience of Europe* . . . data drawn from the history of other continents makes clear the limitations of an approach to world history as a unilineal process . . . . [Emphasis added.]

   See Ernest Gellner, 'The Soviet and the Savage', *Times Literary Supplement*, 18 Oct 1974. This is a long article demonstrating a substantial change of 'line' in contemporary Soviet social anthropology and economic history, with which some of their followers elsewhere may not yet be fully familiar.
7. See B. Hindess and P. Hurst, *Pre-Capitalist Modes of Production* (London: Routledge, 1975). This is a consequence of the application of Louis Althusser's neo-Cartesian methodology to problems of social reality. See further the two authors' auto-critique of their earlier book in *Mode of Production and Social Formation* (London: Macmillan, 1977), where they both modify their general

methodology, and (at pp. 41–3) imply that their earlier 'conceptual' conclusion had been intended not to reject the reality of the Asiatic society itself, but to show the lack of correspondence of that reality with their own definition, or 'concept', of the mode of production. However, both their earlier book and their auto-critique are (in spite of their Marxist jargon) very reminiscent, in both spirit and method, of modern mathematical economics.

8. See Macpherson's 'A Political Theory of Property' in his *Democratic Theory: Essays in Retrieval* (London: Oxford University Press, 1973).
9. Some authors have tended to confuse the institution of domestic slavery with a slave-based system of political economy. For example, an Iranian sociologist has remarked that a group of village labourers, whom he identifies as serfs *as well as* domestic slaves, engaged in 'the advanced *sale* of their labour to landlords or feudals, in order to earn their living – thus demonstrating a total lack of distinction between slaves, serfs, and even workers, who (according to the author himself) *were free to sell their labour on advanced contracts*. However, the author later refers to the same group of people as being 'the same as *serfs*, who were also regarded as *domestic slaves*, i.e. slaves [who were] *bonded* to the interest of the feudal household, *tied to the land*, and obliged to supply *corvée labour*'! See G. Ensāfpour, *Tārīkh-i Zindigī-yi Iqtisādī-yi Rūstā'īān va Tabaqāt-i Ijtimā'ī-yi Iran* (Teheran: Intishār, 1971) pp. 159 and 236. (Emphasis added.)

   Another Iranian author, of similar views, has emphasised the indisputable fact that Iranian peasants 'were not citizens', while overlooking the equally clear fact that *no* Iranian individual or social group had ever been *citizens*: in spite of extreme differences in income and status. See Farhad Nomani, 'The Origin and Development of Feudalism in Iran . . .', *Tanqīqat-e Eqtesadi*, IX (Summer and Autumn 1972) pp. 5–61.

   On the whole, the impression given by such Iranian authors is that their main purpose is to point out that Iranian peasants were no less exploited than their European counterparts, although one is at a loss to know why such a perfectly valid point of view should require so many mistakes and mystifications for it to be 'proved'.

   In his *History of the Medes* (Persian translation, Teheran, 1966), Diakanov speaks of a 'semi-patrimonial, semi-slavery' system, and refers to the use of *domestic* slaves as *corvée* labour as part of the evidence for this classification. In *The Heritage of Persia* (Cleveland, Ohio: World Publishing Co., 1963), Richard N. Frye claims that the fact that the king was above the law and, therefore, could assign land to his loyal servants, led to the foundation of a feudal system. Such 'arguments' and 'observations' may be found in many a learned piece of writing on the subject.
10. The organised and efficient network of state posts and communications, as well as the countrywide system of travellers' inns, built and organised by the state, are perhaps even better evidence for the *economic* role and significance of the Persian state. See Herodotus, *The Histories* (Hamondsworth: Penguin, 1954), Book I.
11. The original of 'satrap' is more likely to have been *shatrapāt*, where *pāt* (or *pād*) is of the same Indo-European origin as the Latin *pater*.

   Later, under the Ashkānids, this system was somewhat 'decentralised', in so far as regional governors enjoyed a measure of autonomy, as well as security of tenure, as long as they rendered the required (especially financial) obligations to the king–emperor. For this reason, the Ashkānid system became known, in the post-Islamic era, as *mulūk al-tavāyefī* (or government of communal/tribal rulers). The late nineteenth-century *translation* of the European term and concept of feudalism into this Perso-Arabic word has caused untold confusion among educated Iranians about the nature and significance of both European feudalism and the Ashkānid *mulūk al-tavāyefī* system. In fact, it may be argued that, depending on the economic and military power of the Iranian state (among other factors), the Achiminid (satrapic), and Ashkānid (*mulūk al-tavāyefī*) forms of regional administration have intermittently survived in the country down to the present day: for example, the Sāsānid, Ṡafavid and modern Pahlavi systems resembled the former, while the Ghaznavid, Afshārid, Zand and Qajar systems were more like the latter. In either case, however, the nature of despotic relations between the king–emperor, his provincial appointees or dependent rulers, and the mass of the people was fundamentally the same.

12. Some of these terms have acquired the social significance described above only in the last two centuries, while in this century some of them have been losing their historical meanings because of mistranslations of European words and misapplication of European ideas.
13. Until a couple of decades ago, a state hospital, school, or whatever, was referred to as *dawlatī*, and their private counterparts as *mellī*. The Iranian national railway system is still officially described as *dawlatī*.
14. See further Ch. 4, below.
15. See, for example, Nomani, in *Tahqiqāt-e Eqtesadi*, IX.
16. This was, and still is, true of *all* other forms of property and possession. In recent years, many well-to-do Iranians have been known to hide their valuable possessions (antique jewellery, carpets, and so forth) for fear of having to 'present' (*pīshkish*) them to a royal person, or a powerful potentate, upon discovery.
17. See, for example, Ahmad Ashraf, 'Historical Obstacles to the Development of a Bourgeoisie in Iran', in M. A. Cook (ed.), *Studies in the Economic History of the Middle East* (London: Oxford University Press, 1970), who puts a rather lop-sided emphasis on the nature and role of traditional Iranian guilds (*aṣnāf*) as a barrier against the development of industrial capitalism in Iran.
18. This was a main cause of traditional merchant charity (unknown in Europe), which has survived down to the present day: periodic public feasts, and distribution of both cooked and uncooked food among the needy on religious and other occasions. It would be a mistake to regard this as an inevitable consequence of the teachings of Islam, if only because such teachings are common to many religions, including Christianity.
19. The whole of Iranian history bears witness to numerous, as well as continuous, instances of *arbitrary* violations of life, limb and property. Apart from usurpations of possession and property, this was a country in which kings and royal persons were regularly killed, blinded, castrated, and so forth, by their own relatives as well as enemies. The number of Sāsānid kings and princes who were 'eternally lost' (or 'drowned in a swamp') during hunting expeditions, or arrested, blinded and killed by their own kinsmen is quite considerable. In post-Islamic Iran the same tradition continued throughout the centuries which ended with the Ṣafavid Reunification in the sixteenth century. Ṣafavid history itself is one continuous story of killing and blinding royal persons, not to mention state officials, and ordinary people. For example, Ismā'īl II was assassinated by his own relatives, Muhammad Khudābandeh had been blinded, and 'Abbās I did not leave a single able-bodied son of his own to succeed him.

    Nādir Shah Afshār, the captive slave of a tribe, later to become a common bandit, a great general, and the founder of the Afshārid 'dynasty', blinded his own son and heir in a fit of paranoiac rage. His grandson Shāhrukh (already blinded by others) was tortured by Āghā Muhammad, the first Qajar king, so savagely, in an effort to make him reveal the hiding place of *all* his treasures, that he did not survive, in spite of a full confession. Āghā Muhammad himself had been castrated when, as a boy, his tribe had been defeated by another. When he captured the old Iranian city of Kirmān, he plundered so much and blinded so many of its people that the city has not managed to recover from its devastating effects. The Zand 'dynasty', which was finally toppled by Āghā Muhammad, were, in spite of popular myth, masters of fratricide, and treachery against their own kinsmen. As late as 1848, Muhammad Shah II's second and favourite son, 'Abbās Mīrzā Mulk-ārā, a boy of eleven, was nearly killed at the hands of his elder brother, Nāṣir al-Dīn, who succeeded to the throne and – according to his own, now publicly available, memoirs – was greatly indebted for his survival to the intervention of important foreign emissaries and their governments. However, all of his own personal possessions were confiscated, and his household effects were looted by his brother's guards.

The case of state officials is yet another large chapter. The hair-raising treatment of the grand vazīrs Majd al-Mulk Yazdī, Khājeh Shams al-Dīn Juvainī (who was himself a party to the gruesome fate of the aforementioned) and Khājeh Rashīd al-Dīn Fażlullah by successive Ilkhān rulers is too well known to elaborate. This is also true of the treacherous massacre of Imām-quli Khān (the great Ṣafavid general who recaptured the isle of Hurmuz, and became governor of the Fars province) together with his kindred, on the order of Shah Ṣafī; the terrible end of Hāj Ibrāhīm Kalāntar, the *I'timād al-Dawleh* (or 'Trust of the State'!), at the hands of Fatḥ 'alī, the Qajar king; the official assassinations of Qā'im Maqām and Amīr Niẓām (popularly known as Amīr Kabīr), by Muhammad Shah II, and his son, Nāṣir al-Dīn; the official assassination of Taimūr-Tāsh, Nuṣrat al-Dawleh, Sardār As'ad, and others, on the orders of Reżā Shah (Pahlavi); and so on and so forth. Besides, the fact that state officials from the Grand Vazīr to the common doorman could be publicly flogged, at a moment's notice, while still holding office, may provide yet another set of evidence for the absence not only of an aristocracy, or citizenship, but of *any* legal framework, *any* traditional code of conduct, whatsoever.

A study of Persian literature in general, and of the great Persian chronicles in particular, would supply many more examples of this permanent state of lawlessness, and, more importantly, afford insight into social life, and social relations, in Iranian history. Here is a sample of the chronicles: Baihaqī's *Tārīkh-i Mas'ūdī*, Nāṣir Khusraw's *Safar Nāmeh* (a travelogue), 'Ibn Balkhī's *Farsnāmeh*, Juvainī's *Tārīkh-i Jahāngushā*, Khājeh Rashīd al-Dīn's *Jami'al-Tavārīkh*, Hamdullah Mustawfī's *Tārīkh-i Guzīdeh*, Iskandar Munshī's *'Ālam Ārā*, Istir-ābādī's *Durreh-yi Nādirī*, Lisān al-Mulk's *Nāsikh al-Tavārīkh*, 'Abdullah Mustawfī's *Sharh-i Zindigānī-yi Man . . .* (historical memoirs), Dawlat-Ābādī's *Hayāt-i Yaḥyā* (historical memoirs) and Hedāyat's *Khāṭirāt va Khaṭarāt* (historical memoirs).

20. The Persian language and literature are full of such instances. For example, the Perso-Arabic word *bakhīl*, or 'miser', is used both of one who is envious of other people's fortune, and of a parsimonious person who neither consumes his own wealth nor donates to others, but simply accumulates. In a folkloric expression such a person is described as he who 'neither eats it himself, nor allows it to others, but would let it rot, then bestow it to dogs'. In his famous *Gulistān*, Sa'dī remarks that 'a *bakhīl*'s money will be unearthed only when he is himself inside the earth'; somewhere else, he advises his (rich) readers 'to consume as well as give, so as to inherit both worlds'.
21. See, for example, Barrington Moore Jr, *Social Origins of Dictatorship and Democracy* (Harmondsworth: Penguin, 1967); and Anderson, *Lineages of the*

Absolutist State. We have already emphasised the historical and analytical distinctions between dictatorship and absolutism on the one hand, and despotism, on the other: in an absolutist state, there *may* be a monopoly of power, but its exercise is bound by contracts and conventions.

There is one other point arising from Anderson's book which it is important to mention. His emphasis on the role of Islam as a main cause of Middle Eastern 'absolutism' seems to invert the 'causal' relationship: Islam emerged in the midst of a nomadic and tribal people, who conducted their 'social affairs' on the basis of a primitive democratic tradition; and there is nothing in its basic tenets and doctrines which should have resulted in the foundation of a despotic system, even though parts of its civil code (for instance, its *toleration* of polygamy, and its egalitarian laws of inheritance) were not helpful for the emergence of a feudal–aristocratic system of political economy. If we have to identify any causal connections at all, then it looks more likely that it was the despotic systems of the conquered territories – in particular, Iran and Egypt – which moulded the Islamic (Umayyid, 'Abbasid, Fāṭimid, as well as Andalusian or 'Moorish') politiconomic systems in their own image.

In his *Islam and Capitalism* (London: Allen Lane, 1974), Maxime Rodinson is right in pointing out that Islamic *doctrines* cannot have provided a serious barrier against the rise of capitalism in Muslim countries, although his implicit view that they could even have *encouraged* the development of (industrial) capitalism is less acceptable. However, the weakness of Rodinson's whole argument is owing not so much to the points that he discusses as to the points that he ignores: in particular, the absence in his book of an analysis of those factors which discouraged the development of capitalism in Muslim societies, and of which the origins must be sought in the *pre*-Islamic era.

22. See, however, Ch. 15, below, for my rudimentary development of the concept of the 'aridisolatic society'. See also, my 'The Aridisolatic Society: a Model of Long Term Social and Economic Development in Iran' (mimeo).

3 Developments in the Nineteenth Century

Introductory Remarks

The nineteenth century coincides with the *effective* period of Qajar rule; the first quarter of this century covers the *effective* period of its death agony. The tale of Iran's social and economic developments in the nineteenth century is, briefly, as follows: there is a secular tendency for population growth, trade expansion, price inflation and a decline in the domestic and external values of 'the' national currency; there is growing contact with European countries, affecting the composition of foreign trade, the balance of payments, the pattern of consumption and – subsequently – the internal power structure, mores, norms, ideas and institutions, culminating in the struggles against trade concessions to foreign countries as a prelude to the Persian Revolution.

Here, I do not intend to reiterate this tale in greater detail, but seek to assess its implications for the dynamics of the Iranian political economy with some regard for analytical rigour and precision. Commentators have hitherto tended to view the situation in two conflicting ways: according to the 'traditional' view, Qajar Iran was a clear example of backwardness, in contrast to European progress; according to the 'modern' view, there were dynamic forces at work which led to (at least creeping) economic progress, the emergence of a 'bourgeois' class, the breakdown of the 'feudal' (or whatever) system, and so on. Both these views contain some elements of truth; but neither is entirely acceptable. Nineteenth-century Iran was certainly 'backward' in comparison with European socio-economic developments; but it was far from *static*, unchanging or unchangeable. Yet the changes which did occur were by no means necessarily 'progressive' if, as is normally the case, progress is associated with the growth of economic welfare, the accumulation of capital, the invention or absorption of new techniques, the rise in productivity, the expansion of productive industry, the greater integration of the productive sectors of the economy, the emergence of a considerable industrial class, the enactment of serious social and political reforms, and so forth.

In what follows I shall argue that the major socio-economic changes of the last century were to a large extent due to uninvited, and partially harmful, intervention by European countries in the Iranian political economy, and that it was the combination of economic depression, political subjugation and social destitution – combined with greater political awareness, and imperialist rivalries – that led to the collapse of the old order.

A Periodisation

To begin with, it would be helpful to divide the century into three successive periods: 1800–50; 1850–70; 1870–1900. Period I corresponds, roughly, to the reign of Fatḥ'ali Shah, and Muhammad Shah II; Period II separates the accession of Nāsir al-Din Shah (in 1848) from the events of the early 1870s – the famine, the decline of Persian silk, the ill-fated Reuter Concession, and so on; and Period III covers the rest of Nāsir al-Dīn's reign, until his assassination in 1896.

Period I is, in some *relative* sense, a period of stabilisation and consolidation: for once, after a long interval, there was some considerable socio-political continuity throughout the country, even in spite of the Russo-Persian wars, which led to considerable loss of territory. The latter events must be viewed more as a consequence of the long-term weakening of the traditional Persian Empire, a tendency which dates back to the decline of the Ṣafavid dynasty. Such events, although catastrophic in themselves, did not cause the kind of *internal* upheaval, instability and insecurity which was characteristic of the second half of the eighteenth century. Leaving aside Fatḥ'ali's unheroic attitude towards foreign aggression, his insatiable appetite for public revenues – raised by heavy taxation and extortion – must have been a less destabilising factor than the previous state of chaos, disorder and plunder. At any rate, most of the consequences of his inglorious reign made themselves felt towards the end of this period, symbolised by the predominantly urban revolt of the 1840s, which is sometimes incorrectly regarded as a purely religious event.

The second half of the century left Nāṣir al-Dīn with the unenviable task of holding the country together, *within the old framework*, in a period of intensifying economic unhappiness, increasing foreign imperial intervention and rising domestic political discontent. It is often claimed that, but for the loss of his reforming first Chief Minister and brother-in-law, Mīrzā Taqī Amīr Niẓām, popularly known as the Amīr Kabīr (whom he first dismissed, then banished and later had executed near Kāshān), Iran might have made rapid progress towards industrialisation and modernisation along the road which was taken by Japan some twenty years later. Even putting aside such grotesquely overt proclamations, it is unlikely that the merits of Amīr Niẓām – not to mention his defects – would have led to a significant change of direction for the Iranian political economy. This, however, is another, though highly important, matter.[1] Yet, the general impression gained from the available evidence – including anecdotes, memoirs, travelogues and what numerical data there are – strongly suggests that the socio-economic situation was somewhat better in the period 1850–70 than in the following thirty years. Indeed, it is in these last three decades that the process of socio-economic disintegration clearly reveals itself, in the growth of foreign imperial power, the sale of trade concessions, the accumulation of foreign debt, the widening balance-of-payments deficits, the rapid decline in the value of money, the growing socio-political unrest, the weakening of central control over the provinces, and so forth.

The Growth of Population

Until the past few decades, when the growth of world population has been owing more to the application of technical progress in preventive medicine than to a general rise in material prosperity, population growth had been regarded as – at least – a qualitative indicator of the state of a country's relative prosperity. Whatever the causal relations, it is generally assumed that periods of progress and prosperity, not to mention industrialisation and economic growth, usually witness high population growth rates, through a decline in the death rate and sometimes also a rise in the birth rate. The available estimates for the Iranian population at some arbitrary dates in the nineteenth century – notoriously unreliable, and sometimes even contradictory, as they are – have given the general impression that there must have been an approximate doubling of the population (from about 5 million to 9 million or more) over the century as a whole, indicating an average annual growth rate of about 1 per cent. This, by modern standards, looks like a convincingly modest rate of increase, but, within its proper context, it would have to be viewed with greater caution than it has hitherto received. For example, Issawi has observed that this figure, being appreciably less than the *compounded* annual rate of population growth for Egypt, may be fairly accurate. But, apart from the difficulties facing the Egyptian estimate itself, the comparison is not very helpful, if only for the fact that the income per capita of Egypt at the end of last century was much higher than that of Iran. However, a closer analysis of the available estimates for the Iranian population itself would tend to weaken the hypothesis of an annual average growth rate of 1 per cent in more direct ways. First, this hypothesis appears to be inconsistent with the belief, also held by Issawi (and Keddie), that the *nomadic* population stayed constant at about 2.5 million, *unless it is further assumed that the nomadic tribes lost most of their population growth to the rest of the country through settlement.*[2] This is a highly unlikely assumption which they do *not* make. Therefore, we are left with the implicit hypothesis that the *settled* population – of both the urban and rural variety – grew from 2.5 million in 1800 to 6.5 million in 1900; that is to say, by an *average* annual rate of 1.6 per cent. Yet it is unbelievable that in such socio-economic conditions the *average annual* growth rate of *any* section of the population could have been as high as this, because any average growth rate implies much higher actual growth rates in periods when, in the absence of cholera and famine outbreaks, the population could begin to make up for its perennial losses.

Secondly, the existing data for the years 1838, 1867 and 1869 make it clear that by the mid nineteenth century the Iranian population could certainly not have been any more than 6 million and was probably less (see Table 3.1), which would imply an even higher rate of increase, both on the aggregate and for the settled population, in the latter half of the century, and especially in the last three decades – that is, in the period which suffered the most from famine, inflation, economic poverty and political insecurity. What can we make of all this?

At the outset some attention ought to be paid to the distinction between *cyclical* and *secular* changes in population, particularly in conditions, such as these, where the volatility of both the natural and the socio-economic circumstances could play a very significant role in determining significant short-term variations. For example, at the beginning of our Period I there could have been a cyclical tendency for population growth, making up for the cyclical decline in the previous periods, in response to the relative socio-economic stabilisation which we have already mentioned. This should have reinforced any secular tendency for the growth of population. On this basis, Gardane's estimate of 9 million for 1807 may not be as gross an exaggeration as is generally held. But there were other factors, including counter-cyclical tendencies, working in the opposite direction. First, there was significant loss of territory in this period, especially of the provinces ceded to the Russians, which, being one of the economically most well-endowed regions of the Empire, must have contained a high ratio of the total population, probably amounting to not much less than 1 million people. This important fact seems to have been overlooked by the commentators on population change. Secondly, there was the notorious series of cholera outbreaks, extending from mid-1830s to mid-1860s and cyclically upsetting the long-term secular tendency. These – we know at least qualitatively – took a very heavy toll, but that is not all.[3] Indeed, it is likely that they also tended to reduce the birth rate below the rate which would have corresponded to the normal state of the political economy. Therefore, it is not unlikely that between 1800 and 1870 the figures for total population remained stationary at around 6 million, even though the general socio-economic conditions in 1800–70 may have been better than in Period III (1870–1900); for the loss of population due to epidemics and foreign expansionism is not correlated to ordinary birth and death rates.

In Period III, however, the negative weight of such cyclical and exogenous factors eased considerably, reducing the death rate and even probably increasing the birth rate at the same time, while the secular decline in the socio-economic 'incentives' in the same period had not yet had sufficient time to make a negative impact on the general secular tendency of birth and death

TABLE 3.1 Population estimates ('000)

	1800s	*1812*	*1838*	*1867*	*1869*	*1884*	*1888*	*1891*	*1909*	*1910*
Gardane	9,000	–	–	–	–	–	–	–	–	–
Thompson	–	–	–	4,400	–	–	–	–	–	–
Houtum-Schindler	–	–	–	–	–	7,654	–	–	–	–
town	–	–	–	–	–	(1,964)	–	–	–	–
village	–	–	–	–	–	(3,780)	–	–	–	–
nomadic	–	–	–	–	–	(1,910)	–	–	–	–
Zolotoliv	–	–	–	–	–	–	6,000	–	–	–
town	–	–	–	–	–	–	(1,500)	–	–	–
village	–	–	–	–	–	–	(3,000)	–	–	–
nomadic	–	–	–	–	–	–	(1,500)	–	–	–
Curzon	–	–	–	–	–	–	–	9,000	–	–
town	–	–	–	–	–	–	–	(2,250)	–	–
village	–	–	–	–	–	–	–	(4,500)	–	–
nomadic	–	–	–	–	–	–	–	(2,250)	–	–
Medredev	–	–	–	–	–	–	–	–	10,000	–
town	–	–	–	–	–	–	–	–	(2,500)	–
village	–	–	–	–	–	–	–	–	(5,000)	–
nomadic	–	–	–	–	–	–	–	–	(2,500)	–
Be'mont	–	5,000	6,000	–	5,000	–	–	–	–	8,000

Source: based on Charles Issawi, *The Economic History of Iran 1800–1914* (Chicago and London: University of Chicago Press, 1971).

rates on its own account. Therefore, there could have been a relatively rapid rise in population from about 6 million in the mid-1860s to 8 million in 1900. In summary, the population of Iran probably grew from about 6–7 million at the beginning of the nineteenth century to something like 8–9 million at the end of it, most of the increase occurring over the last few decades.

Putting aside the differences in figures, this general conclusion does not seem to vary much from the prevailing views which we discussed earlier in this section. But there is an important difference in the interpretation of the course of events. The rise in population in the nineteenth century cannot be put down mainly to a *secular* tendency due to an improvement in the social and economic conditions. This applies particularly to the last decades of the century, in which it mostly fell. And this conclusion, tentative and largely speculative as it inevitably is, seems to correspond more consistently with our total knowledge of the political economy of Iran in the last century than does any significantly different interpretation.

Taxation, Inflation and Foreign Trade

The Iranian political economy in the nineteenth century was, in purely empirical terms, a typical example of a traditional autarky. There did not exist an absolutely large bureaucratic apparatus radiating from the centre to the provinces, although it is still unlikely that the relative size of the bureaucracy, and the army, was as consistently insignificant as is sometimes made out. Whatever the political system, the country was still desperately poor even by the standards of the Turkish metropolis and Egypt. And this general state of poverty clearly must have made itself felt on what the central authority could, or could not, afford to spend on itself.

But, in any case, the sum total of rules, regulations, interventions and restrictions which were in force clearly make up the hallmark of a centrally controlled political economy. One wonders what the reaction of an Adam Smith would have been to a system of 'mercantilism' which imposed duties on the *internal* movement of commercial goods, even at a time when foreign powers had typically forced it to restrict its external tariff rate to a maximum of 5 per cent.

Taxes consisted mainly of the land tax, the poll tax, the tax on the profit of master craftsmen, and customs duties, with land tax undoubtedly contributing the lion's share.[4] In addition, the so-called 'irregular' extortions (which were otherwise pretty regular in their own right) provided supplementary revenues for the local and central purses. Other non-fiscal methods of raising revenues – such as sales of trade concessions to foreigners, direct foreign loans, and sales of public offices – appear to have increased in relative significance towards the end of the century. But this does not imply an easing-off of taxes on the agricultural sector.

The true rate of land tax – like so many other things in this case – is a source of mystery. The few estimates that have been produced are neither very reliable nor consistent with each other. Gardane put it down to 10 per cent for the beginning of the century, while Curzon later claimed that it had been increased to 20 per cent at about the same time; according to Malcolm, it varied between 5 and 20 per cent. Theoretically, this makes sense. The productivity of land and the quality of the agricultural produce still varies quite considerably from one part of the country to another. It is therefore quite likely that, whereas in the poorest regions a 5 per cent tax rate (to which the 'irregular' extortions must be added) might have been sufficient to keep peasant consumption at subsistence, a higher rate of, say, 15 or 20 per cent could have done the same for the more productive provinces.[5] Such a practice would, of course, have left little room for positive incentives towards greater regional productivity, but we may safely assume that nothing could have been further from the thoughts of the central authorities, and their local exploitative agents, than considerations of this nature. Thus, it may be inferred that the *weighted* average rate of land tax for the whole of the country was around 15 per cent of the agricultural produce. The burden of 'irregular' extortions must have been somewhere in the region of a further 10–15 per cent, so that the overall rate of agricultural exploitation for the first few decades of the century – probably covering the whole of Period I and Period II – must have been around 25–30 per cent. But this seems to have intensified in Period III. By all accounts, it looks as if Curzon's report of a 25 per cent 'regular' tax rate for the 1880s (in addition to the relative intensification of 'irregular' extortionism) should be taken seriously. Hence the total burden must, *in percentage terms*, have increased to around 35 to 40 per cent in the last few decades of the nineteenth century. A high – and increasing – rate of inflation is sometimes blamed for this, as in such situations there would be a relative decline in the purchasing power of total revenues based upon a constant (flat) rate of taxation. But it must be remembered that some of the tax was collected in kind, and, in any case, if the rise in taxation was encouraged by a relative depression of the food-producing sector of agriculture (because of the shift to profitable cash-crop farming), the direction of causation may have been the reverse: i.e. a lower marketable food surplus for the urban sector adding fuel to the inflationary spiral!

Inflation, however, had other, more immediate and more effective, causes than this. Of these, the deliberate debasement of the local currency, the fall in the international price of silver and, consequently, the decline in the external value of the currency must be regarded as the most important 'monetary' factors. There are a number of interesting questions even at this broad and aggregate level: to what extent was inflation due (a) to successive debasements of the local currency, (b) to a continuous decline in the exchange rate caused by factors *other* than debasement and the fall in the price of silver, and (c) to structural and other non-monetary factors reinforcing the monetary trends; and what was the *relative* significance of each of these variables in the three periods which we have identified? It is clear that a satisfactory solution to all of these questions would be difficult to find even if we were in possession of more and better data. They are nevertheless too important to ignore altogether.

'The' Iranian currency – consisting, in fact, of a conglomeration of gold and silver coins (with smaller sub-divisions of copper and nickel), many of which had been in circulation, either locally or globally, since as far back as the sixteenth century – was nominally based on a bimetallic standard. But, for the best part, Iranian money was in fact based on silver, and the rial – which had been borrowed from the Spaniards (as had the name of its Persian translation, *shāhi*, which was a different and less valuable coin) – became the principal silver coin in the nineteenth century. This had originally been the equivalent of one-eighth of a tūmān, but probably from 1816, when it was reissued as a *ṣāḥib-qarānī* coin, or simply *qarān* (or *krān*), it was devalued to one-tenth of a tūmān. Throughout the century, debasement took two different forms: the official reduction of the *weight* of the coin; the 'unofficial' deterioration of the *fineness* of any given weight. This latter cause of the decline in the intrinsic value of Iranian money was later blamed on malpractice alone, and it led to the centralisation of the Mint towards the end of the century; but, in any case, it would be impossible to quantify its effect separately. Fortunately, we can say a little more about the official reduction of the silver content of the krān. According to Nafīsī, the krān contained the equivalent of 9.2 grams of silver 'in the beginning' (presumably the first decade); a little while later, this was reduced to 6.9 grams, and subsequently, under Muhammad Shah II (1834–48), to 5.75 grams. At the beginning of Nāṣir al-Dīn Shah's reign (1848) it was further reduced to 5.37 grams, and subsequently it was brought down to 4.98 grams; in 1910, it stood at 4.54 grams.[6] This is interesting. It shows that in the course of the century the official silver content of the currency fell by about 50 per cent, with about four-fifths of the fall occuring in Period I, and just about one-fifth in the latter half of the century. We shall examine the significance of this in a moment; meanwhile it is worth noting that an *official* debasement of 50 per cent over the whole of the century does not by itself appear to have been as dramatic as it might appear from the more qualitative statements concerning the issue. On the other hand, Joseph Rabino's detailed numerical discussion of debasement (in his article of 1892) should be treated with some caution, as he gives the impression that he does not distinguish carefully between the total depreciation of the *external* value of the Iranian currency in general (to which other, more important factors had also made a contribution), and the effects of its debasement in particular.[7]

In pre-industrial economies debasement was the standard method for an arbitrary expansion of the money supply. It enabled governments to spend more, and this – with a given aggregate supply of goods and services, and a probably stable velocity of circulation – tended to push up the price of domestic goods. Therefore, it was an invisible tax on the mass of the population, as it resulted in a transfer of real resources from them to the government. In addition, official debasements of the local money tended to devalue it relative to foreign currencies, although its precise consequences for the balance of trade cannot be known *a priori*, as this would also depend on the elasticities of demand for exports and imports (assuming, as is likely, that any possible income effects were insignificant). However, the domestic inflationary consequences of moderate debasement for our period should not be exaggerated. For this was an economy in which hoarding was the rule, banking habits and facilities almost non-existent, and public revenues were spent mainly on services and a few 'luxury' items. It is true that in conditions of low per capita incomes the income-elasticity of demand for food is likely to be high, so that increases in aggregate spending would automatically tend to put pressure on food prices; but this is unlikely to have been accompanied by any significant multiplier effects. Therefore, all things considered, the inflationary effect of official debasement *alone*, for the whole of the nineteenth century, cannot have been very significant – although, as we have seen, it must have made a much greater impact in the first half of the century. Thus, if there is evidence of high inflation – especially in the latter half, and particularly during the last three decades, of that century – we have to look for other factors (including the non-monetary factors) which were responsible for it (see Table 3.2).

During the nineteenth century the external value of Iranian currency fell by 410 per cent. But its distribution was very uneven. Table 3.3 shows that over 60 per cent of the total decline in the rate of exchange took place in the last three decades of the century: an annual percentage fall of 8.3 per cent for Period III as compared with 2.3 per cent for the whole of Periods II and III taken together.[8] In order to 'neutralise' the influence of debasement, Table 3.4 has been worked out, in which each figure is simply the difference between the corresponding figures in Tables 3.2 and 3.3.[9] It can be seen that, *putting aside the influence of debasement*, the annual *fall* in the exchange rate was just about 1.6 per cent over the period 1800–70, but it rose to 8.2 per cent for the remaining thirty years. In other words, in the first seven decades (and especially in Period I), when most of the debasement took place, 'the other factors' causing the overall depreciation of the local currency must have been relatively weak, while in Period III, when debasement was insignificant but the rate of depreciation was truly rapid, these 'other factors' must have been very strong indeed. Of these, the fall in the international price of silver after 1870 was certainly the most significant. But there had been a prelude to this which, in the context of our topic, is usually overlooked: between 1848 and 1867, following the North American and Australian gold discoveries, there had been an upsurge in the world supply of gold which resulted in an *appreciation* of silver in terms of gold, and this was accompanied by a sharp rise of about 25 per cent in world commodity prices. This trend was reversed, however, when the relative price of the two metals first stabilised around their former ratio of 1 : 16, in the latter half of the 1860s, and then began to fall from the mid-1870s, when fresh supplies of silver began to flow onto the world market. In

TABLE 3.2 Percentage distribution of debasement: selected periods

	1800–1900	*1800–50*	*1800–70*	*1850–70*	*1850–1900*	*1870–1900*
Total	50.0	40.0	45.9	5.9	10.0	4.1
Average per annum	0.5	0.8	0.6	0.3	0.2	0.1

Source: based on Sa'īd Nafīsī, *Tārīkh-i Ijtimā'ī va Iqtiṣādī-yi Irān dar Qurūn-i Mu'āṣir* (Teheran: Bunyād, 1965) pp. 20–1 and 220–1.

TABLE 3.3 Percentage rate of currency depreciation: selected periods

	1800–1900	*1800–50*	*1800–70*	*1850–70*	*1850–1900*	*1870–1900*	*1800–92*	*1870–92*	*1892–1900*
Total	410	120	160	140	290	250	260	100	150
Average per annum	4.1	2.4	2.3	2.0	5.8	8.3	2.8	4.5	18.8

Source: based on Issawi, *The Economic History of Iran*, pp. 343–4.

TABLE 3.4 Percentage rate of currency depreciation 'net' of debasement: selected periods

	1800–1900	*1800–50*	*1800–70*	*1850–70*	*1850–1900*	*1870–1900*	*1800–92*	*1870–92*	*1892–1900*
Total	360.0	70.0	114.1	34.1	280.0	245.9	210.0	96.0	146.0
Average per annum	3.6	1.4	1.6	1.7	5.6	8.2	2.3	4.4	18.7

Source: Tables 3.2 and 3.3 above.

fact, the relative price of silver fell by over 100 per cent by the end of the century.[10] But most of this dramatic fall was concentrated between 1889 and 1893, when silver prices relative to gold fell from 1 : 22.10 to 1 : 32.57 – that is, by over 47 per cent! It is therefore not surprising that in Table 3.4 the annual rate of depreciation for the period 1800–92 is just 2.3 per cent, while for the remaining eight years of the century it is equal to 18.7 per cent.

To summarise, the average annual rate of currency depreciation ('net' of the effects of official debasement) was about 3.6 per cent for the century as a whole. This is a fairly high rate for an economically backward country, and it cannot be merely or mainly explained by the fall in silver prices in the international market, because: (a) the rate of depreciation for the first half of the century, *when silver prices were almost constant*, was only 1.4 per cent per annum; (b) it rose to 1.7 per cent in the following two decades, *when silver prices were moderately rising*; (c) it increased dramatically to 4.4 per cent per annum between 1870 and 1892, *when silver prices were moderately falling*; (d) it galloped to 18.7 per cent in the remaining few years of the century, *when silver prices were declining sharply*. In fact, if we remove the combined effect of *rising* silver prices (for 1850–70) and *falling* silver prices (for 1870–92), we are left with an average annual rate of depreciation of 2.1 per cent for 1850–90, which is neither explained by debasement nor by the change in silver prices. This leaves us with only one possible explanation: this 2.1 per cent annual rate of depreciation was almost entirely due to a structural balance-of-trade deficit, which was further reinforced by the local debasements and, especially, the international decline in the price of silver. Indeed, figures in Table 3.5 show that the Iranian trade deficit was much higher between 1868 and the 1880s, when silver prices were falling moderately, than in the following decades, when silver prices declined dramatically. By all accounts, it looks as if the usual explanation of Iran's growing trade deficit with reference to the decline in silver prices alone is unacceptable.

Issawi and Entner have already discussed Iran's foreign trade fairly extensively, but there is still some considerable scope for analytical and numerical comments. They may be right in thinking that the *volume* of Iran's foreign trade grew substantially throughout the century, though Issawi's estimate of a twelvefold increase must be treated with caution.[11] But, in any case, the following important (and interconnected) points must be kept in mind: (a) the growth of Iran's foreign trade is unlikely to have been due to any significant domestic economic development – on the contrary, it must have been the result of the growth of European demand for primary products and the pressure of European powers (both directly and through the imposition of preferential tariff rates) to sell their manufactured products; and (b) this altered not only the *volume* but also the *composition* of Iran's exports and imports, with generally undesirable consequences for the national economy.

Table 3.5 brings together some estimates of Iran's total foreign trade in the nineteenth century, which, as we have already indicated, are not very reliable.

TABLE 3.5 Imports, exports and the balance of trade[a] ('000)

	1800s	*1820*	*1830*	*1857*	*1868*	*1880s*	*1900*
Imports	–	–	2,000 (3,800)	3,000 (6,840)	2,500 (6,250)	4,669 (14,660)	5,000 (25,550)
Exports	–	–	–	–	1,500 (3,750)	2,331 (7,319)	3,000 (15,330)
Total (imports plus exports)	2500 (2500)	–	–	–	4,000 (10,000)	7,000 (21,980)	8,000 (40,880)
Balance (exports minus imports)	–	–	–	–	−1,000 (−2,500)	−2,338 (−7,341)	−2,000 (−10,220)

[a] The top figures are expressed in terms of sterling, and those in parentheses give the corresponding tūmān values, which have been calculated according to the ruling rate of exchange at, or near, each date.

Source: based on Issawi, *The Economic History of Iran*, various tables and observations.

But, provided that the degree of unreliability is fairly evenly spread, we may be able to make some useful observations on *changes* in foreign trade and the balance of payments. Until the 1860s even what little information there is is insufficient to indicate movements in Iran's total balance of trade. We know from Entner's study of Iran's trade with Russia that, although Iran seems to have had a surplus on this account right up until the end of the century, the surplus tends to rise from 1830 to a maximum of 4.4 million gold rubles in 1864, and decline thereafter continuously (with one significant exception) until it turns into a deficit at the beginning of the twentieth century. Indeed, it is almost possible to fit a normal distribution curve to the figures for the period 1830–4 to 1890–4.[12] There are other indications that the period 1830–65 must have been a relatively happy one for Iran's foreign trade, even in spite of the 5 per cent *ad valorem* tariff rate which had been imposed on her, first by Russia and subsequently by the other imperial powers. But, from sometime in the 1860s until the end of the century, there developed a relatively large, and growing, deficit in Iran's foreign payments. It would be wrong to blame this wholly, or even mainly, on the fall in silver prices, since, as we noted earlier, this assumed dramatic proportions only in the last decade of the century, whereas the increase in the payments deficit reached its peak in the 1880s and fell to a lower level in 1900 (see Table 3.6). In percentage terms, this shows an

TABLE 3.6 Imports, exports and the balance of trade: rates of change (per cent)

	1830–57	*1857–68*	*1868–85*	*1885–1900*
IMPORTS				
total	50	−16.6	88.0	7.1
	(80)	(−8.3)	(134.6)	(74.3)
average per annum	1.8	−1.5	5.2	0.47
	(3.0)	(−0.80)	(7.9)	(4.9)
EXPORTS				
total	–	–	55.4	28.7
			(95.2)	(109.4)
average per annum	–	–	3.3	1.9
			(5.6)	(7.2)
DEFICIT				
total	–	–	−134.0	−14.5
			(193.6)	(39.2)
average per annum	–	–	−7.9	−0.96
			(11.4)	(2.6)

Source: Table 3.5.

annual average *increase* of 7.9 in the payments deficit, reckoned in sterling, between 1868 and 1885, but a *decline* of 0.96 between 1885 and 1900 (see Table 3.6). Indeed, the widening gap between imports and exports for the period 1868–85 could be put down mainly to the significant differential between the rates of increase of imports and exports – apparantly rising at 5.2 and 3.3 per cent, respectively – which may be contrasted with the corresponding rates of 0.47 and 1.9 for the remaining fifteen years of the century, when the rate of exchange was rapidly depreciating in response to the sharp decline in the price of silver (see Table 3.6). Long and short, the evidence provides some definite indication of the turn in the wheels of misfortune for Iran in the last three decades of the century.

There remain some remarks on the change in the composition of foreign trade. The rise in the production and export of cash crops, at the expense of other products, has been noted by some commentators, including Issawi and Keddie. But it is necessary to emphasise that the shift in Iran's pattern of trade was not simply, or significantly, the case of a relative increase in the export of cash crops and decline in the export of food crops. That apart, the main plot of the scenario falls over a substantial shift between the export of *processed* and *primary* products. Let us attempt a brief analysis of the figures in Table 3.7. The breakdown of imports shows that in percentage terms the import of clothing material fell slightly (from 66 to 63 per cent) between the 1850s and 1880s. Given a substantial increase in *total* imports in the latter twenty years or so of this period, this of course indicates a very considerable *absolute* growth. On the other hand, the percentage share of textile products in Iranian exports fell sharply, from 61 to 19 per cent, over the same period. Even if we allow, as we must, for some contribution of raw silk exports to this total (in addition to the fact of the general decline in silk production due to the devastating silkworm disease which started in the middle 1860s), this is still a remarkable observation. Take the case of cotton and woollen products alone. It can hardly be a coincidence that the contribution of this sector to total exports should have declined from 23 to a mere 1 per cent, while at the same time the share of raw cotton in the same total had increased from 1 to 7 per cent. And it may be instructive to note that this change in the pattern of exports took place over a period for the best part of which the international terms of trade were turning against primary and in favour of finished products. Furthermore, the fall in the exports of Iranian cloth was not just relative but also absolute. On the other hand, there was a rapid increase in the absolute level of textile imports. The two observations put together give us some indication of what the 'law of comparative advantage' must have been doing – in an almost unprotected domestic market – to the weak and ailing Iranian textile industry at a time which many writers believe to have witnessed the growth of the Iranian 'bourgeoisie'. And to pay, so far as possible, for this substitution of foreign for domestic goods, there had to be a very substantial

TABLE 3.7 The composition of foreign trade: percentage distribution by various categories

	1850s	*1880s*
IMPORTS		
Cotton cloth	43	48
Woollen and silk cloth	23	15
Total cloth imports	*66*	*63*
Tea	9	2
Sugar	2	8
Metal goods	2	2
Paraffin	–	1
Others	21	24
Total	*100*	*100*
EXPORTS		
Silk and products	38	18
Cotton and woollen cloth	23	1
Total cloth exports[a]	*61*	*19*
Cereals	10	16[b]
Fruits	4	6
Tobacco	4	5
Raw cotton	1	7
Opium	—	26
Total primary exports	*19*	*60*
Carpets	–	4
Others	20	17
Total	*100*	*100*

[a] This should include raw silk.
[b] Mainly rice.

Source: based on Issawi, *The Economic History of Iran*, pp. 135–6.

increase in the production of cash crops, chiefly opium but also rice (which is even now locally regarded as a luxury food product), cotton, tobacco, and so on. This, in a period of doubtful productivity growth, institutional rigidity, and lack of technical progress, should have meant a decline – and very probably an absolute decline – in the production of staple food for domestic consumption. And, given that population was increasing at a significantly positive rate, we have another clue to high inflation rates, perennial food shortages, and the growth of abject poverty. No wonder that by the end of the century Iran had become dependent on the importation of sizable quantities of food products in the hope of maintaining internal equilibrium.

Public Revenues and the National Product

The main sources of public revenues were briefly mentioned in the previous section. Table 3.8 summarises some estimated data for taxes and revenues in the nineteenth century. It is difficult to make much of such a pitifully small number of observations – which, in any case, may not be very reliable – but it may still be worth a try. Gardane and Malcolm's figures for the beginning of the century are very significantly different. All things considered, it may be nearer the truth to assume that the regular and the 'irregular' tax on agriculture amounted to about 20 million tūmāns each. Thus, the money value of the regular tax probably grew, apparently fairly smoothly, from 20 million tūmāns in the 1800s to about 50 million tūmāns at the close of the 1880s. Even though the figures may not be very reliable, they can throw some light on the *change* in total land tax, and other economic categories, on the assumption that any possible errors would be fairly systematic. The figures for 1886 and 1888–9 are in some sense more reliable than others, partly because, though

TABLE 3.8 Taxes and revenues ('000 tūmāns)[a]

Original sources	*1800s*	*1836*	*1867*	*1886*	*1888–9*
Gardane	3000	–	–	–	–
'regular'	(2000)	–	–	–	–
extortion	(1000)	–	–	–	–
Malcolm	6000	–	–	–	–
'regular'	(3000)	–	–	–	–
extortion	(3000)	–	–	–	–
India Office	–	2461.0[b]	–	–	–
UK Parliament (*Accounts and Papers*)	–	–	4912.5	5500	–
direct in money	–	–	(3825.0)	(4850)	–
direct in kind	–	–	(550.0)		–
customs	–	–	(537.0)	(650)[c]	–
Curzon	–	–	–	–	5537
'regular'					(4837)
extortion					(700)[c]

[a] Revenue figures, excluding customs revenues, must reflect the total land tax fairly accurately, although they include other taxes, such as taxes on the profits of the artisans, but notably poll tax, which, although levied independently from agricultural output, exclusively affected the peasant community.

[b] This is probably an underestimate for *total* revenues.

[c] My estimate (probably lower than the true figures).

Source: Issawi, *The Economic History of Iran*, Ch. 8.

they are quoted by two independent sources, there is a very close correspondence between them. And, on the whole, the rest of the observations do not seem too out of joint with these two figures. Unfortunately, it is difficult to know the real purchasing power of these nominal figures in the corresponding periods. But a two-and-a-half-fold increase in public revenues over eight more-or-less inflationary decades is not very impressive. Other things being equal, an average annual rate of inflation of about 2 per cent (which is a wild guess, but probably not an overestimate) would have sufficed for the real value of public revenues to have remained constant from the beginning to the end of the period. In this connection, Issawi's expression of surprise at the relatively small difference between the respective figures for 1867 and 1888, 'at a time when the real national product of Iran had probably increased appreciably', seems to be unjustified: it is based on an assumption which the figures themselves tend to disprove.[13] In fact, from our earlier analysis of foreign trade, inflation and currency depreciation, it looks as if these estimates are well in keeping with the economic conditions of the last few decades of the century, when the combination of high inflation rates and currency depreciation probably tended to increase the burden of 'irregular' extortions, in the hope, at least, of maintaining the real value of public revenues. We shall not attempt a lengthy discussion of the disbursement of public revenues, beyond observing that, according to estimates for 1867, 1868 and 1885, less than 60 per cent was spent on the army and the 'bureaucracy' (the army taking 40 per cent), and the rest was allocated to the privy purse, pensions for the 'nobles' and divines, and other, *ad hoc* disbursements. Although the sums involved were not absolutely considerable – thus reflecting the country's general poverty – their percentage distribution indicates the *relative* significance of the army and the 'bureaucracy' as organs of the state. There was, in any case, little or no expenditure on public services beyond the allocation to the 'colleges', amounting to 6 per cent of the total, recorded for 1884 – 5.[14]

This brings us to our last attempt at numerical bravery, with regard to the most significant, and the least clear, questions for Iranian economic developments in the last century: changes in the national output, per capita output, economic structure, aggregate consumption and saving, and the distribution of income. Figures for the national product are frankly non-existent, but, assuming that the weighted average rate of land tax, at 15 per cent of the agricultural output, was fairly uniform throughout the century, we may obtain some estimates for the value of total agricultural output in the corresponding years. These figures may be examined in Table 3.9, where figures for the national product are estimated on the assumption that agriculture had a constant 80 per cent share in the national output (we shall discuss the implications of this assumption later). An examination of the estimated figures for agricultural output, calculated by the above procedure, conveys an impression similar to our earlier discussion of public revenues. Agricultural products cannot have experienced a very significant growth even

TABLE 3.9 Some estimates of land tax, agricultural output and the national output ('000 tūmāns)[a]

	1800s	*1836*	*1867*	*1886*	*1888–9*
Land tax	1,700.0	2,091.8	2,719.0	4,122.0	4,111.0
Agricultural output	11,333.3	13,945.3	24,793.3	27,480.0	27,406.6
National output	14,166.6	17,431.6	30,991.6	34,350.0	34,258.3

[a] Land-tax figures have been calculated on the assumption that they constituted 85 per cent of public revenues (excluding customs). This would imply a constant 15 per cent share for other taxes. It would make no difference to our comparative observations through time if shares other than 85 and 15 per cent were assumed. It may be argued that the share of other taxes may have increased at the latter dates (for instance, by an increase in the total poll tax due to the growth of population); but this would result in even lower estimates of land taxes for these dates, implying an even lower agricultural output than shown in the table.

Agricultural output has been calculated on the assumption of a 15 per cent weighted average rate of land tax. The basis for this assumption has been discussed in the text.

National output has been estimated on the assumption that the share of agriculture in total output was 80 per cent. This has also been discussed in the text.

The figure of land tax for 1836 may be either an underestimate or, for some reason, unrepresentative for the period. But, if neither was the case, it would tend to confirm the general hypothesis that, in any case, the period 1848–67 must have been a relatively prosperous one, as, among other things, world commodity prices, and not only the price of silver, rose in this period.

Source: Table 3.8.

in Period III, when inflation rates were high and there was a significant switch to the production of cash crops. And this tends to confirm our earlier conclusion, that over this period the real value of the staple food crops probably fell absolutely. Clearly, our assumption of a uniform tax rate of 15 per cent for all the observations may not be correct. Yet the contemporary reports indicate *higher* tax rates for the latter half of this century (for instance, Curzon's claim of 25 per cent), which would imply even *lower* figures for the agricultural output in the last few decades than shown in Table 3.9. Thus, if we are to take the available figures at all seriously, our conclusion with respect to the agricultural sector seems to be almost inescapable.

The figures for the national product are recorded merely to indicate similar tendencies for the economy as a whole. It may be objected that the assumption of a 20 per cent contribution by industry and services (which has been plucked out of the air) may not be accurate. But it does not make any difference at all what the true figure might have been, so long as we keep our observations to *changes* in output. In addition, the assumption of a *constant* share (of 20 per cent or whatever) for the non-agricultural sectors throughout the century may be questioned on the ground that the share of these sectors might have been increasing in the latter half of the century; but this is very doubtful. We have already seen that the forces of 'comparative advantage' were busy driving the Iranian textile industry from both the foreign *and* the home market. And this alone was probably the most important sub-sector of manufacturing industry. There could have been some increase in the share of trade offsetting a possible tendency for the share of the non-agricultural sectors of the economy to decline. Yet a rise in the share of the non-agricultural sectors could not have increased their share to more than 30 per cent of total output; and, even on this extremely optimistic assumption, the real value of the national output in the inflationary years of the last decades cannot have been much greater than in the earlier periods. Hence, by any reckoning, it is hard to see what significantly positive economic development took place in the latter half of the century.

Not much can be said about such categories as consumption and saving, even on the aggregate, except that for the mass of the population the former must have been near subsistence (and sometimes below it) and the latter non-existent. Most of what little saving there could have been was probably made by a few 'enlightened' big landlords and, especially, a few big merchants, the increase in whose fortunes has led some historians to believe that the last few decades of the century witnessed significant economic growth and the rise of an incipient capitalist class. However that may be, our analysis indicates that the standard of living of the mass of the people must have dropped, perhaps even significantly, in the last few decades of the century. This was the period, we may recall, when the rate of inflation was high, the Iranian textile industry in retreat, and the production of staple food probably in decline; in addition, the international prices of silver and commodities were falling, and the Iranian population was rising.

A Brief Appraisal

This account, like its political counterpart, is a story of almost unmitigated failure. However, the 'rate' of failure was clearly not uniform either in its impact through time, or in its consequences for *all* the categories and sectors of the political economy. The Qajar period was generally not a happy period for the Iranian political economy. Indeed, it is difficult to see any considerable period of *economic* happiness since the decline of the Ṣafavid dynasty. Things naturally got worse, for two fairly closely related reasons: on the one hand, the perpetuation of socio-economic disruption and malady became cumulative in its long-term effects; on the other hand, the development of other political economies both enhanced the *relative* poverty of a backward economy, and affected it *absolutely* as a consequence of the inevitable shift in the international balance of power.

The Iranian economy, as also its polity, was inescapably jolted out of 'equilibrium' in the nineteenth century, when the agents of imperial rivalry, free trade, modern technology, political democracy, and so forth, made their presence felt in the country. Loss of territory reshaped the map of the country, robbed it (sometimes) of some of its best human and other resources, diminished both its productive capacity and its internal market, and reduced its political power. This, among other things, resulted in the preferential tariff treaties which left the economically weak and technologically backward native industry naked in competition with cheap machine-made products, which, in turn, led to a loss of manufactured exports, a shift to primary cash-crop production, a possible decline in staple-food production, and a general rise in imports. The payments deficit and the inflationary consequences were reinforced, as if through the hands of Providence, by the dramatic fall in the price of silver in the last three decades of the century. Meanwhile, population growth had had a further depressing effect on the standard of living of the mass of the people. There was clearly no technical progress, in the strict economic sense of this term, worth talking about. If anything, there are signs of technical *regress*, by which we mean the loss of a self-developed know-how, refined over the centuries, without the acquisition of a suitable substitute which, in its economic consequences, would be at least equal with the fore-gone technique. In fact, Iranians tended to acquire the habit of *consuming* the products of modern technology much more successfully than applying or adapting the technology itself – a tendency which has persisted well into the present century. This is a fact which, like so many other things, stands in total contrast to the reaction of Japan to foreign economic and political pressure of a similar kind in the same period. The 'technical progress' to which political historians usually point refers almost entirely to minority *consumption* of the products of foreign technology. The same goes for aggregate saving and accumulation. While lacking data for these important categories, we have enough indirect information to make it very difficult to believe that there could have been any remotely significant amount of capital accumulation, apart from some notable cases of hoarding and/or *investment in trade*. For it is difficult to suppose sizable physical accumulation, on the aggregate, over a period in which, on the one hand, production techniques had not improved, the internal market – in spite of population growth – possibly diminished, and the external market (for manufactured products) declined; and in which, on the other hand, taxes and extortions became more and more oppressive, debasement and other causes of inflation reduced the real standard of living, and socio-political insecurity (which, even at the best of times, has been a remarkable feature of the Iranian political economy) rapidly increased. Thus, in spite of the growth in population – which may not have been as large as is sometimes supposed – and a substantial increase in 'trade', a comprehensive analysis shows that there was little economic progress worthy of considera-tion, while in many areas there is evidence of fundamental decay and decline. This, by the way, indicates not a *static* state of 'lack of social integration', but a dynamic and/or cyclical tendency for socio-economic *dis*integration.[15] It is sometimes presumed that there had been a tendency for the growth of a 'national bourgeoisie' which, when threatened by foreign economic com-petition, and enlightened by foreign political teaching, led the Persian

Revolution (1905–9) against 'feudalism'.[16] Yet there is no quantitative or qualitative support for such presuppositions. We cannot identify any considerable accumulation of capital in the production of industrial goods; on the contrary, both the export and the import figures, as we saw, indicate a decline in the main traditional Iranian crafts (except carpets). But, if this so-called 'bourgeoisie' refers to those engaged in domestic and foreign *trade*, it is very difficult to assess the situation. The growth in foreign trade clearly tended to increase the size and significance of its middle-men, but to what extent this meant a *net* increase in merchant capital, and to what extent it involved a mere diversion of such capital from *domestic* to *foreign* trade activities (and, hence, its concentration in fewer hands), it is difficult to know.

Appendix: An Application of Myrdal's Concept of Circular and Cumulative Causation

It would be useful to analyse the interaction of these major tendencies in the Iranian economy – and their immediate net consequences for the whole of the country – in terms of Gunnar Myrdal's suggestive theory of 'circular and cumulative causation'. Briefly, Myrdal's theory proposes a new model of inter-industry and interregional change, in place of the standard neo-classical model of equilibrium analysis. It emphasises divergence, as opposed to convergence on socio-economic equilibria, of sectors, regions and national economies, in the absence of exogenous equilibrating forces, such as the intervention of national states in their interregional and international trade. Once a state of aggregate – or sub-aggregate – equilibrium has been disturbed by the free play of market forces, the theory predicts a circular and cumulative tendency to reinforce that disturbance unless conscious policy intervenes to counteract its effects and enforce macro-economic balance within (and, as far as possible, between) various national economies.

The process of circular and cumulative causation itself is made up of two sets of major, but opposing, effects. First, there is what Myrdal describes as the 'backwash effects'. For example, the opening up of a backward national region (or economy) to trade with another, more forward region or country would result in a cumulative transfer of resources (capital, labour, and so forth) to the latter region, and would consequently reinforce the poverty of the backward region and the state of interregional inequality. The second set of major effects is what Myrdal calls the 'spread effects', which make up the sum total of all the possible benefits spilt over from the forward and progressive to the backward and declining region, in the process of interchange between them. For example, the expansion of the former may widen the market for the products of the latter, and at the same time make it possible for some of its inhabitants to enjoy better and/or cheaper 'foreign' products. Myrdal maintains, however – and this seems to be borne out by a good deal of historical evidence and empirical observation – that the spread effects are bound to be much weaker than the backwash effects, and the balance of the two forces is, therefore, very likely to lead to the decline of the backward region.[17]

It is possible that the theory of circular and cumulative causation is more readily applicable to the contemporary as well as historical analysis of *interregional* than to that of *international* trade. For example, the movements of labour and capital are much freer across the regional boundaries of a single national economy than they would be across the national economic (and political) boundaries themselves – although, at least in the contemporary world, such international backwash effects may be observed in the net transfer of capital and *skilled* labour resources from some developing to some advanced countries. But it is likely that, at least in the case at hand, such direct transfers from Iran to the European countries were quite negligible. Nevertheless, the matter does not rest at this point.

Indeed, many of the features of economic change in nineteenth-century Iran, especially during the second half of the century, and particularly its last three decades, may be characterised in terms of the Myrdalian backwash effects. The diplomatically imposed preferential tariff treaties, the deterioration of the terms of trade (resulting in an indirect transfer of real resources from the country to its major trading partners) and the cumulative balance-of-payments deficit may all be regarded as such adverse effects of the greater integration of the Iranian economy in world trade. More importantly, the decline of indigenous manufacturing production and traditional technology, the greater shift of resources to primary production in the hope of meeting the growing import bill, the loss of self-sufficiency in food production as a result of the growth of exportable cash-crops, the expansion in the (specific as opposed to nationwide) consumption of (largely imported) goods and services, through the demonstration effect, which the country could ill afford, were perhaps the more subtle, and also the more enduring, backwash consequences of this unequal partnership.

Against these backwash effects must be set the possible spread effects of the greater internationalisation of the Iranian economy. One such spread effect is the so-called commercialisation of the Iranian economy, the growth of international and, *probably*, domestic trade; and the possible, though by no means certain, extension of *total* commercial capital, and its greater centralisation and concentration. Here, it may be noted parenthetically that it would be a mistake to regard this as a 'stage' of development in the Iranian economy along the lines of the rise of commercial capitalism in sixteenth- and seventeenth-century Western Europe. For, apart from many other considerations, the latter development was a unique and progressive event unprecedented since the fall of the Roman Empire and the corresponding rise of European feudalism, while the principles of a commercial political economy had been long established in Iran (as also the rest of the Middle East), and the decline in commerce in the eighteenth and early nineteenth century was a *cyclical* experience reflecting the general decline in the fortunes of the country. Thus, the so-called 'commercialisation' of the latter period cannot be regarded as a 'stage of development' in a series of progressive socio-economic transformations comparable to the European experience. But, in any case, what of it? This, after all, was the very instrument through which all the backwash effects mentioned above were brought about![18]

The second spread effect, the significance of which cannot be underestimated, was the impact of Western political ideas and practices on the Iranian intelligentsia, and their influence in broadening and increasing the latter's criticism of the state of affairs in Iran – criticisms which themselves were not independent of those backwash effects. Thirdly, the improvement in the means of communication, especially through the construction of telegraph lines, clearly hastened the greater integration of the political economy as a necessary catalyst of the first two spread effects. Fourthly, the appearance or increase, in the Iranian market, of some new – and, perhaps, somewhat 'superior' – consumer products, such as electricity, foreign fabrics and shoes, may by themselves be regarded as such spread effects, although, as we have seen, they led to even stronger backwash effects by destroying the local industry and technology, thus weakening motives for saving and accumulation, and increasing the deficit in the country's international payments.

In this respect it is worth taking issue with one particular, though in my view insignificant, piece of observation. It is often claimed that the casual remarks of foreign travellers to Iran, in the late nineteenth century, about the spread of tea-drinking, even to some villages, must be taken as indirect evidence for the growth of public welfare. In our scheme, this would be regarded as one example of the fourth group of spread effects mentioned above. However, let us note that, first, such casual observations, based on very small samples and made by observers who were not usually well informed about the country's circumstances – *and the changes therein* – cannot, in principle, be taken too seriously; secondly, given the inevitably small sample of observations, generalisation is a near impossibility; thirdly, putting aside the above objections, such observations could only be generally true of the *regions* from which the samples were taken: in an economy with such great regional imbalances in welfare, resources and technology as that of Iran (both now and especially then) such countrywide generalisations would be little short of analytical absurdity. We noted above that the process of circular and cumulative causation is particularly strong between the regions of a changing economy, so that, while a privileged region may be making a net gain, many regions may be incurring a cumulative net *loss*, more than counter-balancing the net welfare gain of the privileged region. And this could well have been an effect of the growth of 'commercialisation', centralisation of trade and improvement in communications, in the late nineteenth century. Therefore, while villagers around Mashhad, Tabriz and Teheran may have been enabled to drink tea, or whatever, the peasants of Kirmān, Kurdistan and elsewhere could well have been going without their daily bread. In a comprehensive study of the dynamics of a political economy, it is not the welfare of the privileged minority which should be the exclusive focus of attention. Fourthly, it is no new discovery that the opening up of a backward economy, anywhere, will result in the importation and consumption of hitherto non-existent or luxury products by a small percentage of the population, usually to the detriment of its balance of payments, its local industry, its future growth, and the welfare of the majority of its inhabitants. Indeed, this is a familiar picture in many parts of the Third World at present. But by itself it is hardly evidence of 'progress' and 'improvement' in anything at all. Last, but certainly not least, these observations mainly refer to the close of the nineteenth century, when, as an examination of the figures in Table 3.7 above – the only 'hard' evidence at our disposal – reveals, the percentage share of tea in total imports *fell* from 9 per cent (in the 1850s) to a mere 2 per cent (in the 1880s), while population was growing faster than ever before! Unfortunately, we are not in possession of *absolute*, as distinct from *percentage*, figures for imports in the latter period, and this makes it difficult to know exactly whether tea imports had absolutely declined between the two dates. But, on the assumption that total imports rose from the 1850s to 1880s by no more than 400 per cent, it would appear that the absolute level of tea imports would even have slightly declined by the latter date. This makes Issawi's remark that the import of 'tea . . . expanded greatly' rather puzzling. In any case, on the above assumption and the further (conservative) estimate that the average population growth rate over these three decades was about 1 per cent per annum, it would follow that the per capita import and consumption of tea (which, in this context, is the appropriate index) *fell* by about a quarter from the 1850s to 1880s![19] The figures speak for themselves.

NOTES

1. Those who are familiar with the state of the Iranian political economy in the nineteenth century would benefit from some information on the Japanese socio-economic position, as well as the changes it underwent, in order that the comparison might be seen in a more realistic perspective – see, for example, W. W.

Lockwood, *The Economic Development of Japan . . . 1868–1938* (Princeton, NJ: Princeton University Press, 1969). Amīr Niẓām, however, bears a curious resemblance to Reżā Khān Pahlavi, in his social background, military position ('Amīr Niẓām' was a special title created for him to indicate his supreme command of the armed forces, in much the same way as 'Sardār Sepah' was created for Reżā Khān), personal ambitions and pseudo-modernist methods and aspirations. We need have little doubt that, had he survived, Iranian historical mythology would now regard him as an agent of some foreign power, and a ruthless despot, just as Reżā Khān, had he not managed to succeed (or survive) in his earlier years, would doubtless now be held to be a great hero who had fallen victim to foreign imperialism and internal reaction. Such are the ironies of history, which, in this case, cannot be further pursued here. See, however, Chs 5 and 6, below, for some more references to this subject.

2. See Charles Issawi, *The Economic History of Iran 1800–1914* (Chicago and London: University of Chicago Press, 1971); and Nikki R. Keddie, 'The Economic History of Iran 1800–1914, and its Political Impact: An Overview', *Iranian Studies*, Spring–Summer 1972, pp. 58–78.
3. In a recent article, G. G. Gilbar (using some detailed provincial statistics and other information) has shown that periodic famines and epidemics, as well as ordinary endemic diseases, took a heavy toll in the nineteenth century. See his 'Demographic Developments in Late Qajar Persia, 1870–1906', *Asian and African Studies*, XI, no. 2 (1976).
4. For a more elaborate discussion of the tax structure, see Issawi, *The Economic History of Iran*, Ch. 8.
5. This does not, however, mean that the general standard of living should have been the same in all provinces; for the notion of 'subsistence' refers to a biological minimum as well as to a sociological limit, and the latter could vary (even significantly) between different countries and regions, reflecting the productivity of nature and the traditional standards enjoyed or suffered.
6. Sa'īd Nafīsī, *Tārīkh-i Ijtimā 'ī va Iqtiṣādī-yi Irān dar Qurūn-i Mu'āṣir* (Teheran: Bunyād, 1965) pp. 19–20 and 220–1. It is not clear whether the devaluation of the rial, relative to the tūmān, also dates from 1816. However, many traditional shopkeepers still persist in referring to the equivalent of 2.5 official rials as 2 rials! On the subject of Iranian currencies, see further, H. L. Rabino, *Coins, Medals and Seals of the Shahs of Iran, 1500–1941* (Hertford, 1945).
7. See his 'Banking in Persia', in *Journal of the Institute of Banking*, 1892.
8. It is significant to note that between 1834 and 1864 the rate of exchange of the rial merely fell from 20 krāns to 22.5 to the pound sterling, the lowest exchange rate for any one year over the period being 22.8 krāns to the pound in 1856.
9. This method of isolating the effect of debasement is not accurate, as it is based on the assumption that all other factors are given, and it ignores the secondary repercussions of debasement itself. Yet it is useful as a crude indicator, especially as our interest is in *changes*, over time, in the influence of different variables.
10. See, for example, S. E. Clough, *European Economic History* (London: McGraw-Hill, 1968).
11. Issawi's method of estimating the trade figures is not very reassuring. However, it is important to note that (a) figures for foreign trade refer to both imports and exports, and rapid increases in a pre-industrial country's imports at the cost of inflation, a trade deficit and foreign debts are hardly evidence for 'economic development'; and (b) Issawi's estimate of £5 million worth of foreign trade for the 1860s, together with all other information available, would indicate an export coefficient of 0.15 and import coefficient of 0.22, which are unbelievably high for Iran's circumstances at the time. (Our procedure for estimating the above

coefficients is too elaborate to discuss, especially as the point itself is not all that important.) See Issawi, *The Economic History of Iran,* pp. 131–2.

12. See Marvin Entner, *Russo-Persian Commercial Relations* (Gainesville, Fla, 1965); and Issawi, *The Economic History of Iran*, p. 142, Table 1.
13. Ibid., p. 337
14. See ibid., and the references therein.
15. Our references to 'lack of social integration' are related to some popular but not so helpful 'structural functionalist' theories of 'the political sociology of development', much in vogue in the 1960s but unfashionable at present. For an application of one such 'theory' to an aspect of modern Iranian politics, see E.Abrahamian, 'Kasravi, the Integrative Nationalist of Iran', *Middle Eastern Studies*, Oct 1973, pp. 271 – 95; and H. Katouzian, ' "Kasravi, the Integrative Nationalist of Iran". A Comment' (mimeo., June 1974). See further Chs 5 and 6, below.
16. See further the appendix to this chapter, as well as Chs 4 and 5,below.
17. See Gunnar Myrdal, *Economics Theory and Underdeveloped Regions* (London: University Paperbacks,1957).
18. In particular, see Vahid F.Nowshirvani *et al.*,'The Beginnings of Commercial Agriculture in Iran' (mimeo., n.d.).
19. Let us, however, emphasise that this conclusion is based on the assumption of a fourfold increase in total imports over the period, and that we do not wish to insist that the consumption of tea did not increase in those decades, even though such an increase may have been exaggerated. Our main argument is that, even if this is true, it cannot be regarded as evidence for an increase in per capita incomes and welfare.

4 *Mashrūṭeh* and after: Revolution and Depression, 1900–18

In 1896 Nāṣir al-Dīn Shah, the last effective ruler of Qajar Iran, was assassinated. The assassin was both a victim of the corruption and lawlessness of the degenerating despotic state, and a devout follower of the Islamic political thinker and leader Sayyed Jamāl al-Dīn Asad-ābādī (better known outside Iran as 'Afghānī'). The Shah's assassination was the final act in a sorry tale of political agitation and perennial revolt, in which the Tobacco-Régie affair had been the most significant incident: in 1891 public rebellion had forced the Shah to withdraw his concession granting a monopoly of the tobacco trade to a foreign company.[1] In retrospect, this had been a momentous achievement: for the first time within memory, the state had been compelled to bow to popular opinion in response to a widespread urban rebellion.

Mashrūṭeh: The Revolution Against Despotism

There have been numerous accounts, in a variety of languages, of the Persian Revolution and its various aspects.[2] Yet, the merits of these works notwithstanding, a definitive history of the revolution still remains to be written. Here, our interest in the subject is purely analytical. In this section I shall try to present an analysis of the tendencies and forces which led up to the revolution; its objectives and achievements; and the socio-economic make-up of its human agents. This will be followed by a brief review of the state of the Iranian political economy in the decade which separates the end of the revolution from the conclusion of the First World War.

THE CAUSES OF THE REVOLUTION

A theoretical explanation of the Persian Revolution could be formulated along the following lines. Economic development in the nineteenth century had led to the growth of an urban bourgeoisie who were not – or could not be – accommodated within the existing feudal (or 'semi-feudal') system: in the well-known Marxist terminology, the forces of production (that is, the combined effects of capital accumulation and technical progress) had developed to the extent that the relations of production (the prevailing class structure, and the moral and social institutions corresponding to it) could no longer contain them. The resulting conflict between the technological base and the institutional superstructure – the socio-economic reality and the ideological appearance – eventually manifested itself in a political upheaval for the establishment of a new (and historically relevant) institutional framework.

This is a familiar model for the original formulation of which the French Revolution had supplied the basic empirical data. It involves many unsettled, controversial questions, such as whether or not the revolution would be caused by wholly impersonal forces or effected by the conscious effort of human agents in pursuit of their personal and class interest. These issues, though highly significant in their own context, are outside the scope of our present task. Fortunately, however, they are of little relevance to the problem in hand. For, whatever the 'correct' solution to these finer problems, the question of primary interest to us is whether or not the Persian Revolution was a bourgeois revolution.

The model – in its crude and basic form presented above – has been a popular explanation of the revolution among Persian intellectuals. It has been also held by some historians and sociologists, with some (occasionally significant) qualifications. For example, the latter have tended to place more emphasis on the accumulation of *financial* (merchant) as opposed to *physical* (industrial) capital in nineteenth-century Iran, or they have considered the role of imperialist powers, and European ideologies, as important supplementary factors. Few would deny that all of these observations on socio-political development must be included in *any* realistic assessment of the forces behind the Persian Revolution. Yet the dogmatic *or* flexible application of the basic Marxist *model* – as opposed to the broader Marxian *approach and method* – would be irrelevant to this case.

On the basis of the arguments and evidence of the previous chapters we make the following assertions: (a) Persia was not a feudal society; (b) during the nineteenth century there had been very little industrialisation and technical progress in production; (c) there is little or no evidence for a systematic growth of per capita income; (d) there was a shift of resources away from the production of food and traditional manufacturing products; (e) this structural change did not stimulate growth of productivity in agriculture, and technical progress in manufacturing, but led to greater food and machine-made imports; (f) there was a growing inflation and balance-of-payments deficit. These observations alone should make it *difficult* to apply the above model to the Persian Revolution; the rest of the analysis in this section would, I believe, make it *impossible*.

There can be little doubt that the increase in the volume of foreign trade had led to greater concentration and centralisation of commercial capital. Yet, this was neither due to an indigenous expansion, or a greater integration, of the national economy; nor the result of an autonomous discovery of new methods and markets by Iranian merchants.[3] For these reasons, if none other, an analytical comparison of nineteenth-century Iran with the period of the rise of commercial capitalism (or 'mercantilism') in western Europe is not justified: whereas the commercialisation of European society proceeded through centuries of effort and struggle by the burghers – the emerging bourgeoisie of the 'free towns' – with increasing support from the state against the feudal aristocracy; towns, commerce and the state have always been significant features of life and labour in Iranian society.

Nevertheless, it is true that the growth of foreign trade benefited the big Iranian merchants; and by increasing their actual fortunes it directly increased their potential political power, at the expense of the state. It also played a role in weakening Iranian despotism in a number of indirect ways. First, the foreign imposition of commercial treaties by itself exposed the relative weakness of the Iranian state in relation to the international powers. Secondly, some of the steps involved in proposing and concluding such treaties – for example, illicit payments to the Shah and high officials, intensification of bureaucratic factionalism, and so forth – tended to weaken the unity of the despotic structure and apparatus from within. Thirdly, the greater specialisation in the production and export of raw materials, the relative decline of traditional manufacturing, the use of modern means of communication, such as the telegraph, the high rate of inflation (which, in the case of food products, was almost invariably blamed on speculation by merchants), the crippling deficit in foreign payments and the resulting accumulation of foreign debts – these were some of the causes of a complex structural change in the political economy which the traditional bureaucracy could not even comprehend, let alone cope with.

The growth of foreign trade was only one aspect of Iran's greater contact with European countries. The Anglo-Russian rivalry weakened the Iranian state without replacing it by direct colonial rule. It laid bare the helplessness of the Shah and the bureaucracy, and it humiliated the Iranian people, who blamed the political system as the sole reason for the country's subjugation. It demonstrated European standards of living, education, and so on, which the intelligentsia thought as being exclusively the result of constitutional forms of government. It taught them that, in an alternative system, private property could be safe and powerful, political power could be shared, official posts could be less insecure, and life and limb could be better protected against arbitrary decisions. And this, they thought, was all that was necessary for a free, powerful and prosperous Iran.

The causes of the Persian Revolution must be sought in a combination of such inseparable mental and material processes, rather than in an uncritical application of a theoretical model, or models, which refer to a significantly different historical reality.

THE OBJECTIVES OF THE REVOLUTION

There are always gaps between the objectives and the achievements of every successful revolution, although this does not mean that there is little correspondence between them: on the contrary, the achievements of a revolution are the real, concrete counterparts to its ideal, abstract objectives. The objectives of the French Revolution were symbolised in the famous motto 'Liberty, Equality and Fraternity'; its achievements eventually led to the political supremacy of the bourgeoisie, greater individual liberties, freer trade, and equality before the law – in short, the destruction of the institutional framework of French feudalism. A casual acquaintance with the demands and slogans of the Iranian revolutionaries would give the impression of a great deal of similarity between them and the aims and aspirations of a bourgeois revolution. For they too asked for greater freedom, justice and democracy. Yet, on closer examination the appearances would prove to be deceptive: beneath the layer of words and concepts, which are rendered synonymous by formal translation, there lie the differences in their real social and historical significance.

Mashrūṭeh is a Perso-Arabic word meaning 'conditioned', 'constrained' or 'qualified'. The central demand of the Persian Revolution was the establishment of a constrained or qualified monarchy; it was also the revolution's greatest – though not lasting – achievement. It meant the abolition of 'the rule of force' (a well-known Persian phrase) and its replacement with a government legitimised by popular consent. More precisely, the revolutionaries demanded a system of government in which the widespread absolute *and* arbitrary exercise of power would be impossible; the executive would be appointed, and its activities checked and balanced, by elected representatives of the people; the judiciary would be an independent body guided by civil and criminal codes of justice. Inevitably, these demands found symbolic expression in a campaign for a written constitution based on the separation of powers.

In the European languages, the struggle for *Mashrūṭeh* is generally described as the Constitutional (or, more correctly, the Constitutionalist) Revolution of Iran. This is symbolic of some serious confusions which go beyond wasteful semantic squabbles: the confusions arise from differences in historical experience, cultural visions and conceptual frameworks, which are reflected in the use of language. The Persian Revolution was not fought for a *social* contract; rather, it aimed at a contract – a legal framework – which would make life and labour less insecure and more predictable. The revolutionaries did not demand equality before the law, for there existed no law (in the European sense of this term) before which men could be equal. That is, 'the law' itself was the expression of the arbitrary whim of those in positions of power, each of whom – according to his station – could decide to treat different men differently at different times. Thus, the law itself was as changeable as the law-giver, his interest, his mood and his pleasure. By fighting against despotism, the revolutionaries fought for law itself.

Iranian despotism was not a tyranny or dictatorship in the Graeco-Roman senses of these terms which have been passed on to modern Western culture. It described a monopoly of *arbitrary* power, at each and every level of public life, 'legitimised' by the monopoly of one man alone. It was not a system in which tradition, custom, morality and law constrained freedom of thought, expression or participation in social processes in a predictable – even unchanging – fashion. It was a state of lawlessness; of the theoretical equality of all the subjects before the decisions of the ruler; and their actual inequality according to those arbitrarily changeable decisions – they were equal before absolute power because even their actual inequalities could not be regarded as stable and lasting. It was a social framework which combined the weakness of *all forms* of private property with a high degree of socio-political mobility, where a man possessed of good health and great wealth could not know whether he would enjoy either or both the day after.[4]

The Iranian revolutionaries struggled for freedom; but the meaning which this conveyed to them – that is, their *understanding* of the concept of freedom – was neither bourgeois nor the higher forms of liberty. It would be best to discuss this subject with reference to Isaiah Berlin's suggestive – though controversial – distinction between the 'negative' and the 'positive' concepts of freedom. Briefly, *negative* freedom describes absence of restraints; the removal of legal barriers against the activities of the individual; the antithesis of law, though not of a legal framework. It implies, in the well-known saying, a state of individual liberty which may be constrained only in so far as it may prevent others from enjoying the same degree of freedom. In such a state the existence of a legal framework is justified only to the extent that it enables *everyone* to benefit from the maximum possible freedom from restraint. By contrast, the *positive* concept of freedom defines not so much a situation in which there exist few barriers to individual activity, as a state of affairs where men would enjoy the power *to* act: here, the emphasis is not on a passive, potential permission to eat or starve, employ or be unemployed, fit or be a misfit, but on an active, real, power *to be able* to eat, find employment, or – in Harold Laski's words – 'realise one's best self'. For negative freedom, the existence of a legal framework with provisions for equality before the law is all that is necessary and sufficient, so long as the law does not restrain freedom beyond the minimum compatible with the enjoyment of negative freedom by all. For positive freedom, the law must intervene – even constrain the (negative) freedom of some – in order to make at least a minimum amount of *social* equality possible; at the political level, this would mean the existence of a democratic system through which people could *participate* in political processes; at the socio-economic level, it would mean laws which would mitigate, or 'remove', inequalities in social opportunities, incomes and welfare. Negative freedom is freedom in the most obvious, common sense of this term, *constrained* by *legal* equality; positive freedom is the existence of legal *rights*, *guaranteeing* various degrees of *social* equality.[5]

The concept of freedom for which the Iranian revolutionaries fought was neither of these two, nor their synthesis. The Iranian revolutionaries demanded freedom not from legal restraints, but from organised and official *lawlessness*; not to enjoy socio-economic equality, but to *divide* the absolute *power* of the state, and share it out between them. In its 'negative' aspect, their concept of freedom involved a positive demand for a legal framework – for law itself; in its 'positive' aspect, it involved neither more nor less intervention by the state in the political economy, but a hierarchical and geographical division and democratisation of state power. It was freedom from political impotence, social indignity and economic insecurity. It was a struggle by 'subjects' and 'servants' – including landlords, merchants and others alike – to become not so much citizens (in the strict European sense of this term) as *persons*. It was a demand for *all* to enjoy security of life, limb and property from unconstrained and unpredictable bureaucratic licence. That is why the revolutionaries simply assumed that all other social and political desiderata – economic progress, social welfare and national integrity – would be ensured by their triumph against despotism.

Berlin's two concepts of freedom are products of European liberal thought, developed in the successive periods of emerging and mature capitalism. Neither the philosophy nor the related social environment is of much relevance to the Persian Revolution, its agents or its social context.

THE EVENTS AND THE AGENTS OF THE REVOLUTION

The social and intellectual forces of the revolution, which had been developing for a long time, were called into action when, in 1905, two respectable members of the merchant community – the *bāzār* – were publicly flogged. These were two sugar merchants accused of *ihtikār*, or speculation in trade, by the governor of Teheran, who ordered the punishment. In this case, the 'state' had apparently acted in 'the public interest'. But the public reacted with total condemnation, because they presumed the merchants to be not only innocent, but also victims of personal enmity; or scapegoats for official inefficiency and corruption.[6] This, in any case, would be the normal response of a people who had always viewed the organs of the state as the agents of brute force and heartless injustice. Clearly, the episode itself could not have surprised a public used to many similar experiences: the caning and flogging of victims of unconstrained power, ranging from bureaucratic officials to domestic servants. Yet it was immediately seized upon as a pretext for demanding the establishment of an *Idālat-khāneh* (literally, House of Justice). The Shah himself was feeble, ailing and weak; in fact, all available evidence suggests that he must have been subnormal in intelligence. But his lackeys (*nawkarān*) quickly grasped the implications of this demand; and they did their best to prevent its final victory. The series of street demonstrations, mosque meetings, political leaflets and proclamations, and 'sit-ins' in sanctuaries (*bastnishīnī*) which followed were met with the resistance of the ruling bureaucratic elite, and led to some violence and bloodshed.

As the movement spread to the provinces – and notably to the progressive and relatively prosperous province of Azerbijan – attitudes hardened, and revolutionary demands were extended to no less than a constitutional government. In retrospect the initial success of the revolution was too easy; and – apart from the revolutionary effort itself – this was due partly to the personal weakness of the Shah, and partly to the British government's active support for the revolution, through their diplomatic legation in Teheran and other cities. The British support for the revolution was consistent with both their interest and their ideology: by supporting the revolution they were both scoring diplomatic points against the Russian government, on whom the Iranian court had become increasingly dependent, and siding with the cause of freedom and democracy, with which they identified the British system. Indeed, this is the light in which their role and position were viewed by Iranian intellectuals at the time. In any case, the later conspiratorial theory according to which the British government through their Iranian agents or spies 'created', 'led' and 'concluded' the Persian Revolution is one which can be safely laughed out of court: at its best, this is a flight of fancy in reading history backwards – that is, interpreting past reality merely in the light of later experience; and, at its worst, shows a complete disregard for the effects of social forces and human consciousness in historical situations.

At any rate, a constitution was hastily drafted; and it received royal assent shortly before the Shah's death. But, as the revolutionary leaders had rightly expected, his son, Muhammad Ali, who was sworn in as the new (constitutional) monarch, would not give up despotic rule without a bloody struggle.[7] Indeed, he wasted no time in trying to undo the achievements of the revolution: he conspired with foreign governments (mainly the Russians), provincial governors and big landlords; he tried, with some success, to divide the revolutionary leadership by buying some of them off, and frightening others into inaction. More significantly, he opposed the revolutionary goal of *Mashrūteh* not to *istibdād* (or despotism) but to *Mashrū'eh*, or the rule of Islamic law: in theory, this could mean a political system in accord with the principles of Islamic law and jurisprudence; in practice, it would have led to the restoration of despotism, somewhat modified by the direct participation of a few religious dignitaries in its processes. The main slogan of a large street procession organised by the Shah's agents (in which the Jewish community was forced to take part) was as follows: 'We support the Prophet's religion. *Mashrūteh* we do not want.'

In 1907, a secret agreement between Britain and Russia set up two – British and Russian – spheres of influence, divided by an Iranian buffer zone. This was probably the most important reason for the withdrawal of active British support for the Persian Revolution, and the intensification of Russian backing for the Shah. These domestic moves and external events, combined with the defiant and uncompromising attitude of the revolutionaries, encouraged the Shah to lead a military coup against the constitutional government: the National Assembly was bombarded, and the revolutionary leaders were arrested, murdered, or forced into hiding. Without doubt, it was the heroic resistance in the city of Tabriz, capital of the Azerbijan province, that in the first crucial months following the coup saved the revolution from total collapse. By holding out, the Tabrizis inflicted defeat and humiliation on the enemy, and encouraged resistance in the capital and elsewhere. In 1909, the revolutionary armies from Gīlān and Iṣfahān joined forces and, after routing the government troops, entered Teheran in triumph. The Shah was forced to abdicate and go into exile, and his young son Ahmad was put in his place under the supervision of a regent.

The nature and purpose of a revolution is identified both by its aims and by its agents. The participants in the Persian Revolution – the social classes which were represented among its leadership, rank and file and sympathisers – came from all walks of urban life except for the military–bureaucratic establishment. The peasantry were neither specifically represented in the objectives of the revolution nor autonomously took part in it: there were no demands whatever for greater social and economic justice for the peasants; and on the occasions when a peasant group took part in the struggles they were almost invariably mobilised and led by their own landlords. Merchants, landlords, lower administrative ranks, modernised intellectuals, Qajar noblemen, religious dignitaries, theological scholars and common preachers all took part in the revolution, with the single unifying aim of destroying despotism and replacing it by a constitutional government. Inevitably there were exceptions. But, as social classes and professional groups, these strata of the urban people were on the side of the revolution, because, for the reasons we have already discussed, they all stood to lose nothing, and gain something, from its triumph.

The revolutionary triumph promised law, political participation and greater personal security to all. This would automatically ensure greater economic safeguards, (and, hence, more political power) for all forms of private property. It also promised greater freedom and a more open society, which was cherished by writers, poets and journalists both for ideological and for professional reasons. Besides, this group – more than any other – expected a quick rise in Iran's fame and fortune in consequence of the fall of despotism.[8] Thus, the revolution against despotism was not fought for purely 'idealistic' reasons – that is, merely because the revolutionaries disliked despotism and preferred a 'democratic' system; its triumph promised real economic, social and personal gains for the participating classes and individuals.

It would be impossible, within the present compass, to do analytical justice to the complex role of religion and religious leaders. However, the results of the arguments and evidence of such an analysis may be summarised in the following points.

1. Islam is not a purely mystical and spiritual religion; it is also a way of life. It is not an other-worldly, but a synthetic 'both-worldly' vision and doctrine.
2. Shī'ism – the distinct visionary and doctrinal interpretation of Islam held by the great majority of Muslim Iranians – incorporates strong, somewhat Messianic, mystic elements; but these are such that can be used both in inducing passivity and submissiveness, and in promoting activity and revolt.
3. Whatever the initial historical causes of Shī'ism may have been – and this is subject to a good deal of intellectual and theological dispute – it very quickly became a means for the rejection, by Iranians, of Arab (and, later, Turkic) rule and hegemony over the entire Muslim community.
4. Its 'political theory', or 'theory of the state', drew on the original Shī'ite belief that the practical leadership of the Islamic community had been *usurped*, against the will of God, by others. In time, the state itself became symbolic of the usurpation of the kingdom of God on earth. It was 'the rule of force'. In the Shī'ite principle, nothing is Caesar's; everything is God's through his preordained representatives on earth.[9]
5. Thus, Shī'ism evolved into a revolutionary ideology, both in theory and in practice, until a Shī'ite order – the Ṣafavids of Ardabil – reunified Iran through a series of protracted military campaigns at the beginning of the sixteenth century and proclaimed Shī'ism as the state religion.
6. The superficially theocratic Ṣafavid state overshadowed the radical quality of Shī'ism and reduced it to docility and submission. The Ṣafavids succeeded in establishing their (unjustified) claim to direct descent from the seventh Holy Imām of the Shī'ite faith; they integrated the Shī'ite religious dignitaries, theologians and scholars into the organs of the state; they disguised their political conflicts of interest with the orthodox Islamic Ottoman Empire in religious dressings; and they were successful on the socio-economic front. For a period in its history Shī'ism became less of a dynamic ideological force and more of 'an opium of the masses'.
7. Shī'ism, like the rest of Islam, lacks church, hierarchy and order. This makes it easier for both saints and demons, the very learned and the nearly illiterate to become religious preachers and dignitaries. It is nonsense to contrast such concepts as 'secular' and 'religious' – not to mention 'clerical' or 'ecclesiastical' – in this context. At any moment the *interpretations and modes of application* of the Shī'ite Islamic principles can be as numerous as the number of divines and theologians with a reasonably large following among the faithful.

8. In the first half of the nineteenth century, the socio-political passivity of Shīʿism was shaken up by the heterodoxy of the Shaikhīs, and the heresy of the Bābīs. This was accompanied by a series of significant urban revolts and disturbances, which could not have been purely due to sectarian religious sentiments. But their subsequent defeat, and the banishment of the Bābī leaders, led to developments which emphasised the movement's sectarian religious character, and destroyed its dynamic socio-political quality.[10]
9. By contrast, in the latter half of the nineteenth century Shīʿite leaders and preachers participated in the struggles against the state without proposing any substantial change in the existing principles of the faith. Thus their confrontation with the state was direct, and its purpose – expressed within religious terms of reference – explicit. The Tobacco-Régie incident was the most significant of these direct confrontations.
10. The basic demands of the Persian Revolution were well within the theory and history of Shīʿism. Their success could have meant a greater voice for Shīʿite leaders in the affairs of the state. The state itself was weak, divided and dominated by foreign powers. The religious leaders could not possibly have remained passive towards the vocal and active movement of the majority of their followers. The mosques, theological colleges and religious charities were financed mainly by regular payments and posthumous endowments of the propertied classes behind the revolution. Therefore, in the first few years, Shīʿite leaders and preachers were almost totally united in supporting the revolutionary cause.
11. The Persian Revolution, like all others, had its own moderate and radical tendencies. Therefore, it was not surprising that after its initial successes factionalism began to develop within its leadership and among its ranks. There were also personal rivalries (which did, and do, matter). But among those religious dignitaries (as distinct from common preachers, some of whom were simply bribed by Muhammad Ali into changing sides) who first began to doubt, and then oppose, the revolutionary cause, fear of damage to the faith itself must have played an important role. They were afraid, not without cause, that constitutionalism would lead to European modernism, which would weaken religious faith in the community. Yet it remains true that, both in number and in authoritative weight, the great majority of religious leaders remained faithful to the revolution until its final triumph in 1909.

In its first stage, the revolutionary movement had enjoyed the support of many prominent religious leaders, as well as ordinary preachers and theological scholars. Among the leading *ʿulamā* of Teheran, Sayyed Muhammad Ṭabāṭabāʾī and Sayyed ʿAbdullah Behbahānī remained faithful to the revolution until its final triumph; Shaikh Faẕlullah Nūrī went along with it until the succession of Muhammad Ali Shah, having been a somewhat reluctant fellow-traveller of the revolutionary leaders; and Sayyed Abulqāsim Imām Jum'eh quickly changed sides even before the revolution had achieved anything. However, when Muhammad Ali began to conspire against the constitution, and the National Assembly (*Majlis*) which it had created, it was Shaikh Fazlullah Nūrī who led the reactionary 'religious' front against the revolution, and in favour of his own obscure notion of *Mashrū'eh.*

The *Majlis* tried to do its best to accommodate Nūrī's and Muhammad Ali's combined pressures, by taking them at their word, and making provisions for a greater supervision of statutory legislation by the most prominent leaders of the Shī'ite community. But neither those two nor their domestic and foreign (i.e. Russian) supporters could be satisfied by such compromising measures. It is unlikely that Muhammad Ali, his despotic henchmen or his Russian allies were unduly worried about the possible damage caused to the Shī'ite faith by a system of constitutional monarchy. This leaves us with Nūrī, and the small group of religious leaders and preachers gathered around him.

To begin with, Nūrī's slogan of *Mashrū'eh* lacked a clear content: it involved criticisms of *Mashrūṭeh*, and allegations that it would harm the faith; it was expressed in passionate statements denouncing the revolutionary leaders as Bābīs, heretics, infidels, and so forth, but it did not contain a description of *Mashrū'eh* as an alternative system of government. It could not possibly have led to the unprecedented situation of a system of government by Shī'ite leaders, for this would have been even less acceptable to the Shah – the most powerful supporter of *Mashrū'eh* – than constitutional monarchy. Therefore, it could only have been a device for the Shah to re-establish a somewhat modified form of traditional despotism; for some religious dignitaries to add to their social and political power and influence; and for Nūrī himself to defeat his rivals, especially Behbahānī, and become the most important political *mujtahid* in the country. Indeed, Nūrī must have entertained the illusion of sharing power (either on his own, or as a member of the religious leadership) with Muhammad Ali. Yet this was an illusion which could not have materialised, even if they had succeeded in defeating the revolutionary movement: in a despotic system of whatever form, ultimate power is neither divisible nor subject to contract; therefore, once a person (or a group of people) is associated with the state, his political as well as economic power cannot be *independent* from it. Indeed, Shī'ite leaders had enjoyed their independent power and prestige precisely because of their usual lack of direct association with the despotic apparatus.

While Nūrī was apparently concerned about the ill effects of *modern legislation* on the faith, it is likely that he was more worried about the inevitable reduction in the judicial powers of religious leaders, in consequence of the establishment of a *modern independent judiciary*. For, apart from trying the less important penal cases (and especially those of a 'moral' nature – drinking, petty theft, adultery, and so on) many religious leaders had developed the habit of judging private civil litigations concerning property, trade, and the like. The latter was technically known as *tarāfu'* (or 'settlement [of disputes]'), and it had become so notorious for bribery and corruption, that the self-respecting religious leaders usually refused to be involved in it. This does not mean that all of those involved in the practice were corrupt, or that Nūrī was in favour of such corruption. Corrupt or uncorrupt, it was an important factor in the social prestige and power of religious leaders (even including those who did not practice it), and would have disappeared, as it did, with the foundation of a modern judicial system.

Finally, Nūrī's campaign for *Mashrū'eh* also had a purely personal side to it; for both he and Behbahānī regarded themselves as worthy of being the most powerful *mujtahid* in Teheran, and – as Sa'dī has aptly put it – 'no two kings can live in the same realm'. Behbahānī's more prominent position in the leadership of the revolution first alienated, then angered Nūrī, and the latter's full collaboration with the Shah and involvement in the coup (as well as the murders and prosecutions which followed it) left no room for a future rapprochement. Nūrī was hanged after the fall of Muhammad Ali, and Behbahanī must have been very influential in deciding his fate.

Yet the greatest moral and social support among the Shī'ite leadership came not from the religious leaders in Teheran and other Iranian cities, but from the holy city of Najaf in Iraq. Traditionally, the most eminent Shī'ite leaders, the *Marāji' al-taqlīd*, or Supreme Sources of Religious Guidance, were located in that and, occasionally, other holy cities in Mesopotamia. At the time, there were four such most eminent religious leaders in Najaf, Hāj Mīrzā Ḥusain Teherānī (the Senior *Marja'*), Ākhūnd Mullā Muhammad-Kāẓim Khurāsani (the Most Learned *Marja'*), Shaikh 'Abdullah Māzandarānī, and Sayyed Muhammad-Kāẓim Yazdī. The first three gave total support to the revolution in all its stages, by issuing edicts and public statements, communicating with religious and other leaders of the revolution, sending acrid letters and telegrams to the Shah, and responding to his (and Nūrī's) humble pleas for support with contemptuous rejection. Indeed, at one stage, in a joint telegram to Ṭabāṭabā'ī and Behbahānī, they 'unfrocked' Nūrī, and effectively damned and excommunicated him, in the following words: 'Since Nūrī is a disrupter of life, as well as a corrupter[of the world], his authority in the Affairs [of the Faith] is forbidden [*ḥarām*].'[11] Yazdī was the only great *mujtahid* who supported Nūrī and the Shah. But, with the other three *Marāji'* and especially Teherānī and Khurāsanī, on the side of the revolution, he could not have carried sufficient weight, and, in fact, did not do so. It would be no exaggeration to claim that, without the persistent support of those three *Marāji'*, the revolution could not have succeeded when and how it did.

To conclude the arguments of this section, the *Mashrūṭeh* Revolution was fought against traditional despotism, for political, social and economic reasons, by all the classes and individuals who hoped to gain from its results. It was not a bourgeois, nor a 'semi-bourgeois', revolution.

After the Revolution: The Political Economy in Turmoil

Once the passions were spent and the euphoria was over, political chaos, social disorder, economic poverty, national disintegration, parliamentary factionalism and imperialist interventions brought the truth home to the people. There has been no genuine revolution in history which has not been followed – at least for a time – by socio-economic slump and psychological depression: there are always significant gaps between the theoretical expectations and the practical (indeed, the maximum possible) achievements of a revolution; and, even within the constraints of real possibilities, it takes time, toil and trouble to establish a new socio-economic equilibrium. But the Iranian people had to take a much stronger dose of depression, disappointment and disillusion than is usually the case. For obvious reasons the country was unprepared for an orderly and fruitful participation in the new system; the new system itself carried within it much of the old methods and habits of conduct; the economic conditions had been worsening, both for domestic and international reasons; greater regional and provincial autonomy quickly degenerated into nomadic tribal feuds and organised brigandage; and tacit and explicit interventions of imperialist powers reinforced the above tendencies, and intensified factionalism and corruption within the new political elite.

It was out of the ashes of the most noble, though unrealistic, hopes and aspirations of the Persian Revolution that the various strands of modern Iranian nationalism rose into being (see Ch. 5). The origins of the exceptionally strong and persistent xenophobia of modern Iran must also be sought in this period: that is, the universal myth – believed by almost every order of urban Iranian society – that any event of the slightest political significance must be the result of a carefully conceived and meticulously executed conspiracy by foreign powers; the unimaginable fatalism which ascribes little or no role to domestic social and economic events, nor the power of ideas and the will of the people in determining social processes, and their change.

The First World War was the last straw; and it nearly broke the camel's back. The people's historically rooted anti-Russian and more recent anti-British sentiments automatically placed them on the side of the Central Powers. The Turks – especially now that they too had set up a crypto-democratic political system – were no longer regarded as the age-old Sunni enemies of the Shī'ite community, but as 'our Muslim brothers' fighting against European imperialism.[12] Russian troops had already been stationed and active in the northern parts of the country; and a British police force – the South Persia Rifles – was hastily organised and led by British officers in the Fars province: true to the letter of their 1907 agreement, the imperial powers were busy safeguarding their respective 'zones of influence'. In the circumstances there were only two choices available to the Iranian Government: either to remain formally neutral or to declare war on the Allies.

The problem was intensively debated; but, after some hesitation and indecision, the government decided to remain 'neutral', or, more accurately, to stay *passive* and watch the events. There were three distinct tendencies within the broad political and intellectual elite: the radical minority counselled an open alliance with the Central Powers; the conservative group claimed that it was in the country's best interest to co-operate with the Allies by remaining passive; and the 'moderates' – who were no less resentful of the Anglo-Russian interventions than the radicals, but more cautious in their choice of tactics – believed that open hostility against the Allies would risk total colonisation and dismemberment for the country. The radicals were thus isolated as a minority; therefore, they decided to 'go it alone'.

In 1916, the radical politicians and intellectuals moved ('migrated') to the western regions of Kirmānshāh and Kurdistan, where they set up a rival, provisional government, and entered the war against the Allies. This was a strategic mistake which exposed the country to greater and less obviously illegitimate military interventions by the Allies; and it turned her western regions into a free battle zone between the Turks and the Russians. When the war ended, Iran was in political and economic ruins.[13]

It is only within such a socio-political perspective that the country's economic situation may be intelligently – indeed, intelligibly – discussed. This was a period not of continuous (rapid or gradual) change, but of unsystematic and uneven upheavals brought about by domestic conflict and foreign interference. A country no less desperately poor and undeveloped than before – with no industrialisation or growing middle class, such as current historical mythologies attribute to it – had become conscious of itself, its destiny, its dignity and its place and position in a selfish and turbulent world. It was a situation in which politics and literature were experiencing genuine revolutionary changes on the basis of the same set of economic 'facts' and data, though not the same state of equilibrium in socio-economic relations.

'The facts' – recorded and reiterated in many publications with varying detail – were as follows. Population grew slowly from about 9 to 11 million with an almost unchanging distribution (of about 85 and 15 per cent, respectively) between rural and urban communities. The balance of payments remained in chronic deficit throughout, and foreign debts went on accumulating. Iran exported oil and industrial raw materials (mainly to Britain), and traditional manufactured products, notably carpets (primarily to Russia). Likewise, she purchased between 80 and 90 per cent of her imports from the Russian and British empires.

There were no significant changes in the economic structure or technology. About 90 per cent of the country's labour force was involved in agricultural production and rural handicrafts; the remaining 10 per cent in commerce, state and other services, and urban manufacturing. Accumulation of physical capital was very limited, and most of the investment in new plant and equipment was in domestic (as opposed to imported) capital goods, using traditional techniques of production. Expansion in roads, communications, health and other infrastructural facilities was insignificant; investment in modern secondary education advanced, in purely relative terms, somewhat more rapidly than did investment in the other basic sectors.

The 'budget' – there was, of course, no such thing as it is normally understood – was made up of a series of revenue and expenditure estimates, and in no year were these fulfilled. There was a chronic 'budget' deficit, but not simply in the sense of a planned or expected surplus of expenditures over revenues: both receipts and disbursements were usually short of expected estimates, even though actual disbursements were invariably in excess of actual receipts. The result was that the government habitually failed to meet its financial obligations and redeem its debts. Yet about 50 per cent of government expenditures was allocated to the army and other security forces.

The national currency was – both internally and internationally – still based on silver. Paper money, for which the (British-owned) Imperial Bank had the monopoly, was very scarce, and almost entirely backed by metallic cash reserves. Modern 'banking services' were limited to the activities of the Imperial Bank and the (Russian) Banque des Prêts de Perse ('Loan Bank of Persia'), neither of which acted as an agent for domestic credit creation. The latter function was still carried on by traditional 'goldsmiths' (ṣārrāfan) pawnbrokers, and urban and rural money-lenders, who demanded considerable amounts of assets, and charged usurious rates of interest, against their loans.

In the period 1900–18 a new factor emerged in Iran which was destined to dominate almost every aspect of the political economy in the following decades: the discovery, production and export of petroleum. In 1900 a concession was granted to William D'Arcy (and his partners) for £200,000 (paid in 1903) for the exploration and subsequent production of oil – effectively covering the whole of Iran except the Russian zone of influence – until 1960. The resulting activities began to bear full fruit in 1908, when the Anglo-Persian Oil Company was set up, 51 per cent of whose shares were quickly acquired by the British government. All major decisions concerning the rate of output, pricing, marketing, refining, and so on, were left to the discretion of the company, against which (apart from some residual payments) it agreed to pay the Iranian government 16 per cent of its annual net profits. This afforded the government some room to breathe, as a source of domestic expenditure and foreign exchange. But the oil revenues were meagre both in absolute and in relative terms. Between 1912 and 1919 nearly 2.9 million long tons of oil were produced at a rapidly growing rate; on average, Iran's share amounted to £250,000 per annum. Clearly, these payments had been short even of the letter of the agreement, or the company would not have paid a further compensatory £1 million (in 1920) under pressure from the Iranian government. Whether or not the compensation was adequate must, for want of genuine information, be left to speculation.[14]

Domestic volatility and foreign intervention had created a state of social, economic and psychological insecurity which was manifested in the moral and financial greed and corruption of the post-revolutionary governments. It was never clear whether departmental estimates were related to real (actual and planned) expenditures, or to the size of the pockets of the departmental heads and their assistants. Usually, the more politically powerful a departmental head, the larger the allocation actually made to the department and/or to his privy purse. In his classic work *The Strangling of Persia*, Morgan Shuster, the conscientious American financial adviser (who was officially appointed in 1910 in order to modernise Iranian public finance) has given us a vivid account of this and many other aspects of the Iranian political economy: on many occasions he would have to spend hours haggling with powerful Iranian officials over their allocations, for he knew that much of the payments would eventually find an illicit outlet, one way or another. His own mission was abruptly terminated in 1911, when a Russian ultimatum for his dismissal obliged the government to comply, in spite of an unyielding resistance by the National Assembly. Those indigenous Iranian elements who saw in Shuster an incorruptible technocrat threatening their financial 'interests' must have heaved a sigh of relief. If we have to search for a Thermidor after the Persian Revolution, then this episode is the nearest to such a betrayal of the ideals of the revolution. For on that fateful day a great revolutionary general (Ephrim Khān) led the troops which occupied the National Assembly and brought its resistance to the ultimatum to a forceful end. Yet, it is both ironic and illuminating that the Thermidor of a genuine historic revolution had to be strongly associated with – though not entirely determined by – the wishes of a foreign power.

Henceforth, the Iranian people's vision of every aspect of social and economic reality – its agents, defenders and critics – was primarily and profoundly determined by an assessment of three basic elements: official bribery and embezzlement, imperialist conspiracies, and the activities of the domestic allies, agents or spies of imperialism. This simple model has remained the most popular means of social and economic analysis down to the present day: there is, at any time and with regard to any general or partial problem, a well-designed foreign conspiracy (sometimes going back several years, if not decades) which controls the situation and determines the outcome with the help of the domestic, indigenous agents of imperialism, who make up the bulk of the corrupt and embezzling public officials. Iran has been exposed to many imported modern ideologies since the First World War. Yet a careful study and analysis of the practical attitude of even the most rigorous ideological movements would betray the strong influence of the above historical vision merely disguised in complex and mystifying forms.

NOTES

1. See Aḥmad Kasravī, *Tārīkh-i Mashrūṭeh-yi Irān* (Teheran: Amīr Kabīr, 1968); Nikki Keddie, *Religion and Rebellion in Iran* (London: Frank Cass, 1966), and *Sayyid Jamāl al-Dīn al-Afghānī* (Berkeley and Los Angeles, Calif.: University of California Press, 1972); Hamid Algar, *Religion and State in Iran 1785 – 1906. The Role of the Ulama in the Qajar Period* (Berkeley and Los Angeles, Calif.: University of California Press, 1972).
2. For example Kasravī, *Tārīkh-i Mashrūṭeh*; Keddie, *Religion and Rebellion*; E. G. Browne, *The Persian Revolution 1905 – 1909* (Cambridge, 1910); Mehdī Malik-zādeh, *Tārīkh-i Inqilāb-i Mashrūṭīyat-i Irān*, vols 1–7 (Teheran, 1949–56); Firaidūn Ādamīyat, *Fikr-i Demukrāsī-yi Ijtimā'ī der Nihzat-i Mashrūṭīyat-i Irān* (Teheran, 1975); Ibrāhīm Fakhrā'ī, *Gīlān dar Jumbish-i Mashrūṭīyat* (Teheran: Jībī Books, 1972); Nāẓim al-Islām Kirmānī, *Tārīkh-i Bīdārī-yi Irānīyān* (Teheran, n.d.).
3. These are some of the well-known characteristics of the rise of 'commercial capitalism' in western Europe. See, the appendix to Ch.3, above.
4. See Ch.2 above, and especially some of the notes concerning the absence of socio-economic security or predictability for all individuals, owing to the arbitrary nature of despotic power. The high degree of social mobility was an inevitable consequence of this system. Iranian history is full of examples of individuals who, either on their own merits, or through personal favours, or indeed because of circumstances, have risen from the lowest 'ranks' to the highest positions. Nādir Shah Afshar, Amīr Niẓām, and Reżā Shah Pahlavi are only the most well-known examples of this regular pattern.
5. See Isaiah Berlin, *Two Concepts of Liberty* (Oxford: Clarendon Press, 1958). For a constructive critique of Berlin's argument (within its own, European context) see 'Berlin's Division of Liberty' in C. B. Macpherson's *Democratic Theory: Essays in Retrieval* (London: Oxford University Press, 1973).
6. The immediate cause of the flogging was the governor's personal anger at the intervention of some influential people on behalf of one of the two merchants. However, when this merchant's son broke down at the sight of the beating, the governor ordered him to be flogged as well, even though there had been no charges of speculation against him. The other merchant was also a colonel in the army! The governor himself ('Ata 'al-Dawleh) later became a supporter of the revolution, and was duly flogged for it on the orders of Muhammad Ali Shah. Such small details may be helpful in gauging the nature of Iranian society, and its history. See Kasravī, *Tārīkh-i Mashrūṭeh*.
7. Muhammad Ali had already made his reputation when, as the Crown Prince and governor of Azerbijan, he had ordered the murder of three prominent intellectuals (Rūḥī, Kirmānī and Khabīr al-Mulk), who had been accused of complicity in the assassination of Nāṣir al-Din. Sayyed Ḥasan Taqī-zādeh, a leading young revolutionary radical, had later told Sayyed Muhammad Ali Jamālzādeh (the aged Iranian writer) that he and other younger revolutionaries had been so worried about the Shah's death (and, therefore, Muhammad Alī's succession) before his approval of the draft constitution that they had begged the Shah's personal physician to try to keep him alive until the document was ready for the royal assent. (The story was quoted to me by Jamālzādeh himself.)
8. For a description and analysis of the hopes and aspirations, as well as confusions and illusions, of the modernised younger intellectuals, see Chs 5 and 6, below.
9. However, God's rule on earth will be fulfilled only through the advent of the Twelfth Imām, the Mahdī or Redeemer. This automatically rules out the

establishment of a theocratic state led by religious leaders who do not regard themselves as representatives of God or the Mahdī, but see themselves as merely the latter's worldly deputies by virtue of learning and the adherence of the Shī'ite community. There have been a number of heterodox or heretical Shī'a movements whose leaders have claimed to have special callings beyond those of the ordinary religious leaders, often ending up by claiming to be the Mahdī himself. Such was the well-known case of Sayyed Ali Muhammad Shīrāzī, known as the *Bāb* (i.e. the 'link' between the Mahdī and the faithful), and the less well-known case of Sayyed Muhammad Musha'sha', who founded a local dynasty in eastern Khūzistan in the fifteenth century. For further information on the latter case, see Aḥmad Kasravī, *Tārīkh-i Pānṣad Sāleh-yi Khūzistān* (Teheran: Gām-Pāidār, 1977).

10. The circumstantial evidence strongly suggests that the Bābī uprising of the mid-nineteenth century was an anti-despotic political movement dressed (as usual) in a religious garb, though this does not mean that those who participated in it did not believe in the early Bābī ideas. It was the first countrywide politico-religious movement since the rise of the Ṣafavids, whose earlier pseudo-theocracy, and later integration of the religious leadership into the state, had stripped the Shī'ite faith of its historical anti-establishmentarian force for three centuries. In fact, with the degeneration of the Ṣafavid state, some worldly religious leaders gained a great deal of political power, and their influence was the cause of a lot of political mistakes which weakened the state, and helped the Afghan invasion of the Iranian hinterland. The most well-known example of these religious dignitaries was Mullā Muhammad Bāqir Majlisī, who, apart from his disruptive political influence, has had the greatest share in proliferating unreliable *akhbār* (or Shī'ite 'traditions' as opposed to *uṣul* or doctrines), and promoting superstitious beliefs, through his writings.

    Therefore, it was not surprising that Bābism, itself an offshoot of the Shaikhīs, was both a social movement against the state, and a religious heresy within the broader Shī'ite faith. Indeed, if the early Babīs had chosen their tactics *vis-à-vis* the religious community and its leaders more carefully, avoiding the appearance of a heretical sect, and attracting the general sympathy of the community as a whole, it is likely that the impact and outcome of the movement would have been significantly different. However, the subsequent division of the sect into the Azalīs (or Babīs), and the Bahā'ī's, reduced the former (Bābī/Azalī) group to a small band of fundamentalist Bābīs who, *as individuals*, supported the *Mashrūṭeh* Revolution. But the Bahā'ī community was opposed to *Mashrūṭeh*. For earlier (Iranian) accounts and interpretations of these movements and events, see Lisān al-Mulk's *Nāsikh al-Tavārīkh*, and Aḥmad Kasravī's *Bahā'igarī*. See also Muhammad Ali Khunjī, 'Taḥqīqī darbāreh-yi Mazāhib-i Bābī va Bahā'ī', *Andīsheh-yi Naw*, I, no. 3 (Bahman 1327 AH/January 1949 AD). For two different, but equally valuable, European approaches to the subject, see E. G. Browne in H. M. Balyuzi (ed.), *Edward Granville Browne and the Bahā'ī Faith* (London: Ronald, 1970); and Algar, *Religion and State in Iran*.

11. Quoted in Kasravī, *Tārīkh-i Mashrūṭeh*, p.528. Khurasānī, who was regarded as the Most Learned *Marja'*, was even more committed to the revolutionary cause than his two colleagues, and this involved a lot of real hardship, even to the extent of putting his life in danger. See Kasravī, *Tārīkh-i Mashrūṭeh*, pp. 380–5. Nūrī's most important ally among the religious leaders in Teheran was Ākhūnd Mullā Muhammad Āmulī. For a specimen of the views of the supporters of *Mashrū'eh*, see their long public statements, reprinted in Kasravī, *Tārīkh-i Mashrūṭeh*, especially the one on pp. 432–8, where they attack the proliferation of newspapers, the provision for the representation of Jewish, Christian and Zoroastrian

minorities, and so on; describe any group of ten members of the *Majlis* as comprising 'four materialists, one Bābī, two European types, and three Twelver Shī'ites who are absolutely ignorant or completely illiterate'; and claim that, because of the slogans of 'liberty and fraternity', 'a Jewish man now sodomises a Muslim boy, and another assaults a chaste woman'.

12. This change of attitude is clearly noticeable in the works of the political poets and writers of the period, such as 'Ishqī and 'Ārif.
13. The leaders of the Provisional Government themselves later realised their own mistake. This was implicitly admitted by Sayyed Ḥasan Mudarris (the Minister of Justice in that government, who later became the leader of the opposition in the *Majlis*) in a meeting of the Sixth Session of the National Assembly. See Ḥusain Makkī (ed.), *Duktur Muṣaddiq va Nuṭqhāy-i Tārīkhī-yi Ū* (Teheran: 'Ilmī, 1946) pp. 96–8. Another leading figure of the Provisional Government was Sulaimān Mīrzā Iskandarī, who, as one of the earliest (though honest) victims of Iranian pseudo-modernist ideas, later became a leading advocate of Reżā Khān, and opponent of Mudarris, in the Fourth and Fifth Sessions of the *Majlis*. See further Ch.5, below.
14. For more detailed data and information on economic matters, see Charles Issawi, *The Economic History of Iran, 1800 – 1914* (Chicago and London: Chicago University Press, 1971), and J. Bharier, *Economic Development in Iran, 1900–1970* (London: Oxford University Press, 1971), as well as their references. See further Muṣṭafā Fāteḥ, *Panjāh Sāl Naft-i Irān* (Teheran, 1956).

Part II

The State and Counter-Revolution: 1921–41

5 From Reżā Khān to Reżā Shah: Preludes to the Despotic Counter-Revolution, 1918–26[1]

When the Great War ended, the fate of Iran was in balance. At the centre, the old Iranian despotism had been replaced by a disunited – almost incoherent – plutocratic 'system'. In the provinces, the centrifugal regional and tribal forces were threatening to tear the land asunder: a familiar situation in Iranian history upon the collapse of an established order, the fall of a dynasty or the death of a powerful despot. The presence of British troops in different parts of the country had removed any trace of Iranian sovereignty and independence. There was national disunity, political conflict, economic disruption and poverty, social insecurity; and administrative corruption and incompetence. At the same time the geopolitical situation of the Middle East was being radically transformed. The balkanisation of the Arab lands, and the Bolshevisation of the Russian Empire introduced important new factors into the balance sheet of international power-politics in the area. Iran and the Iranians were, once again, caught in the middle.

The Jangal Movement

The formation of the 'rebellious' Provisional Government in Kirmānshāh had been followed by an armed insurrection in the Caspian province of Gīlān. This was organised and led by a group of younger *Mashrūṭeh* revolutionaries from the region itself. It was headed by Mīrzā Kūchik Khān – a former scholar of a traditional college – who had fought for the revolution in various capacities. A Shī'ite Muslim and an unyielding patriot, Kūchik was an indefatigable fighter and an incorruptible leader whose sole ambition was to rid the country of foreign imperial domination and domestic administrative corruption. The Jangal (Forest) Movement – as the Gīlān Revolution has come to be known in history – was neither a 'separatist' nor a 'bourgeois nationalist' nor a communist revolution. It predated the Bolshevik Revolution in Russia; and it was a genuine reaction to the disillusionment and depression which had followed the triumph of 1909.[2]

The Russian Bolsheviks got involved with the movement when, in May 1920, Soviet troops entered the Caspian port of Enzeli in order to reclaim the Russian naval vessels abandoned by the forces of the White-Guard General Denikin upon his defeat in the southern theatre of the Russian Civil War. This came as a complete surprise to the British expeditionary force occupying the port and the provincial capital, Rasht, and it responded by a swift evacuation and retreat, very probably both for logistic and for strategic political reasons. Yet, in addition to securing the repatriation of their naval vessels, the Russian occupation became, by accident or design, a useful instrument for Soviet diplomatic manoeuvring: the Russians were as anxious to secure their own backdoor from British-inspired interference in Russia as were the British government to curb the spread of Bolshevism southwards. The Russians had already sent a note of protest to the Iranian government against the proposed Anglo-Iranian treaty, known as the 1919 Agreement, initiated and actively canvassed by the British Foreign Office

The Russian landing in Enzeli provided the Soviet government with an excellent opportunity to counteract the British tactics. To this end it helped forge a coalition between Kūchik and a group of Azerbijani 'Marxist' revolutionaries, led by Ḥaidar Khān, which, with moral, material and technical support from Russia, occupied Rasht and declared a revolutionary republic.[3]

Ḥaidar Khān Tāriverdiev – variously known as *Bumbīst* (Bomb-maker), *Chirāq-barqī* (Electrician) and *Amū-ugulū* (Cousin) – had been a radical *Mashrūṭeh* revolutionary who had specialised in underground activity and distinguished himself in the use of urban guerilla tactics against Muhammad Ali Shah and his gang. He was a strong personality, a heroic figure, and a revolutionary democrat no less committed and incorruptible than Kūchik.[4] In reality there was, and could not be, much difference between him and Kūchik in terms of their basic goals and aspirations for the Iranian political economy; but he probably regarded Kūchik as a 'bourgeois nationalist', and certainly viewed himself as a revolutionary Marxist. At any rate, political prejudice, vested interest and theoretical misunderstandings have now built up this mainly formalistic division into an indisputable historical metaphysic. The real difference was that Ḥaidar was an early representative of revolutionary Westernism (or modernism) and Kūchik an example of revolutionary Persianism: that is, they were men with similar revolutionary *aspirations* for the country but with different, at times contradictory, *understandings* of Iranian society, and, hence, dissimilar *approaches* for its revival and re-organisation. Otherwise, the adoption of a revolutionary Marxist model, or the use of Marxist jargon by Ḥaidar and by his subsequent – noble and ignoble – political imitators was much more a question of form than of substance. To put it briefly as well as bluntly, a typical Iranian Marxist–

Leninist was then as now simply a revolutionary with some (usually superficial) knowledge of Marxist theory and tradition, wishing to rid the country of imperialism and to promote rapid national economic development by the use of modern technology; this has usually been combined with an emotional commitment – sometimes even subservience – to the Soviet Union and other communist powers.[5]

The establishment of the Gīlān republic was accompanied with the formation of the Communist Party of Iran (CPI), in Enzeli in July 1920. Alarmed by these developments, the central Iranian government lost no time in negotiating for a general settlement which would normalise Russo-Iranian relations. The Russian response was rapid as well as positive: within only a few months of its formation, the CPI 'concluded' that the Iranian revolution must await the full bourgeois development of the country! In January 1921 the Russians declared that they would evacuate their troops and personnel from Gīlān once all British forces had been withdrawn from Iran. On 24 February a military *coup d'état* 'toppled' the Iranian government and assumed control. Two days later, the celebrated Russo-Iranian treaty of 1921 was concluded and signed in Moscow. In May, the British forces left Iran, but the expected march of the Gīlān revolutionaries on Teheran was inexplicably postponed until October, during which time the Russian personnel and technical advisers were withdrawn from the province. The delay in acting and the physical withdrawal of the Russians may have already sealed the fate of the revolution. But these events had some moral and 'ideological' implications which probably did more to spell the doom of the revolutionaries of Gīlān. For, just as the main Iranian army was advancing on the provincial republic, the Gīlān coalition collapsed, and the two ('nationalist' and 'Marxist') factions of the revolution engaged in a civil war between themselves. The Jangalis were routed; Ḥaidar was killed in prison; Kūchik retreated and froze to death; and the remaining revolutionary leaders either capitulated or crossed the border into the Soviet Union. Few could have realised that the gruesome public display of Kūchik's head in Teheran was an ominous symbol of the emerging new order in Iran.[6]

The 1919 Agreement

The British government was anxious to stabilise the Iranian political economy so as to safeguard its own regional as well as local interests. This desire had become more intense and more urgent as a result of the October Revolution in Russia. The Iranian plutocracy (many of whom were not, as has generally been thought, mere 'British agents') were equally anxious to pull the country together and normalise the situation. Yet the coincidence of national poverty, political disorder, social disunity, tribal and ethnic conflict, and the economic disruption and dislocation which had followed *Mashrūṭeh* and the Great War was likely to render the achievement of this very difficult.

Therefore, the British government (in fact Curzon, the Foreign Secretary) decided to provide a catalyst to enable the Iranian elite of the right administrative calibre and political colour to approach this difficult task. To this end, the Foreign Office entered into negotiations with the cabinet of Vusūq al-Dawleh – an intelligent and strong but unpopular politician who was, mainly as a result of this particular move, regarded as a British 'spy' – for a bilateral treaty of technical assistance and economic co-operation. This resulted in the notorious 1919 Agreement.

The main points of the agreement were the provision of a loan by Britain to Iran, and the employment, by the Iranian government, of British military and civil technical advisers to help reorganise Iran's army and state administration. This looks like the first formal attempt at the provision of financial and technical assistance from a 'developed' to a 'developing' country (or 'foreign aid'), a form of assistance that has become widespread since the Second World War. Yet it was rejected by the Iranian political public with an emotional (and, occasionally, physical) violence which bears no comparison with contemporary attacks on foreign aid by dissenting political groups and parties in the countries of the Third World. The British Foreign Office, and Curzon in particular, were genuinely unable to understand the significance of this reaction; consequently, they made the habitual mistake of all arrogant powers (or 'superpowers') who would blame the results of their own ignorance of an alien culture on the activities of 'a few rabble-rousers', 'the mob', 'subversive elements'.[7] The overwhelming rejection of the 1919 Agreement by the Iranian political public was not so much because of the letter, or even the spirit, of the treaty. In fact, the agreement had been rejected even before its contents were known to any number of people; and it is likely that most of those who have regarded it as a great conspiracy against Iranian national sovereignty and territorial integrity have known very little of its contents.[8]

By the time the 1919 Agreement was concluded, the Anglo-Russian secret treaty of 1907 had become well known; the subsequent role and tactics of the British government in Iran, including political and military intervention, had robbed British claims of good will towards Iran of all credibility; the British replacement of Ottoman suzerainty over the neighbouring Arab lands, and especially Iraq, was far from reassuring; and the thinly disguised British support for Shaikh Khaz'al, the ruler of Muḥammeh (later Khurramshahr), who was suspected of secessionist designs for the oil province, was alarming. A detached analysis, based not only on the agreement but also on a knowledge of subsequent developments (including the publication of the relevant documents thirty years later, and of other revelations through memoirs, biographies, and the like) shows that the worst fears of the Iranian people were unfounded; in particular, it is now almost certain that the British did not intend to use the 1919 Agreement as a vehicle for *increasing* their hold over Iran, let alone colonising it directly. But this guarded analytical conclusion, sixty years after the event itself reveals the extent to which the British government had acted, and reacted, with real ignorance.

And, true to their misunderstanding of the situation, the British had made a mistake in dealing with men who were least suitable for the peaceful implementation of such a policy, although perhaps in this regard they had had very few options: by definition, popular politicians scarcely take unpopular political decisions, especially in a 'developing country'. For, apart from his own unpopularity, Vusūq was – willy nilly – allied with two other politicians, Nuṣrat al-Dawleh (Fīrūz) and Ṣārim al-Dawleh (Mas'ūd), whose personal integrity and administrative ability fell far short of his own. Perhaps the charge of being British agents has been more just against these two men than any other Iranian politician of this century, if only because future events proved that, in pursuit of their narrow self-interest, they would be ready to offer their services to *any* person or power. At any rate, such a triumvirate was wholly anathema to the political public, even without their involvement in the agreement!

The *Coup d'État* of 1921

The period 1921–6 was a period of dual sovereignty : a period of intense struggle for political power both between rival men and between competing political visions. It was inaugurated by the *coup d'ètat* of February 1921 (3 Isfand 1299 AH in the Persian calendar), when a professional 'Cossack' brigade, led by Reżā Khān, who was later to found the Pahlavi dynasty, marched from the provincial town of Qazvīn, occupied the capital almost without bloodshed, declared martial law, and appointed Sayyed Żīā' al-Dīn (Ṭabā-Ṭabā'ī), a hitherto obscure journalist, to the office of Prime Minister. At least a few days before its commencement the imminence of the coup had been known in Teheran; indeed, the Shah had ordered the capital's garrison that no resistance should be offered to the intruders. Furthermore, the Qajar monarch immediately recognised the coup and thus, as the *Majlis* was still in recess, gave it some retrospective legitimacy.[9]

In fact there had been no government to topple: Vusūq's cabinet had already been replaced by a 'caretaker' government led by Sepahdār-i Rashtī (Akbar), a man hardly capable of taking care of anything even at the best of times. His so-called government was already withering away when, in anticipation of the coup, he resigned from office. In retrospect it is clear that the coup was intended as the alternative route to the achievement of the spirit of the 1919 Agreement – that is, a political stabilisation in Iran which would not pose a threat to the main local regional interests of the British Empire. It is equally clear that Britain was somehow involved in the conception of the coup, although it is improbable that the British Foreign Office itself conceived the idea. The full facts of the matter are not yet known; but it is certain that the commander of the local British forces, General Ironside, was directly involved in the conception and execution of the coup. According to both written and spoken memoirs, there were at first other civilian and military nominees for the leadership of the coup than those who finally led it; many are said to have turned down the suggestion. At any rate, it is certain that Reżā Khān was hand-picked by Ironside, who was impressed by the man's personal and martial qualities.[10]

The coup-makers immediately declared martial law and interned nearly all the conventional politicians of *all* political persuasions, not even excluding Nuṣrat al-Dawleh, the opportunistic member of Vusūq's triumvirate, who, returning from London had fancied himself as the natural candidate for premiership in the new set-up. This was, as we shall see later, the beginning of an entirely new era in Iranian history, in the profoundest sense of the term. Yet, it is a sign both of the anti-authoritarian nature of the Iranian public, and of the political atmosphere to which they had become accustomed, that next to the opening words 'I command' of Reżā Khān's martial-law declaration, printed on the city walls everywhere, there appeared overnight the taunting response 'Go to hell' ('Guh mīkhurī'). They found it not only unacceptable but also incredible that Reżā Khān, or anyone else, would seriously presume to take *command* of their lives. They were soon to know better.

But it would be a mistake to think that the coup was greeted merely with a mixture of apathy and hostility: on the contrary, for reasons which will become clear in a moment, it was given an enthusiastic, even euphoric, reception by many younger political activists, including scores of poets and essayists, belonging to a revolutionary trend in Iranian nationalism. For example, the poets 'Ishqī and 'Ārif, both of whom had previously been imprisoned for their outspoken opposition to the 1919 Agreement, wrote songs, poems and articles in support of the coup and its twin leaders; the political elite had been locked up; the communiqués issued by Sayyed Żīā and Reżā Khān were couched in unprecedented radical and vitalistic nationalist terms, ending with slogans such as 'long live the Iranian nation'; and within a month the new Prime Minister had declared the 1919 Agreement – which he himself had previously supported in his journal – dead and buried. In fact, when three months after the coup Sayyed Żīā 'inexplicably' resigned from premiership and left the country, this was seen by the radical nationalists not as an internal coup by Reżā Khān (which is the more likely explanation) but as a subtle counter-coup by the hated political elite – the more so, as it was followed by the release of the prisoners from that elite, who were still in gaol, and by general elections.[11] The deceptive normalisation appeared, both to the opponents and to the supporters of the coup, as a return to the *status quo ante*.The song of lament written by Abulqāsim 'Ārif for the departure of Sayyed Żīā ('I would forfeit my life for your Black Cabinet, return!') is still remembered.

Dual Sovereignty: The Contest of Men and Visions

There were to be five more cabinets, led by elite politicians of varying political tendencies and methods before Reżā Khān, the *de facto* permanent Minister of War, became Prime Minister towards the end of 1923. In this period he rapidly consolidated his position in various fields: he tightened his command over the expanding professional army and gained total popularity among both officers and men; he personally commanded the troops which finally routed the Janglis in Gīlān; he began to put down tribal and regional rebellions, highway robbery and brigandage; he established *non-committal* contacts with the political elite, posing as an honest broker who was above conventional political intrigue and petty rivalry; he gathered around himself younger men of the civil service and the professions – many of them with modern, Western-style if not truly Western, educational backgrounds – who made up the emerging techno-bureaucratic elite of the country; he presented himself as an able and honest patriot to the country at large; and, finally, he managed to win over the majority of the deputies of the *Majlis*. In a short and decisive period he dug in deep roots, while the political elite – contemptuous of 'the illiterate former private soldier' – were engaged in their conventional cut-throat competition. They woke up to reality when it was too late.[12]

The clash of ideas, and the unfolding of events, in this crucial quinquennium have been little understood *in relation to the time and place in which they occurred,* either because inappropriate models or analogies have been applied to them, or because they have been evaluated merely in the light of subsequent events – that is, by reading history backwards. For example, according to some models Reżā Khān appears as a 'strong' nationalist leader determined to effect social progress in a country not yet ready for 'Western-style parliamentary democracy'; indeed, this was the view of the British legation in Teheran, and, through it, the Foreign Office in London. According to some other models, Reżā Khān was a 'bourgeois nationalist' leader confronting 'reactionary feudals' and their 'religious supporters'; this was the view of the Soviet embassy in Teheran, and, through it, the People's Commissariat for Foreign Affairs in Moscow. In fact, there is very little difference of *substance* between these two views: they are both generalisations from the European social and intellectual experience merely couched in different ideological *terms*. According to a third (and much more Iranian) model, the Iranian public had *from the beginning* regarded Reżā Khān as a British 'spy' who would fulfil his mission in the service of British imperialism. Yet anyone who would care to examine the vast political, journalistic and artistic (mainly poetical) literature of this period would soon realise that this is mainly a projection backwards of later emotions. Even Sayyed Ḥasan Mudarris, the most tenacious opponent of Reżā Khān, did not accuse him of being a British 'spy', and, in any case, did not oppose him merely for this reason: indeed, with a rare clarity of vision he saw the real threat as lying in Reżā Khān's bid for *total* power.[13]

This subject is important in its own right; but it is indispensable to an analytical understanding of the development of the Iranian political economy since the foundation of the Pahlavi dynasty. Therefore, it deserves more detailed discussion, which will also aid appreciation of the theories and arguments advanced in the rest of this book.

Three basic political tendencies may be identified since the triumph of the *Mashrūṭeh* Revolution, regardless of the many more guises in which they appeared. Furthermore, *all* three tendencies may be described as 'nationalist' from the viewpoint of *European* history and social science. The first tendency may be called 'modern', 'progressive', 'radical' or 'forward-looking' nationalism; the second, 'liberal', 'democratic' or 'bourgeois' nationalism; and the third either 'conservative', 'insular', 'backward-looking' nationalism, or indeed, 'obscurantist', 'pro-feudal', 'black reaction'! It is sufficient to employ the above terminology in order to show up the *conceptual* misunderstandings that it formalises.

In fact, only the first tendency can be clearly identified as having a kind of nationalist vision similar to its European counterpart. The reason is that it drew considerably – though not entirely – on European cultural and historical sources which had lately impressed the Iranian intellectual consciousness. It was hard-headed, modern-minded, impatient and acutely conscious of the ancient – that is, *pre-Islamic* – glories of the Persian Empire. It wanted to remove the barriers which it believed religion had put in the way of Iran's cultural and technological progress. It was weary of the slow processes of parliamentary and judicial deliberations, and it scorned the corruption and selfishness which they sometimes involved. It matched the learning, urbanity or parliamentary sophistication of the other tendencies in its liveliness and energy, both in journalism and in military and administrative activities. It was vocal, forthright and positive in action; meritocratic in attitude, and contemptuous of the old 'aristocratic' and religious values. It consisted of an amalgam of journalists, political poets and essayists, Westernised bureaucrats and military leaders. They were heterogeneous in their educational, technical and socio-economic backgrounds, and otherwise unhomogeneous in their motives and aspirations; in any case, not all of them continued within this broad tendency until the end. But there is a sufficient amount of similarity in their methods, ideas and temper to justify grouping them together within a distinct tendency.

Hard-headed nationalist sentiments began to be expressed in a scattered fashion in the first instance by poets and journalists as early as the beginnings of the First World War, though they can even be traced to the revolutionary period itself. The poets Muhammad Reżā 'Ishqī, Abulqāsim 'Ārif (Qazvīnī), Farrukhī Yazdī and Abulqāsim Lāhūtī are but a few well-known examples of the literary group within this tendency. Later, a number of distinguished intellectuals, lawyers and soldiers, including Sulaimān Mīrzā Iskandarī, Ali

Akbar Dāvar, ʻAbdul-Ḥusain Taimūr-Tāsh, Farajullah Bahrāmī, Ali Dashtī, Colonel Ḥabībullah Shaibānī, Generals Amīr-Aḥmadī, Yazdān-Panāh and Amīr-Ṭahmāsibī, and so on, were added to the list and increasingly gathered around the personality of Reżā Khān.

The literati filled in books and journals about bygone glories which had ended in total poverty and helplessness. They popularised the stories of the Achiminid and Sāsānid military and cultural achievements and, in the process, stumbled upon Iran's historic defeat by the Arab nation, which in turn they held responsible for all the religious superstition and obscurantism that plagued the country at the time. Many of them were not anti-religious, but nearly all were contemptuous of religious leaders and preachers. Ārif Qazvīnī wrote,

> Ever since the Arabs got a foothold in Iran,
> No word of happiness has been heard from the land of Sāsān.[14]

ʻIshqī wrote the 'opera' of the Resurrection of the Persian Emperors and reacted sharply, in a poem, to a suggestion apparently made by some Turkish journalists that Zoroaster had been a Turk and not an Iranian. He was so earnestly full of nationalistic fervour that he once wrote, referring to the depth of his patriotic feelings,

> I am in love, let my dismembered heart bear witness,
> I hold no other evidence but this shredded document.[15]

Farrukhī Yazdī, a nationalist poet, whose career was to embrace membership of the *Majlis* and death in prison, wrote almost nothing but patriotic political pieces, of which this is a specimen:

> We are the dear ones of Kaikāvūs
> The sons of Jamshīd and of Cīrūs [Cyrus]
> The offspring of Kāran, Gīve and Tūs,
> But as we are deeply disappointed in England,
> Lord Curzon has been visited with anger,
> He has now resorted to passion plays.[16]

Once the poets and essayists had set the stage in this fashion, the politicians and military leaders entered the scene. The latter were naturally more aware of the practical constraints on the restoration of some of the past glories, but these aspirations provided them with the ideal goals towards which they should strive, and the methods of reform which they should employ. For it is a commonplace – although, curiously, this was unknown to most of the intellectual stage-managers – that the pursuit of such goals usually requires means incompatible with the kind of civil liberties, and sometimes even licence, which the nationalist writers had taken for granted. Thus, gradually a dividing line began to appear between the pragmatic realism of the politicians and the abstract idealism of the intellectuals within this political tendency; and, as so often happens, these two groups, which were so close to each other in terms of ideas and aspirations, eventually became each other's deadly enemies.

With the benefit of hindsight, it seems inevitable that the practical leadership of this tendency should have been assumed by a military leader, and Reżā Khān emerged as the obvious choice. A native of Savād Kūh in the province of Māzandarān, Reżā was a brigadier who had risen from the ranks during the post-revolutionary period. He had participated in a number of counter-insurgency campaigns against restorationist attempts by the relics of the old despotism; and, in particular, he had distinguished himself in action in the successful campaign led by the great revolutionary generals Ephrīm Khān ('the Armenian') and Sardār Bahādur (later, Sardār As'ad) against Sālār al-Dawleh, the brother of the fallen monarch. His rapid promotion owed a lot to his professional merits, the meritocratic character of revolutionary armies, and the Iranianisation of the officers' corps in the 'Cossack' brigade, especially after the rise of Bolshevism in Russia had led to the disappearance of the Imperial Russian officers previously 'seconded' to it. Brigadier Reżā Khān, later known as the Sardār Sepah – a title approximately translatable as the 'Lord General' – was intelligent, hardworking, forthright and ruthless, with an astonishingly powerful memory, and a high degree of self-confidence that through success degenerated into arrogance. He had had very little formal education, but he had accumulated a good deal of experience in military organisation and leadership. He was nationalist in sentiment, pragmatic in choice of means, and ruthless in the application of methods that he thought necessary for the achievement of both personal and national objectives. He had an iron will that on a number of occasions helped him to save his own life, or a cause that otherwise might have been totally lost. He successfully combined two conflicting qualities which are very rarely found in the same person: a short temper and directness to the point of rudeness – and sometimes even obscenity – with an ability to hold views, plans and even personal grudges so close to his chest that he would catch almost everybody by surprise each time he decided to reveal his hand. He had no time for freedom, but at the time pretended to operate within a framework of law and order; he was not democratic in attitude but there was an element of populism in his behaviour. Like his main rival and adversary, Sayyed Ḥasan Mudarris (some of whose personal qualities he must have secretly admired), he was contemptuous of the old nobility, and he regarded them as utterly incapable of saving the situation. Mudarris may not have been guilty of too much exaggeration when he said, at about this time, that there were only two men of political courage and real masculinity left in the country: Reżā Khān and himself.

The second – the so-called 'liberal' or 'bourgeois nationalist' – political tendency was more directly a product of the *Mashrūṭeh* Revolution. This took the form of a fairly genuine synthesis between Shī'ite anti-despotism and Western pluralism in support of personal freedom, legal justice and political power-sharing. It was not predominantly or significantly religious in character. But it realised that in the circumstances an attack on religion, its historical origins and social traditions would be incompatible with the spirit of the institutional framework which it wanted to preserve for the body politic. It was symbolised by such respectable and popular political figures as Mīrzā Ḥasan Mushīr al-Dawleh, Mīrzā Ḥusain Mu'tamin al-Mulk, Mīrzā Ḥasan Mustawfī al-Mamālik and Dr Muhammad Muṣaddiq al-Ṣalṭaneh (who was destined to lead the campaign for the nationalisation of Iranian oil twenty-five years later). These men were deeply committed to the preservation of the constitutionalist achievements of the Persian Revolution; yet, at the same time, they were not averse to a certain amount of house-cleaning, especially for the establishment of law and order throughout the country. Their European education and experience added to their upbringing in enlightened and sophisticated Muslim households had, in the first instance, impressed a deep sense of legalism on their minds which did not make it impossible for them to reach compromises within a broadly legalistic framework. Personally, they were not, so long as they could help it, the stuff of which martyrs are made; but their conduct was at times so correct, so apparently open and indiscriminate, that it earned some of them the ambiguous – if not mildly pejorative – title of *vajīh al-melleh* ('national goody-goody'). Their 'nationalism' was to a large extent empirical, and, therefore, had less to do with the greater glory of the Iranian nation than with a reassertion of the civil and national dignity of the Iranian people. This outlook was even more true of the third political tendency, which we shall discuss in a moment. In a purely relative sense, they had been the Presbyterians of the Persian Revolution, and they became the Directoirists of its aftermath: they were equally opposed to Jacobinism, restorationism and Bonapartism.

The third and last major political tendency was much more radical, less flexible, more obstinate and more entrenched in the old Iranian civil and religious culture, less Europeanised and, therefore, less acutely conscious of nationhood but more conscious of the community of Iranians. They were not religious obscurantists who might have been harking back to the early or middle Qajar socio-cultural arrangement. On the contrary, they were quite uncompromising on the issues of the defence of parliamentary government and decentralisation of power. Indeed, in terms of technical skill, a few of them must be ranked among the greatest parliamentarians that Iran has ever seen. They were the inheritors of the early Shī'ite opposition to centralised political authority; they were Shī'ite Muslims who realised that their opposition to arbitrary power, and their commitment to the defence of personal liberties and independent judicial procedures was, in the context of

Iranian politics, the nearest thing to what might be described as the Shī'ite political doctrine.[17] In practice they normally found themselves in alliance with the second political tendency, with whom they shared a good many political objectives; and, like them, they drew their public support from the *bāzār* community and the urban crowd. They included such men as the poet Muhammad Hāshim Mīrzā Afsar, Mīrza Hāshim Ashtīyanī, Sayyed Ibrāhīm Żīā'al-Vaīẓīn, Shaikh Muhammad Ali Tehrānī, Fīrūz-Ābādī, Hāyerīzādeh, Kāzirūnī, the manoeuvrable poet-laureate Bahār, and, above all, Sayyed Ḥasan Mudarris, who in almost every respect was the very personification of this movement. Many of its adherents, including some of those mentioned above, later changed course or withdrew from the public scene, but Mudarris remained adamant until the bitter end.[18]

Mudarris was a native of Qumsheh (now Shahreżā), a small town in the central province of Isfahan. He was educated first at a madriseh (or traditional college) in the city of Isfahan, then in Najaf. He gained his entrance into Iranian national politics when he was selected as a *ṭarāz-i Avval*, nominated by religious leaders, in the *Majlis*. In no time this unknown provincial *'ālim* who had brought along with him little more than a sharp wit, and an even sharper tongue, made a considerable reputation in the political circles of the capital. The First World War and the long parliamentary recession it brought found Mudarris in the Provisional Government of Kirmānshāh as Minister of Justice. When that government finally dissolved itself he was among those of its leaders who thought it safer to spend a period of grace in Istanbul before returning to Teheran. On his return he opposed the 1919 Agreement, although his personal relations with Vusūq al-Dawleh – the Prime Minister on whom the fate of the treaty directly depended – remained on the whole cordial. On the morrow of the 1921 coup, when on the order of Sayyed Żīā (Ṭabā-Ṭabā'ī) almost every conventional politician was arrested, Mudarris found himself in prison. And a few months later, after the rapid disappearance of Sayyed Żīā from Iranian politics (at least for some considerable time to come), he secured a seat for himself in the newly elected *Majlis*. It was from this time onwards that the battle-lines for the final confrontation less than five years later became more and more clearly drawn.

Mudarris was an accomplished parliamentarian, with electrifying oratorical powers, who on a number of important occasions turned the parliamentary tide in his own favour by the sheer weight of a speech or two full of common-sense, wit and, sometimes, moral intimidation. He was in contact with people of all classes and, if anything, was noticeably less warm in his attitude towards the nobility than he was towards the common people. He was democratic in his political attitude, and he had no use either for high posts or for worldly possessions. Indeed, Flaubert's remark about Renan – 'If a man is *someone* why should he want to be *something*?' – fits his case perfectly. But, at the same time, he loved to enjoy personal power, especially in a 'king-making' capacity. He was self-assured to the point of being incautious and even tactless at times, and this was an important factor in his downfall. He was a man of principles, but, unlike some of the leaders of the second tendency, he was not too particular about the means he employed for the attainment of his objectives. Even when he used tactics which could be easily taken as evidence of hypocrisy and inconsistency, however, he applied them in a way that would largely preempt such accusations. For example, he surprised many by his defence of Nuṣrat al-Dawleh's credentials for commission to the *Majlis* barely six months after the latter's activities in favour of the 1919 Agreement. But, at the same time, he spoke with such contempt both of him and of his role in that episode that it was difficult to accuse him of inconsistency.[19] Or when, in a moment of despair, he made the tactical mistake of contacting Khaz'al, the Shaikh of Muḥammarreh, who stood accused of being a separatist, a tyrant, and an agent of imperialism all at once, he still made no bones about his sentiments towards him. He wrote,

> I have, on two or three occasions, mentioned in my letters that the people of Teheran generally do not think well of you; that you do not have a good reputation in the country, and that all the people have a sense of hatred and dislike towards you. Therefore, if you would like your past to be forgotten, you will have to compensate for it with good deeds . . .This is the day on which you are being put to the test . . . if you pass it well, your wrong-doings will be inevitably mitigated. . . . otherwise it is not possible to deceive the people of Teheran with words alone. . . .[20]

This small passage is in fact highly representative of some of his prominent personal characteristics: in particular, his directness, his inflexibility on points of principle, and a self-assurance which sometimes bordered on arrogance. He, reputedly, once sent a message to Sayyed Żīa saying, 'You should have killed us all, if you wanted to be allowed to succeed.' And he later proved – even though in another context – to be as good as his word. He did not quite understand the modern processes of politics and government, and yet he was a great *politician*; he was dictatorial in personal manners but democratic in social spirit. He was pragmatic in his choice of means but rigid in the defence of his principles. Mudarris was a star of the post-revolutionary 'liberal anarchism'; he fell when the 'liberal-anarchist' age was over.

The Unequal Confrontation

Through the Fourth Session of the *Majlis* (1923–5) it became gradually clear that Reżā Khān was bidding for a complete takeover. In fact, Mudarris and his followers became alive to the threat and its *full* implications earlier than others. The popular politicians of the second tendency were, at first, not entirely convinced that this was so; and, in any case, they were rather impressed with Reżā Khān's positive achievements (both then and even later). This was in part a reflection of differences in vision. For, what Mudarris and his tendency were (rightly) most afraid of was a restoration of functional despotism. They cared much less about the maintenance of law and order in the provinces, the revival of 'the past Iranian glories', and so forth than about the defence of the hard-won achievements of *Mashrūṭeh* against the increasing threats of revivalist nationalism. On one occasion, Mudarris told one of his own sympathisers (who had pointed out Reżā Khān's merits to him) that after all the people had to be safe 'from those whom they supply with a few rifles'![21]

The illegal activities of the police and the gendarmerie, both of which the War Office had quietly brought under its own command, were increasing daily; and it was becoming less and less possible to indulge in free (and sometimes licentious) political activity and journalism, which had been generally – but not always – possible since the First World War. Besides the annual budgetary increases in the allocation for the army, there were illicit financial appropriations by the Ministry of War. This issue came to a head particularly when, in a parliamentary speech, a *Majlis* deputy (Mu'īn al-Tujjār, a leading *bāzār* merchant) complained against it. Mudarris took up the theme and pointed the attack at Reżā Khān himself with reference to the manipulations by the War Office of the *khāliṣeh* (state) properties and indirect taxes. The confrontation that followed was finally settled with a tactical retreat by the Minister of War.

In time, the leadership of *both* anti-despotic tendencies found themselves in opposition to Reżā Khān's tactics and aspirations. But it was Mudarris and his group who took a consistent and wholly intransigent stand against him. Mudarris in particular resorted to almost every possible tactic to prevent the Sardār's assumption of complete power. He unsuccessfully tried to move the Prince Regent into action. He rallied the leaders of the *bāzār* and entered into negotiations with individuals whom he would otherwise have not regarded as natural allies. In this way he managed to alienate – at least for a critical period – leaders of the second political tendency, whose sympathies were generally much closer to his own than the other party's. For example, late in 1922 he managed to bring down the government of the popular and highly respected Mīrzā Ḥasan Mustawfī al-Mamālik by his masterly parliamentary tactics, and tried to put the highly unpopular Mīrzā Aḥmad Qavām al-Salṭaneh in his place. His own justification for this was simple and pragmatic: he likened Mustawfī to a 'jewelled sword' which, however, was only useful during peace-time; and Qavām to a 'sharp sabre' which was absolutely indispensable for war. But this did not prevent the national-revivalist poets 'Ishqī, 'Ārif and Farrukhī from showering him with a barrage of abuse and obscenity. Yet, by will and by circumstance, Reżā Khān's fortunes continued to rise, in spite of occasional setbacks: the *Majlis* elected him to the premiership in October 1923, mainly because of the spinelessness of Mushīr al-Dawleh (a popular 'goody-goody'), though this would have happened sooner or later;[22] he overthrew, and arrested, Khaz'al, the tyrannical Shaikh of Muḥammareh (who had been enjoying British protection), hence enhancing his stature among his supporters and bystanders, and throwing his opposition into confusion or silent admiration; he bought off a number of politicians and journalists from the opposite camps, frightened some others into inaction, and won over many others who, in such circumstances, always judge the 'truth' by the relative power of the contenders.

Reżā Khān Becomes Reżā Shah

The final battle was fought in two stages. Early in 1924 telegrams began to arrive from all over the country for the establishment of a republic. Demonstrations and meetings were held, leaflets distributed, concerts given and speeches delivered proclaiming the virtues of a republican system. Reżā Khān pretended to be neutral, but the active involvement of the army in the republican camp was symbolic. The opposition to republicanism, which included the leaders and supporters of the two anti-despotic political tendencies, also closed ranks. In fact, it was clear to many of the latter that Reżā Khān's republic was the first step towards the foundation of the Pahlavi dynasty.[23] Some national-revivalist intellectuals – notably the poet 'Ishqī, who had increasingly been showing signs of a change of heart – defected to the opposition. But the government already enjoyed quite a sizable majority in the new (i.e. Fifth) session of the *Majlis*, and it would not be an exaggeration to claim that, but for the exceptional energy and astuteness of Mudarris, the campaign would have been an undiluted success. It failed ingloriously. Matters came to a head when, in a sitting of the new session of the *Majlis*, Mudarris was physically attacked by Dr Iḥyā'al-Salṭaneh (Bahrāmī), a lesser light among Reżā Khān's supporters in the National Assembly. The news of a physical assault on the leading *mujtahid* exploded in the city like a bombshell. There were public demonstrations at the gates of the *Majlis*, involving physical struggles between supporters of the opposition and the much fewer people shouting for the government. When Reżā Khān arrived on the scene (apparently without knowledge of the blow to Mudarris), he was furious, and ordered the Assembly guards to disperse the crowd. A protracted and bloody battle was fought in which the Sardār himself became personally involved ('not flowers but bricks did they throw at him', wrote 'Ishqī in a semi-colloquial poem which made a significant contribution to his death by assassination a few months later).[24]

The next public figure to lose his temper was the respected *Majlis* President, who publicly abused Reżā Khān for his order to the Assembly guards to use force in dispersing the crowds, because the guards were, *ex officio*, under his own direct command. Reżā Khān, whose star had now reached its nadir everywhere except in the army, resigned his office, and retreated to his recently acquired rural estate near Teheran. However, the provincial army commanders began to send threatening letters to the *Majlis*, and, apart from that, many of its independent members were not altogether convinced that Reżā Khān's complete withdrawal would be in the country's best interests. Thus, a delegation of *Majlis* deputies, led by highly respectable independents such as Mustawfī al-Mamālik, Mushīr al-Dawleh and Dr Muṣaddiq, ceremoniously visited Reżā Khān at his retreat and brought him back to Teheran.

The republican movement was scrapped, and Reżā Khān, now reinstated in office, paid a visit to Qum (where – after the formation of the new kingdom of Iraq – many of the *Marāji' al-taqlīd* now lived) and made his peace with the leading religious dignitaries. Furthermore, he adopted a very conciliatory attitude towards Mudarris, and in a private conference conceded some of his political demands.[25]

This was a major defeat for Reżā Khān, but not a complete triumph for Mudarris, who seems to have overestimated the significance of his success for a brief, but crucial period: Mudarris had won the battle, not suspecting that he was about to lose the war. Between April 1924 and November 1925, when the Qajar dynasty was overthrown, Reżā Khān played his hand very carefully, especially with regard to religious affairs and, above all, his relations with Qum. For example, he himself, at the head of a group of army generals, participated in the annual religious processions mourning the martyrdom of Imām Ḥusain, and organised a number of the mourning services which are traditionally held on such occasions.[26]

Meanwhile, a bizarre episode occurred which has never been satisfactorily explained. In July 1924, rumours that a *saqqā khāneh* (public fountain founded by charity to commemorate the martyrs of Karbila) had performed a miracle were quickly followed by passionate public demonstrations in which most of the slogans were against the Bābīs (by whom were meant the Bahā'īs), and in the course of these the American vice-consul, taking photographs of the crowd, was lynched and killed. Both Reżā Khān (in league with 'the British') and Mudarris and his followers (also in league with 'the British'!) were, at the time, accused of instigating the disturbances. Whatever their origin, it is highly unlikely that there was a specific plot against the life of the American diplomat (which is a favourite view of all the commentators), but the event played into the hands of Reżā Khān, whose domestic and foreign well-wishers (including Moscow Radio) described it as the work of the feudal reactionary opposition. It led to the declaration of martial law, and further restrictions on the press.[27]

By the time the opposition woke up to Reżā Khān's new strategy of a direct bid for total power, it was too late to do much about it. In August 1924 they tabled a motion of censure against the very person of the Prime Minister, accusing him of 'active rebellion against the Constitution'. The motion was debated in a charged atmosphere, involving physical struggle both inside and outside the *Majlis*, but it was eventually withdrawn, because of the strength of the majority and the fears of some opposition deputies for their own safety. It was after this failure that Mudarris tried to use Shaikh Khaz'al of Muḥammareh by encouraging him to challenge Reżā Khān as a usurper, and invite Aḥmad Shah (the Qajar monarch) to return home from Paris *via* his own stronghold in Khūzistan. But Reżā Khān moved quickly, went to the province, effectively arrested Khaz'al and returned to Teheran a national hero.[28] Meantime, he played on Mudarris's vanity by making an honourable peace with him – a fatal mistake which the self-assured opposition leader must have bitterly regretted within a few months.

In mid-October 1925 a simple motion – signed by a number of deputies, including some who until recently had been in opposition – was tabled in the *Majlis* demanding the abolition of the Qajar dynasty and the temporary transfer of the royal title to the Prime Minister, until (according to the provisions of the Constitution) a constituent assembly had ratified the decision. The opposition – now sunk to a handful of deputies, some of whom had decided not to attend, with or without apologies – desperately tried to use delaying tactics, but to no avail. Of the fourteen deputies led by Mudarris, *he alone* raised his powerful voice, shouting that even if they took 'a hundred thousand votes it would still be illegal', and stormed out of the *Majlis* without delivering a formal speech. Four of the independents – Taqī-zādeh, 'Alā, Muṣaddiq and Dawlat-Ābādī, in that order – delivered speeches against the resolution. All these speeches were reasoned, and, in that sense, moderate. They all included praise for the achievements of the Prime Minister and support for his continuation in office, but they argued that the proposed resolution would be of no practical benefit, or that it had to be applied according to proper constitutional procedures. In particular, Muṣaddiq, who delivered an extremely well-prepared, reasoned, and yet emotional speech, said that he was opposed to the move because, if it turned the Sardār into a powerless constitutional monarch, the country would lose the leadership of a very able politician, and if it turned him into a despot (which he very well knew would be the case) it would be against the achievements of the Persian Revolution: he would not support such a cause no matter whether he was 'abused', 'cursed', 'killed' or even 'mutilated'. The speeches were answered, one by one, by four members of the majority faction, in a moderate tone. The assembly divided, and the motion was carried overwhelmingly. The Qajars fell, and an exciting chapter of Iranian history ended.[29]

Both the elections for the Constituent Assembly and its deliberations, which ratified the previous decision of the *Majlis* and conferred the royal title on Reżā Khān and his male issue, were no more than a farce: they can have surprised few men other than Sulaimān Mīrzā Iskandarī, the parliamentary socialist leader, who only then discovered that he had been deceived by the 'bourgeois nationalist leader' whom he had so consistently supported.[30] Yet it is also true that only a few men – this time Muṣaddiq among them – could conceive of the long-term implications of this event. In fact, just after Reżā Khān's coronation, early in 1926, the light-hearted urban crowd made up another of their habitual anti-authority slogans (though, in this case, not so offensive as usual): 'That which they've put on your head – they've just been pulling your leg!' They would soon learn who was pulling whose what. For this was a crucial strategic success for the despotic counter-revolution.

The Economic Scene

After the war the devastated Iranian economy gradually began to recover and, to some extent, reintegrate: the conclusion of the war itself was a stabilising factor; the growing extension of effective central authority, from 1921, at least made the roads and tracks more passable and less exposed to brigandage, thus reducing costs of transport and risks to trade; the growth and stabilisation of oil revenues (relative to the previous period) provided a boost to the economy by increasing home demand and relieving the balance of payments; the greater sense of economic security and expectations of better prospects were encouraging to traders and small investors; the state expenditure on some (though limited) infrastructural and industrial (mainly mining) projects was helpful both to immediate recovery and greater expectations; the budgetary and fiscal reorganisation helped reduce public debt and, more significantly, put the government accounts in much better order. None of this, however, implies a glaring economic improvement, much less economic development. It merely indicates gradual recovery from the previous state of total economic and financial, as well as socio-political, chaos. Recovery from total chaos is one thing, social and economic progress another.

OIL

It is from this period onwards that oil production and oil revenues become a key factor for the vicissitudes (including both the fortunes and misfortunes) of the Iranian political economy: by maintaining Iran as a country of vital interest to multinational oil companies as well as to Western governments, thus provoking their systematic intervention in the domestic affairs of the country; by tying the home demand, the level of state expenditure and the balance of payments to the variations in the price and quantity of oil exports, which, until recently, have been out of the control of the domestic political economy; by increasing (and sometimes reducing) the economic and political power of the state, which has been solely responsible for the receipt and the disbursement of oil revenues; by creating an autonomous economic sector, alienated from the rest of the political economy, combining minimal employment opportunities with a highly disproportionate financial return; by affording an *invisible* (and, productively, unearned) source of imports, consumption and general welfare – mainly for the privileged urban classes – which would otherwise not have been possible, and hence creating a gulf between real effort and actual earnings that gave rise to further expectations on the part of both the already privileged and the aspiring classes of the urban population; by making it *technically* easier to achieve economic 'progress', 'industrialisation' or 'modernisation', but *socio-economically* more difficult and even detrimental to the Iranian political economy – its productivity, cohesion, stability, integrity and survival – as a whole. It took over fifty years, including many years of interruptions, reversal and euphoria, for the full effects of the ahistorical and asocietal agencies of oil production and oil revenues to bear their sour fruits *in toto*. Yet the process had already begun in this period: the revenues were both absolutely and relatively small; but they were entirely received by the state; and they grew faster than any other economic category.

Table 5.1 contains some interesting observations. First, column (5) of the table shows that, from 1919, the physical output and export of oil increased every year without exception until 1926, when it was over four times the 1919 figure; secondly, column (3) indicates that the *value* of oil exports likewise rose to under twice the figure for 1919 (though, in this case, the increase was not continuous in every year); thirdly, from column (2) we see that Iranian oil revenues fluctuated a good deal, but, in any case, they reached much higher levels between 1924 and 1926 (i.e. in the years of Reżā Khān's bid for complete ascendancy); fourthly, there are greater variations in Iranian oil receipts when these are shown as a percentage of the total value of oil exports, in column (4), which shows that the Iranians were paid between a minimum of 5.05 per cent

TABLE 5.1 Oil revenues, oil exports, etc., 1919–26

(1) *Year*	(2) *Oil revenues (£ m.)*	(3) *Value of oil exports (£ m.)*	(4) *Oil revenues as % of oil-exports value*	(5) *Volume of oil exports ('000 long tons)*	(6) *Oil revenues per long ton (£ sterling at the 1919 exchange rate)*
1919	0.47	7.24	6.49	1106	0.42
1920	0.59[a]	6.88	5.57	1385	0.58
1921	0.59	6.54	9.02	1743	0.67
1922	0.53	7.73	6.85	2327	0.43
1923	0.41	8.11	5.05	2959	0.23
1924	0.83	12.30	6.75	3714	0.39
1925	1.05	12.53	8.10	4334	0.43
1926	1.40	13.43	10.42	4556	0.60

[a] Excludes the lump-sum payment of £1 million in lieu of outstanding accounts.

Source: columns (2) and (5) – J. Bharier, *Economic Development in Iran 1900–1970* (London: Oxford University Press, 1971) tables 8.4 and 8.3; columns (3), (4) and (6) computed on the basis of figures in tables 6.4, 6.9 and 8.3, ibid.

and a maximum of 10.42 per cent of the value of the exports of their own oil. Finally, since both the total quantity of exports, and exchange-rate variations, would affect the sterling value of oil receipts, column (6) was calculated to show the annual oil revenues per long ton, *assuming that* the rate of exchange between rial and sterling had remained constant since 1919. Thus, the variation in the figures of this column indicate all other influences, of which oil-price variations, erratic payments, illicit book-keeping tactics (or 'creative accounting') and statistical errors must be the most important.

Meanwhile, there were two abortive attempts to grant concessions for oil exploration and exploitation in Iranian Azerbijan to American companies: the first, in November 1921, to the Standard Oil Company; and the second, in 1922, to the Sinclair Consolidated Oil Corporation. The Soviet government strongly protested against both: according to the Irano-Soviet agreement of February 1921, the Soviet Union had cancelled all concessions granted to Tsarist Russia, and Russians, on the condition that these concessions would not be transferred to the government or citizens of another country. These included the north Iranian oil concession, which had previously been granted to a Georgian subject of Tsarist Russia; therefore, the 'transfer' of this concession to an American company would violate the terms of the Irano-Soviet agreements. In fact, neither of the two attempts were successful, though not directly because of the Soviet protest: the first attempt failed almost certainly because the southern Anglo-Persian Oil Company quickly entered into an agreement with the Standard Oil Company for joint exploitation, and the British government acquired a majority shareholding. This was unacceptable to the Iranian government, *Majlis* and public, who would never grant such a concession to a *British* company. The second attempt failed apparently

TABLE 5.2 Non-oil exports and the balance of trade, 1918–26

(1) *Year*	(2) *Volume of non-oil exports ('000 tonnes)*	(3) *Value of non-oil exports (million rials)*	(4) *Value of non-oil exports (£m.)*	(5) *Balance of trade, including oil exports (million rials)*
1918	49	115	4.2	–205
1919	103	187	7.48	–262
1920	49	137	4.03	–111
1921	84	179	3.62	–108
1922	115	305	5.49	115
1923	147	385	8.10	87
1924	211	485	11.55	207
1925	229	515	13.45	178
1926	152	450	9.24	324

Source: columns (2), (3) and (5) – Bharier, *Economic Development in Iran*, tables 6.4 and 6.6; column (4) – computations from the data in tables 6.4 and 6.9, ibid.

because the Soviet Union made it plain that, in the event of successful exploitation, it would deny transit facilities for export; but it is not unlikely that the British government also played a role in forestalling the second attempt.[31]

There are signs of recovery and revival in the domestic – i.e. non-oil – economic sectors which were not entirely unconnected with the oil receipts. No reliable (and little *un*reliable) data exist for aggregate agricultural output and its distribution by crop or region. Yet, qualitative evidence indicates that this sector was performing better than in previous years. There is also some indirect quantitative evidence: agricultural production was still largely divided between cash crops (cotton, opium, tobacco and dried fruits), which were mainly exported; and food crops (wheat, barley, rice, fruits, etc.) produced for domestic consumption. Furthermore, most of the non-oil Iranian exports consisted of agricultural products. Therefore, given the fact that over this period the country was generally self-sufficient in food, and its non-oil exports began to recover in volume and value, it follows that agricultural output must have been moderately increasing (see Table 5.2). In fact, the main items of agricultural imports were tea and sugar. Thus, agricultural recovery and growing oil receipts improved the balance of trade, and turned its chronic deficit into a surplus.[32]

There were also some developments in manufacturing and non-oil mining. The expansion of manufacturing took place predominantly in the 'private' sector.[33] For that reason it tended to be oriented towards local consumer demand, and it consisted mainly of small traditional plants and workshops employing unskilled and artisan labour in the production of such goods as soap, glass and textiles. Larger plants in the production of sugar, matches, textiles and similar 'light' consumer products – using *modern manufacturing techniques* – had already been set up by foreign investors and, sometimes, the state, but had mainly failed. It is certain that carpets still made up the bulk of Iranian manufacturing exports. Carpet weaving was still a village-based cottage industry; but there is qualitative evidence that some other rural and semi-rural industries, such as soap manufacture and some textile and footwear production, had begun to move to towns. This was the beginning of the institution (though not yet the technology) of modern factory production in manufacturing: that is, production by labour employed on monetary wage-contracts. In contrast to manufacturing, the expansion of non-oil mining – mainly salt and coal – was almost entirely due to state investment. But perhaps the most important area of public investment relative to others was in the expansion of modern (as opposed to traditional) education: the growth in the number of secondary schools, which were mainly concentrated in the capital.

These relatively minor economic improvements (most of which went unnoticed) hardly met the expectations of the Iranian intellectuals – and especially the dominant national-revivalist group among them – and their obsessive and emotional socio-economic cravings for, in particular, the foundation of a national bank, the construction of railways, the rapid expansion of modern primary and secondary education, the establishment of a European-style university, the extension of manufacturing production *based on modern technology*, a large increase in the provision of electricity and telephone services, the provision of modern urban public transport, and so forth. Many of them did not realise that the rapid fulfilment of these superficial *desires* (in place of an approach to socio-economic progress based not on an inverted sense of national inferiority, but related to the realities of the country's past and present) would take no less than a counter-revolution. This, in short, was Reżā Shah's 'mission for his country'.

NOTES

1. A substantial part of this chapter has been published in my 'Nationalist Trends in Iran, 1921–1926', *International Journal of Middle Eastern Studies*, Nov 1979. But even this part of the chapter has undergone some significant revisions.
2. See Ibrāhīm Fakhrā' ī, *Sārdār-i Jangal* (Teheran, 1965), a political biography of Kūchik, which, in spite of its shortcomings, is a more reliable source than the writings of Kūchik's rival comrades after emigration to the Soviet Union.
3. See ibid.; and E. H. Carr, *The Bolshevik Revolution* (Harmondsworth: Penguin, 1966) vol. III.
4. See Kasravī, and other Iranian sources on the history of the *Mashrūṭeh* Revolution cited in ch. 3, above. For a relatively new, and valuable, source on Ḥaidar's life, ideas, and activities, and on various socialist tendencies and groups in the period 1903–33, see D. Bozorgue (ed.), *Historical Documents: The Workers', Social Democratic, and Communist Movement in Iran* (Florence: Mazdak, 1976). The documents are in Persian.
5. The arguments about Ḥaidar's 'Marxism–Leninism' and Kūchik's 'bourgeois nationalism', still rage among Iranian intellectuals, as evidence that the same ideological and political *formalism* is still very much with us. This pseudo-ideological classification was first developed by some Jangalī émigrés in the Russian journal *Novyi Vostok*, and, through that, in the French journal *Revue du Monde Mussulman*. See Carr, *The Bolshevik Revolution*, vol. III.
6. See further Fakhrā'ī, *Sardār-i Jangal*; Carr, *The Bolshevik Revolution*, vol. III; and Victor Serge, *Memoirs of a Revolutionary* (New York: Oxford University Press, 1963), who quotes Blumkin, the Bolshevik intelligence officer among the Jangalīs, to the effect that the Gīlān revolution was called off from Moscow. Blumkin was the first Bolshevik to be arrested and shot by the Soviet Secret Police (GPU).
7. See relevant documents quoted in Gordon Waterfield, *Professional Diplomat, Sir Percy Loraine* (London: John Murray, 1973), especially Curzon's telegram to Loraine in 1923 in which he incidentally refers to the 1919 Agreement by saying that 'I attempted to help Persia with the Anglo–Persian Agreement, but was defeated and flouted by the Persians themselves. . . . I am becoming sadly tired of Persian suspicions, Persian intrigues, and Persian machinations . . . if [Persia] chooses to alienate us, she does herself no good, and us no harm' (pp. 79–80).
8. The political poet 'Ishqī accused Vusūq of selling the country to Britain and, in a scathing poem addressed to Vusūq, told him that 'Iran was not your daddy's

property'. Dawlat-Ābādī, a leading independent politician, told Sir Percy Cox, the British *chargé d'affaires*, that there was nothing wrong with the articles of the agreement, but everything wrong with the agreement itself. When Mudarris (of whom more below) was told by a supporter of the Agreement that its first article guaranteed Iran's independence, he said if the country was independent it would need no such guarantee. 'Abdullah Mustawfī, a one-time Persian diplomat in London, wrote a whole pamphlet against the Agreement, entitled *'Ibṭāl al-bāṭil* ('Refuting the Untruth'). See 'Ishqī's *Kullīyāt*, ed. A. A. Salīmī (Teheran: Amir Kabir, n.d.); Dawlat-Ābādī, *Ḥayāt-i Yaḥyā* (Teheran, 1950) vol. IV; Ḥusain Makkī, *Duktur Muṣaddiq va Nuṭqhā-yi Tarīkhī-yi Ū* (Teheran: 'Ilmī, 1945); and Mustawfī, *Sharḥ-i Zindigānī-yi Man . . .* (Teheran, 1962) vol. III.

9. See Ḥusain Makkī, *Tārīkh-i Bīst Sāleh-yi Irān* (Teheran: 'Ilmī, 1945) vol. I; Ibrāhim Khājeh Nūrī, *Bāzīgarān-i 'Aṣr-i Ṭalā'ī* (Teheran, 1942–3); and G. Arfa', *Under Five Shahs* (London: John Murray, 1964).
10. See especially Makkī, *Tārīkh-i Bīst Sāleh-yi Irān*, vol. I; and Khājeh Nūrī, *Bāzīgarān-i 'Aṣr-i Ṭalā'ī*
11. The Shah, and the entire opposition to the coup, particularly disliked Sayyed Żīā, and regarded him as the source of all their troubles since the coup. This played into Reżā Khān's hands, and made it easier for him to get rid of the Sayyed. The popular myth that 'the British' themselves decided to get rid of the Sayyed in favour of Reżā Khān entirely overlooks the role of the Shah and the leading politicians; besides, there is no real argument or evidence in its favour. See especially Makkī, *Tārīkh-i Bīst Sāleh-yi Irān*, vol. I.
12. At about the same time, Stalin and Hitler too were helped in usurping total power by their own opponents' overemphasis on their humble backgrounds, and underestimation of their qualities.
13. Both Rotstein and Shumyatsky, the successive Russian *chargés d'affaires* in Teheran between 1921 and 1925, regarded Reżā Khān as the leader of a 'bourgeois democratic' revolutionary movement, and his opposition as a combination of 'feudal' or 'semi-feudal' and religious reactionaries. Several articles in various Soviet journals described Reżā Khān in such terms – for example, an article in *Novyi Vostok* (1924) in which Reżā was represented as 'the leader of the Persian national-revolutionary movement, who succeded in securing Persia's independence'. In an interview in October 1924, Shumyatsky himself identified Reżā and his band as 'the genuine supporters of centralisation and bourgeois democratic progress, the nationalists', whose progressive government was opposed by 'feudalists' backed by 'the English'. According to a Soviet report on the proceedings of the Fifth Comintern Congress (held in June 1924), the Communist Party of Iran had actively participated in 'the intensification of the struggle of national democratic elements against feudalism and its backer, British imperialism'. This Russian attitude towards Reżā Khān remained basically the same even in November 1925, after he had overthrown the Qajars in order to establish his own dynasty: they were still hoping that, 'by proclaiming himself president of a Persian republic, [he] would place himself at the head of a "national-revolutionary movement"'. See E. H. Carr, *Socialism in One Country* (Harmondsworth: Penguin, 1972) vol. III, pp. 659–65, and *The Bolshevik Revolution*, vol. III, pp. 463–8; and Makkī, *Tārīkh-i Bīst Sāleh-yi Irān*, vols II and III.

The British view was less euphoric, and (incidentally) more in line with the *critical* sympathy of the *Majlis* independents, such as Mushīr al-Dawleh, Muṣaddiq and others, who appreciated Reżā Khān's efforts to establish law and order in the country, but disliked his dictatorial tendencies. This is best represented in the attitude of Sir Percy Loraine, who believed that 'this is the way to deal with these people as long as there is no brutality. . . . The common people are delighted to have at last a strong man at the head of affairs.' Loraine's *personal* role was decisive in making the British Foreign Office accept Reżā's overthrow of Shaikh Khaz'al (in 1924) in spite of pressures brought by Sir Percy Cox and others in favour of the latter. The Foreign Office documents show that Shumyatsky's belief that Khaz'al's open challenge to Reżā Khān had been part of a British conspiracy to mobilise 'the feudalists' against 'centralisation and bourgeois democratic progress' was completely unfounded. They also refute the later Iranian view that 'the British' had simply decided to sacrifice one of their agents (i.e. Khaz'al) in favour of another (i.e. Reżā). Indeed, those who 'analyse' modern Iranian history purely in terms of perpetual foreign conspiracies may be surprised to know that, at the news of Reżā Khān's coronation, the head of the Eastern Department of the Foreign Office described him as 'a usurper'. Early in 1923, Curzon himself had warned Loraine not to trust Reżā Khān, who was, in Curzon's words, 'quite capable of talking sweet and acting sour'. Still earlier, Armitage-Smith, the British Financial Adviser to Iran, had described Reżā to the Foreign Office as a person who 'betrayed everyone who has been with him, and hates H. M. G. [His Majesty's Government]'. See Waterfield, *Professional Diplomat*, esp. Chs 6–12. See further Makkī, *Tārīkh-i Bīst Sālah-yi Irān*, vols I–III.

There can be no doubt that both Britain and Russia were keen to preserve and promote their respective interests in Iran. My emphasis on the above issues is intended to show their errors of judgement, which were mainly due to their misunderstanding of the nature of Iranian society through theoretical preconceptions based on European history and experience. Furthermore, I wish to provide evidence for Iranians themselves that (a) the *uncritical* application of such theories by Right and Left alike is bound to be misleading; and (b) that for a real understanding of the forces and events of the Iranian political economy, both in the past and at present, a knowledge of the *internal* factors and tendencies is absolutely indispensable.

14. *Dīvān-i Mīrza Abulqāsim 'Ārif-i Qazvīnī* (Teheran: Saif-i-Āzād, 1946) p.270.
15. 'Ishqī *Kullīyāt*, pp. 222–32, 350, and 334.
16. See *Dīvān-i Farrukhī*, ed. H. Makkī (Teheran: 'Ilmī, 1953).
17. In a speech in the *Majlis* in 1921, Mudarris said that 'Muslim Persia must be Muslim and Iranian', and in another (1923) speech he said that he had once told the Ottoman Prime Minister, 'If anyone crosses Iranian borders without our permission we shoot him, if we can, irrespective of whether he wears the [Persian] *kulah*, the religious *turban*, or the *chapeau*. . . . Our religious practice is our very politics, and our politics are our very religious practice . . .' (quoted in Makkī, *Tārīkh-i Bīst Sāleh-yi Irān*, vol.II).There is a great deal of further evidence which shows that Mudarris was neither a modern nationalist *nor* a religious fanatic, but a democratic Shī'ite political leader.
18. He was murdered (in 1938) on the orders of Reżā Shah, after nine years of solitary confinement in a desert citadel in the province of Khurāsān.
19. See Khājeh Nūrī, *Bāzīgarān-i 'Aṣr-i Ṭalā'ī*, pp. 159–63.
20. See, Makkī, *Tārīkh-i Bīst Sāleh-yi Irān*, vol. III, pp. 172–3.
21. See, Mustawfī, *Sharh-i Zindigānī-yi Man*, vol.III.
22. He was 'insulted' by Reżā Khān, and resigned in protest, even though Reżā tried, by modifying his words, to persuade him to stay in office. See ibid.; Makkī, *Tārkhi-i Bīst Sāleh-yi Irān*, vol. III; Khājeh Nūrī, *Bāzīgarān-i 'Aṣr-i Ṭalā'ī*.
23. For example, in a poem on the subject, the poet-laureate wrote, 'Dar pardeh-yi jumhūrī, kūbad dar-i Shāhi; / Ma bīkhabar u dushman-i tammā' zirang ast' ('In the guise of republicanism, he is trying to become king; we are naïve, and the

greedy enemy is canny'). See M. T. Bahār, *Dīvān* . . . (Teheran: Amir Kabir, 1954) vol. I.

24. See further M. T. Bahār, *Tārīkh-i Muktaṣar-i Aḥzāb-i Sīyāsī dar Irān* (Teheran, 1944); Khājeh Nūrī, *Bāzīgarān-i 'Aṣr-i Ṭalā'ī*; Dawlat Abādī, *Ḥayāt-i Yaḥyā*; Makkī, *Tārīkh-i Bīst Sāleh-yi Irān.*
25. See, for example, ibid., vol. III; and Khājeh Nūrī, *Bāzīgarān-i 'Aṣr-i Ṭalā'ī.*
26. In fact, leading religious dignitaries in Qum and Iraq were on good terms with Reżā Khān, and at no time did they make any public move against him. On the contrary, in 1922 he was honoured by being sent a sword from the treasury of a holy shrine in Karbila, and even in May 1924 he was further sent a 'picture' of Imām Ali from the treasury of the Imām's own shrine in Najaf (accompanied with a letter from a *Marja'* in Qum), which were delivered with pomp and circumstance. See especially Makkī, *Tarīkh-i Bīst Sāleh-yi Irān*, vol. III.
27. One of the slogans of the demonstrators – 'This unprincipled Bābī has rebelled against the people' – was definitely aimed at Reżā Khān. The popular view that this had been a British plot to prevent American companies from being granted concessions to explore for and exploit oil in northern Iran is all the more remarkable in that the proposed concessions had fallen through over two years *before* this event. However, a comprehensive trade treaty with Russia had been concluded in June 1924, and this *may* have been in the minds of some of those who organised and led the demonstrations. On the basis of all the existing evidence, it looks as if, whether or not there had been an organised plot, various conservative, democratic, and opportunistic factions opposed to Reżā Khān – perhaps including the Royal Court – took advantage of the demonstrations in order to attack him. It is extremely unlikely that either he or any of the foreign powers was involved in the episode.
28. Contrary to the speculations of Makkī, Khājeh Nūrī and others, and, of course, the Iranian popular myth, the overthrow of Khaz'al was not a political manoeuvre designed by the British government and executed by Reżā Khān. On the contrary, all the available evidence shows that the move was made by Reżā himself, the British Foreign Office was divided on how to *respond* to his move, and only Loraine, who as early as 1922 had described Reżā Khān as 'the winning horse', had, with some qualification, believed that the Foreign Office should not honour the British government's earlier commitment to defend Khaz'al. See further 13, above.
29. See Makkī, *Duktur Muṣaddiq*, as well as all the other Persian sources cited in the above notes. The night before, an assassination attempt on the life of poet-laureate Bahār had led to the murder of a journalist who had been mistaken for the leading opposition deputy. That same night, some wavering supporters of Reżā Khān in the *Majlis* were 'invited' to a private meeting where they were made to pledge their support for the motion that was to be tabled next morning.
30. The socialist leader had candidly believed that Reżā Khān would honour his agreement with him, and become an *un*hereditary royal dictator. But, once he had discovered his 'mistake', he refused to vote for the ratification of the *Majlis* decision in the Constituent Assembly, and disappeared from Iranian politics until 1941. A number of leading opposition figures, in and out of the *Majlis* – for example, Ḥāyerī-zādeh and Sayyed Abulqāsim Kāshānī – were both 'elected' to the Constituent Assembly, and voted for the establishment of the Pahlavi dynasty.
31. The British were also claiming that any such agreement would be unacceptable, because the same (Tsarist) Russian subject who had acquired a concession before the First World War had sold it to a British subject.
32. In this period, the Perso-Soviet trade agreement concluded between Reżā Khān

and the Soviet government in June 1924 (which would have resulted in a much greater exchange of goods between the two countries) was not ratified by the *Majlis*. See further Makkī, *Tārīkh-i Bīst Sāleh-yi Irān*, vol. III; and E. H. Carr, *Socialism in One Country*, vol. III.

33. For a specimen of the state's budgetary statement in this period, see Bahār, *Tārīkh-i Mukhtaṣar*, pp. 259–64. In 1922, land tax made up over a quarter of government revenues, and the Ministry of War claimed 40 per cent of the budgetary allocations (other than the improper use of state-land revenues, and suchlike, by the army). There was a 'budget deficit' of about 15 per cent of revenues, for the financing of which no provision, or possibility, existed.

6 The Triumph of Pseudo-Modernist Absolutism, 1926–33

The fifteen years which separate Reżā Shah's accession and abdication can be divided into two parts: the period 1926–33, when his power was absolute; and the period 1933–41, when it was both absolute and arbitrary. The year 1933 marks a watershed because it witnessed two important, and related, events: the fiasco of the new oil agreement, and the fall of 'Abdulḥusain Taimūr-Tāsh, the powerful Minister of the Imperial Court. In the first seven years, a number of important socio-economic changes were effected; the Shah's power was still subject to some – increasingly weakening – challenge from the opposition; his decisions were taken, or modified, in consultation with his personal confidants; and the lives, dignity, security and property of the people were not yet completely at the mercy of the whims of the Shah, or the will of his servants.

Yet the year 1926 marks the beginnings of the supremacy of pseudo-modernism in Iran, which, though with interruptions and variations, has lasted until the time of writing, when a revolutionary movement is quickening the pace of its undignified death agony. For this reason, it is absolutely indispensable to begin this chapter with a brief discussion of the meaning and significance of our concepts of modernism and pseudo-modernism, and their relevance to the present study of modern (i.e. twentieth-century) Iran.

Modernism and Pseudo-Modernism

A NOTE ON MODERNISM

Modernism is a synthetic vision of both science and society which has gradually emerged from European developments in the past two centuries. It is a general attitude which reduces science to mechanistic or technological universal laws, and social progress to the purely quantitative growth of output and technology. In this respect, the modernist vision is not ideological, for a mechanistic and universal attitude to science, and purely quantitative and technological aspirations for society, may be contained and pursued within conflicting ideological frameworks. Ideological beliefs and issues do matter a great deal, but conflicting ideological theories and policies can be (and, indeed, have been) formulated within the spirit and vision of this European modernism.[1]

An aspect of this broad European modernism which is most relevant to the present study is the way in which European (including American) thinkers, statesmen, journalists, and so on, have tended to study, approach, and report on the countries of what is now known as the Third World by an *uncritical* application of techniques, theories, methods and aspirations drawn from the experience of advanced countries.[2] Many examples may be found in the works of scholars, assessments of diplomats (as well as intelligence agents), blueprints of technical experts, and so forth. Indeed, the voluminous literature of contemporary development economics alone can supply massive evidence for this modernist approach to an important aspect of life and labour in 'developing' countries. The problem has two interrelated sides to it: first, a mechanistic and universal view of modern science automatically excludes a search for those social and historical features of the developing countries which, with the aid of modern scientific *methods* and progressive *values*, could result in fruitful analyses of the relevant problems, and attempts at their solution; and, secondly, the exclusion from theory and policy of such important indigenous values, techniques, institutions and historical perspectives produces results which are often irrelevant – they are analogous to laboratory tests based on incorrect specifications of the problems.[3]

It has now become fashionable among many non-European (including Iranian) intellectuals to claim that 'outsiders' are incapable of understanding their cultural and social problems, although, curiously enough, they do not normally extend their claim to the case of those 'outsiders' who have the 'right' ideological colourings. Indeed, the new fashion has even been used by the Shah and Queen of Iran and their domestic apologists – i.e. Iranian pseudo-modernists *par excellence* – to their own political advantage. I do not agree with this new trend, and in particular see no inherent reason why 'outsiders', of whatever nationality, should be incapable of meaningful studies of the developing countries. For, if it is merely a question of prejudice, then that is not necessarily determined by a person's nationality; and, if, as I believe, it is a question of irrelevant generalisations from *existing* knowledge and experience, then there is no reason why anyone could not formulate relevant theories and policies, by an appropriate application of those methods and ideas which have thus far developed science and society in advanced countries. The problem, I repeat, has its roots in an implicit belief in the *homogeneity* of social experience everywhere in the world, and the related universality of scientific laws, which (though contrary to the spirit of the founders of modern science and society) have created their own problems in the advanced countries themselves.

A NOTE ON PSEUDO-MODERNISM

Indeed, many intellectuals and political leaders of the Third World itself are voluntary victims of a *superficial* version of this European modernism – that is, of pseudo-modernism. The modernism to which we have briefly referred is a product of certain developments in advanced countries, even though it is subject to criticism within its own context. Pseudo-modernism in the Third World, however, is the product of this product: it is characteristic of men and women in those societies that – regardless of *formal* ideological divisions – are alienated from the culture and history of their own society, both in intellectual ideas and in social aspirations, but, unlike the European modernists themselves, they seldom have a real *understanding* of European ideas, values, and techniques. Thus, Third World pseudo-modernism combines the European modernist's lack of regard for specific features of Third World societies with a lack of proper understanding of modern scientific and social development, their scope, limit, and implications, and whence they have emerged. That is how modern technology (which is often confused with modern science) is seen as omnipotent, and capable of performing miracles which would solve any and all socio-economic problems once purchased and installed; why traditional social values and production techniques are regarded as inherent symbols, indeed causes, of backwardness, and sources of national embarrassment; and why industrialisation is viewed not as an objective but as an object, and the installation of a modern steel plant not as a means but as an end in itself. This subject is vast, and the full discussion of its various aspects would require a separate treatment. Some of these aspects, however, will become clear, in the specific case of Iran, in the course of this study.

Modernism and Pseudo-Modernism in Iran

THE BACKGROUND

The foregoing chapters, especially Chapters 2–5, include scattered remarks on the various effects of Iran's exposure to modern European countries, ideas, and techniques since the middle of the nineteenth century. On the whole, the economic consequences of this exposure were damaging, but the economic damage itself, combined with the influence of modern science and ideologies, made an important contribution to the overthrow of traditional despotism. There were many Iranian politicians and intellectuals who began to formulate ideas, and develop social aspirations, which had been profoundly influenced by their knowledge of European (including Russian) societies. Among the relatively early 'modernisers' Mīrzā Malkum Khān Nāẓim al-Dawleh is a well-known example. It is impossible to generalise about the specific views of the various individuals involved in the process, who, in any case, came in different generations. There were some like Fatḥ'alī Ākhūnduf, who denounced almost every Iranian tradition, was vehemently anti-religious (though this hostility was in fact directed against Islam, which he regarded as a cause, if not *the* cause, of the country's backwardness), and was totally captivated by all things European.[4] There were many more, like Malkum himself, who took a more sophisticated view of the problem, and this included some leading younger intellectuals of the *Mashrūṭeh* Revolution, such as Sayyed Ḥasan Taqī-zādeh, Mīrzā Jahāngīr Khān Shīrarāzī (Ṣur-Isrāfīl) and Alī Akbar Dehkhudā. The movement included many religious leaders and preachers – for example, Ḥaj Shaikh Hādi (Najmābādī) and Sayyed Jamāl al-Dīn Isfahānī – who, at different levels, adapted modern ideas to their own specific realm of religious thought and action.

Thus, during the *Mashrūṭeh* Revolution and its immediate aftermath three major attitudes towards modern ideas and methods were prevalent: the dominant modernising views of both 'lay' and religious groups who were nevertheless firmly rooted in Iranian culture and history, and would not easily 'throw the baby out with the bath-water'; the traditionalist and reactionary zealots who were opposed to any application and adaptation of modern values, techniques and institutions to Iranian society; and a small (but growing) band of pseudo-modernist Europeanisers, from the midst of whom a right-and left-wing later developed. An Iranian playwright of the period has authentically contrasted the traditionalists and the pseudo-modernists of the time in the play *Ja'far Khān az Farang Āmadeh* ('Ja'far Khān Has Returned from Europe').[5]

It is also from this period that 'social democratic', 'socialist' and later 'communist' tendencies begin to develop, although – for a variety of reasons – they did not manage to become a major political force until the 1940s. Not surprisingly, many of the earlier Iranian 'socialist' groups developed in the province of Azerbijan, where there was a great deal of physical and intellectual movement across the border with the Russian colonies of northern Azerbijan, Georgia, and so on. It is not possible to produce even a cursory discussion of these various groups, and their ideas, in the present work. A striking feature of many of them, however, is that (a) they display very limited knowledge of Iranian history and society, and hence there is very little *adaptation* of socialist theories to their own environment; and (b) they betray little knowledge and understanding of socialist theory and history itself. For example, in 1908 the Tabriz Social Democratic Group wrote a letter to 'Citizen' Kautsky asking for guidance in a socialist analysis of the Persian Revolution. The letter refers to two Iranian socialist views of the revolution. The first regarded it as 'lacking any progressive content [because the revolutionary] movement is against foreign capital, i.e. the only factor which can help break up the economic formations of our country: *in simple words, the aim of this* [*revolutionary*] *movement is to block the way to European civilisation*'. According to the second, the movement was a bourgeois revolution directed against *the feudal system*, notwithstanding its 'retrogressive tendencies, emanating from reactionary elements'; *in defence of this view*, its upholders point out that, 'despite the so-called struggle against foreign capital, in the blossoming period of the revolution, 1906–7, when we had a National Assembly, imports of European products increased'.

It is clear from the above that, in the midst of the revolutionary struggle against serious attempts at despotic restoration (especially in Tabriz, whose people had become heroic symbols of resistance), Iranian socialists were preoccupied with the 'correct' ideological analysis of the movement; both tendencies regarded economic protectionism as anti-socialist, because it would *block the way to European civilisation*; and neither of them took notice of the fact that the revolutionary objectives were not opposed to the interest of Iranian landlords as a class. Kautsky's reply contained a measured Marxist analysis, and it pointed out that opposition to foreign capital was not necessarily reactionary. Yet, in a subsequent letter to Plekhanov, the group expressed their disagreement with Kautsky's comments. One wonders what they would have been told had they written their original letter to Rosa Luxemburg or Lenin.[6]

This is just a single example from a lot of evidence which shows that Iranian pseudo-modernism has not been confined to a given (right-wing) ideological outlook, and has been a large trap into which many individuals and groups with claims to radical ideologies have also fallen.

THE RISE OF PSEUDO-MODERNISM IN IRAN

The rise and supremacy of official, as well as unofficial, pseudo-modernism in Iran was based on, first, an uncritical rejection of all existing Iranian traditions, institutions, values, and so on, as 'backward' and a source of national humiliation, and, secondly, a superficial zest, an emotional fever, for the imitation and emulation of all things European within the narrow confines of a small, but increasing, group in the urban community. That this pseudo-Europeanism itself was based on the ancient institution of Iranian despotism shows up the true 'modern and progressive' content of official pseudo-modernism; but the apologetic arguments of both domestic and foreign well-wishers of such systems (who in effect argue that you 'need' an iron dictatorship in order to achieve democracy!) is too infamous to be worth further discussion.

This irrational attitude of cultural self-denigration and capitulation was, however, combined with an equally irrational sense of Iranian chauvinism and self-glorification. The transplantation of European vitalistic nationalism helped the romantic rediscovery of the ancient, pre-Islamic Iranian civilisation, whose achievements were then blown up beyond reasonable recognition, and whose failures and defects were buried in the pseudo-modernists' 'collective unconscious'. Slowly but surely, the impressive and comprehensive social and cultural achievements of post-Islamic Iran were either submerged or repudiated; but the despotism and imperialism of Sāsānid Iran were – as a model of total virtue – elevated. In a country in which the term 'nation' and the European concept of nationhood had never existed, a narrow concept of 'the Iranian nation' was fabricated. This had no beneficial results whatsoever; but it sowed division among the Iranian cultural entities, which had always made up a coherent *community of Iranians.*

It was by no means a one-man operation, for not only the organs of the state, but also scores of journalists, writers, poets, intellectuals, teachers and academics made significant contributions towards its realisation. Furthermore, it was not the creed only of those holding power and privilege, because a major segment of the opposition consciously or unconsciously adhered to a thinly disguised version of it. Iranian liberals (not to be confused with men such as Dr Muhammad Muṣaddiq), communists and other Marxists have – with just a few minor exceptions – often shared this basic outlook with their adversaries and persecutors. They have merely used liberal and Marxist jargon to dress up their own versions of Iranian pseudo-modernism: their anti-Islamism (and anti-Arabism) derived from much the same sentiments as that of the other side; their rejection of Iranian cultural traditions had the same socio-psychological origins, even though they camouflaged it by the application of pseudo-radical terminology;[7] their vitalistic nationalism was disguised in their emotional zest for 'economic progress', 'industrialisation' (especially the construction of a steel plant), and so on; their *étatiste* attitudes to modernisation were disguised in the name of a non-existent 'proletariat', and against a non-existent 'bourgeoisie' (a concept which they no doubt associated with traders, money-lenders and even embezzling bureaucrats!); and their avowed hatred of 'bourgeois freedom' – where it did not exist (and, had it done it would not have been *bourgeois* freedom) – was, in spite of its ideological trimmings, a genuine product of Iranian despotism and European nationalism. No wonder that so many of them later found themselves in a perfectly natural environment – whether in the SAVAK (the Shah's secret police), the Plan Organisation or the Prime Minister's office – when the oil revenues finally enabled the state to fling its gates wide open.[8]

For reasons which will become clear through the rest of this book, it took many decades for the reaction against Iranian pseudo-modernism to be formulated in ideas and translated into action. One of the earliest manifestations of this reaction is the late Jalāl Āl-i Aḥmad's *Gharbzadehgī*, published in 1962. The most literal translation of the term *gharbzadehgī*, which the writer himself invented, is 'West-struckness'; its most authentic translation is 'occidentitis', implying an infection, as in the medical terms tonsil*itis*, bronch*itis*, etc.; but perhaps a good compromise between authenticity and familiarity is simply the term 'Westernism'. Āl-i Aḥmad's insight and intuition are – especially for their time – admirable; but his argument suffers from factual and historical errors and omissions, analytical limitations and empirical casualness which cause – and to some extent have already caused –

a confusion of the issue. For example, he is oblivious to the historical roots of European modernism *within its own, European context*; his emphasis on *the West*, meaning western Europe and the United States, diverts attention away from the *general* European (as well as American) characteristics of modernism; his concentration on the case of Iran (and, to a lesser extent, the East) overlooks the pseudo-modernist infection of nearly all 'developing' countries; his portrayal of Iranian, and Eastern, Westernism as the product of an external, Western, conspiracy, pure and simple, is not only naïve but also sidesteps the significance of the domestic Iranian forces (reaching far beyond the agents of imperialism) which played an important role in its propagation and imposition; and his discovery of its 'origins' in such events as the travels of Marco Polo betrays analytical simplicity and sociological xenophobia. Āl-i Aḥmad's early insight is evidence for his native ability – so uncharacteristic of modern intellectuals of his generation – to rise above petty squabblings and grasp the essential. But this does not mean that his impressionistic diagnosis should be uncritically accepted, and – worse still – used as an anti-intellectual weapon with which to brush aside all reasonable arguments, or promote xenophobia and pseudo-traditionalism.

The antithesis to the mindless pseudo-modernism which has dominated Iran for the past fifteen years, has now been formulated in a general tendency towards a rediscovery of Iranian traditions. In the nature of things this was inevitable; and it would be a mistake to dismiss it as nothing but a nostalgia for medieval obscurantism. Yet it would be equally dangerous to go to the other extreme, for such a counter-euphoria would bring its own destruction. There is everything wrong with the pseudo-modernism that has so signally failed Iranian society, body and soul. But there is nothing wrong with the idea of openness and progress, both in the intellectual and in the material sphere of life and labour. Furthermore, it was not European ideas and techniques *in themselves* that played havoc with the whole social fabric. It was the failure to understand and criticise those ideas and methods within their own, European context, first; and to use, not emulate, those of them that, in a sensible synthesis with Iranian social and historical realities, could serve the cause of social reconstruction and progress.

If, at long last, Iran is to achieve a normal social and economic system within a genuinely progressive cultural framework of its own, then there must be a realistic synthesis of *modern* (not pseudo-modernist), and *traditional* (not pseudo-traditionalist) ideas, values, methods and techniques.

The New Bureaucracy: The Men and the Machine

THE MEN

The rapidly increasing power of the state was inevitably bound up with the growth and centralisation of the military and administrative apparatus. In the pre-revolutionary Qajar era, though the power of the state had been absolute and arbitrary, there did not exist a vast, centralised bureaucratic network. This was partly owing to the relative poverty of the state and society; partly owing to the traditionalist nature of the state; and partly because of the associated lack of modern means of communications and modern technology. Whereas the new state aspired to the positive assertion of state power to bring about social and economic change, it was also relatively richer, mainly because of its exclusive command over the oil revenues, and, it was therefore both willing and able to employ modern technology in pursuit of its objectives for the Iranian political economy. Hence, the Pahlavi state began by extending, modernising and centralising the army and the bureaucracy, concurrently with investment in activities which would complement such a policy: roads, railways, telecommunications, higher education, and so forth.

The men around Reżā Shah, those who had played a crucial role in putting him on the throne, were by no means faceless and dependent lackeys and clients. On the contrary, some of them were among the most able politicians, administrators and army generals in the country. For example, 'Abdulḥusain Taimūr-Tāsh was a man of exceptional ability and intelligence, which, together with his unusually good looks and European-style finesse, had made him a victim of narcissism and arrogant conceit. He displayed a curious amalgam of practical and intellectual ability, Napoleonic self-confidence and ruthlessness, and despotic cruelty.

By contrast, Ali Akbar Dāvar, whose ability, intelligence and intellect were no less (if not more) than those of Taimūr-Tāsh, was a dedicated and almost selfless lawyer whose main ambition was to serve the country to the best of his ability. He was an entirely self-made man who had taken advantage of a favourable opportunity to study law in Switzerland. Dāvar was the one and only personage in Reżā Shah's personal entourage whose ability and integrity were, and remained, beyond objective dispute: he made many mistakes, the greatest of them being his genuine belief – which he later regretted – that Reżā Khan was the only available route to Iranian salvation; but he was caught in circumstances unsuitable to men of his integrity and ability, and he always tried to make the best of a bad job, even including the moment when he took his own life.

Nuṣrat al-Dawleh (Fīrūz), a member of Vusūq's triumvirate, and the go-between in the negotiations over the infamous 1919 Agreement, was able and self-reliant, but entirely amoral, exceptionally selfish, and shamelessly opportunistic. By alienating Vusūq and, later, dropping Mudarris, he had already demonstrated that he would be ready to sell his soul to the highest bidder. Farajullah Bahrāmī (Dabīr-i A'ẓam), though not a distinguished administrator or politician, was an intellectual and literary figure who had been Reżā Khān's *chef-de-cabinet* ever since the latter's appointment to the Ministry of War; for a time he wrote literary essays and reviews under the pen-name of 'F. Barzigar' ('Farmer'). Ali Dashtī, a former common preacher in Bushihre, who had been thrown out of that small southern Iranian port for his notorious promiscuity, had already established himself as a 'progressive' journalist in Teheran. He was a 'romantic' writer of some value for his own time, and an intellectual gangster who suited his later position as chief literary censor perfectly.

General Amīr-Aḥmadī (formerly Brigadier Aḥmad Āqā Khān) was an exceptionally able and ruthless military commander, both of which characteristics helped him in putting down insurgencies and brigandage in the turbulent western and south-western regions of the country with efficiency and cruelty. General Amīr Ṭahmasibī – a former superior of Reżā Khān – was able and intelligent but, in contrast to Amīr-Aḥmadī, educated, polished and sympathetic. There were a few other generals close to the Shah, of whom Yazdān-Panāh, Āyrum, Ḥabibullah Shaibānī and Amīr-Khusravī were the most important.[9]

There were others who were not so close to Reżā Shah, some of whom had had records of active or passive opposition to his rise to power. Mirza Ḥasan Mustawfī, the aged and popular politician, co-operated for a short period and quickly withdrew to the background shortly before his death. Mehdīqulī Hedāyat (Mukhbir al-Ṣaltaneh) – a relatively conservative leader of the *Mashrūṭeh* Revolution – persisted throughout this period, but faded out in the ensuing period of hard-headed pseudo-modernism, with which he did not agree. Ja'farqulī Bakhtīyarī (Sardār As'ad, previously Sardār Bahādur) a leading revolutionary general – under whose command Reżā Shah had once fought as an army corporal – co-operated until his apparently inexplicable arrest and murder in prison. Sayyed Ḥasan Taqī-zādeh – a leading radical member of the *Mashrūṭeh* Revolution – rose to become Minister of Finance, and ended by going into voluntary exile. Bāqir Kāẓimī, (Mu'azziz al-Dawleh) a centrist *Mashrūṭeh* supporter, became Foreign Minister and finished with a shadowy existence until the Shah's abdication in 1941. He was destined to become Minister of Finance in Dr Muṣaddiq's government twenty years later. There were still many others: for example, Muhammad Ali Furūghī, who combined a high degree of learning with a servile attitude towards his political master.

It is significant that, by 1933–4, of the men of special ability and independence in Reżā Shah's immediate entourage, only Dāvar had survived in office. Others had been dismissed, arrested, assassinated, or killed in prison. These were the beginnings of the rule of authentic Iranian despotism – that is, the combination of both absolute and arbitrary power.[10]

THE MACHINE

Such were the men who helped provide the state machinery with which Reżā Shah destroyed first themselves in order to establish his undisputed despotic rule over the Iranian lands and their peoples. The new military–bureaucratic network closely resembled the ancient imperial Persian system. The country was divided into a number of provinces, some of whose boundaries were arbitrarily defined to suit the strategic purposes of the state. The system of dual military and civil governorship for each province was intended both to divide labour and to provide a check on the activities of each governor by the other. This was paralleled by a centralised urban police force, directly under the command of the chief prefect, usually an army general, in Teheran; and a rural police force (gendarmerie) which was likewise led by an army general with headquarters in the capital. This system has survived till the time of writing, except that the oil-revenue boom of the past fifteen years produced an explosion in the personnel, the weaponry and the technology used by the agents of despotism.

In the sphere of social, economic and judicial legislation, certain relatively significant bills were enacted in order to modernise the civil, financial and judicial services. Here, Dāvar played a particularly active role, the most important of his administrative reforms being the reorganisation of the Ministry of Justice and the establishment of an office for the registration of urban and rural property. For this purpose, he employed a group of French legal and judicial experts, a decision which provoked Dr Muṣaddiq's opposition in his first and last term of parliamentary office under Reżā Shah: in a typically long, humorous but reasoned speech, he argued that foreign experts could cause more harm than good, because they would tend to generalise from their own, irrelevant social framework. This simple but profound warning went unheeded, both then and for a long time to come.[11]

The idea of formal property registration was clearly a good one, as it could – and, to some extent, did – promote much greater legal, judicial and economic efficiency. But, inevitably, it became a powerful means whereby some state property, especially uncultivated and semi-urban land, and a lot of rural smallholdings were usurped and registered by those who had an advantage in knowledge, power, or both. It did not even provide a general security for property-ownership, as it could have done, since in no time the Shah and the state became so powerful that no one could dispute their private and public expropriations of private (especially rural) property. Even such an astute and well-meaning reformer as Dāvar could not realise that laws and regulations by themselves can provide little protection in a social system which is founded on military–bureaucratic lawlessness.

A good example of bureaucratic reformism and mindless vandalism was the state expenditure on the modernisation and 'beautification' of the capital and other towns and cities. In principle, such reforms and reconstructions were badly needed: the construction of wider streets, their pavement with cobbles and asphalt, the regulation of means and methods of traffic, and so forth. The actual reforms, however, tried to fulfil these tasks in the most superficial, arbitrary and – in fact – vandalistic manner. The old city walls and gates of

Teheran were pulled down for no reason other than that they were regarded as shameful symbols of backwardness. In the construction of new streets, or the extension and widening of the old, the policy was to demolish any and all buildings – residential, monumental, historical or whatever – merely in order to keep them straight. The vandals played havoc with community life and historic architecture at will.[12]

Among the more important items of social legislation in this period were the series of bills concerning the promotion of higher education. In 1925 the first group of sixty state scholars was sent to European countries – especially France, Belgium and Germany – to study a variety of scientific, technical and other subjects. The exclusion of Britain is politically significant: in the whole of the Reżā Shah period not a single state student was sent to Britain; nor was a single British expert or company employed to assist in the realisation of state projects. Many of these students had been sent as part of a teacher-training programme aimed at manning the rapidly increasing state and private secondary schools, and, later, the newly established University of Teheran. Once again, the educational policy was consistent with the general attitude of pseudo-modernist *étatisme:* whereas over 90 per cent of the population were illiterate, expensive educational projects were carried out in order to supply state officials and take pride in the growing number of modern Iranian doctors, engineers, teachers, and so on.

The Political Economy

Economic development, in the sense of a quick and comprehensive socio-economic transformation, is essentially a post-colonial fever: it dates back to the end of the Second World War. In the 1920s the idea of social and economic progress in predominantly rural societies was still novel, vague and untried. Even the Soviet Union – the inheritor of a vast empire, with unusually rich and diverse human, agricultural and mineral resources, dominated by a semi-industrialised European country – was engaged in technocratic trial-and-error and political controversy in its efforts to discover an appropriate method for comprehensive economic development. It finally (in 1928) settled for comprehensive planning and the collectivisation of Soviet agriculture; and it took at least two decades to prove that, whatever its sociological merits, Soviet planning could be technologically successful.

For the national-revivalist Iranians, western Europe was certainly the model of hopes and desires for the future. But their more immediate aspirations centred around a number of piecemeal and partial 'improvements', in education, transport and communications, health and other social services, and the bureaucratic and military networks. In the literature of economic development such activities are now described as investment in 'social overhead capital' or 'infrastructure', and are generally regarded as prerequisites for a conscious and comprehensive development effort. The Iranians had no such model in mind. In fact, the model itself is more of an *a posteriori* generalisation and rationalisation of what has already happened in 'developing' countries, rather than an *a priori* hypothesis for the strategy of economic development.

In attempting to fulfil many of its immediate aspirations, the new régime was helped by a combination of self-reinforcing favourable factors: it was receiving substantial amounts of oil revenue, which were paid directly into the Treasury; it had the power to impose and collect high (and sometimes punitive) customs and excise duties, and was relatively efficient at doing so. It also enjoyed the approval and co-operation of the new intellectual, professional and bureaucratic classes of the society. State expenditure became the main instrument for piecemeal development.

MONEY, BANKING AND FINANCING

The establishment of a national Iranian bank had been a national-revivalist dream, and the new régime lost little time in acting for its fulfilment. This led to the foundation of Bank Melli Iran, with the help of a German 'expert' who was later to stand trial on charges of corruption. The monopoly of issuing notes, hitherto enjoyed by the British-owned Imperial Bank of Persia, was transferred to the new bank; and there was to be a complete metallic (mainly silver) coverage, later reduced to 60 per cent, of the notes in circulation. The creation of Bank Melli was symptomatic of all initial steps at stimulating development, both in Iran and elsewhere: they create capacity where there will be little output, and they expand supply where there is little demand. This by itself may not be an incorrect policy, assuming that (a) complementary policies result in the expansion of other activities which can use the goods or services produced by the initial projects (that is, there exists a strategy which promotes *interdependent* activities); and (b) the creation of modern firms and institutions does not simply duplicate existing traditional and indigenous production and technology. In this case, as is often the case in 'developing' countries, neither of these conditions was fulfilled. At the time, and for a long time afterwards, the Iranian merchant community was dependent on the traditional *ṣarrāfān* (the Iranian counterparts to the old European goldsmiths) for its 'banking' needs. The institution was well-developed, and its working thoroughly understood by both the *ṣarrāf* and the merchants. Furthermore, there existed mutual trust and security in transactions between the two sides. By contrast, the new state bank brought to bear no experience and little expertise in running its affairs; and it was something alien to both the bureaucrats who manned it and the public whom they were supposed to serve.

It may be argued that the *ṣarrāfi*s charged high interest rates, restricted credit, often demanded substantial collateral, and so forth – all of which would inhibit business expansion and economic efficiency. But the fact is that the new bank, and the few other banks which were later established in the same spirit, did not, and *could not*, fare any better in these regards: they charged high interest rates, they were very selective in their choice of clients, and they therefore granted little credit. The difference was that, where the *ṣarrāfī*s would discriminate on grounds of the business creditworthiness of their clients alone, the banks – being bureaucratic institutions – discriminated through nepotism and privilege. The devastating social, institutional and technological dualisms which the pseudo-modernists have created in 'developing' countries has its origins in such an approach and attitude to economic development. Let there be no misunderstanding. Our criticism is not directed against genuine efforts at social and economic progress; it is levelled at senseless, even harmful, pseudo-modernist emulations. It may have been useful to overhaul and update banking services in Iran. But it would have been cheaper and better to encourage the expansion and evolution of the existing *ṣarrāfī* network, perhaps even involving the foundation of a model state *ṣarrāfī*, organised and managed by men of experience in the business.

The sources of state revenue were oil receipts, customs revenues, other indirect taxes, and income tax. The direct and indirect revenues from oil made up the largest single source of income for the Treasury. Furthermore, the rise in oil receipts rapidly increased the relative significance of this source of state revenue to about one-third of total government expenditure. Yet, the perennial volatility of oil revenues began to cause irritation and anxiety; and this – as we shall shortly see – led to the abrogation of the D'Arcy concession, and the conclusion of the 1933 oil agreement. There were a series of income-

TABLE 6.1 Budgetary allocations, 1928–33 (million rials)

Department	*1928*	*1929*	*1930*	*1931*	*1932*	*1933*	*Average, 1928–33*
War	112	141	147	179	186	215	163.3
Finance	61	81	82	77	124	94	86.5
Interior[a]	25	36	38	36	41	49	37.3
Posts and Telecommunications	22	28	20	19	24	26	23.2
Education	18	21	22	24	36	42	27.2
Justice	15	16	18	16	19	23	18.0
Imperial Court	12	13	12	12	13	13	12.5
Foreign Affairs	9	11	12	9	18	19	13.0
Industry, Trade and Transport[b]	3	3	1	1	20	26	9.0
Agriculture	–	–	1	1	2	2	1.0
Total	276	350	353	374	483	509	391

[a] Includes expenditure on public health.
[b] Up to and including 1931, figures refer to expenditure on transport (other than railways) only; from 1932, they refer to industry and trade, almost exclusively.

Source: based on Bharier, *Economic Development in Iran*, table 4.1

tax measures, but the consequences were neither progressive in theory, nor significant in practice. The burden of domestic taxation was still largely shouldered by excise, lump-sum and other indirect taxes, which were invisible to the masses of the people who paid them and inoffensive to the privileged classes, who could well afford payment.

The pattern of state expenditure was entirely consistent with its aspirations: the extension, centralisation and modernisation of the military–bureaucratic network, as well as expenditure on 'infrastructural' services. Tables 6.1 and 6.2 show the absolute and percentage budgetary allocations for different departments, in descending order of magnitude. The bulk of the military–

TABLE 6.2 Budgetary allocations, 1928–33 (percentage share of the total)

Department	*1928*	*1929*	*1930*	*1931*	*1932*	*1933*	*Average, 1928–33*
War	40.4	40.3	41.6	47.9	38.6	42.2	41.8
Finance	22.0	23.1	23.2	20.6	25.7	18.5	22.2
Interior	9.0	10.3	10.8	9.6	8.5	9.6	9.7
Posts and Telecommunications	8.0	8.0	5.7	5.1	5.0	5.1	6.2
Education	6.5	6.0	6.2	6.4	7.4	8.3	6.8
Justice	5.4	4.6	5.1	4.2	3.9	4.5	4.6
Imperial Court	4.3	3.7	3.4	3.2	2.7	2.6	3.3
Foreign Affairs	3.3	3.1	3.4	2.4	3.7	3.7	3.3
Industry, Trade and Transport	1.1	0.9	0.3	0.3	4.1	5.1	1.9
Agriculture	–	–	0.3	0.3	0.4	0.4	0.2
Total	100.0	100.0	100.0	100.0	100.0	100.0	100.0

Source: Table 6.1.

bureaucratic network – War, Finance and the Interior – received over 70 per cent of the allocations, with the Ministry of War alone spending over 40 per cent of the total budget; yet this figure excludes other military expenditure, illicitly financed from sources such as the income from state property (the *khāliṣeh*). The other areas of higher priority were Posts and Telecommunications, Education, Justice and, from 1931–2, Industry. Agriculture, however, was characteristically left to its own devices.

THE 'INFRASTRUCTURE'

We have already seen that, outside the predominantly military and bureaucratic expenditures, Posts and Telecommunications and Education were given high priority in the state budget: between 1928 and 1933, the average expenditure on these two categories was 6.2 and 6.8 per cent of the budget. In the case of Education, the proportional budgetary allocation increased from

6.5 per cent in 1928 to 8.3 per cent in 1933 (see Table 6.1). In any budget these would be very impressive *percentage* figures for educational expenditure, even though the corresponding absolute amount of funds spent might fall short of higher aspirations. Yet, as mentioned earlier, most of the educational funds were spent on expensive modern 'prestige' projects; and, in particular, not a farthing was spent on raising the literacy rate or the intellectual consciousness of the vast majority of the people.

The other major 'infrastructural' investment of this period was the construction of the Trans-Iranian Railway, running from Bandar Shah, a Caspian port, through Teheran, the west and the south-west to Ahvāz, near the Persian Gulf – a distance of about 1400 kilometres. Construction began in 1927, but it took eleven years for the whole project to be completed. It was financed mainly by a special tax on the consumption of tea and sugar – two indispensable and complementary items in the daily diet, 'bread-and-cheese and tea', of the mass of the people – and the deficit was made up by bank loans and state grants. The project was an unmitigated economic folly, though this is not how it was viewed at the time by the majority of the politically-conscious public. The criticisms levelled against this project can be summarised by two basic questions: 'Why from the centre-north to the south-west?'; and, 'Why a railway and not a road?'.

Both questions were raised by Dr. Muṣaddiq at the very moment when the railway construction bill was submitted to the *Majlis*. He argued that an alternative route across the north-central regions – connecting Tabriz and Mashhad through Teheran – would be much more sensible; and he was right: this would have been cheaper to construct and maintain, for geophysical and other reasons; it would have reduced domestic *and* international transport costs across the country; and the higher freight and passenger demand would have led to greater capacity utilisation.[13] However, the popular view, that the sole reason for the choice of the less sensible route was to enable the British to deliver war supplies to the Russians fourteen years later, is not convincing.

First, in 1927 there was not the slightest probability of an Anglo-Soviet military alliance against Germany. Secondly, if it is held that the railway had been originally intended for British use in possible future hostilities with Russia, it still makes no sense: in such an event, it could be cut off, destroyed, and even used much more quickly by the Russians themselves; if it were to have been at all effective, it should have connected Bandar Abbas to Astara or Ardabil, not the south-eastern corner of the Caspian Sea to the end of the Persian Gulf; and, finally, it is worth noting that, as in all such projects, not a single British consulting firm was employed, from start to finish.[14]

The second question, 'Why a railway and not a road?', was equally valid. There can be little doubt that a well-constructed modern highway would have been cheaper – both in domestic and in foreign currency – to build and maintain; and it would have been ready for full utilisation earlier.[15] The following suggestions may help provide some reasonable answers to both questions.

The southern stretch, from Teheran to the Persian Gulf, must have been suggested by considerations of *domestic* military strategy: it made the main regions of ethnic and nomadic trouble much more easily accessible; indeed, it is likely that Reżā Shah conceived the idea in his earlier mission to Khūzistan to overthrow Shaikh Khaz'al. The northern stretch, from Teheran to Bandar Shah, must have appeared to serve a dual purpose: it connected Teheran to Reżā Shah's own province of Māzandarān – where he had acquired extensive estates, and was about to confiscate many more – and beyond it, on the edge of the Iranian Turcomanistan, with the lucrative cotton-producing estates he was to purchase, usurp or requisition. It was also truly a *trans*-Iranian railway, which was part of the total vision. For similar reasons, a railway was preferred to a road: both the state and its clientele badly wanted a *railway*; a mere road would simply not have been good enough. Apart from that, the same considerations of domestic military strategy may have favoured the construction of a railway: usually, the transfer of heavy military equipment, and personnel, by railways is faster and more efficient; and this was certainly then the case in Iran.

Apart from the railway project, the state made some relatively considerable investment in building, extending or renovating ordinary roads. Over this period, around 13,000 kilometres of new roads of various descriptions were constructed, connecting the main cities, or feeding into smaller towns.

INDUSTRY, AGRICULTURE AND TRADE

This period, as we have seen, is not marked by any considerable drive towards the expansion and modernisation of manufacturing industry. But, especially towards the end of the period, the state began to make some direct investment in modern manufacturing plants, particularly sugar mills. According to official records, some twenty-four new enterprises, each of them employing ten or more workers, were founded. These enterprises were mostly, though not wholly, state-owned. But the classification according to the minimum number of workers employed is very likely to understate the expansion of the manufacturing sector: it reveals the natural bias for the larger and more modern plants and factories; it also reflects the difficulty of collecting data for the smaller, traditional craft and repair shops. Yet qualitative evidence – the growth of direct state expenditure, and the expansion of the military–bureaucratic apparatus – would indicate a commensurate rise in general manufacturing output and employment.

Similarly, although agriculture was in any case not a favourite sector, there are several indications that aggregate agricultural output must have been slowly increasing. This is a period in which (a) incomes, population and home demand were rising; (b) there were few *structural* shortages of food products;

and (c) Iran's volume of non-oil exports – almost exclusively comprised of agricultural cash crops, and carpets – was, on average, maintained.

The state's expenditure on its modernising projects led to the steady growth of Iranian imports, and oil revenues had to be increasingly relied upon to finance the consequent rise in foreign-currency requirements. Yet this cannot have been the main reason for the Shah's unease over the apparently inexplicable variations in the annual oil revenues paid by the Anglo-Persian Oil Company (APOC): the Iranian visible trade balance was in surplus, and the invisible account – for which data do not exist – cannot have shown a larger deficit. This, among other things, reflects the well-known cautious, even miserly, attitude of Reżā Shah towards expenditure. But, precisely because of this miserly attitude, he was unhappy about the level and the volatility of the oil revenues: he believed that Iran was receiving a raw deal, both by the terms of the original D'Arcy concession, and – within those terms – by arbitrary decisions of the APOC. The matter reached its climax in the unilateral abrogation of the D'Arcy concession, followed by the anti-climax of the 1933 oil agreement.

OIL AND THE 1933 AGREEMENT

It will be helpful to begin with a review of the figures in Table 6.3. Column (1) of this table shows that, whereas, with the exception of 1931, the oil output had been increasing every year, oil revenues were subject to dramatic variations over the period. For example, in 1927 there was an increase in oil

TABLE 6.3 Oil output and direct revenues[a]

	(1) *Annual amounts*		(2) *Annual changes*	
Year	*Output*	*Revenue*	*Output*	*Revenue*
1926	4556	1400	–	–
1927	4832	500	276	–900
1928	5358	530	526	30
1929	5461	1440	103	910
1930	5929	1290	468	–150
1931	5750	310	–179	–880
1932	6446	1530	696	1220
Net change 1926–32	–	–	1890	230

[a] Output figures are in thousand long tons; revenue figures are in £'000. Figures exclude later adjustments under the 1933 agreement.

Source: based on Bharier, *Economic Development in Iran*, tables 8.3, 8.4, pp. 157–8, and the sources cited therein.

output, but there was nearly a two-thirds *decrease* in revenues. Column (2) shows these annual changes in output and revenues in detail. The Shah was very unhappy about this situation, and the company responded to official complaints by emphasising the effects of the world depression and various other 'causes'.

The year 1931, when the revenues fell to the ridiculously low level of £310,000, was the straw that broke the camel's back. Given (a) such an apparently inexplicable fall in the revenues, (b) the Shah's characteristic suspicion of everyone and everything, which was already developing into a pathological paranoia, and (c) the purely conspiratorial theories of politics, of which both Reżā Shah and many other Iranian political leaders, as well as the political public, have been prisoners, the Shah was convinced that the British government itself had prompted the company to reduce payments, because – so the Shah believed – it was either displeased with him or wished to exert pressure on him for some reason.

He instructed the cabinet to conduct formal negotiations with the company; and the chief negotiator was the most powerful man in the country after the Shah himself: 'Abdulḥusain Taimūr-Tāsh, the almighty Minister of the Imperial Court. Taimūr-Tāsh was in fact more radical in his view of the situation; he even believed that the government should make friendly overtures to the Soviet Union, in order both to frighten Britain and improve Irano-Soviet relations. The negotiations dragged, and the Shah lost control of his nerves: one day he stormed into the cabinet room while the cabinet was in session, threw the oil file into the heater, and ordered his ministers 'not to leave' until they had prepared the draft of the (unilateral) abrogation the D'Arcy concession.[16] This was the typically rash behaviour of a despot who was getting more and more used to imposing his own will in all situations. This time, however, he had overreached himself: in this case, the Shah's will could not be imposed absolutely, and by his usual methods, if he still wanted to survive on his throne. The D'Arcy concession was duly abrogated, but the Shah realised – and/or was made to realise – that he had to enter a new agreement: the Iranians lost the initiative, and the 1933 Agreement was concluded. This was inevitably hailed as a great triumph; but it was an abysmal failure.

The area covered by the new agreement was only a quarter of the D'Arcy concession; but it included all the areas under exploitation, and most of the proven reserves. It also extended the concessionary period from twenty-seven to sixty years. The basis of revenue payment was changed from the previous 16 per cent of the company's annual net profits to 4 shillings per barrel produced: it was by no means certain that this would improve Iran's share over the concession period; but it ensured that changes in the market price, and/or the company's tax obligations to the British government, could not be used as reason for dramatic declines in the revenues paid to the Iranian government. There were also some changes in the minor provisions of the former concession. Finally, to sweeten the pill, the company agreed to pay an extra £1 million for 1931, and a further £1 million for the conclusion of the treaty. Yet it is significant that no firm procedures were laid down for future revisions and renegotiations of the Agreement: the Iranians were expected to be bound by the letter of this unfair agreement for sixty years.

It was a fiasco; but it is both simplistic and tautological to blame it all on the British imperialist power. This power was real enough. But there can be no doubt that, if the negotiations had been conducted with the care, delicacy and diplomacy which they demanded, the Iranians would have got considerably better results. To the extent that this was not achieved, Reżā Shah's despotic, arrogant and ignorant methods of conducting anything and everything must be held responsible. It was in this sense that the Finance Minister, Sayyed Ḥasan Taqī-zādeh, who officially signed the agreement (shortly before going into voluntary exile because of his unhappiness with the Shah's growing despotism and megalomania), declared, fourteen years later, that in signing the 1933 Agreement he had been merely 'an instrument'.[17]

The episode did not end without claiming an important casualty, although, with or without the oil crisis, the trend of events had made this inevitable: the fall, trial, conviction, imprisonment and subsequent murder in prison of Taimūr-Tāsh, the demigod of the new régime. The Shah had suspected him of double-dealing during the negotiations; he had also become nervous of his contacts with Russians, thinking – though this is very unlikely – that Taimūr-Tāsh was preparing the ground for his own succession. It is also possible that the APOC and/or the British government, which must have been weary of Taimūr-Tāsh's toughness in the negotiations, and his overtures to the Russians, indirectly helped, or quickened, his downfall.[18] He was both a cause and a product of the new despotic régime. And he perished by the same sword by which he had lived, and let others die.

The fall of Taimūr-Tāsh was symbolic of Reżā Shah's assumption of total and arbitrary power. For, from that moment until his own day of reckoning, the Shah became the undisputed arbiter over the lives, freedoms, rights and properties of the Iranian people.

NOTES

1. Some aspects of this general issue have been developed in detail in my *Ideology and Method in Economics* (London: Macmillan, 1979).
2. Take the simple but significant fact that, in their reports on politico-religious affairs in Iran since 1977, some foreign journalists have been referring to 'the Mosque' (implying a clerical hierarchy and tradition, analogous to the Christian Church), although mosques are no more than religious *buildings* for *voluntary* meetings and communal prayers of the faithful, and neither Islam, nor, especially, its Shī'ite sect has a clerical hierarchy. That also goes for the regular usage of such terms as 'the clergy', 'the Āyatullah of Teheran' (or elsewhere), and so forth, which

convey to the European reader an incorrect image of religious institutions and relations in Iran.

3. For more details concerning the Third World, see my 'Peasant Societies and Industrialisation: A Critique of Modernism and Pseudo-Modernism in Economic Development', a paper presented to the Berlin Institute of Comparative Social Research symposium 'Three Worlds or One?', June 1979 (forthcoming in the proceedings of the symposium).
4. This is in contrast to another, and a much more accomplished, writer of Ākhūnduf's generation, 'Abdurraḥīm Ṭālibuf, who maintained an admirable sense of balance in all his writings.
5. See, in the notes to Chs 4 and 5 above, the Iranian works cited with reference to the *Mashrūṭeh* Revolution and its aftermath, and the references therein.
6. See, D. Bozorgue (ed.), *Historical Documents: The Workers', Social Democratic, and Communist Movements in Iran* (Florence: Mazdak, 1976) vol. VI, pp. 24–6. The fact that they addressed Kautsky as *citizen* (translated into a newly coined Persian term, *shahrvand*, which, of course, is void of all real meaning in the Iranian social context) had not been meant as an insult to the leader of the almighty German Social Democratic Party of the time; it is probably evidence that they were not quite up-to-date with modern European jargon.
7. For example, the reader will find all of these anti-Islamic, anti-Semitic, anti-traditional, as well as chauvinistic Iranian tendencies based on romantic glorifications of pre-Islamic Iran in the writings of Sādiq Hedāyat, the great Iranian writer of the period, whom no one can accuse of collaboration, even passive agreement, with Reżā Shah and his despotic machine. See his plays *Māzīyar* (written with M. Mīnuvī) and *Parvīn, the Sasanian Girl*, his travelogue on a journey to Isfahan, as well as short stories such as 'Ākharīn Labkhand' and 'Talab-i Āmurzish'. This is by no means confined to Hedāyat or a small number of writers and poets, and in general there are few exceptions to it (Jamālzādeh is probably the best example). Furthermore, other Iranian intellectuals, both then and later, have displayed similar tendencies, even though they happened to be in opposition to the official champions of pseudo–modernism.
8. See further Part IV, below.
9. Many of these men have been portrayed in Khājeh Nūrī's biographical sketches *Bāzīgarān-i 'Aṣr-i Ṭalā'ī* ('Actors of the Golden Era') although this source must be used with caution, in regard to both fact and judgement.
10. All of the able Iranian politicians who were either independent from or opposed to Reżā Shah had already been completely chased out of public life, put in prison, or exiled abroad. These include Sayyed Ḥasan Mudarris, the brothers Mushīr al-Dawleh and Mu'atamin al-Mulk, Dr Muhammad Muṣaddiq, the brothers Vusūq al-Dawleh and Qavām al-Salṭaneh, Sulaimān Mīrzā Iskandarī and Qavām al-Dawleh, who, in spite of their different political views and temperaments were all opposed not only to Reżā Shah's despotism, but to despotism itself. See further Ch. 7, below.
11. The speech is reprinted in Ḥusain Makkī, *Duktur Muṣaddiq va Nuṭqhā-yi Tārīkhī-yi Ū* (Teheran: 'Ilmī, 1945).
12. The process had already begun during Reżā Khān's premiership. In a *Majlis* speech in 1925, Mudarris had pointed out that modernisation had to be distinguished from such lawless acts against the people and their possessions. A barely literate general, Karīm Āqā Būzarjumehrī, the appointed Mayor of Teheran, should take much of the 'credit' for this wholesale official vandalism.
13. See Muṣaddiq's extremely well-reasoned argument and evidence (Makkī, *Duktur Mūṣaddiq*) as a supreme example of how a progressive Iranian who both was

rooted in his own society, and properly understood (and applied) European ideas and methods, approached the issue of social and economic progress as early as 1926–7.

14. Various American, Swedish and German firms were involved at different stages of the project.
15. In his parliamentary speech, Muṣaddiq supplied detailed facts and figures from the official consultant's estimates, which show that the cost of constructing a good road could have been 10 per cent of the cost of the proposed railway.
16. For an eyewitness account of this and related episodes, see the memoirs of the then Prime Minister, Mehdīqulī Hedāyat: *Khāṭirāt va Kaṭarāt* (Teheran, 1946).
17. See further Muṣṭafā Fāṭeh, *Panjāh Sāl Naft-i Irān* ('Fifty Years of Persian Oil') (Teheran, 1955), and Hedāyat, *Khaṭirāt va Kaṭarāt*, which almost conclusively show that the fiasco of the 1933 Agreement was due not to a conspiratorial design, but to the Shah's own arrogant stupidity. Taqī-zādeh's comment means that, as Minister of Finance, he had been no more than a tool of the Shah's despotic decisions. Shortly after signing the agreement, he was honourably discharged by being appointed Iranian ambassador to France, but in 1935 his description of the Shah as a 'land-eating wolf' would have cost him his life had it not been for a coded telegram from Bāquir Kāẓimī, the Foreign Minister, advising him not to return to the country. Kāẓimī's warning was discovered by the Shah's agents, and nearly cost him his own office.
18. *The Times* had published rumours that during his visit to London *via* Moscow, Taimūr-Tāsh's attaché case (containing important documents) had been inexplicably lost. Whatever the truth of the rumours, the paranoiac Reżā Shah must have suspected that the documents had contained secret deals between the Court Minister and the Soviet authorities. The fact that Taimūr-Tāsh was sympathetic to closer Iranian ties with the Soviet Union is beyond serious dispute; he was murdered in gaol when the Soviet Deputy Foreign Minister, Kara Khan, visited Iran in a bid to intervene on his behalf. A few years later, Kara Khan himself disappeared in Stalin's purges.

7 The Rise and Fall of Pseudo-Modernist Despotism, 1933–41

The Suffocating Socio-Political Atmosphere

In the first parliamentary session which followed Reżā Shah's coronation, a few genuinely-elected deputies, all of them in opposition, managed to get back into the *Majlis*; among these, Mudarris and Muṣaddiq were the most able and the most uncompromising. At first, Mudarris tried by his usual pragmatic tactics to control the situation as much as possible; but he soon realised that the Shah was in no mood for a genuine compromise. Muṣaddiq, on the other hand, took a consistent, tough and courageous oppositionist line: one way or another, he opposed nearly all the bills which the cabinet submitted to the *Majlis*, if only because all such legislation had originated with the Shah; that is, whatever the bills' contents, the procedure for their conception and formulation had been unconstitutional. The régime did not have much joy from Mudarris either: he once publicly explained that the reason why he had supported the bill for compulsory military conscription was that it would enable the people to use guns, and so bring down the new régime! Although they did not normally co-ordinate their activities, the two men together caused a considerable amount of embarrassment, even anxiety, to the Shah during this session. Muṣaddiq's last parliamentary speech under Reżā Shah was a fierce, sarcastic, factual and documented attack on the way in which the army, the police and the gendarmerie were engaged in determining the full outcome of the impending general elections.[1] Shortly afterwards, both Muṣaddiq and Mudarris found themselves without parliamentary seats.[2]

Muṣaddiq withdrew to his private estate, a couple of hundred kilometres west of the capital, until eleven years later, when the agents of despotic persecution caught up with him: he was, and always remained, a man of open and public action; and, in the circumstances, he had no channels left for communicating with the public. Mudarris, however, was a different sort of person; and as a religious leader, he had his own channels. He therefore stayed in Teheran, at his modest home in a traditional district (in Dardār Alley, off Ray Street), and he continued his activities in a semi-clandestine fashion. The details of his activities at the time are not yet known with precision or certainty. For example, it is claimed that a mosque in Chirāq-gāz (later, Chirāq-barq) Street – which he supervised, in his religious capacity – had been used for training an armed group, whose mission was to shoot at the Shah's carriage on the occasion of the formal opening of the new session of the *Majlis*.[3] But one thing is certain: Mudarris was definitely busy trying to cause trouble, and the agents of the régime knew, and probably even exaggerated, this. In 1929 he was arrested and imprisoned in an old citadel on the edge of the Lut Desert in the Khurāsān province, with no legal or judicial procedures whatever. Nine years later he was murdered (indeed, martyred) in cold blood, on the direct orders of Reżā Shah himself.[4]

Meanwhile the Shah organised and promoted his own police state as a more powerful parallel to the civilian government. First, he hounded and/or frightened into inaction the few remaining elements of the former parliamentary opposition, as well as the larger group of the old plutocracy, including Vusūq, his brother Qavām, his former associate Ṣārim (al-Dawleh), and a good many others. Next he began to destroy anyone who, for real or imagined reasons, he regarded as a potential threat: he started with some of the more independent members of his retinue, such as Sardār As'ad, and Shaikh Khaz'al, and ended with his own close hatchetmen and confidants, such as Brigadier Dargāhī, the criminal police chief, and Taimūr-Tāsh. In some cases, he would even send organised gangs of police assassins to raid his victim's house, or the temporary gaol in which he was kept, and murder him with their bare hands: such were the fates of Nuṣrat al-Dawleh and Khaz'al.[5] In the meantime, his machine persecuted, imprisoned or drove into exile the few remnants of the old Communist Party, which was already weak and demoralised.

As the Shah's power became wholly absolute, and more arbitrary, he increasingly became a prisoner of the few, now mainly gutless and self-seeking, lackeys about himself, and a victim of his own propaganda. Not only argument and criticism, but even independent thought and action ceased to exist. Crude and ugly public propaganda deceived him into regarding himself as the symbol of perfection, a god incarnate, to the extent that even his own personal megalomania could not have managed it. The notorious Institute for the Guidance of Thoughts, led by spineless and demoralised intellectuals, was only the formal institutionalisation of this policy.[6] The *Majlis* became a redundant rubber-stamp; ministers degenerated into the Shah's own house-boys, and their departments became – in the first instance – instruments for the promotion of the Shah's public wishes and private property. Both the person and the property of landlords and, to a lesser extent, big businessmen, became fair game for persecution and expropriation by the Shah, his henchmen, and his army. The judiciary, the most important achievement of the revolution, was its last bastion to weaken and, finally, surrender. When the loop of the police state finally closed, the Most Powerful Imperial Majesty himself lost real control, because he had no independent access to data and information: he expected to hear what he already believed; and, therefore, he had no choice but to believe what he heard. Such are the simple dialectics of absolute and arbitrary power.

It was a similar dialectical process which led to the disaffection of many young students whom the new régime had proudly sent to European countries for higher studies. They compared European technology and material prosperity with Iranian backwardness and poverty, and they became more radical and impatient modernists than the Shah and his servants. They contrasted the relative openness of European societies with the absolute closedness of the despotic state in Iran. They sympathised with European socialist and communist movements, because these movements identified themselves with the downtrodden, both in Europe and in the colonial countries. Thus, the few who were converted to active Marxist opposition did not, as one of them was to remark later, *choose* communism, but *were chosen* by it.[7] Given the circumstances, there simply was no alternative.

These young men believed they were Marxists, or Marxist–Leninists; and they used 'theories' – in fact jargon – in their analysis of the Iranian political economy. But in reality, they were usually converted emotionally, on the basis of a few slogans. Many of them did not learn much Marxism, even afterwards; and, in any case, their theoretico-historical perspective had little to do with Marxism, or Iran. Necessity is the mother of invention: the Iranian landlord whose life, freedom and property were constantly at the mercy of the despotic state became a *feudal* (though this is not to deny that he was, in any case, an exploitative agent); the despotic state which did as it pleased became the *executive committee* of the 'bourgeois–feudal' classes; the Iranian merchant – with a history which goes back to several centuries before the rise of capitalist individualism in Europe – became a *bourgeois*; and the motley group of domestic servants, craftsmen, repair workers, petty traders and street beggars became the Iranian *proletariat*! Such is the combined power of subjective ideas and objective necessities. And it still goes on both in Iran and elsewhere. Needless to say, Marxist and other alien theories, ideas, techniques and so forth are *not* useless in understanding and developing Iran, and other non-European societies. They become useless and misleading when they are used as bodies of mechanistic dogma; when they lose their critical dynamism and degenerate into static and irrelevant articles of faith.

However, the young Iranian 'Marxists' were, in fact, socially conscious modernists who wanted modern industry and technology as well as freedom from repression and poverty. The few 'party cells' which, on their return to Teheran, they managed to set up, mainly discussed 'theoretical' issues, which were covertly publicised in their periodical *Dunyā* ('The World'). Early in 1937, both they and some of the sympathetic readers of *Dunyā* – who did not even know that this was supposed to be a Marxist journal – were arrested, tried for 'rising against the system of constitutional monarchy, and adhering to the collectivist doctrine', convicted and gaoled. Altogether, they were fifty-three in number; and, since then, they have been known as the Fifty-Three. They suffered indignity, violence and torture both before and after their trial; and their most senior member, Dr Taqī Arānī, a chemist of exceptional intelligence and impeccable morality, was indirectly killed in prison.[8]

Three years later, the agents of arbitrary despotism interrupted Dr Muṣaddiq's self-imposed exile on his estate, and arrested him without the slightest provocation. They ransacked his home for 'incriminating' evidence without success. He was subsequently banished to a gaol in the Khurāsān province, to which Mudarris had been transferred shortly before his murder the year before. Muṣaddiq might possibly have been visited with the same fate had it not been for the personal intervention of the young Crown Prince, the future Muhammad Reżā Shah, on his behalf. The Crown Prince did not know Muṣaddiq at all. He intervened at the request of a Swiss citizen, a man called Ernest Péron, the nature of whose very close relationship with the Prince is not yet completely clear. In turn, Péron had been asked to act by Muṣaddiq's son, a doctor who had treated Péron at the Najmīyeh hospital, a public endowment by Muṣaddiq's mother. The intervention resulted not in Muṣaddiq's release but in his house arrest until 1941, when the Most Powerful Imperial Majesty literally ran away from his Aryan Country.

Social Progress or Sartorial Terror?

We have already argued that both the European modernists and their superficial emulators in 'developing' countries are universalisers in science and homogenisers in society. And the pseudo-modernists of the developing countries, who suffer both from cultural alienation and from a national inferiority complex, jealously try, by all possible means, to create miniature show-pieces of 'homogeneity' with European societies. Hence the persistence of real backwardness, and the superimposition of the destructive socio-economic 'dualism' which is observed in many such societies. In the previous chapter, we discussed a few prominent examples of this in the economic and bureaucratic fields. Here we shall devote a few pages to the much more grotesque and arbitrary examples in the social and institutional context.

Traditionally, social propriety had required male Iranians to wear a headdress, both outdoors and, in formal gatherings, indoors. These headdresses varied from the *'ammāmeh* (the religious 'turban'), its non-religious version, the *dastār*, the common skull-caps, the *shab-kulāh* and the *'araq-chīn*, to the official–'aristocratic' *kulāh*, a sheepskin hat a version of which (made of synthetic material) has now become popular in Western countries. From the beginning, Reżā Shah and his fellow pseudo-modernists decided that (a) it was a disgrace that people wore such a *variety* of headdresses; and (b) that these headdresses were all representative of Iranian backwardness. They therefore designed a new hat, which they called the Pahlavi hat and which closely resembled the French military cap, and ordered everyone to wear it. This, however, did not go down too badly, especially as it bore a resemblance to the traditional *kulāh*. Likewise, the use of European suits, jackets and trousers, already common in the higher social circles, was made compulsory for civil servants and professionals, and encouraged among other social strata.

However, a few years later the Shah decided that the Pahlavi hat was not sufficiently modern. Therefore, orders were sent out for everyone to wear the currently fashionable hat in Europe and America, the 'French' *chapeau*, known in Iran as the 'basin hat'. This was a little too much, and the people began to become restless. In particular, a preacher by the name of Buhlūl began to attract large crowds in the city of Mashhad when he publicly protested against this piece of undiluted arbitrary tyranny. It led to an infamous massacre, and hundreds of arrests. The paranoiac Shah was later told that Asadī, the provincial governor, who was a prominent traditional (but lay) man of the same province, had been implicated in the 'uprising'. There was little or no evidence, but Asadī was publicly hanged none the less. Such were the preludes to Reżā Shah's greatest achievement for 'social progress', praised by friend and many foes alike: the 'emancipation of women'.

On 7 January 1936 Iranian women were formally, ceremoniously, indiscriminately and forcibly 'unveiled'. Both official and officially inspired meetings were held everywhere in order to celebrate the 'liberation' of Iranian women. Thenceforth the use of the Iranian *chādur* – a long overdress covering the woman's head and body, and incorrectly referred to as a 'veil' – was *forbidden*. And so was the use of *any* form of headscarf or headdress, except for European hats. Those who dared defy this piece of violent lawlessness would not be arrested, tried, imprisoned and/or fined upon conviction: they would be victims of physical assault by police*men* (for there were no policewomen), who would simply pull the *chādur*, or the scarf, off their heads in public, and, with a torrent of loud abuse, tear it into shreds.

Many, indeed most, women over the age of forty became 'voluntary' prisoners in their own homes. To them, this was exactly the equivalent of a sudden 'law' which would compel European women to wear 'topless' dresses. Yet even this enforced self-imprisonment did not completely solve their problem. For example, there was the problem of going to the public bath at least once a week: before the rapid march of pseudo-modernism, Iranians of all social classes had been dependent on highly elaborate public baths, a tradition developed over the centuries – for Iran's was a communal, not an individualistic, society. Those who happened to have rooftop access to their local baths through the neighbouring houses were lucky. Those who did not took grave risks and, when caught, suffered the prescribed indignities.

It was indeed a great triumph for human rights, personal dignity, individual freedom, private security, public propriety, legal rights and social justice – let alone the emancipation of women! Yet, multitudes of right-thinking – 'highly progressive' – foreign and Iranian commentators have described this act of arrogant tyranny, unsurpassed by any comparable act in the whole history of Iranian despotism, as the moment of Iran's emergence from the 'Middle Ages'. Such is the weight of evidence – for anyone who cares to examine it – against ignorant modernism, and its destructive effects for human life and culture everywhere in the twentieth century.[9]

The 'veil', which like any form of dress had seen many variations in the course of history, dated back to the pre-Islamic Sāsānid (Persian) Empire, which allowed not only polygamy, but also incest and concubinage for the few who could afford it. Thus, it had always been an entirely urban phenomenon. The conversion to Islam had been a great liberating force for Iranian women: they could not be forced to marry against their own will; they had a *right* to inherit from their fathers, mothers, husbands, sons and other relatives, up to one-half the inheritance of the male decendants; they could independently own, and dispose of, property; upon being divorced, they were entitled to dowry payments by their husbands, if these had not already been met. The social and economic participation of Iranian women had been greater than their European sisters for most of the period since the rise of Islam. At the time when the Iranian 'Emancipation Law' was enforced, many younger women of the upper social circles already mixed with men, without scarfs and the like, in private parties and gatherings; many girls went out to school; other women, far from being chained to their beds or 'kitchen sinks', would go out almost every day, wearing their *chādur*, for shopping, visits to friends and relatives, and so on; and, in general, socio-psychological prejudices had begun to relax.

This is not to paint a rosy picture but to put the subject in its true perspective and context. No one can deny that women were, and still are, unequal to men, both in Iran and elsewhere. Likewise, there existed much social prejudice and injustice – including discrimination against women – for which religion *as such* cannot be held responsible: at their worst, religious *and* other ideologies can be used to justify disagreeable habits, customs, norms and prejudices; they do not bring them about. But, in a society where men themselves were helpless objects of manipulation by the organised lawlessness of the state, would it not be grotesque to regard this act of persecution of women as their emancipation? Not to mention the superficiality of the move itself, however it was made: while everything else remained the same – and the Shah himself treated his own three wives as his personal chattels – would women be emancipated by going out without headscarfs?

There can be no doubt that by a process of genuine education, and social and moral suasion, Iranian women would have gradually 'unveiled' themselves with dignity and consent. What happened was neither emancipation nor progress; it was a shameless act of ignorant self-indulgence by a despotic pseudo-modernist, and the few rootless zealots who applauded him as the 'Redeemer of Persia'.

Social Progress or the Monopoly of Power?

The attack on religion was inevitable. But this was not provoked by an organised religious 'resistance against social progress'. Most of the religious dignitaries and preachers had supported the *Mashrūṭeh* Revolution, even against Muhammad Ali Shah's petty cleverness in offering his alternative of *Mashrū'eh*. Some of them had even paid with their lives in defending the revolution. That apart, religious leaders and the community of believers had not put up any organised resistance against the acts of pseudo-modernistic vandalism, ranging from the demolition of old mosques and private houses for extending the streets, to the 'emancipation of women'. No doubt they disapproved and earnestly prayed for the advent of the Mahdī; but they did so in cautious conversations, and silent prayers.

Reżā Shah's religious persecutions had two real aims, and none other: to destroy Iranian Shī'ism, and its practices, as shameful evidence for the backwardness of his great Aryan Country; and, to remove any *independent* social institution, and all autonomous channels of public association and communication. The customary public processions during the first ten days of the Islamic month of Muḥarram, in which the Shī'ite faithful mourn the martyrdom of Imām Ḥusain, were outlawed. Furthermore, all religious gatherings where the preacher relates the life and works of Muhammad and the Shī'ite martyrs (especially Imām Ḥusain and his father, Imām Ali) were banned, both in mosques and in private houses, all the year round. Indeed, if a preacher was seen running during the Muḥarram peak period, he was in danger of arrest on suspicion that he was bound for a secretly held gathering of this sort (commonly called *rawżeh-khāni*). At times, houses in which people were mourning their newly dead relatives were raided on the presumption that they were holding a *rawżeh-khānī* session. Every Muḥarram many people would end up in police stations on true or false charges of holding such a session in their own homes. So successful was pseudo-modernism in Iran that members of the gendarmerie could loot and rape the peasants with impunity by day; and people were arrested for holding religious meetings in their own homes at night!

By 1939 the Shah was entertaining the thought of forbidding the publication of the Islamic lunar calendar, so that the people would not know the dates of religious mournings and festivals.[10] Fortunately, the day of his own downfall was not too far away.

Economic Policy and the Political Economy

THE BROAD VISION

The reader who has understood the logic of pseudo-modernist despotism will be able to predict the resultant trend of economic events and policies even without any factual knowledge of them: the growth of manufacturing industry; a rise in its scale and capital-intensity as a result of the growing application of foreign technology; an increase in the number and share of state and private monopolies in industrial and commercial output; the greater bureaucratisation of economic life and labour; the creation of excessive productive capacity, because of a disregard for industrial interdependence in the state's investment policies; the dual waste of investment in expensive educational projects where, on the one hand, there was no adequate productive outlet for the new graduates, and, on the other hand, the state was obliged to create unproductive employment by increasing the number of bureaucratic desks and offices; and so on. Apart from all this, increases in the land tax squeezed the landlords in favour of the state; and the state monopoly of foreign trade, as well as important areas of domestic trade, cheated the merchant community out of a vast domain of economic activity. There were tariffs on internal trade, and everyone had to have an official permit for travelling from one city to another!

OIL, THE STATE AND THE ECONOMY

The 1933 Agreement, and the beginnings of the world economic recovery, followed by general rearmament and the Second World War, ensured the stability and, later, growth of Iranian oil revenues. It is worth emphasising that these revenues were paid directly to the state. On the whole, oil receipts provided over 20 per cent of total budgetary *allocations*; but, given the fact that actual expenditures almost invariably fell short of planned allocations, it is certain that the share of oil revenues in state *expenditures* was higher than this. In addition, since the oil revenues were paid out in foreign exchange, they more than balanced the current account in the balance of payments. Hence, the state had a sizable source of revenue and foreign exchange *outside* the indigenous political economy and its productive performance: it was neither due to customs and taxes levied on the public, nor a consequence of exports produced by the domestic means of production and, in particular, labour force.

A review of the annual budgetary allocations will provide some indications of the broader trends of state policy and macroeconomic activity, especially as departmental expenditures covered both current spending and investment projects. Tables 7.1 and 7.2 contain, respectively, the various departmental allocations and their shares in the total. First let us make some general observations on the data: the total allocations (though normally short of actual expenditures) increased very rapidly; for example, the total budgetary allocation for 1939 (2613 million rials) is more than four times the corresponding figure for 1934 (625 million rials) (see Table 7.1). Given that the average rate of inflation in these five years was low, these observations show a

TABLE 7.1 Budgetary allocations 1934–41 (million rials)

Departments	*1934*	*1935*	*1936*	*1937*	*1938*	*1939*	*1940*	*1941*
War	239	256	275	319	403	380	485	593
Finance	172	176	197	216	275	90	146	266
Industry and Trade	22	68	76	150	320	459	751	1006
Education	47	57	68	72	81	84	132	195
Interior	40	44	52	56	70	108	110	123
Posts and Telecommunications	28	28	34	37	43	58	71	90
Justice	25	28	29	33	43	56	64	79
Foreign Affairs	22	25	27	26	30	27	33	31
Health	13	19	24	34	37	88	65	83
Imperial Court	14	13	14	16	16	16	16	17
Agriculture	3	17	27	34	48	54	72	122
Communications	[a]	21	179	256	161	854	999	1092
Other	–	–	–	–	–	339	168	477
Total	625	753	1002	1249	1527	2613	3112	4174

[a] Included in the figure for Posts and Telecommunications.

Source: based on Bharier, *Economic Development in Iran*, pp. 65–6, tables 4.1 and 4.2.

TABLE 7.2 Budgetary allocations 1934–41 (percentage shares in the total)

Departments	*1934*	*1935*	*1936*	*1937*	*1938*	*1939*	*1940*	*1941*	*Average*[a] *1934–41*
War	38.3	34.0	27.5	25.6	26.5	14.5	15.6	14.2	19.6
Finance	27.5	23.4	19.6	17.2	18.0	3.4	4.7	6.4	10.2
Industry and Trade	3.5	9.0	7.6	12.0	21.0	17.6	24.1	24.1	19.0
Education	7.5	7.7	6.8	5.8	5.3	3.2	4.2	4.7	4.9
Interior	6.4	5.9	5.2	4.5	4.6	4.1	3.5	2.9	4.0
Posts and Telecommunication	4.5	3.7	3.4	3.0	2.8	2.2	2.3	2.2	2.6
Justice	4.0	3.7	2.9	2.6	2.8	2.2	2.1	1.9	2.4
Foreign Affairs	3.5	3.3	2.7	2.1	2.0	1.0	1.1	0.7	1.3
Health	2.1	2.5	2.4	2.7	2.4	3.4	2.1	2.0	2.4
Agriculture	0.5	2.3	2.7	2.7	3.1	2.1	2.3	2.9	2.5
Imperial Court	2.2	1.7	1.4	1.3	1.0	0.6	0.5	0.4	0.8
Communications	[b]	2.8	17.8	20.5	10.5	32.7	32.1	26.2	23.7
Other	–	–	–	–	–	13.0	5.4	11.4	6.6
Total	100.0	100.0	100.0	100.0	100.0	100.0	100.0	100.0	100.0

[a]Figures in this column are percentage shares of average allocations in the mean of total budgetary allocations for the whole period. They do not represent the simple average of the preceding columns.

[b]Included in the figure for Posts and Telecommunications.

Source: Table 7.1.

large increase in real expenditure by the state. Consequently, the allocation of nearly each and every department went on increasing (with very few exceptions) every year; but the rates of increase were very uneven, so that, whereas the *share* of some departments in the total rose over time, that of others declined (see Table 7.2).

However, the rapid, and steady decline in the *percentage share* of the War Office, from 38 per cent in 1934 to 14 per cent in 1941, must be treated with caution: first, it is certain that the military network spent appreciably more than the budget allocation for the War Office, partly because this department did not cover the entire activities of the military network, and partly because income from other sources, such as state property, was used for military purposes; secondly, even the legal allocations for the War Office alone (in Table 7.1) are suspect, because it is very likely that from 1936 onwards items under 'communications', and 'other expenditures' conceal payments for military activities. Finally, the figures and percentage shares for 1939, 1940 and 1941 are not readily comparable with the corresponding figures for the previous years, because of a change in departmental responsibilities and expenditures in 1939. These redefinitions and rearrangements must particularly have affected the nominal allocations and expenditures of the Ministries of War and Finance: for example, the Ministry of Finance lost some of its gigantic empire to the Ministry of Industry ('manufacturing and mining').

It is hardly necessary to emphasise the sudden, and cumulative, boost that industry received over this period: in 1941, the allocation to Industry was nearly fifty times what it had been in 1934 (see Table 7.1), with the result that the percentage share of Industry and Trade rose from 3.5 (in 1934) to 24.1 per cent of the total budgetary allocations. Most of the expenditure was on the establishment of modern mechanised factories, mainly in the production of sugar, cotton and silk products, building materials, and – to a lesser extent – glassworks, matches, leather products, and so on. But the addition to the industrial labour force was not as significant as the general increase in the manufacturing capacity, because of the capital-intensity of the larger factories: in 1941 the industrial workforce, excluding the oil sector, was nearly three times what it had been ten years earlier.

The state factories were managed by state officials and departmental bureaucrats; and their rules of appointment, hierarchy, and general conduct were almost exactly the same as those of any other bureaucratic office. There was as much corruption as elsewhere in the state apparatus; managerial positions were insecure, and the frequency of change was ridiculously high; production targets and pricing were arbitrary and haphazard.

The tendency towards larger plants using imported technology is evident, even though the initial expansion was in the 'light' consumer industries. Yet this was only the beginning, and, if Reżā Shah's régime had had a longer lease of life, it would quickly have switched its 'strategy' towards heavy industrial production. Indeed, the Germans had already delivered most of the blast furnaces for the construction of a modern steel plant – one of the greatest cravings of *all* strands of Iranian pseudo-modernism – when the intrusion of the war into Iran postponed the fulfilment of this psychological need for another twenty-five years.

The Trans-Iranian Railway remained under construction until 1938, and work was started on another (less vigorously pursued) railway project, aimed at linking Tabriz, in the north-west, through Teheran to Mashhad, in the north-east of the country. In practice, it went as far as connecting Teheran – through Karaj, Qazvīn and Zanjān – to Mīyāneh, until it was completed in the late 1950s. Likewise, road-building projects were continued, but with less urgency and emphasis than in the period 1926–33. Education, however, was given almost the same priority as before: even though the percentage share of education declined over the years (see Table 7.2), the absolute sums were increasing considerably; and, in any case, an average percentage share of nearly 5 per cent for the whole period is a respectable figure. As mentioned before, the problem about the state education policy was that it concentrated its investment in expensive (i.e. capital-intensive) education – a strategy which was socially unjust, economically wasteful, and technologically irrelevant.[11]

Reżā Shah's Economic Balance Sheet

It is not as if one can separate the 'purely' economic policies and consequences of a régime from the rest of its decisions and outcomes. And this is the view which we have so far taken in the present study. Yet many educated Iranians have – overtly or covertly, in writing or by word of mouth – tended to distinguish sharply between the various consequences of Reżā Shah's despotism: for example, by denouncing his 'dictatorship' (the wrong term) and/or his attack on religion, but acknowledging or praising his nationalist sentiments and aspirations, and/or his 'modernising' policies. Often, they overlook the fact that that 'dictatorship' and this 'industrialisation' – or that attack on all tradition, and this 'modernisation' – are the integrated products of one and the same system.

Nevertheless, it would serve a useful purpose to assess the 'purely' economic consequences of Reżā Shah's despotism. Within a period of less than twenty years there was a considerable increase in the roads and communications network, the industrial capacity, the application of modern technology, modern secondary and higher education, and so on. Therefore, would it not be fair to say that – 'at least from the economic point of view' – Reżā Shah left the country appreciably better off than he had found it? The answer is no, for the following reasons.

Reżā Shah's 'economic achievements' were not the consequence of a reasonable and relevant, let alone successful, approach to economic progress; and they were all paid for by the oil revenues, and the burden of indirect taxes borne by ordinary people. Any investment expenditure would result in the building of roads, factories, schools and banks; but an appropriate investment strategy is one which results in the allocation of the national resources to their best possible use. In simpler words, what matters is what the national economy gets from what it spends on building a factory, not the mere fact that a factory, *any* factory, has been built for everyone to see. Yet, on the basis of the evidence it is clear that in his economic policies Reżā Shah wasted the national resources by investing them in projects which involved high costs and low returns.

However, 'purely' economic questions also involve such things as income, consumption, welfare – and their distribution among the people. There exist no output and income series for this period, let alone numerical data on consumption, distribution, and the rest. Yet there is no doubt that aggregate output and income grew considerably; but the chief beneficiaries of it were the more privileged people of Teheran and a few other major cities. And among the latter, though merchants and traders must generally have benefited, the greatest advantage was taken by the higher echelons of the state bureaucracy, and their business associates. Agriculture as a whole was given very little assistance, and the tenural arrangements remained exactly as they had been for centuries. But the persistent and comprehensive discrimination against the rural population went far beyond the simple concentration of state investment in industry.

The state acted as the sole buyer and distributor (i.e. a 'monopsonist') for the main agricultural products, including wheat and barley, which were and remain the staple food of the population. Thus, by acting as a monopoly buyer they kept agricultural prices as low as possible, and turned the domestic terms of trade persistently against the rural population. The idea was not to obtain a higher real surplus from agriculture – a kind of 'forced saving' – in the interest of capital accumulation. On the contrary, the sole purpose of this unjust policy was to force consumption away from the peasant, in the interest of Teheran and a couple of other cities. In other words, the state monopoly was used to subsidise a few privileged cities at the expense of the rural society. Furthermore, the policy deliberately discriminated against some provinces, and particularly the north-western province of Azerbijan. Indeed, the Azerbijanis – who happen to make up some of the most able and productive human resources of the country – were subjected to such a degree of discrimination that they were led to wholesale migration to Teheran itself.

Apart from that, nearly all welfare services, and especially education and health services and public utilities, were concentrated in Teheran and, to a somewhat lesser extent, a few other cities. Thus, the Iranian peasantry was penalised in every possible way.

The Hour of Reckoning

Reżā Shah was both pro-German and pro-Nazi. For he was an *étatiste*, a militarist, a despot, a racist and pan-Iranist; and, in spite of owing his initial rise to Ironside (and probably other British agents in Iran), he liked neither Britain nor the British role in Iran. It would be wrong to think that he was an agent or 'spy' of the British Empire, if only because the weight of detailed evidence of all kinds is against this very popular theory.[12] To the extent that he tolerated the British influence in the Iranian political economy, his main motive was to protect his own position; for he too, like the rest of the Iranian political public, believed that the British could do what they liked in Iran (and elsewhere) by a wave of their magic wand. That is why, at the rapid growth of the rival power of Nazi Germany in the 1930s, he thought it both safe for himself and desirable for Iran to manoeuvre his foreign policy in favour of the Germans; already he was relying more and more on German technical advisers for his military and civilian projects, and Germany was becoming the most important single exporter to Iran.

When the war broke out, Iran remained officially neutral, but the Shah, his army and his henchmen clearly wished the Germans total success. As a matter of fact, in adopting this attitude they had the support of the majority of the Iranian political public. The latter were not so much pro-Nazi as anti-imperialist and, therefore (in this sense), anti-British. But it is fair to say that they also enjoyed some of the racist Nazi propaganda about the Aryan race, to which they thought they belonged.

The British strategists had already become nervous about the possibility of a German drive through Egypt and Iraq to the Persian Gulf, supported by local well-wishers, cutting off the Suez Canal and the Iranian oil supplies in a major strategic offensive. Rashīd 'Ālī Gīlānī's uprising in Iraq must have reinforced these anxieties, and the attitude of the Iranians cannot have been reassuring. In July 1940, Germany attacked the Soviet Union in three directions: to the north, the centre and the south. The southerly offensive quickly led to the capture of the Ukraine, and threatened to cut through the Caucasian oilfields on the north-western border of Iran. The situation must have looked desperate, both in Moscow and in London.[13]

The Allies began to issue warnings to the Iranian government – at first, in informal and private contacts, but later in formal and public notes – that, unless the activities of the German agents in Iran were curtailed, they would take a very serious view of the situation. This referred to the presence of several hundred German technical and military advisers in Iran, some of whom are bound to have been undercover agents for various German intelligence services. The Iranian response was, for some time, cool and dismissive, merely reassuring the Allies of their own neutrality, and the harmlessness of the German nationals. However, in the summer of 1941, it became clear that the Allies were intent on taking a tough line with the Shah and his servile government. It is typical of absolute and arbitrary despots that they begin to feel the gravity of a serious situation too late to be able to manoeuvre themselves out of it; for they are victims of a belief in their own invincibility, and of flattering misinformation from their servants. At the eleventh hour, some radical steps were taken in the hope of forestalling an Allied invasion of Iran. But it was too close to the high noon; the Allied forces entered Iran on 25 August 1941. Reżā Shah took the foolish step of ordering a general mobilisation, which was followed by a few days of resistance by the 'Imperial armed forces'. This exposed the complete hollowness of the glorious Iranian army – the costs of whose existence and extra-legal powers had been borne by the Iranian people – and quickly led to its demoralisation and disorderly retreat. Senior officers are reported to have escaped by wearing the hitherto forbidden women's 'veil', though this may be just a caricature of the truth about the army, the most cherished product of the 'Redeemer of Persia', the 'Architect of Modern Iran'.

His Most Powerful Majesty abdicated and was taken abroad a British vessel to Mauritius, and later to Johannesburg, where he died – probably of depression – in 1944. It is not yet absolutely clear how he was made to take this inevitable decision. The likeliest explanation is that the British refused to promise protection to him in the event of a Russian drive on Teheran.[14] Thus ended the inglorious career of an able, intelligent and self-made man who had let himself be thoroughly corrupted by a combination of the ancient institution of Iranian despotism and the contemporary ideas and techniques of pseudo-modernism. The lesson to be learnt here is that there can be no socio-economic stability and peaceful progress in Iran until their most tenacious enemy – Iranian despotism – has been uprooted for ever. It must not be allowed to shelter under the umbrella of modernism, reformism, Marxism, traditionalism, or whatever – which merely give the basic forces of despotism the chance to reassert themselves.

NOTES

1. See its reprint in Ḥusain Makkī, *Duktur Muṣaddiq va Nutqhā-yi Tārīkhī-yi Ū* (Teheran: 'Ilmī, 1945).
2. Years later, Muṣaddiq was to recall that, for window-dressing purposes, the state had included a few independent political figures in its list of the new *Majlis* 'deputies', but many of them, such as the brothers Mushīr al-Dawleh and Mu'tamin al-Mulk refused to be drawn, and resigned their 'seats'. See Ḥusain Kay-ustuvān, *Sīyāsat-i Muvāzineh-yi Manfī*, vol. II (Teheran, 1950; rprt Paris: Muṣaddiq Publications, 1977).
3. See Ibrahīm Khājeh Nūrī, *Bāzīgarān-i 'Aṣr-i Ṭalā'ī* (Teheran, 1943–4).
4. See Shaikh al-Islām Malāyerī's speech in the Thirteenth Session of the *Majlis* (1941), quoted ibid.
5. See Ch. 6, above.

6. It would be embarrassing, and probably a little unfair, to mention the names of some of the literati and scholars who let themselves be used in this way: these were not intellectual gangsters as others were; they were victims of their own lack of heroism in circumstances in which only saints and heroes remain unpolluted.
7. Khalīl Malekī has made this point in many of his articles and essays, including his political memoirs. See *Kāṭirāt-i Sīyāst-i Khālīl Malekī*, edited with an introduction by Homa Katouzian (Teheran: Ravāq, 1980).
8. See Buzurg 'Alavī, *Panjāh-u-seh Nafar* ('The Fifty Three') (Teheran, 1944; 2nd edn Teheran: Uldūz, 1978); Khalīl Malekī's scattered writings on the subject, as well as his memoirs.
9. Compare with the attitude of Muṣaddiq (whom no one can accuse of having been a 'reactionary'), who said, in a parliamentary speech a decade later, that, although he himself had worn the European hat, and his wife had gone without a scarf, when they had both been in Europe, he had confined himself to his home for eight months in order to avoid the compulsory wearing of the Pahlavi Hat (until at least some sort of a law made it look a little less arbitrary), and he had been opposed to Reżā Shah's 'emancipation of women', because this should have come 'through an evolutionary process, through the progress of the people . . . not because somebody has become powerful. . . [and says] I want things to be this way, and they must be this way. . . . Everyone in his own way should have principles. . . . One ought to have personal dignity, and not submit to [the language] of sticks and clubs' – see Kay-ustuvān, *Sīyāsat-i Muvāzineh-yi Manfī*, vol. II, pp. 78–9.
10. This was told by Dr Aḥmad Matīne-Daftary, then Prime Minister, to M. H. T. Katouzian, who in turn related it to me. Matīne-Daftary had ignored the Shah's instructions to this effect, and later pretended to him that he had forgotten them.
11. For more data and information on economic events and issues, see M. Fāṭeḥ, *Panjāh Sāl Naft-i Irān* (Teheran, 1956); V. Conolly, 'The Industrialisation of Persia', *Journal of the Royal Asiatic Society*, 1935; A. Banani, *The Modernisation of Iran, 1921–1941* (Stanford, Calif.: Stanford University Press, 1961); M. Āgāh, 'Some Aspects of Economic Development of Modern Iran' (unpublished D. Phil. thesis, University of Oxford, 1958); R. Arasteh, 'Growth of Modern Education in Iran', *Comparative Education Review*, III (Feb 1960); Z. Khosroshahi, 'The Politics of Education under Conditions of Economic Growth, with Special Reference to Iran' (unpublished Ph. D. thesis, University of Sheffield, 1978).
12. We have already presented and analysed the evidence in the previous chapters. According to both Dawlat-Ābādī, in *Ḥayāt-i Yaḥyā* (Teheran 1949) vol. III, and Muṣaddiq (in Kay-ustuvān, *Sīyāsat-i Muvāzineh-yi Manfī*, vol. II) as early as 1924, Reżā Khān himself had said that 'The British brought me [to power] but they did not realise whom they were dealing with.' This is obviously a double boast, and it cannot mean more than the fact that General Ironside, Howard and other British officials in Iran, had been behind the 1921 coup, and had picked Reżā as the military backbone of Sayyed Zīā's dash for power. What followed from then onwards was in the first place determined by the interaction of the internal forces, and Reżā Khān's cleverness in dealing with both the British and the Russian government. It is certainly true that Sir Percy Loraine did not realise whom he was dealing with.
13. See, for example, William Shirer, *The Rise and Fall of the Third Reich* (London: Pan, 1964).
14. Strong rumours had it that the British government, through Sir Reader Boulard (their *chargé d'affaires* in Teheran) actively canvassed the abdication of Reżā

Shah. In his biographical sketch of Ali Suhailī, Iranian Foreign Minister at the time, Khājeh Nūrī implies that he heard from Suhailī himself that this is what the British had demanded (*Bāzīgarān-i 'Aṣr-i Talā'ī*). On the whole there can be little doubt that the British played an important, perhaps decisive, role in the Shah's abdication, even though they might not have demanded it in so many words. Apart from that, the British embassy in Teheran boycotted the official ceremony for swearing in Muhammad Reżā, the Crown Prince, as the new king. See further ibid.

Part III

Interregnum, Democracy and Dictatorship, 1941–61

8 Occupation and Interregnum, 1941–51

Reżā Shah's departure was greeted with public euphoria: the despot had fallen, and the empty despotic machine had automatically collapsed, though its foundations remained as firm as ever. The situation was rather comparable to the fall of Napoleon III in 1870: in both cases the collapse of tyranny had been a consequence of foreign occupation, but the people were at least happy to be rid of their respective tyrants. The difference was that, unlike the French experience, the occupation of Iran was not the consequence of defeat in a war with the occupying countries, and it was not followed by a class struggle for political power.

Political prisoners were freed; political, religious and other meetings could now be held openly; newspapers and books could be published without political censorship; people could speak freely in their homes, unafraid of being reported by a servant or relative; women could wear the *chādur* and go to the public bath, if they so wished. Those landlords and farmers whose properties had been usurped by the Shah or his *apparatchiki* filed petitions to the courts and recovered their assets. Some people who had suffered gross personal injustices, or whose relatives had been murdered in prison, sued the official agents of injustice. A few well-known official murderers, such as the bogus doctor who specialised in injecting political prisoners so as to cause their death, were publicly prosecuted, convicted and executed. Others, such as the criminal police chief, Mukhtārī, were merely imprisoned and later released – in this case, through the intervention of Muhammad Reżā, the new Shah, who apparently even arranged a pension for the culprit from his own resources. In fact, very little punishment was meted out on the direct and indirect agents of Reżā Shah's despotic apparatus. This is partly commendable, for it is consistent with the Iranian people's historical trait of not being vindictive; yet, it is not completely defensible: there did not have to be a general witch-hunt, but it was absolutely necessary for the full horrific story of fifteen years of pseudo-modernist despotism to be openly told and examined in some detail. The political establishment, headed by the new Shah, had an obvious stake in minimising the scale of such an exposure.

The Occupation and the Political Economy

The occupation forces had promised non-intervention in the country's internal affairs, total and immediate withdrawal at the end of the war, and full payments for reparations as well as for their use of the country's economic resources. In practice, non-intervention was a myth, for two entirely different reasons: first, indirect interference, at least, was to some extent inevitable, precisely because the occupying forces needed to use Iranian resources, ranging from foodstuffs and raw materials to roads, railways and telecommunications; secondly, there was also a lot of unjustifiable interference, induced by rivalry among the occupying countries themselves, with an eye to postwar prospects. Thus, the British and the Russians both tried to set up or support political groups, tendencies and figures which they regarded as their own natural allies. But, for the time being, their most important, common objective was to promote their war effort, and for this reason they did their best to prevent serious political conflict and instability in the country. It was later, in Teheran, Yalta and Potsdam, that the Allied chiefs came to an agreement about their respective spheres of influence.

The economic impact of the occupation was devastating. The Allies needed food, tobacco, raw materials, and so forth, both for the use of their troops in Iran and for general use. Therefore, they effectively forced the Iranian government to put the country's resources at their disposal. The operation was carried by means of monetary 'policy': in particular, the devaluation of the Iranian currency, the expansion of the money supply, and the extension of credit to Russia and Britain.

First, the Iranian currency was devalued by more than 100 per cent, from 68 to 140 rials to the pound sterling. Depending on the circumstances, devaluation may have beneficial or damaging effects for a given political economy. When the Iranian currency was devalued, foreign demand for Iranian exports – i.e. the demand of the occupation forces for Iranian goods and services – was virtually unlimited, while the possibility of expanding the supply of these goods and services was extremely limited. These two facts put together imply that the devaluation by 100 per cent of the Iranian currency reduced Iran's earnings from the sale of her goods (or exports) to the Allies by almost half of what they would have been had the currency not been devalued. On the other hand, as Iranian imports were highly specific in nature and could not be significantly reduced now that foreign exchange (and, hence, foreign goods) were dearer, the value of Iranian imports could not have been much less than they would have been without the devaluation. These observations together mean that the devaluation was detrimental to Iran's export earnings as well as to her balance of trade, and had a devastating inflationary effect which further impoverished the already poor Iranian people.[1]

Secondly, the *fourfold* expansion of the money supply in the circumstances described above was entirely inflationary, because there could be no question of hoarding paper money, and, in any case, the increase in the money supply had been expressly intended to meet the Allies' local currency 'requirements', enabling them to pay for their expenditures in the country.

Thirdly, according to separate agreements with Britain and the Soviet Union, 60 per cent of Iran's annual trade surplus with Britain, and the whole of the annual credit given to Russia were to be frozen until the end of the war, when they would be repaid, in gold, according to the new (devalued) rate of exchange of the rial. In plain language, the whole thing – the devaluation, the printing of money and the lending to Britain and Russia – was a case of armed robbery against a desperately weak and poor nation. A disinterested reader may simply put this down to the much more important need to defeat the Axis Powers, and regard it as a 'necessary evil'. However – leaving aside the double standards implied when the same 'disinterested' parties comment on similar Nazi robberies in their own conquered territories – one may wonder why it was necessary for the Allies to force an over 100 per cent devaluation of the Iranian currency, so as to pay only half the value of their purchases of Iranian goods and services, *once the war was over*, and meanwhile to sell their own goods to Iranians at double the price.[2]

The full inflationary consequences of these impositions are not difficult to imagine, even though they cannot be quantified with precision. Between 1936 and 1941, the wholesale price index had risen from 100 to 176, both in consequence of the continuous growth in state expenditure, and as a result of the rapid rise in international demand for primary goods brought about by the war.[3] However, in 1944, in a measured and well-argued parliamentary speech, Dr Muṣaddiq estimated that prices had increased tenfold (i.e. by 1000 per cent) since the occupation of 1941, and this was not challenged by the then Minister of Finance.[4] What is certain is that the above 'policies', combined with trade speculation and a decline of the marketed agricultural surplus of peasants and landlords alike led to a great scarcity of goods and to hunger and famine in towns. The long queues for the purchase of a loaf of normally inedible bread (a mixture of wheat and barley with a good proportion of sawdust) are still remembered by many of the ordinary urban people.

Iranian goods and currency apart, the Trans-Iranian Railway, mainly used for supply deliveries to the Soviet Union, made the single most important Iranian contribution to the Allies' war effort. This necessitated the extension of the line from the Ahvaz terminal to the port of Khurramshahr on the Persian Gulf, as well as some repair and maintenance works elsewhere, which were carried out and paid for by the British forces. In the same parliamentary speech cited above, Muṣaddiq calculated that, on the basis of a 6 per cent rate of interest on the capital, the Allies owed the country $140 million, whereas they were prepared to pay, and the Iranian government was ready to accept, only $5.2 million. Even if one accepts the Allies' claim of $21 million for repair, maintenance and other costs (as well as a number of used lorries, which they simply expected the Iranians to buy from them), the Iranians were still robbed of at least $100 million. Let us emphasise that all such calculations exclude the effects of the devaluation and the crippling inflation rate, and are entirely based on the nominal value of Iranian money and its rate of exchange in 1944.

Brute force was brought to bear, and both Right and Left – both conservative politicians and Tūdeh Party 'Marxist–Leninists' – concurred in the resulting expropriation of the Iranian people.

At the end of the war the British and American forces withdrew from Iran in accordance with the initial agreement, and the British paid back the full amount of the credit that had been advanced to them during the occupation. But the Soviet forces refused to withdraw until they had been served with an American ultimatum and had obtained the promise of the north Iranian oil concession from the Iranian government. Furthermore, they delayed repayment of the Iranian credit granted them during the war, using it as an instrument of diplomacy until early in 1955, when they negotiated payment with the Zāhedī government and, a couple of months later, paid the money to the new government, led by Ḥusain 'Alā.

Politics and Problems

The fact that Reżā Shah's departure did not create a power vacuum was almost certainly due to the Allied occupation of the country: it was clearly not in the interests of the occupying forces to encourage, or even tolerate, a revolution which would try to uproot the despotic régime and dismantle its apparatus completely. Instead, the hitherto servile *Majlis* deputies suddenly found themselves with the unexpected, and wholly unjustified, authority to appoint and dismiss governments. Yet this itself automatically implied a diffusion and fragmentation of *despotic* power, although it was far short of a democratic system. Furthermore, the judiciary recovered a good deal of its power and independence. The old 'establishment' – the spineless landlords, bureaucrats, journalists and intellectuals, many of whom must have been secretly unhappy with their own demise and loss of dignity under the old Shah – rallied around the new Shah in the hope of minimising their actual or potential losses. Characters such as Ali Dashtī, the old chief censor, even had the iron nerve to become great advocates of democracy and freedom.

Nevertheless, the situation was ripe for competitive political groupings, and it led to the organisation of rival political factions and parties.

THE TŪDEH PARTY

The Tūdeh Party was founded in a memorial gathering at the graveside of Dr Taqī Arānī, the outstanding senior member of the Fifty-Three, who had been led to his death in prison. The meeting was attended by nearly all the remaining members of the group, as well as a host of older and younger politicians, political activists and intellectuals who had been more or less genuinely opposed to Reżā Shah and his despotic rule. Symbolically, it was addressed by Sulaimān Mīrzā Iskandarī, the aging Qajar nobleman and former parliamentary socialist leader, who to his great regret had allowed himself to be used by Reżā Khān ('the bourgeois nationalist leader') until the moment of the latter's accession to the throne. Thus, at the time of its foundation, the Tūdeh Party was, both symbolically and in reality, a coalition of various progressive, anti-despotic and libertarian tendencies: it was a popular (or national) democratic front, rather than an ideological political party. The broader objectives of the party were the establishment of parliamentary democracy, the reconstruction of the political economy, and greater public welfare and social justice.

In the circumstances, it was inevitable that the 'Marxist' faction of the party should predominate in the party leadership: the men of the Fifty-Three had a halo of innocence around their heads; their impressive educational qualifications commanded respect among the people; they were younger, more energetic and better at organisational matters; and they possessed an ideological framework which seemed capable of explaining every phenomenon, and resolving any and all problems. In addition, the Soviet Union had become popular (not only in Iran, but even in England and America), mainly because it had demonstrated its might in meeting the German avalanche.

From the beginning, there were some internal party disagreements – including within the Marxist faction itself – mainly because of the way in which the party bosses tended to concentrate powers of decision-making in their own hands. This fact alone, like any other dictatorial relation, led to avoidable tactical and strategic mistakes, resulting in the greater frustration and criticism of the younger party activists, which in turn posed a greater threat to the leadership, inducing it to tighten the grip further – and so on. It was the logic of the old Iranian despotism all over again. The critical activists, who dominated the party cells in the capital, gathered around the personality of Khalīl Malekī, a prominent member of the Fifty-Three, who had developed some reservations about the personalities of a few of his colleagues while they were all in prison.

The internal party struggle – focused on the issue of the annual party conference (or 'congress' as they called it), which the leadership, year after year, refused to hold – became more acute in consequence of the uprising, and the declaration of provincial autonomy, in Azerbijan. The latter episode led to a quiet withdrawal of many other, non-Marxist tendencies from the Tūdeh Party, making it look increasingly like a communist party, though the party did not openly declare itself communist until after it had been banned (early in 1949) by an act of the *Majlis*. Meanwhile, the internal party disputes and struggles led to the famous party split of early 1948. With the internal opposition thus chased out, and its leaders characteristically described as traitors, agents of imperialism, enemies of the masses, and the like, the party leadership imposed its iron grip on, and indisputable rule over, the entire party membership. It is well known that, in the party conference which was hastily called to condemn the splinter group, Dr Faraidūn Kishāvarz, a leading member of the party establishment (who has been alienated from the party since the end of the 1950s) sighed with joy, saying, 'What a relief!' (Rāhat shudīm').[5]

THE CONSERVATIVE PARTIES

The Tūdeh Party began as a national democratic front and not as a communist party. Yet it was clear to many landlords, remnants of Reżā Shah's higher bureaucracy, and the like, that that party posed a threat to their economic and political interests. The first attempt to set up a conservative grouping led to the foundation of the 'Idālat (i.e. Justice) Party. When Sayyed Zīā al-Dīn Ṭabā Tabāī', the infamous Prime Minister of the 1921 coup, returned from exile, he took over the mantle of the conservative leadership by founding the Irādeh-yi Mellī (or Popular Will) Party. In fact, these political groupings cannot be described as proper parties: they lacked organisation, programme and regular meetings; they were centred around one or two personalities who appeared to be actually or potentially powerful; and, therefore, their 'membership' rose and declined with changes in the direction of the political wind. It is well known that when, in 1946, Qavām al-Salṭaneh became Prime Minister and put Sayyed Żīā in prison, the latter was left as the sole member of his own 'party'![6]

Qavām al-Salṭaneh was the strong old-school politician who, after plotting with Mudarris and others to overthrow Reżā Khān, had been forced into exile even before the Pahlavi dynasty was founded. His Democratic Party, though broadly conservative, was not as wholly establishmentarian a collectivity as 'Idālat and Irādeh-yi Mellī. Qavām was not a democrat, but he was opposed to despotism, and he certainly believed that the Shah (for whom he had little personal respect) should act as a constitutional monarch.

The combination of deep-seated habits of political thought, emotional assessments, simplicity of analytical methods, and so forth, led to the popular belief, both then and later, that *all* the Iranian conservative politicians were 'British spies'. This is very unlikely, and it is contradicted by a systematic examination of facts. There are bound to have been some direct British agents in Iran: that is, men in the pay or favour of the British government in order to serve its interests in Iran. But many of the conservative politicians were simply ready to depend on Britain as a countervailing power against the Soviet Union. Still others – such as Sayyed Ḥasan Taqī-zādeh, who had also returned home from exile – were pro-European, or pro-British, mainly because they genuinely admired European social, political and cultural arrangements. This does not mean that these men's ideas, objectives and methods, which were by no means uniform among themselves, were desirable or acceptable; it simply means that not every undesirable politician, in Iran and elsewhere, was necessarily the 'lackey' or 'spy' of a foreign power.

The same is also true of the leadership of the Tūdeh Party, who have been described *en bloc* as the 'lackeys' and 'spies' of the Soviet Union, by members of both conservative and democratic and left-wing tendencies. It is likely that a couple of Tūdeh leaders were directly in the service of the Soviet Union; but a lot of them were merely weak, or misguided, or arrogant, or power-hungry, or simply corrupt men who would have revealed these qualities in any framework: take Dr Murtizā Yazdī, whose total corruption is now incontrovertible, although his is by no means the only case. Still, there were other members of the Tūdeh Party leadership – such as the Qajar nobleman 'Abduṣ-ṣamad Kāmbakhsh – who, apart from ideological commitments, had a deep emotional attachment to Russia and Russian culture.[7]

OTHER GROUPS AND PERSONALITIES

There were other, smaller political groupings, of which the Iran Party was the most important. Once again, this was not so much a political party, as a collectivity of mainly European-educated younger technocrats with European-style liberal and social-democratic leanings: Allāhyār Ṣaleh, Kāẓim Ḥasībī, Dr Karīm Sanjābi, Dr Bayāni, Ghulām-alī Farīvar, and so on, who were destined to supply many of the personnel of Dr Muṣaddiq's future government. Another grouping was the small band of very young men, dominated by Muḥsin Pizishkpūr and Dārīyush Furūhar – with extreme nationalist sentiments and pro-German leanings – who called themselves the Pan-Iranist Party. They were mainly involved in street battles, usually against members of the Tūdeh Party, until the movement for the nationalisation of Persian oil, when they supported Dr Muṣaddiq and the National Front. Shortly afterwards, the party split into two factions: the faction led by Furūhar continued its support for Muṣaddiq and became less chauvinistic in its political vision, especially after the 1953 coup; the faction led by Pizishkpūr supported the Shah, and persisted in its crypto-fascist overtones, which rendered it a useful propaganda instrument for the 'imperial order' from 1963 to 1978.

Meantime, a small fundamentalist and radical group of Muslim activists known as the Fadā'īān-i Islām (Selfless Devotees for Islam), led by Navvāb Ṣafavī and Sayyed 'Abdulḥusain Vāḥidī, began to make its presence felt, mainly by resorting to public assassination. This movement was somewhat analogous to the contemporary Egyptian 'Ikhwān-al Muslimīn, or Muslim Brotherhood, although its membership was insignificant and it lacked a popular base. It is illuminating, as well as tragic, that these men too were regarded as 'British spies' by their opponents, though this is not to express approval for their ideas or methods. The Fadā'īān were politically indiscriminate in the choice of their targets: they assassinated Sayyed Aḥmad Kasravī, a leading scholar and a critic both of Shī'ism and of Bahā'īsm; 'Abdulḥussain Hazhīr, a leading conservative politician; and General

Razmārā, the army chief of staff and Prime Minister (of whom more later). They also made an unsuccessful attempt on the life of a leading journalist and politician, Dr Ḥusain Fāṭemī, shortly before he became Muṣaddiq's Foreign Minister and official spokesman. A few of their leading members met their end in front of a firing squad after the attempt by one of them, in 1956, to assassinate Ḥusain 'Alā, the Prime Minister, who was both a conservative politician and a close adviser to the Shah. Perhaps 'the British' had decided to destroy this group of their 'spies' by some of their other 'spies'!

It is unlikely that the Fadā'īān enjoyed much support, or approval, from the established religious leaders, particularly those in the holy city of Qum.[8] But it is certain that they maintained some relations with Sayyed Abulqāsim (Āyatullah) Kāshānī, a leading *mujtahid*, resident in Teheran. Kāshānī had had a long record of anti-British struggle: after the fall of Mesopotamia (later Iraq) to the British forces during the First World War, he had been arrested and held in a steamship bound for Baṣra when at Kūt he had managed to jump overboard and swim to safety under a hail of bullets. He had then managed to find his way through the Kurdish mountains to Iran, and finally Teheran. With the rise of Reżā Khān, he had provided back-room support – especially in organising street demonstrations – in favour of Mudarris and the *Majlis* opposition, although in 1926 he became a member of the Constituent Assembly and voted for the establishment of the Pahlavi dynasty. During Reżā Shah's reign he had not been involved in any direct political activity. Yet, with the Allied occupation of Iran, the British forces put Kāshānī under arrest, without any provocation, as a potential troublemaker. Kāshānī was too pragmatic a politician to be a fanatical or fundamentalist Islamic leader, but he did have a commitment to Iranian Shī'ite traditionalism. There is no doubt, however, that one of his main political commitments was to the removal of the British influence from Iranian politics. It was this, more than anything else, that made him a natural ally for Dr Muṣaddiq over the nationalisation of Iranian oil, though the two leaders fell out afterwards, both for personal and for doctrinal reasons (see Ch. 9).

Last, and truly not least, there was Dr Muṣaddiq, the able statesman who never had been, and never became, a party politician. He had had an excellent record as minister and provincial governor in various governments before Reżā Khān's premiership. His courageous stand against Reżā Khān's assumption of the royal title, and his later victimisation by Reżā Shah, were well known. He was a popular democrat, but not a pseudo-modernist (or Westernist) of any description. He had studied law in Europe, but he always spoke as an educated man who was deeply rooted in Iranian cultural traditions. He was a man of principles, but not an idealist who would easily confuse theoretical models with existing realities. He was not faultless; but he was better than any comparable political leader that Iran has seen in this century. We shall have other occasions to discuss Muṣaddiq's strengths and weaknesses, and for the moment it may be noted that it was the sum of the above qualities, and their demonstration in practice, that drew larger and larger crowds behind him. In 1949, while conducting a campaign against the Anglo-Iranian Oil Company (the former APOC), he led a large crowd to the royal palace, in protest against the government manipulation of the general elections. Their aim was to demonstrate their grievance by the traditional Iranian method of sitting-in (*bastnishīnī*). After negotiation with the court authorities, a delegation of nineteen leading members, headed by Muṣaddiq, was admitted into the palace garden. Later, these men issued a public communiqué and declared the formation of the National (in fact, Popular – *Mellī*) Front. Among the signatories were Dr Alī Shaīgan, Dr Muẓaffar Baqā'ī, Ḥusain Makkī, 'Abdulqadīr Āzād, Maḥmūd Narīmān, Dr Ḥusain Fāṭemī and Dr Karīm Sanjābī.

Azerbijan and the Northern Oil

THE PROBLEM

Azerbijan had always been a relatively prosperous province, because of better natural endowments, and a favourable location – in the north-west of the country *en route* both to Russia and to central and western Europe – resulting in greater economic and cultural contacts with European countries. But, because of its sensitive location, it had also been exposed to invasion and occupation – by the Ottomans and the Russians – and this had given it a greater sense of belonging to the Iranian socio-cultural entity. The people of Azerbijan speak a Turkic language, not too different from that of the neighbouring foreign lands, though it includes a good many loan-words from Persian. Therefore, the Azerbijanis' sense of attachment to the rest of Iran finds its strongest expression in their deep commitment to the Shī'ite sect of Islam.

The people of Azerbijan had made the greatest, and sometimes also the most enlightened, contributions to the *Mashrūṭeh* Revolution. During the revolution, the Azerbijanis had initiated the establishment of a provincial assembly, or *anjuman*, which ran the affairs of the province. We have already noted (in Chs 3 and 4) that during the Qajar era, Iran was not dominated by a vast *bureaucratic* machine; and this has misled some historians into the belief that – in contrast to the Ottoman system – Qajar despotism was decentralised. This is not correct. For, in this case, as in the other, the chain of command emanated from the centre; the provincial governors were appointed by the Shah himself, regardless of whether or not they had any knowledge of the province, let alone were natives of it; the governor's power *vis-à-vis* the province was as absolute and arbitrary as the Shah's *vis-à-vis* the whole country; and the people of the province, as such, had no access to the roles of decision-making, and no influence in decisions concerning their own life and labour. That is why a most cherished objective of progressive revolutionaries (and especially those in the provinces) was to diffuse the central despotic power, and also change the nature of the provincial power, by setting up permanent provincial, and city, assemblies. This idea had found an inexact expression in the Constitution.

Yet in no time power was restored to the centre, and the deep-rooted historical system of provincial governorates run by centrally appointed bureaucrats reasserted itself. The abortive uprising led by Shaikh Muhammad Khīyābānī, leader of the Azerbijani Democrats, in the early 1920s, was due to the denial of this constitutional right to Azerbijan (and elsewhere). Yet, many commentators – of both the apologetic and well-meaning but mistaken varieties – have accused Khīyābānī, who met a tragic death as a result of the uprising's failure, of 'separatism'. At any rate, Reżā Shah's despotism was both central and bureaucratically centralised. Furthermore, the Shah, being a pseudo-modernist and, in the worst sense of the term, nationalist despot, was particularly contemptuous of linguistic minorities, especially the Turkic-speaking groups, who are the most numerous and socio-economically the most advanced of them all. The Kurds come next; but they are 'Aryans', Kurdish is an Iranian language, and, though their martial qualities are impressive, they are economically less developed than the Azerbijanis. Under Reżā Shah, there was military–bureaucratic injustice everywhere, and in all the provinces; but, on balance, the Azerbijanis got the worst treatment in every respect.

THE AZERBIJANI UPRISING

With the fall of Reżā Shah's despotism, it was inevitable that the Azerbijanis (and the Kurds) should demand greater justice. The movement for home rule gathered momentum, especially as a result of obvious prevarications by the central government. This was a widespread urban movement, and it enjoyed a good deal of support from a wide spectrum of opinion in Teheran itself. The Democratic Party of Azerbijan (Firqeh-yi Demukrāt-i Azerbijan) was reconstituted, and Sayyed Ja'far Pīsheh-varī, an old Democrat later turned communist who had been in prison for twelve years until released by the general amnesty, became its leader. Pīsheh-varī edited the newspaper *Āzhīr*, and openly advocated autonomy for the province. He was elected to the Fourteenth Session of the *Majlis*, but, because of his views on Azerbijan, and the intervention in his favour of the Soviet occupation forces in the elections, his credentials were turned down by the majority of elected deputies. He went back to Tabriz, the provincial capital, and continued to lead the movement for autonomy. Shortly afterwards, a provincial assembly was elected, and, in December 1945, in a short and bloodless move, it managed to disarm the army division stationed in the province. The war had not yet ended; and it was impossible for the central government to send troops to Azerbijan, because both the province and the access areas were still under Soviet occupation.

The Soviet presence was a double-edged blade, one of whose edges eventually turned out to be the sharper: on the one hand, the Russian army could be used at least as a countervailing force against the threat of armed intervention by the centre; on the other, the confrontation with Teheran required both the tacit approval of the Soviet government and protection from the occupying Russian troops – a situation which would inevitably make the Azerbijani Democrats a pawn in international power games. The ultimate failure of the movement owed a great deal to this dependence on Soviet support.

THE MAIN CAUSES OF FAILURE

Yet the primary causes of failure must be sought elsewhere, the following being a brief summary of them.

First, Pīsheh-varī and the Democrats, in a case of too much too soon, allowed a confusion to develop between the overriding short-term political objective – autonomy for Azerbijan – and their own long-term ideological aspirations. Naturally enough, the declaration of autonomy should have been accompanied by a series of reforms in order to give the provincial people some tangible evidence for an improvement in their economic, political and cultural situation. Yet their 'land reform' was too hasty and disorganised; they lacked the time, programme and manpower for an orderly redistribution of land among the peasants, even though their Land Reform Law itself was not unreasonable; and this unleashed both romantic and criminal forces which they could not control. In addition, the radical *manner* in which their land policy was implemented frightened a good many city merchants and others into the belief that they were next on the list for expropriation. This fear was reinforced by some token, yet symbolically ominous, interventions on behalf of factory workers, who must have numbered no more than 1 per cent of the provincial population. Likewise, their emphasis on the teaching and administrative use of the Azerbijani Turkic language was in principle correct, but in implementation wholly misguided. They demanded that all the provincial offices, including judicial courts, should change at once from Persian to Azerbijani Turkic, though knowing very well that a good many existing officials simply did not speak it; they abolished the teaching of Persian in the first few years of elementary education, and this did not go down well in Teheran even among many of those who were otherwise their well-wishers. Worst of all, they began to attack not so much the central government, and the remnants of Iranian despotism, as the rest of the Iranian people; and they openly threatened total separation if all their demands were not amicably met by the central government.[9]

Secondly, their *formal* alliance (instead of a secret concordat) with the Kurdish Democratic Party, which had made a similar move by seizing Mahābād, was a tactical mistake. The nature and history of the Kurdish problem was different from theirs: the Kurds were Sunni Muslims, and so lacked a strong popular bond with the rest of the country, and they may have been much more readily suspected of eventual separatism, if only because of their substantial presence in Iraq and elsewhere. For these reasons, they enjoyed less sympathy elsewhere in the country than did the Azerbijanis. Apart from that, the coincidence of these moves, and the open camaraderie of their leaders gave the distinct impression that there was a concerted action, orchestrated by the Russians, to break up the Iranian lands; and this injured the patriotic feelings of many Iranians, including a lot of Azerbijani people: they would readily support freedom and justice for all; but they would never accept the balkanisation of their country, especially if they felt that this was owing to the machinations of a foreign power.

Thirdly, the foreign power was the Soviet Union. It had enjoyed a good deal of popularity earlier, mainly because of its heroic war effort and dazzling successes against the enemy. But, on the one hand, they could, and did, quickly remind the majority of the Iranian public that these were still 'the Russians', with all the ugly historic connotations from Tsarist times; and, on the other hand, they were communists, and communism for the majority of both urban and rural Iranians meant little more than official atheism, forced labour camps, hunger and famine, sexual promiscuity, and the collective ownership and use of everything, including one's 'wife'. Clearly, the Azerbijani Democrats could do little to allay such popular misgivings about Russia and communism. What they could, and did not do, however, was to maintain a public distance between themselves and the Russians; and to proceed cautiously with their domestic slogans and programmes. Instead, their jargon, slogans and tactics frightened many, including Azerbijanis, into the belief that 'wife-sharing' was around the corner.[10]

Fourthly, their tactic in forcing the Tūdeh Party (through pressures by Soviet agents, for instance Rustom Aliov, in Teheran) to become fully implicated in, and responsible for, their daily decisions and pronouncements was detrimental both to themselves and to that party. The Tūdeh Party was a countrywide organisation; and, while it had every right to support the Azerbijani movement, it could not afford to be identified with, and answerable for, every specific event arising from the decisions of the provincial government, over which it had no control whatever. Furthermore, the Tūdeh Party was becoming rapidly identified with communism and the Soviet Union; and their full implication in the Azerbijani episode merely strengthened the fear of wholesale communist take over. Many party leaders were aware of these dangers, but their spinelessness led them to submit to Soviet pressure and 'toe the line'. It was an unpopular and an undemocratic decision within the party itself; and it fanned the existing flames of internal dissension and criticism within the party ranks. In the midst of so much trouble, the party itself (to quote Lenin) began to 'shake with fever'.

Finally, both the Azerbijani Democrats and the Tūdeh party failed to realise the power of religion not only over the minds, but also over the daily lives of the Iranian people, including many who belonged to their own social base.

THE ROAD TO DISASTER

Given their tactics and their ideological commitments, the Azerbijani Democrats simply had left no power base for their own survival except Soviet support. And, if they themselves were unaware of this (which, however, is very unlikely), it was well known to all the other parties concerned: the Soviet Union, the central Iranian government, and the Anglo-American powers. The failure of successive Iranian governments to settle the Azerbijani question one way or another meant that it was still unresolved when on 7 February 1946 Ahmad Qavām (al-Salṭaneh) became Prime Minister as the leader of his newly formed Democratic Party (see the discussion of the conservative parties, above). Qavām was an old hand; he had a strong personality; he had been both a personal and a political enemy of Reżā Shah; and, for all these reasons, he was certainly hated by the young Muhammad Reżā Shah. But the latter was still far from being an omnipotent ruler, and, in any case, the circumstances had left him with little choice.[11]

Qavām entered the scene pretending to be an honest broker. There were three main strands to his strategy for meeting the Azerbijani question: to try and appease the Soviet Union directly; to bring pressure on it through the United States and the United Nations for the withdrawal of its occupying troops; and to steer a middle course between the Tūdeh Party and the Azerbijani Democrats, on the one hand, and the conservative groupings, on the other. Eleven days after his appointment, Qavām led a delegation to the Soviet Union, and for three weeks personally negotiated with Stalin and Molotov, without apparent success. But he was keeping the door open. In March 1946, the American government gave Stalin an ultimatum, threatening intervention unless the Soviet Union withdrew from Iran. The news, though not the text, of this ultimatum was released after the temporary failure of Qavām's mission to Moscow. In sum, while the Americans were using 'the stick', Qavām was negotiating over use of 'the carrot' – that is, the north Iranian oil concession, which the Russians had been seeking for some time. The negotiations were continued with the new Russian ambassador in Teheran, and a full agreement was reached by the end of March.

In Chapter 6 we briefly mentioned the unsuccessful attempts in the 1920s to grant the concession to two American companies – a move that was opposed by the Soviet Union. In 1944 Dr Reżā Rādmanish, leader of the Tūdeh deputies in the *Majlis*, categorically stated that the Tūdeh Party was opposed to any grant of oil concessions to foreign powers. Less than a month later, the Soviet government requested the north Iranian concession, including Azerbijan, Gīlān, Māzandarān and northern Khurāsān.

In November 1944, Kaftaradze, a deputy minister for Soviet foreign affairs, arrived in Teheran in pursuit of this demand, and, while he was still there, the Tūdeh Party and the Iranian trade-union leadership (which was controlled by the party) held a demonstration against Muhammad Sā'id, the Prime Minister, who was opposed to the Soviet demand. This made a bad impression on various shades of political opinion, especially as the demonstrators were given protection by the Red Army troops in the Iranian capital.[12] The main reason behind the new Tūdeh Party position was direct pressure on its leadership by the Soviet embassy. But their argument in favour of the Soviet oil deal was not entirely empty: they argued that such a deal could be used as a countervailing force against Britain's power and privilege in Iran.[13] Muṣaddiq, though not entirely unsympathetic to the Soviet demand, disagreed on the grounds that this was analogous to asking 'a person one of whose hands has been amputated to have the remaining hand cut off'.[14] However, Muṣaddiq at first suggested that Iran could enter a contract whereby for a certain period it would sell its northern oil to the Soviet Union alone, and that it could begin exploration and production by raising domestic and international capital and hiring foreign skilled personnel on the international market. Later, he made the alternative suggestion that Iran could sell forward its northern oil to the Soviet government and use the proceeds to finance the project. Neither of the two proposals, which excluded the sale of a concession, or majority shares for the Soviet Union in a joint venture, was acceptable to the Russians and, therefore, the Tūdeh Party. Meanwhile, Muṣaddiq managed to pass through the *Majlis* a resolution prohibiting the grant of any oil concession by the Iranian government unless it was ratified by the *Majlis*. The Tūdeh deputies wavered on their attitude to this resolution, but in the end refused to support it. In any case, the Iranian government shelved the Soviet application until Qavām held out an olive branch by reopening negotiations on the subject.

The fact that for years the people of Azerbijan had been treated with contempt and injustice is not in dispute; and it is very likely that in any case they would have demanded some considerable say in running their own affairs. Indeed, they might have succeeded in this, had not their ambition for autonomy been mixed up with specific ideologies or international power politics. But the Soviet government seized the opportunity to use it as its own stick against Iran for getting the northern oil concession. The uncritical support of the Tūdeh Party for all these policies was a big nail in its coffin as a popular (i.e. *mellī*) movement, because, to qualify for being *mellī*, one must be seen to be independent both of the despotic power of the state and of foreign powers (see Ch. 2, above).

However, the Qavām–Sadchikov agreement of March 1946 granted the Soviet Union a fifty-year concession for north Iranian oil, involving the establishment of a joint-stock company, with 51 per cent Soviet and 49 per cent Iranian shares (becoming 50–50 after the first twenty-five years); it guaranteed the immediate withdrawal of all Soviet troops from Iran; and it anticipated an amicable settlement of the Azerbijani question. This was a complete sell-out by the Soviet Union of the Azerbijani Democrats and the Tūdeh Party. Yet they greeted the agreement with pathetic euphoria: the Azerbijani government sent a delegation, headed by Pīsheh-varī himself, to Teheran, and the 'negotiations' between the two parties finally led to a 'settlement' (involving very significant concessions by the Azerbijani Democrats) in June 1946. On 1 August the Tūdeh Party (and the small Iran Party) entered a formal coalition with Qavām, with the Tūdeh Party holding the Ministries of Commerce and Crafts, Health, and Education, and the Iran Party the Ministry of Justice.[15]

The honeymoon, however, did not last for long. The Azerbijanis had agreed, under extreme pressure, to accept the central government's regional boundary, which excluded Zanjān and the adjacent Turkic-speaking areas from the province. This led to the reoccupation of the area by the central Iranian forces who were stationed on the borders of the provincial hinterland. And the treatment meted out to the freedom-fighters and the people of these areas gave a foretaste of what was yet to come. Meanwhile, the Tūdeh Party had withdrawn its ministers from the Cabinet.

In December 1946 the government declared its intention to send the Iranian army to Tabrīz and elsewhere in order to 'ensure the freedom of the *Majlis* elections' in that province. In vain did the pathetic leaders of the provincial government – in particular, Pīsheh-varī, Jāvīd and Shabistarī – try to reassure the central authorities that this move was unnecessary. Some sections of the Azerbijani provincial army, led by men of principle who were not polluted by the 'art' of political double-dealing, put up a heroic resistance against the advancing central troops. But their politicians had already given up. Shabistarī and Jāvīd capitulated, and Pīsheh-varī went across the border, only to be purged later by his ungrateful allies. After the reoccupation of the provincial cities, the gallant central Iranian troops inflicted mass 'punishment' on innocent and defenceless people on the express orders of their high command and the supreme commander, Muhammad Reżā Shah, himself. There was wholesale killing, burning, looting and rape. For this time Azerbijan had been invaded not by foreigners but by fellow Iranians! Since then, 10 December, 'the day of the Iranian army', has been a public holiday on which 'the liberation of Azerbijan' is celebrated with pomp and circumstance.

THE AFTERMATH

The *Majlis* did not ratify the oil concession to the Soviet Union. But the star of the Tūdeh Party fell to an all-time low, internal party criticism became almost unmanageable, and the party finally split early in January 1948. Thenceforth, the Tūdeh Party became a monolithic communist party. In February 1949, almost exactly a year later, a man by the name of Nāṣir Fakhrārā'ī, posing as a news photographer, opened fire on the Shah and was at once shot and killed. The Shah survived, but the assassination attempt was blamed both on the Tūdeh Party and on Sayyed Abulqāsim Kāshānī! The Sayyed was arrested and banished to Lebanon, without any judicial hearing; and a bill was hastily passed through the *Majlis* banning the Tūdeh Party. Some of the party leaders who did not manage to escape were rounded up for trial, but they were rescued by a regular army lieutenant – a member of the secret Tūdeh Party army organisation led by Khusru Rūzbeh – who produced forged documents commissioning him to transfer the prisoners. They drove in an army van over the border to the Soviet Union. Fifteen years later, the Soviet Union celebrated the rapprochement between the two governments by delivering up that selfless army officer, Lieutenant Qubādī, as a sacrificial lamb to the Iranian régime, which immediately put him against the wall.

The facts about Fakhrārā'ī's assassination attempt, like so many other political matters Iranian, are not yet clear: as usual, there was no official inquiry, and no reports; merely libellous press campaigns against the Tūdeh Party and Kāshānī.[16] There have been rumours that General Ali Razmārā, the strong army chief, had had something to do with it, but the available evidence for this is vague and circumstantial.[17] However that may be, the banning of the Tūdeh Party was to have fatal consequences for the party itself: it gave its leadership a new lease of life, and made it immune from effective criticism and dismissal, because of the conditions imposed by the requirements of semi-clandestine activity; it made some of its leaders – and, later, all of them – dependent on the hospitality of East European countries; it created an atmosphere of fear and suspicion about actual police agents and potential defecters, resulting in the use of hamfisted methods, even including internal party assassinations, against dissidents and waverers. These developments made an important contribution to the party's self-destructive mistakes in the next few years, its basic incapacity to deal with the onslaught against it after the 1953 coup, and its gradual euthanasia afterwards.

Oil and the Economy

This was a period of occupation, instability, conflict, disorder and insecurity. The state apparatus and power had been weakened and thrown onto the defensive. Governments were preoccupied with current political questions, and changed very frequently. The occupation and internal instability had led to supply shortages, which resulted in high inflation rates. Speculative trading and official corruption made the conditions worse. It is almost certain that there was a real decline in *urban* economic activity: state investment expenditure had fallen to negligible proportions; private investment was risky and uncertain; demand was low, unemployment high and poverty widespread; confidence in paper money had greatly weakened; there was a good deal of hoarding and investment in durable assets, such as urban property. What kept the show going was the invisible hand of the oil revenues, which made it possible for the state to meet many of its current obligations and pay for a large proportion of the country's imports.

The situation had a different kind of impact on the agricultural sector: demand for agricultural products was high both at home and abroad; the peasant and the agricultural worker could at least be certain of providing for their own subsistence; the weakening of the despotic apparatus had strengthened the landlords' position. This, in general, could not change the position of the peasantry, for it meant a relative shift of power between the exploitative agents themselves – the landlord and the state; but, in so far as it reduced the social and economic power of the state *apparatchiki* (particularly the gendarmerie) in the village, it must have afforded some benefit to the peasantry.

It was the flow of oil which provided some camouflage for the real depression of the urban sector. But, as usual, oil had two – stabilising *and* destabilising – sides to it. This time, however, the disturbing aspects of the oil sector were more directly political than economic. The fall of Reżā Shah quickly brought up the question of the 1933 oil agreement, which the great majority of the political public regarded as an unjust imposition. And the issue of the north Iranian oil concession focused attention on the whole question of Iranian oil resources and oil revenues. The new freedom had also made it possible for organised labour to participate in industrial and political activities. This was most evident and widespread in the southern oilfields, where the workers were much more effective, because they were the most skilled and prosperous members of the entire industrial labour force. Their many social and psychological grievances stemmed from the comprehensive discrimination against them – not only in pay but even in the bus which took them to work – in comparison with British workers in the fields. There was a great deal of industrial unrest, and in the biggest single event – the oil strike of 1946 – the central government (no doubt under the pressure of the Anglo-Iranian Oil Company and the British embassy) ordered the troops to shoot at the rioting strikers.

Muṣaddiq played the leading role in formulating the oil question – the D'Arcy concession, the 1933 Agreement, and the proposed grant of the northern oil concession to Russia–as a predominantly macropolitical problem. Put briefly, his argument was – and always remained – that, as long as any private or public foreign company had an oil concession in Iran, the country's sovereignty would be in doubt, and its domestic politics would be influenced by outside forces: the existence of the Anglo-Iranian Oil Company (AIOC) had provided a permanent vested interest for Britain in the Iranian political economy, exposing its domestic and foreign political relations to covert British interference and manipulation. If the country wanted to achieve real sovereignty and independence, it had to get rid of this foreign-dominated enclave for ever. That is why he had been in favour of *selling* north Iranian oil, even through an exclusive contract, to the Soviet Union, but he had opposed *the grant of a concession*, or the setting-up of a Soviet–Iranian company for its exploitation.

The AIOC tried to meet the mounting opposition and unrest by offering a package deal, which, however, sought to change the position too little too late. This deal is known, after the chief negotiators, as the Gass–Gulshā'īan, or Sā'id–Gass, Agreement. It was submitted to the *Majlis* for ratification towards the end of its Fifteenth Session. The government of Muhammad Sā'id tried to bulldoze the bill through the *Majlis*. But a combination of powerful filibustering tactics from within, and public opposition from without, prevented its enactment in spite of the government majority inside the Assembly itself. Dr Muẓaffar Baqā'ī Kirmānī, Ḥusain Makkī, 'Abdulqadīr Āzād, Hāyerī-zādeh and Dr 'Abdullah Mu'aẓẓamī, in that order, led the opposition against the agreement in the *Majlis*.

Meanwhile the Shah and the state had been busy trying to strengthen their position. In the spring of 1949 a Constituent Assembly – the elections for which were manipulated by the state – had amended the Constitution to empower the Shah to dismiss one or both of the parliamentary chambers at least twice in his lifetime. There was some public opposition to this; and, in particular, Ahmad Qavām – the famous 'British spy' – wrote an open letter to the Shah from Paris, pointing out that the amendment was against the spirit of the Constitution, and constitutional monarchy. But the Shah responded to him with contempt. Furthermore, the Shah succeeded in having a bill passed through the *Majlis* which effectively transferred Reżā Shah's unlawfully acquired rural properties to himself, in the guise of a foundation under his own guardianship. This would serve two purposes: it would add to his private income; and it would help finance his interference in politics.

When the Sixteenth *Majlis* was opened, the gunpowder was ready to explode both inside and outside the legislative chamber. The situation needed a 'strong man', and so, in the spring of 1950, General Ali Razmārā, the army chief, was appointed Prime Minister. He was an intelligent and well-trained general, an able and sophisticated political tactician, and a skilful diplomatic negotiator. In short, he was the Reżā Khān of his time: a ruthless, efficient and ambitious – but educated and even urbane – politician–general. He betrayed the qualities and aspirations of an Iranian leader who would end up as a pseudo-modernist despot. He was therefore a threat both to the *mellīyūn* (that is, not the 'nationalists', but the democrats), and to the Shah himself. It is remarkable evidence in favour of our evaluation of Razmārā that he was popularly accused of being a Soviet, a British *and* an American 'agent', all at once! In fact, he was nobody's agent but his own; and, precisely for this reason, he tried to make sure that none of these foreign powers would cause serious trouble for him in the country.

He tried to neutralise Britain by taking a soft line over the southern oil issue, to establish warm relations with the Soviet Union (moves of which the Tūdeh Party must have thoroughly approved), and to reassure the Americans that he was a nationalist determined to 'modernise' the economy. According to one of the 'theories' which attribute the cause of every event in modern Iranian history to an elaborate foreign conspiracy, Razmārā was a 'British agent' whom the British were using in order to reach a settlement with the Russians over Iran, to the exclusion of Americans.[18] In this connexion, a lot is made of the fact that, as the army chief, Razmārā had been involved in the removal of an American general who had been seconded to the Iranian Ministry of the Interior as the head of the Iranian gendarmerie. Yet it is certain that Razmārā's move had been intended not so much against 'the Americans', as to bring the gendarmerie back under the army's (that is, his own effective) command – just as Reżā Khān's removal of the Swedish officers in command of the gendarmerie had been intended to extend and consolidate his military command over the whole country. In any case, at least at the time of Razmārā's appointment to the premiership, Muṣaddiq and his few supporters in the *Majlis* were thinking that Razmārā had the support of the Americans, and that is why both Muṣaddiq and Makkī suggested that Razmārā owed his appointment to 'America and Britain'.[19] Furthermore, Razmārā was promised American support over the First (seven-year) Development Plan, already drafted in 1949, which he fully intended to put into operation. (See below, Ch. 10 on the fate of the First Plan.)

To sum up, Razmārā could not have been an agent of any foreign power, but, just like Reżā Khān before him, he was a shrewd and pragmatic politician who was ready to use any and every means to promote his own, and what he believed to be the country's, interests. Therefore, just like Reżā Khān, he tried to give the impression to each of the foreign powers concerned that he would be the best 'solution' for the Iranian situation. We have little doubt that, had he survived, he would have been regarded, at least in the crucial period of his rise to total power, as a 'bourgeois democratic leader' by the Russians as well as the Tūdeh Party, 'the winning horse' by the British, and the strong modernist who would save Iran from communism by the Americans. Razmārā was not a *mellī* personality, not because he was an agent of a foreign power, but because he was an agent of the deep-rooted functional despotism which he wanted to re-establish in his own favour. This is a lesson that many Iranian as well as foreign commentators on modern Iranian history have yet to learn: to be a *mellī* personality, force, party, one has to be both independent from foreign powers *and* opposed to the historic and functional Iranian despotism.

However, these were difficult times, and Razmārā lacked a *popular* power base. Nevertheless, he might have managed rapidly to consolidate his position had he not been singularly unlucky in finding Muṣaddiq at the head of the opposition. He was intelligent enough not to underestimate this formidable opponent and rival, and that is why he tried, unsuccessfully, to make a deal with him.[20] Nevertheless Razmārā might yet have succeeded in his designs had he not met his death by assassination in March 1951. The assassination plot is still shrouded in mystery – as are those involved in it. The self-confessed assassin, Khalīl Ṭahmāsibī, was a member of the small band of Fadā'īān-i Islam. It is likely that Sayyed Abulqāsim Kāshānī had known what was going to happen, though he may not have had a direct hand in organising it. On the other hand, it is also likely that the Shah and his personal confidants had, either independently or through the Sayyed, had prior knowledge of the attempt.[21] Furthermore, there is an old theory (not widely known) that the three bullets found in Razmārā's body did not match; that they were fired from different distances and directions, and that an army sergeant had fired at Razmārā simultaneously with Ṭahmāsibī.[22] It is, however, certain that Muṣaddiq and most of the men around him had not had the slightest information about the plot and those involved. Whether or not the Shah had been involved in the conspiracy, there can be no doubt that he received the news with a great sigh of relief: for the moment, the future of the Pahlavi dynasty looked a good deal less shaky than it had for a couple of years.[23]

The assassination of Razmārā led to the immediate nationalisation of Iranian oil amid public joy and euphoria. There followed two and a half years of dual sovereignty in Iranian politics, ending with the *coup d'état* of August 1953.

NOTES

1. In economic jargon this means that (a) the demand for Iranian exports was perfectly inelastic, and Iran's demand for her imports highly inelastic – hence 'the Marshall–Lerner conditions' could nowhere nearly be met, and there was a great deterioration in the country's external terms of trade, as well as its balance of trade and payments; and (b) since, within the existing technology, the elasticity of the supply of Iranian goods was low, the rise in aggregate demand due to devaluation alone would result in a high rate of inflation, which was further exacerbated by the fourfold increase in the money supply, and the unlimited credit extended to the Allies (see further, the text below).
2. For more details concerning the various 'agreements', and so forth, see Ḥusain Kay-ustuvān, *Sīyāsat-i Muvāzineh-yi Manfī* . . . (Teheran, 1948–50; repr. Paris: Muṣaddiq Publications, 1977) esp. vol. I.
3. See *Iṭṭilā'āt* (daily newspaper) no. 4702, 9 Nov 1941.
4. See Kay-ustuvān, *Sīyāsat-i Muvāzineh-yi Manfī*, vol. II, pp. 82–116.
5. An accurate and balanced account of events leading to the Tūdeh Party split of 1947–8 has yet to be written. Sepehr Zabih's discussion of this episode in *The Communist Movement in Iran* (Berkeley and Los Angeles, Calif.: University of California Press, 1966) contains serious factual and – more significantly – analytical errors: for example, he has applied the model of left and right party opposition (no doubt from the history of the Soviet Communist Party) to this episode, though it is, in fact, absolutely irrelevant to the case. In his recent 'indictment' of the Central Committee of the Tūdeh Party, Dr Firaidūn Kishāvarz almost exclusively confines himself to the misdeeds and 'treasonable acts' of one wing of the party

leadership (headed by Dr Kīyānūrī, the present Party First Secretary) *since* the party split of 1948, and does not discuss those 'mistakes' of the leadership which almost destroyed the party, and led up to the party split, when he himself was still in Teheran and a very important member of the Central Committee. This, of course, is not meant to reduce the significance of Kishāvarz's revelations, but to emphasise the importance of what it is not in his own interest to reveal. See Firaidūn Kishāvarz, *Man Muttaham Mīkunam* . . . ('I Accuse . . .') (Teheran: Ravāq, 1977). For more information on the split, see Eprime (Isḥāq), *Cheh Bāyad Kard*; Ālatūr, *Ḥazb-i Tūdeh bar Sar-i Durāh* (Teheran, 1947); and Yaldā, *Dar Rāh-i Yik Inḥirāf* (Teheran, 1947); *Du Ravish Barāy-i Yik Hadaf* (written, but unsigned, by Khalīl Malekī) (Teheran: Splinter Group, 1948); Khalīl Malekī, *Barkhurd-i 'Aqāyed u Ārā* (Teheran, 1950); Khalīl Malekī and Anvar Khāmeh'ī, *Pas az Dah Sāl Inshi'ābīyūn-i Ḥizb-i Tūdeh Sukhan Mīgūyand* (Teheran: 'Ilm-u-Zindigī, 1957); and H. Katouzian (ed.), *Khaṭirāt-i Sīyāsī-yi Khalīl Malekī* (Teheran: Ravāq, 1980).

6. That is why such 'parties' usually did not have parliamentary groups in the *Majlis* under their own names. The main parliamentary factions in the *Majlis* (apart from the Tūdeh Party's) were Mīhan, Ittiḥād-i Mellī, Āzādī, and so on, as well as the independents.
7. Kāmbakhsh is typical of a few Tūdeh Party leaders, as well as a good number of the party's younger intellectuals, who, in their emotional and romantic attachment to Russia and all things Russian, could be best described as Russian nationalists who happened to be Iranian by birth! His old comrade Kishāvarz has now accused him of being a Soviet agent. See Kishavarz, *Man Muttaham Mīkunam*. . . .
8. As late as 1951, Navvāb Ṣafavī, the leader of Fadā'īān-i Islam, wrote in its newspaper that 'Āyatullah Burūjirdī has not yet broken his silence on this all-important issue [of the oil nationalisation]'. Āyatullah Burūjirdī was at the time (and until his death in 1960) the single universally acknowledged *Marja'al-taqlīd* of the Shī'ites in Iran. See *Nabard-i Mellat*, no. 5, 10 Feb 1951).
9. For example Pīsheh-varī wrote that, 'if Teheran chooses the road to reaction, then farewell . . . let it carry on without Azerbijan . . . [which] prefers to be a free Ireland, instead of being captive like India. . . . If things go on in their present way, we have no choice but to become wholly separate from Teheran and form an independent government.' See *Azerbijan* (newspaper), nos 1, 2 and 84 (1945).
10. According to Khalīl Malekī, who at the time was the chief Tūdeh Party representative in Azerbijan (and an open critic of Pīsheh-varī and his group, as well as the leadership of his own party, in giving them unconditional support), most of the trouble was due to those Azerbijanis who had ostensibly returned from exile in Soviet Azerbijan, and, at another level, the Soviet army, who interfered with the internal politics of the Democrat Party. Malekī's knowledge and views of the Azerbijan situation have found expression on many occasions, including in the military court in which he was 'tried' in 1965 – see *Socialism* (quarterly periodical of the League of Iranian Socialists in Europe), II, no. 7 (1966) 37–56, and his *Khātirat-ī Sīyāsī* (1980). According to Firaidūn Kishāvarz, Mīr Bāqir Bāqirov, the Stalinist Communist Party chief of Soviet Azerbijan, was in control of the Democrat movement in Iranian Azerbijan. See Kishāvarz, *Man Muttaham Mīkunam*. . . .
11. According to Kay-ustuvān, *Sīyāsat-i Muvāzineh-yi Manfī*, vol. II, p. 214, the Soviet Union let it be known that it would be prepared to negotiate with Qavām alone, as the Iranian Prime Minister, and this forced the Shah and 'the pro-British deputies who [had] refused to support his nomination' to yield. See further, Khalīl Malekī's first hand account of this and related incidents, in his *Kātirāt-i Sīyāsī-yi* (1980).

12. The young Jalāl Āl-i Aḥmad, who as a party member had participated in the demonstration, was later to write that he had returned home weeping with shame. See his posthumous *Khidmat va Khīyānat-i Rushanfikrān* (Teheran: Ravāq, 1977).
13. The party leadership, both inside and outside the *Majlis*, adopted this position. 'Iḥsān Ṭabarī and Khalīl Malekī, the latter of whom was not on the party Central Committee, elaborated this point of view, although Malekī's argument was more flexible, and less emphatic, adding that their position on this matter was not substantially different from Muṣaddiq's. We now know that Malekī had been a critic of the party leadership on this as well as other important issues at the time, and his rather mild defence of Tabarī's argument had been intended to preserve the outward appearance of party unity (he has pointed this out in many of his writings, and in his memoirs). See Ṭabarī in *Mardum* (party newspaper) 10 Nov 1944; and Malekī in *Rahbar* (party organ) 28 Mar 1945.
14. See Kay-ustuvān, *Sīyāsat-i Muvāzineh-yi Manfī*, vol. I.
15. According to Kishāvarz, (*Man Muttaham Mīkunam . . .*), who himself was the Tūdeh Minister of Education, the Soviet ambassador was directly involved in the formation of this coalition government.
16. Kishāvarz (ibid.) emphatically claims that an influential faction of the Tūdeh Party, led by Dr Kīyānūrī (the present party leader), had been in touch with Fakhrārā'ī and involved in the assassination plot, though the party leadership was, at the time, unaware of this; he further adds that this was the same faction who had earlier organised and carried out the assassination of Muhammad Mas'ūd, a leading radical and amoral journalist and writer. There is a lot of circumstantial evidence in favour of Kishāvarz's claim that the Kīyānūrī faction was involved in the assassination attempt on the Shah. Since, in addition, I have known for many years (independently from Kishāvarz) that Mas'ūd was certainly killed by this party group, I am inclined to believe Kishāvarz's claim about Kīyānūrī's involvement in the attempt on the Shah's life (which I had not previously known).
17. As Kishāvarz (ibid.) implies, it is even probable that the Kīyānūrī faction of the Tūdeh Party was in league with Razmārā over this and later developments: when the party leaders escaped from gaol, there was a strong rumour that Razmārā had been involved in the escape plan.
18. Kishāvarz (ibid., p.148) puts forward this well-known view, but he cautiously adds the 'hypothesis' that Razmārā may have been playing this game in order to take over the country first, and 'show his *mellī* face' afterwards. Clearly, like nearly all Iranian intellectuals, Kishāvarz regards *mellī* as synonymous with 'nationalist', and, hence, independent of foreign powers. Razmārā might well have succeeded in creating his own despotic nationalism, and pseudo-modernism, but, precisely for this reason (and just like Reżā Khān), he had no '*mellī* face' to show, whether or not he was a 'British agent'. On this point, see further the text below, and Chs 2 and 9.
19. See *Nuṭqhā-yi Duktur Muṣaddiq dar Dawreh-yi Shānzdahum-i Majlis* (Paris: Intishārāt Muṣaddiq, 1969) vol. I, book 1, esp. p. 56.
20. See ibid., books 1 and 2.
21. The fact that Fadā'īān-i Islam later supported the Shah, forcefully, against Muṣaddiq, and that even Kāshānī (with whom he was in contact) threw his weight behind the Shah in 1953, lends support to the possibility of previous collusion. Thus, *Nabard-i Mellat*, published by the Fadā'īān, pronounced, 'God tells the Shahanshah of Iran: you are my shepherd, you are my agent, you are my Messiah' (7 May 1953). In a much earlier issue (12 Aug 1951), Navvāb Ṣafavī, leader of the group, is quoted as saying, 'You lying Muṣaddiq! You have shown your ugly real face to the world, and to the Muslims.'

22. This was related by the presiding judge in the case to M. H. T. Katouzian, who in turn told me. However, the self-confessed assassin was officially pardoned, only to be executed (in fact murdered) together with Navvāb Safavī and other members of the Fadā'īān by the Shah-'Alā government in 1956.
23. Sayyed Żīa al-Dīn Ṭabā-Ṭabā'ī told a number of his friends that he happened to be present when Asadullah 'Alam (the Shah's confidant, who witnessed Razmārā's assassination) brought the news to the Shah, saying, 'They killed him and we are relieved' (*'Kushtand, rāḥat Shudīm*).

9 The Popular Movement of Iran: Oil Nationalisation and Dual Sovereignty, 1951–3

The Iranian Popular Movement was a revolutionary episode; but it failed before it could result in a full-scale social revolution. Such a revolution would have required (a) a satisfactory, even though not ideal, settlement of the oil dispute in the short run; (b) the use of oil revenues together with the people's sense of social involvement, and the newly won international prestige and sovereignty, to uproot the foundations of Iranian despotism, in order to establish a democratic (= *mellī*) political economy; and, (c) social and economic reconstruction and renovation by the application of relevant, and progressive, programmes. Everything depended on the settlement of the oil dispute, and the failure to resolve it was the basic cause of the final disillusionment, disarray and defeat.

Between April 1951 and August 1953, except for a few days, Muṣaddiq was Prime Minister; but he was not in control either of the whole apparatus of the state, or of the entire expanse of Iranian lands: he was merely the leader of a popular (i.e.*mellī*) political movement, and the head of an independent government administration; that is, even at the best of times, he was in charge of *only one organ of the state*. The rest of the state apparatus was still in the hands of despotic agents and institutions, who, in pursuit of their own interests, collaborated with the interested foreign powers against the Popular Movement. The situation was an authentic example of dual sovereignty; and it involved a struggle between the democratic forces led by Muṣaddiq, and the conservative and despotic (and foreign) powers led by the Shah, who eventually emerged the victors.

Yet the fact that the democratic forces were ultimately defeated cannot be entirely explained by the tactics and strategies of their enemies: an army advancing against an enemy would hardly be surprised to meet resistance and retaliation; its success or failure would depend as much on the enemy's decisions as its own; and it can never entirely blame its own failure on the fact that the enemy put up a fight. This is a simple, obvious, but very significant lesson which is yet to be understood by the Iranian political public and – especially – their 'scientific' analysts.[1]

Political Trends and the Balance of Power: An Appraisal

In order to understand the causes and consequences of the political developments of this period, it would be helpful to begin by an assessment of the changing attitudes of various social groups and political groupings towards Muṣaddiq's government.

THE SOCIO-ECONOMIC CLASSES

The fall of Reżā Shah had been followed by an implicit contest for political power between the battered forces of despotism and the anti-despotic forces of both left and right: landlords and big businessmen belonged to the *conservative*, and the middle merchants, retailers, artisans, workers, younger intellectuals and students to the *radical*, wing of this broad anti-despotic tendency. The turn of events pushed the conservative groups – especially landlords – behind Razmārā in the hope that he would stabilise the *status quo* with a 'plutocratic' and authoritarian régime that would recognise the economic and political rights and influence of private property. They would welcome Razmārā's *dictatorship*, just as the Iberian landlords had welcomed Franco's and Salazar's; but they were not in favour of *despotism*, which would monopolise power even to the exclusion of themselves as a social class. Clearly, it was beyond their analytical powers to see in Razmārā not only a dictator, but also a potential despot. At any rate, the assassination of Razmārā amid the movement for the nationalisation of oil threw the conservative social groups into a state of confusion and anxiety, and induced them not to support Muṣaddiq, but to tolerate his government as the least of all potentially successful evils. But, as Muṣaddiq's power began to wane, and the position of the Shah and the Tūdeh Party strengthened, they rallied behind the Shah – who eventually made them pay dearly for their contribution towards the resurgence of his own pseudo-modernist despotism (see Chs 10 and 11).

The attitude of other rentier elements – speculators, big businessmen, particularly in the import–export trade, and so on – was almost identical with the landlords'. But the *bāzār* community, the retailers, the artisans, as well as a large proportion of intellectuals, middle-ranking professionals, students and industrial workers, supported Muṣaddiq, even though they became less and less enthusiastic about the state of the political economy in the last year of his premiership. Those workers, intellectuals, professionals, and so on, who did not support Muṣaddiq were generally either members or sympathisers of the Tūdeh Party.

Finally, the Iranian peasantry, true to its historical tradition, was, *as a class*, politically silent throughout this period.

THE ROLE OF DOMESTIC AND FOREIGN POLITICAL FORCES

(i) *The Tūdeh Party and the Soviet Union.* After the Tūdeh Party had clearly emerged as the Iranian communist party *par excellence*, its social base had been reduced to a proportion of the industrial working class, younger intellectuals and professionals, and university students. At first the Tūdeh Party adopted an unequivocally hostile and destructive attitude towards Muṣaddiq, the campaign for oil nationalisation, and the National Front. The evidence is well known and overwhelming: it identified Muṣaddiq as representative of domestic reactionaries and an agent of American imperialism, and instructed their members, organs and supporters to direct 'the sharp edge of the attack' against the National Front.[2] An extensive analysis of the reasons behind this suicidal confrontation would take us far beyond the scope of this study. For this reason we shall confine ourselves only to a few notes suggesting the outlines of such an analysis.

First, the Tūdeh Party was a self-styled Marxist–Leninist party, with a total commitment to the Stalinist interpretation of this ideology both in theory and in practice. It therefore suffered on two counts: (a) its understanding of Marxism was a second-hand version of Stalin's pragmatic totalitarianism; and (b) its analysis of the Iranian situation bore almost no resemblance to the realities of that country's history, sociology, political economy and institutions. It merely consisted of empty *jargon* which, by changing a few words, could be equally (mis-)applied to Egypt, India, Brazil or wherever.

Secondly, it had whole heartedly accepted the Stalinist myth – which was very useful for the promotion of Soviet interests – that in the interest of 'the world proletariat' the global strategy of the Soviet Union must take precedence over all local issues, tactics and strategies. Accordingly, while the Iranians were directly confronting the Anglo-Iranian Oil Company (AIOC) and the British government, they were more anxious to attack America – the chief adversary of the Soviet Union – even though, in the case of oil nationalisation, the Americans were playing a moderating role against Britain. In addition, the party had uncritically accepted the Soviet division of the world into two camps: friends and foes – that is, 'the progressive forces', and 'the agents of American imperialism' – leaving no place for the non-committed. The tacit and qualified American support for Muṣaddiq, in the first year of his premiership, left no doubt at all for the resident 'progressive forces' that Muṣaddiq was nothing but an 'agent of American imperialism'.

Thirdly, the party specifically interpreted Muṣaddiq's successful attempt to nationalise the entire Iranian oil *reserves* as an imperialist conspiracy against the Soviet Union, which still claimed the concession for north Persian oil.

That is why the Tūdeh party astonished everyone, except its own members and those who regarded them as 'Russian spies', by rejecting the nationalisation policy and instead campaigning for the abrogation of the 1933 Agreement *alone*.

Fourthly, and on a somewhat lower plane, the Tūdeh leadership and the party intelligentsia had nothing but contempt for Muṣaddiq and his supporters, whom they variously described as imperialist agents, forces of reaction, petty bourgeois elements, and the like. They were therefore bitter about the fact that 'this stupid old man who has served imperialism for fifty years' had stolen the show from them.

Finally, the combination of modern totalitarian 'virtues' and traditional Iranian habits of despotism had by then removed all traces of internal party democracy. There were many intelligent critics in the party membership who disagreed with the party line. But they had little chance to express themselves, and when they did they were in danger of repudiation, excommunication and expulsion. Therefore, the party could not even benefit from the sound advice of its own faithful members.

To what extent, if any, the party policy was based on specific directives from Soviet authorities cannot be known. On the whole, it seems unlikely that there were any such open directives: first, the broad principles of conduct mentioned earlier seem to have been sufficient to shape the attitude of the Tūdeh Party; and, secondly, the Soviet Union must have had a few professional agents within the party itself, who would control the situation from within. The official Soviet attitude towards Muṣaddiq was, in principle, consistent with the Tūdeh Party's, but its public expression, in the Soviet press and elsewhere, was much less harsh and more moderate. However, it is certain that, from the point of view of its own global strategy, the Soviet Union would have preferred *any* Iranian government to one which was friendly towards America, and for this reason it could not be happy with Muṣaddiq's government as described by the Tūdeh Party. There have even been suggestions that at this stage Russia had entered a tacit understanding with Britain in order to keep American influence out of the Middle East. The closeness of some leading conservative opponents of Muṣaddiq to the Tūdeh Party and its leadership – for the description of whose motives Muṣaddiq characteristically invented the term 'oil communists' (*Tūdeh-naftī*) – seemed to lend credence to this hypothesis.[3]

To sum up, the Soviet Union was not *directly active* against Muṣaddiq, but it offered him no help either: it could have modified the attitude of the Tūdeh Party; it could have given moral and material support to Muṣaddiq's government; and, at least, it could have paid its war debts to Iran, which were long overdue and in the absence of oil revenues, badly needed. It returned them to the Shah and his dictatorial government less than two years after the 1953 coup, when it was beginning a four-year period of friendly relations with him.

The Tūdeh Party began to moderate the tone of its attacks on Muṣaddiq when he had clearly lost American good-will and the support of some of his own political allies. But this was a relative shift of position, and the party never changed its attitude towards Muṣaddiq even to the level of *constructive* opposition.

(ii) *The Shah, Britain and America.* When Iranian oil was nationalised, Truman of the Democratic Party and Attlee of the Labour Party headed the American and British governments. Both parties were disunited, and both governments were reaching the end of their tether. It was not so much the attitude of the Labour government as the attitude of Britain – and, especially, the attitude of the British establishment and press, which (mis-)guided British public opinion – that played the crucial role.[4] Clearly, British interests were at stake, and it is not surprising that London received the news of the Iranian oil nationalisation, and the subsequent developments, with unmitigated hostility. Yet a person's or a country's defence of vital interests may be based either on a realistic understanding and analysis of the situation, or on misunderstanding and prejudice. Whatever their own interests, the British establishment singularly failed to understand the meaning and significance of the events in Iran. They were therefore ill equipped to deal with them, even in their own best interests.

They saw in Muṣaddiq not a democratic national leader, but at best a nationalist demagogue, and at worst a pro-communist dictator. They regarded Kāshānī as an anti-British, fascist and religious fanatic, even though shortly afterwards he would be described by many of his own previous Iranian sympathisers as a 'British spy'! They deceived themselves into the belief that Muṣaddiq had no genuine popular support, except from 'the rabble' and 'the mob' (the equivalents of the Tūdeh party's pseudo-Marxist 'petty bourgeoisie' and '*Lumpen* proletariat'). They stubbornly refused to understand Iranian habits and methods and so were continuously puzzled by the 'un-British' quality of Iranian tactics and diplomacy. They even regarded Muṣaddiq's occasional breakdowns and faints – many of which were due to his long history of chronic hysteria – as entirely hypocritical, and described them as 'grotesque' and 'ridiculous'. Hostility and prejudice apart, at no time was this total misunderstanding of Iranian culture more evident than in the British press coverage of Muṣaddiq's trial after the 1953 coup: his conduct in this trial was a perfect example of *Iranian* courage, dignity, morality, eloquence, wit, scorn, and so on, synthesised in a great drama; and that is how it was viewed by the Iranian people. Yet the British establishment and public media, using *British* criteria of assessment, saw nothing in it but the clownings of a senile neurotic.

It was on the basis of such a lack of understanding that the British government made the foolish gesture of 'showing the flag' at Ābādān, following the decision of the Iranian government to take control of the oil installations. It is not yet clear whether or not there was a serious possibility of a British occupation of the oilfields, though the later adventure in the Suez Canal gives it a certain degree of probability. However, partly because of American pressure, and partly because of the attitude of the parliamentary Labour Party – and, especially, its left wing – the Labour government accepted the letter of the Iranian oil nationalisation, though, by insisting on full compensation for the abrogation of the 1933 Agreement, it ignored part of its spirit. The fact that a mutually satisfactory compromise was never found owed a great deal to the atmosphere of mutual suspicion and recrimination which had been thus created, in addition to the transparent wishes of the British imperialists (or 'Empire loyalists') to reverse the tide completely. The assumption of power by the Conservative Party after the 1951 general election greatly strengthened both these tendencies.

The American government adopted the role of conciliator, because it was generally against the old-style European colonialism; it regarded Muṣaddiq as the best alternative to the rise of communism in Iran, and it was probably influenced by the American oil companies who were hoping to get 'a foot in the door' in the final settlement. This attitude was maintained to some degree even after the Republican success in the American presidential election, and John Foster Dulles, who, like his (real) Soviet counterpart, Joseph Stalin, divided the world into friends and foes alone, began to run American foreign affairs. But, as Muṣaddiq continued to prove intransigent, Iran's political economy sank into economic depression and political instability, and the real or imaginary threat of a communist bid for power began to grow, the Americans were finally persuaded by their British allies and their Iranian clientele that they had to search for a 'final solution': they discovered it in a *coup d'état*, designed by the American Central Intelligence Agency and executed in collaboration with the Shah, his retinue, and conservative Iranian forces, against Muṣaddiq's government, and the people of Iran. No doubt they believed that this familiar act of great-power arrogance would render the 'free world' even freer than before!

The role and position of the Shah and his retinue are thus clear. At first, they swam with the current of events in the hope of regaining the initiative; but they had underestimated both their rival and the democratic implications of the whole movement. Next, they tried to act with Britain, though not necessarily against America – for example, by trying to use the anti-despotic conservative tendencies as a third alternative: the episode of the abortive premiership of Qavām in June 1952 (of which more below) must be seen in this light. Finally, the deterioration of the country's situation, the destructive role of the Tūdeh Party, the attempts at internal subversion by the Shah and his followers, and external pressures for changing the American attitude bore their sour fruit for the Iranian people.

(iii) *The Zaḥmatkishān and other parties.* As mentioned in the preceding chapter, the Iran Party and one tendency in the Pan-Iranist Party supported the Popular Movement, Muṣaddiq and his government. Yet, although these parties improved their membership because of their pro-Muṣaddiq attitude and the greater political participation of the public, they still remained numerically small and 'ideologically' entirely dependent on Muṣaddiq and the broad Popular Movement behind him. The fact that the Iran Party was disproportionately represented in Cabinet and the *Majlis* was due to its basically elitist and technocratic composition. In general, it is fair to say that, of all the political parties and groups that supported Muṣaddiq's government, there was only one which, in terms of ideas, organisation, publications, activities, membership, and so forth, could offer an alternative to the Tūdeh Party; Zaḥmatkishān-i Mellat-i Irān, or the Toiling Masses of Iran.

The Zaḥmatkishān Party was a coalition of two distinct tendencies: (a) the majority of the Splinter Group of the Tūdeh Party, and their intellectual working-class affiliates, led by Khalīl Malekī; and (b) a motley group of centrist intellectuals, middle and small traders, artisans and common adventurers, gathered around the personality of Dr Muẓaffar Baqā'ī Kirmānī. It was a perfect match: Malekī was an astute – indeed, in retrospect, an unrivalled – Iranian political analyst, an able party organiser, and an *original* socialist thinker – that is, not a mere quotation-monger – with a deep sense of public morality and no personal ambitions whatever;[5] Baqā'ī was an energetic, fearless and ruthless politician, an able public orator, and a charismatic figure with few social and moral principles and a great deal of personal ambition. The coalition worked as long as it suited Baqā'ī to support Muṣaddiq and his government, in which – though not a cabinet member – he was second to the 'Old Man' himself. But when, in mid-1952, he began to waver in his backing for Muṣaddiq (which later developed into outright opposition), the party divided, and the 'Malekī tendency' formed Zaḥmatkishān-i Mellat-i Irān, Nīrūy-i Sevvum: the Toiling Masses of Iran, Third Force. Thenceforth they became popularly known as the Nīrūy-i Sevvum (Third Force) Party.

The Third Force Party was socialist in its ideals, but Iranian in its approach and methods: it was neither a Stalinist nor a social-democratic party; it gave total support to Muṣaddiq's government, though not without systematic constructive criticism. Within less than a year, between its foundation and the 1953 coup, it attracted a large number of students, intellectuals and workers, including a few from the current membership of the Tūdeh Party. It had a number of regular and occasional publications, of which the daily party organ, *Nīrūy-i Sevvum*, which was in fact edited by Malekī himself, and the monthly intellectual periodical '*Ilm u Zindigī* ('Knowledge and Life'), edited by the young Amīr Pīchdād, were the more important. Like the Tūdeh Party, it was instrumental in the development of many intellectual and artistic talents, of whom Jalāl Āl-i Aḥmad, Muhammad Ali Khunjī, Ḥusain Malek, Amīr Pīchdād, Ali Aṣghar Ḥāj-Sayyed-Javādī, Firaidūn Tavallulī and Nādir Nādir-pūr are among the best known.

(iv) *Kāshānī and his following.* There remains Sayyed Abulqāsim Kāshānī, and his sizable following among the more religious urban crowd. To begin with, Kāshānī actively supported the nationalisation campaign and Muṣaddiq's government, but he began to withdraw his support in August 1952, at about the same time as Baqā'ī's alienation from Muṣaddiq. At the outset, it looked as if Kāshānī's personal popularity was as great as Muṣaddiq's: in the large urban demonstrations the pictures of both leaders used to appear side by side. But, as the rift between them became public, Kāshānī's following sank to insignificant proportions. One thing is worth emphasising. At no time did the Shī'ite religious leadership in general, and the only *Marja' al-taqlīd* resident in Qum [there were others in Najaf, Iraq] in particular, voice their opinion about the political situation in the country. There were many younger preachers and scholars who supported Muṣaddiq and the nationalisation movement – in fact, more than they supported Kāshānī. But the silence of the higher religious leaders was not without significance, and it was later broken against Muṣaddiq, under the leadership of the Āyatullahs Behbahānī and Chelsutūnī.

Finally, a word or two about the broader political implications of the Iranian Popular Movement (Nehżat-i Mellī-yi Irān) in this period. *This was not a nationalist movement, and Muṣaddiq was not a nationalist.* It was a democratic (i.e. *mellī*) movement aimed at the establishment of sovereignty without, and democracy within, the country. Iranian nationalism, in the historical sense of this term derived from European experience, has been the ideology of despotism: the ideology of Reżā Shah, his son, and their clientele. At the time, there were only two tiny *nationalist* 'parties' in Iran: Ḥizb-i Pān-Irānīst (the Pan-Iranist Party); and Ḥizb-i Sociālīst-i Mellī-i Kārgar-i Irān (SOMKA – the Iranian Workers' National Socialist Party). The European and Europeanised analysts of all political tendencies have been singularly mistaken in identifying the movement that was symbolised by Muṣaddiq, and the Iranian Popular Movement, as nationalist.

A Summary of Events

Upon the violent death of Prime Minister Razmārā, Muṣaddiq – as the leader of the opposition and the chairman of the National Assembly's Oil Committee – managed to pass his own Nationalisation Bill through both houses of the Iranian parliament by 20 March 1951. Meanwhile, Ḥusain 'Alā, a conservative but meek and mild politician, had formed a caretaker government. The conservative politicians had reluctantly supported the Nationalisation Bill, in the hope that an early settlement would be reached within the letter of the Nationalisation Act. Indeed, only a few weeks after the event, a techno-bureaucratic Anglo-American team, meeting in Washington, resolved that (a) Britain should accept the Nationalisation Act; (b) she should seek a new agreement with the Iranian government, according to which the AIOC would resume activities *as an operating company*, on a fifty–fifty profit-sharing basis; (c) America would support Britain in seeking such an agreement, and, if the Iranian government rejected this solution, she would support Britain's case in the United Nations and the International Court at the Hague ; (d) the Iranian government should compensate the AIOC for its unilateral abrogation of the 1933 Agreement; and (e) America would be ready to grant a loan to Iran for this purpose. These proposals were unrealistic, and they were doomed to failure: characteristically, they missed the predominantly *political* nature of the nationalisation movement, and its distrust of Britain as an imperialist power; they were too rigid on the fifty–fifty profit-sharing proposal; and their reference to 'compensation' gives the impression of lack of seriousness. What other compensation could there be *in addition to* a new, and mutually acceptable, agreement?

Meanwhile, Muṣaddiq had drafted a new bill for the implementation of the Nationalisation Act, which would replace the AIOC by a National Iranian Oil Company (NIOC). He refused 'Alā's bid to support the Anglo-American formula: 'Alā resigned and Muṣaddiq himself became Prime Minister. Muṣaddiq then resolved to implement the Nationalisation Act, although he was prepared to continue oil exports only on the condition that the tankers would give the Iranian authorities a receipt for their loads. Britain's reaction, however, was to withdraw the oil tankers from Ābādān and replace them with the battleship HMS *Mauritius*. From that moment, there was an effective blockade by Britain against the export of Iranian oil.

In July 1951 the International Court, to which Britain had taken her case, decided in favour of the AIOC. The Iranian government rejected this decision on the ground that a dispute between a private company and a sovereign state was out of the court's jurisdiction (this argument was endorsed by the court itself, a year later). In mid-July, Truman sent Averell Harriman to Teheran, in search of a solution. The Tūdeh Party held Harriman's mission as evident proof that Muṣaddiq was a 'traitor', and a 'spy of American imperialism'. It called a massive demonstration on the day of Harriman's arrival, and this ended in bloodshed. This was a calculated blow to the position and prestige of Muṣaddiq, who had expressly forbidden the use of firearms against the demonstrators without prior permission from himself. It almost looked as if his communist and conservative opposition had entered a prior understanding over these tactics; at any rate, the episode was followed by a chorus of condemnation of Muṣaddiq by both the Tūdeh Party and the conservative opposition. This was the origin of Muṣaddiq's coining of the term 'oil communists'.[6]

Harriman's intervention resulted in the agreement of both countries that a high-level British delegation led by Richard Stokes (the Lord Privy Seal in the Attlee Cabinet), should come to Teheran for negotiations, and its members were duly received, early in August, as guests of the Iranian government.

There followed three weeks of protracted, and fruitless, talks between the two parties, for the ultimate failure of which the blame must be placed squarely on the British delegation. According to a series of long, detailed, public and frank reports by Muṣaddiq to the *Majlis*, the Iranians agreed (a) to sell any amount of oil to Britain at Persian Gulf prices (free on board); (b) to enter a twenty-five year contract with the British government, guaranteeing such sales; (c) to let the British, or British companies, provide their own means of transport and other services for carrying their purchased oil; (d) to let Britain provide the same services for any other customers of Iranian oil, if the latter themselves were agreeable; (e) to re-employ the British technical and managerial staff of the AIOC, *other than their directors and chief administrators*; and (f) to pay full compensation for nationalised British property by instalments, in the form either of one-half of the annual value of Iranian oil exports to Britain, or a quarter of Iran's net income from the oil industry, whichever was preferable to Britain.[7]

The British delegation had originally suggested that (a) a (British) marketing firm be created with a twenty-five-year contract with the NIOC to export and market Iranian oil and divide the net proceeds with the NIOC on a fifty–fifty basis; (b) a (British) operating firm be set up which would be responsible for carrying out the entire technical operations (exploration, extraction, refining, and so on) 'for and on behalf of NIOC ', which would be represented on its board of directors (the cost of these operations would be met by the proposed marketing firm); and (c) compensation be paid by the Iranian government for British property used (to that date and after) for the production of Iran's own domestic oil requirements.[8]

In plain language, the British proposal meant that the 1933 Agreement should be revived for another twenty-five (rather than forty) years on a fifty–fifty basis; and it is roughly the 'solution' which Britain imposed *via* the Consortium Oil Agreement in 1954 (i.e. after the coup), although this time it had to share the loot with others, since it held only 40 per cent of the shares in the operating companies then created.

The initial disagreement was followed by two long private meetings between Muṣaddiq and Stokes (in the presence of Harriman, as well as interpreters and others), which were finally broken by Stokes on the pretext that the general manager of the Iranian oil operations must be British and nothing else (Muṣaddiq had suggested someone, or a group, from any other European nationality).[9] It looks as if Muṣaddiq himself may not have realised that this recurring theme (of a British general manager, and so forth) was a mere pretext: the real issue was that, as of right, the British government were demanding 50 per cent of Iranian oil receipts for twenty-five years, because of the fact that the oil nationalisation had put an end to its forty years of exploitation of Iranian oil (and, therefore, the Iranian people).

The D'Arcy concession had been granted by an ailing and moronic Iranian king at the head of a despotic régime; this had led to twenty-five years of

British exploitation (*real*, not imaginary or 'emotional') of the country. The treaty had then been abrogated by an impulsive and arrogant despot in 1933, who had immediately discovered that in order to keep himself on the throne he would have to enter a new agreement, extending the former concessionary period by a further thirty-three years. After all that the British and their wartime allies had imposed on a desperately poor country by the force of military occupation (devaluation, forced credit, famine, inflation, and so on), and all that they and their domestic Iranian allies had done to stem the tide of the Popular Movement of Iran, they were now expecting the movement's government to enter a shabby deal with them – taking and doing a little less than they were used to – through the back door. Such was the real basis of the international legality as well as morality which they claimed for their position (see further the appendix to this chapter). The British demands were impossible, and Muṣaddiq was right not to accept them, although on this occasion he literally bent over backwards in order to reach a reasonable settlement. It is worth noting, however, that the British delegation was evidently unaware of the *political* significance (indeed primacy) of the issue from the Iranian point of view: Muṣaddiq might well have settled on financial–economic terms acceptable to the British; but he would have never agreed to the use of a British company, or general manager, even if it were the one and only demand of Britain. And this, as far as it went, was not the product of an irrational Anglophobia, because, as a matter of fact, both the AIOC and the British government had interfered in internal Iranian politics for too long.

On 25 September, a month after Stokes returned from Iran, the Iranian army occupied the Ābādān oil refinery, and the British expatriates were asked to leave. In view of the International Court's earlier decision, Britain regarded this move as unlawful, and took her case to the UN Security Council. Muṣaddiq led a high-level delegation to New York, and the Security Council resolved that the question of the International Court's jurisdiction in the case must be determined by the court itself. This was a triumph for Muṣaddiq, who extended his American trip in order to explain his position to Truman and obtain firmer American support for the Iranian cause.

In February 1952, in view of the country's desperate economic situation, the government issued 2000 million rials' ($25 million) worth of special bonds, described as Popular Debt, which were redeemable after two years and carried a few prizes. Muṣaddiq personally appealed to the public to buy as many of these bonds as they could, and – in spite of the boycott by the Tūdeh Party and the conservative opposition – they were given an enthusiastic public reception by the *bāzār* community, the enlightened professionals, and the lower ranks of the urban population. None the less, the move failed in its objective, because the rich refused to help.[10] At the same time, Muṣaddiq was struggling with the problems posed by the general elections. The Shah, the security forces under his command, and the provincial magnates had combined to return their own candidates; and the British consulates in major provincial capitals had become centres of anti-government campaigns.[11] This was the reason why the British embassy was asked to close down the consulates, and the British *chargé d'affaires* was recalled to London 'for consultations', after his reluctant compliance with Muṣaddiq's demand.

The election to the Seventeenth *Majlis* was a fiasco: there were both gross illegalities by the alliance between the Shah's retinue and the conservative opposition, and irregularities by government supporters. The situation got so out of hand that Muṣaddiq, supported by the majority of the 101 (out of 136) deputies already elected, had to postpone the rest of the elections indefinitely. It was not a glorious decision, even though it was not illegal; but Muṣaddiq bears the least responsibility for this. Yet, the lesson was not learned that disorganised public support is no match for the combined power of the despotic, conservative and totalitarian opposition against a government that has defied a great imperialist power.

Earlier in the year, the World Bank, in the role of an intermediary, had sent two delegations to Teheran. The gist of its final proposal was that Britain and Iran should agree to resume oil operations and exports, on the condition that the bulk of the output were disposed of by the Bank, which would hold the proceeds until a final settlement were reached. By rejecting this proposal, Muṣaddiq made the greatest mistake of his career – a mistake, moreover, that condemned the Iranian Popular Movement to ultimate failure, and cost the Iranian people, their independence and their democratic movement very dear. Muṣaddiq himself realised that the Bank's proposal could be used as the *beginning* for an honourable settlement from a position of strength; and with consistent support from his associates he would have agreed to it – indeed, he nearly did so. But some of his close advisers pointed out that the Tūdeh Party would seize on such an agreement as evidence of Muṣaddiq's 'treason', and *wrongly* concluded that this would destroy the government's popular support. It was this combination of ill advice from well-meaning but timid and frankly incompetent men, and Muṣaddiq's own unjustified fear of unpopularity, which were the *real* causes of the mission's failure; it was not those matters of detail which were *officially* described as the reasons for disagreement.[12]

The mission failed because Muṣaddiq's advisers had demanded that the words 'on behalf of the Iranian government' should be inserted in the preamble of the draft agreement so that they could bravely face the Tūdeh Party by claiming that the Bank had been employed by the Iranian government itself.[13] Thus, for the sake of a few empty words, and the 'reputation' of a few men, the survival and progress of the Iranian Popular Movement were put in great jeopardy. The Tūdeh Party would have tried to make capital out of *any* agreement, *whatever* its form and content; but the Iranian public was more intelligent, and certainly more loyal to Muṣaddiq, than his close advisers believed them to be. There can be no defence for the Tūdeh Party's hysterical and immoral tactics against Muṣaddiq. But there must be fairness in an objective analysis: Muṣaddiq and his close advisers must also take their share of the responsibility for their decision. The Bank could not possibly have agreed to the insertion of those useless little words, because, as an *intermediary*, it could not claim to be acting 'on behalf of' either side to the dispute! The rejection of the Bank's proposal was regarded as unreasonable by the American government, which, as a result, turned down an Iranian application for financial aid. This latest blow to Muṣaddiq's hopes fell almost on the first anniversary of the Nationalisation Act; there had been no real progress in a year of high hopes and great sacrifices, and there was none in sight.

On 28 May, Muṣaddiq led a delegation to the Hague to open the Iranian case before the International Court. Early in July, he was reinstated as Prime Minister by the new *Majlis*, with a reduced majority. Ten days later, however, he resigned his office because of the Shah's refusal to give up his conventional, but unconstitutional, active command of the armed forces. Aḥmad Qavām – the strong conservative, but independent, politician – became Prime Minister, and in a tactless speech written by Muvarrikh al-Dawleh (Sepehr), a lesser light among his private entourage, he threatened 'the mob' with arrests and executions.[14] The people smelled a counter-revolution; and pro-Muṣaddiq deputies (who had staged a sit-in in the *Majlis*), together with Kāshānī and the pro-Muṣaddiq parties, called a general strike for 21 July (30 Tīr, Persian calendar). In fact, the people's response was spontaneous, and – at the cost of many lives and many more casualties – they fought tanks and bayonets with bricks, stones and bare hands. Qavām was ill in bed, and until early that afternoon he had neither quite understood the gravity of the situation, nor had become conscious of the trap into which 'that brazen young man' (as he himself had once described the Shah) had led him. This was when Ḥusain 'Alā, the polite as well as timid Minister of the Imperial Court, paid him a visit with a message from His Majesty (who by then had become frightened at the scale of the people's revolt), suggesting that he should perhaps step down, 'in the interest of the country'. Qavām listened in silence, and, as soon as 'Alā had finished delivering the Shah's message, he said, in his booming voice, 'His Majesty can go to hell' ("Alāḥażrat guh khurdand'). A few hours later, Qavām resigned office and left home for an unknown destination. This was total triumph for the people, who received the news of Muṣaddiq's return to office, and Iran's success at The Hague, almost simultaneously: the International Court had accepted Iran's argument that the court had no jurisdiction in the Anglo-Iranian oil dispute.

Between August 1952 and March 1953 Iran broke diplomatic relations with Britain; Muṣaddiq lost the support of a few of his associates, the most formidable of whom were Kāshānī and Baqā'ī (none of these, incidentally, was a British or American agent!); the Tūdeh Party shifted its position *tactically*, from downright abuse and libel of the government to unconstructive opposition; in America, Eisenhower and Dulles took over the government, as had Churchill and Eden a year earlier in Britain; the socio-economic situation further deteriorated; the Shah, his clientele and the conservative opposition tightened their resolve to overthrow Muṣaddiq; and the Iranian people frequently took to the streets shouting, 'Death or Muṣaddiq!', but in declining numbers. There were various domestic centres of anti-Muṣaddiq conspiracy, of which the Imperial Court (including the Shah's mother, and his sister Ashraf) and the newly founded Retired (Army) Officers' Association were the most active. Muṣaddiq forced the Shah's mother and sister into exile, but Ashraf went on visiting the country in disguise.

On 28 February 1953 a plot against Muṣaddiq was put into operation by the Shah and a group of conservative politicians and religious leaders. A few days earlier the Shah had informed Muṣaddiq of his decision to go abroad for two months (on a 'pilgrimage' to the holy shrines in Iraq, followed by a visit to Europe for 'medical' purposes), to which the Prime Minister had reluctantly consented. Yet, in spite of previous agreement, the Shah 'leaked' this news to some influential personalities, especially Sayyed Muhammad (Āyatullah) Behbahānī, a powerful *mujtahid* in Teheran.[15] A band of common hirelings and petty criminals, led by the infamous Sha'bān Bīmukh (Sha'bān the Brainless), was organised, and gathered outside the royal palace ostensibly to try to dissuade the Shah from leaving, but in fact in order to assassinate Muṣaddiq, who had been summoned by the Shah for an official 'farewell'. Muṣaddiq managed to escape through a rear gate. The crowd was quickly informed that 'the bird had flown', and immediately went to Muṣaddiq's home, near the palace: they tried to break down its iron gate by driving a jeep against it, but Muṣaddiq had left his home through the roof, and the crowd was attacked both by the Prime Minister's guards from within, and by the people from outside the house. The conspiracy had failed, and, by Muṣaddiq's own acknowledgement, members of the Third Force Party, led by the writer Jalāl Āl-i Aḥmad, played a crucial role in winning the day against the conspirators. However, the failure of the plot forced the Shah to agree to return to the government the extensive rural property that had been usurped by his father, and put back into the Shah's 'care' in 1949 (see Ch. 8).

Meanwhile, the American government had swung to the British position that there could be no deal with Muṣaddiq, whose last desperate request for financial aid was declined by the president. Between March and August 1953, the government simply lost its *raison d'être*: there was nothing to do except keep a watch on potential conspiracies and *coup d'états*. In fact, conspiracies abounded, and the *Majlis* opposition was growing in strength and hostility. On 20 April 1953, Brigadier Afshār-Tūs, the strong but infamous Prefect-General of the police, was kidnapped. A few days later, his body, bearing torture marks, was discovered in a mountain cave near the capital, and a number of disaffected politicians and retired generals were arrested and charged with the crime. Dr Baqā'ī was directly incriminated but, having parliamentary immunity, could not be arrested. The plot was never fully uncovered, because after the *coup d'état* in August the charges were quietly dropped and the case was closed! It is certain that this was only the first of a number of planned abductions and assassinations, in order to force the government to resign. There is circumstantial evidence that not only those publicly charged were involved in the plot, but that the Shah's ruthless brother, Alīreżā, had been the chief conspirator.[16] The Shah himself may have been involved, but, in any case, Alīreżā may have had private designs of his own: the fact that, two years later, his light plane mysteriously crashed in the Māzandarān mountains may not be irrelevant to this case.

On 3 August, Muṣaddiq held a referendum to close the *Majlis* and hold fresh elections. The immediate reason for this was the threat of a censure motion against the government for its unauthorised expansion of the paper money supply; the long-term reason was the threat of further defections which would destroy the government majority in the *Majlis*. The referendum was not consistent with the letter of the Constitution, and it was not conducted in a free and open atmosphere. In any event, it was a tactical mistake and had been opposed by most of Muṣaddiq's senior advisers and supporters – including Khalīl Malekī, Dr Ali Shāigān and Dr Karīm Sanjābī. The *Majlis* was the only organ of the state that still backed Muṣaddiq; without it, he would (and did) lose the rallying point which had been instrumental in the spontaneous uprising of the people in July 1952.

The closure of the *Majlis* provided the conspirators – the Shah, the CIA, the Retired Officers' Association, and the conservative opposition – with an easy method of carrying out their impending coup. On the evening of 15 August a number of leading politicians, including Dr Ḥusain Fāṭemī (the Foreign Minister), were kidnapped from their homes and held at the royal palace. Late that night, the commander of the Imperial Guards, Lt-Col. Naṣīrī (the future SAVAK chief), delivered a royal *farmān*, signed by the Shah, who was 'resting' in a Caspian resort, to the Prime Minister, dismissing him and appointing retired General Fażallulah Zāhedī to the premiership. From the technical constitutional point of view it is not clear whether or not the Shah had the right to issue such a *farmān* in the absence of the *Majlis*; but the government had already smelled a coup, which it had every constitutional right to defeat: Naṣīrī was arrested, the Imperial Guards were disarmed, the prisoners freed from their royal cage, and the Shah – having been warned of the failure – took off for Baghdad and, later, Rome. The news of the coup and its failure resulted in uncontrolled euphoria, jubilant riotings, and public (though not official) demands for the abolition of the monarchy. This by itself did not cause the implementation of the fall-back plan which the conspirators had designed in case of the failure of their first attempt. But the chaos, confusion, sense of insecurity, and fear of anarchy, or an imminent 'Bolshevik' take-over, which it spread among the ordinary public, were one reason for the lack of a spontaneous revolt against the coup-makers during their second attempt, or immediately after its success.

On 19 August 1953 (28 Murdād 1332, Persian calendar) the fall-back plan was put into operation. It involved an open revolt by a section of the army, and a large group of paid rioters led by well-known mobsters and racketeers such as Sha'bān the Brainless and Ṭayyeb, the chief protection-money collector of the Teheran wholesale fruit and vegetable market. The mob had been organised mainly by leading conservative religious dignitaries, such as Sayyed Muhammad (Āyatulla) Behbahānī and Mīrzā 'Abdullah (Āyatullah) Chelsutūnī. The public was stunned and stood by; the loyal political parties could not do much because, by a stroke of misfortune, Muṣaddiq had asked them to send their members home that day, in the hope of curbing the disorganised riotings of the previous days; the Tūdeh Party was the only force which had the civilian and the military means to intervene, but – for reasons which it has not yet adequately explained – it remained neutral. By the evening of that day, Muṣaddiq's home had been captured and looted, in spite of the heroic resistance of his official guards, led by Colonel Mumtāz. He himself had been *forcibly* carried to safety by a handful of close friends. The new government, led by Zāhedī, made a public statement, declared martial law, and imposed a public curfew starting from 8 p.m. that night.

Thus – through the combined onslaught of the conservative, despotic and totalitarian anti-democratic forces, direct foreign intervention, and errors of judgement by the movement's leaders – ended a historic movement for sovereignty and democracy.

The Failure of the Popular Movement: A Brief Autopsy

The failure of the popular democratic movement, which was founded, led and symbolised by Muṣaddiq himself, was a blow to the Iranian political economy from which it would still take years to recover. It was not simply a defeat over the nationalisation of Iranian oil: it was a historic catastrophe concerning the social, political, and economic fate of the Iranian people; it robbed the Iranians of the hope of external sovereignty and internal democracy, which were, and still remain, inseparable national ideals; and it prepared the way for the resurgence of despotism in the most destructive and hideous form Iran has ever experienced. The question is, why?

To begin with, let us dispense with the most popular, and least acceptable, explanations of the failure – that is, foreign conspiracies in alliance with the domestic conservative and despotic forces. The facts of the matter are not in dispute: these foreign and domestic forces did everything in their power to destroy the Iranian Popular Movement, and they finally succeeded. But this was entirely expected of them: it was clearly in keeping with their various interests to prevent Iran's assertion of full sovereignty, and her development into a democratic society. This argument can be put in an alternative way: to claim that the basic causes of the movement's failure lay outside the movement itself, would mean that *in any case* the movement had been doomed to failure; that its failure was absolutely inevitable; that its foreign and domestic enemies were so powerful as to prevent its success in any and all circumstances. But this is incorrect: it flies in the face of the facts; it leaves nothing for the art of leadership, and the will of the people; it is a recipe for inaction and/or surrender before 'the forces of imperialism and their lackeys'! The enemies of the movement fought tooth and nail against it; but there is no reason why it could not have won the war in spite of them. The same goes for the role of the Tūdeh Party: politically, there can be no justification whatever – only repentance – for its destructive role, which reinforced those of the other domestic and foreign enemies of the movement; analytically, no better role could have been expected from a Stalinist party led by men of few principles. But its destructive opposition merely made the movement's failure more likely; it did not make it inevitable.

The question we must ask of ourselves is this: what could have been done by the movement and its leadership to ensure the long-term success of the Iranian people and their political economy? The answer is, it should have come to an honourable solution over the oil dispute, and immediately proceeded to carry out the basic political and economic reforms in order to raise the people's standard of living, isolate and defeat the conservative minority, and uproot the age-old Iranian despotism once and for all. Curiously enough, after many years of simply blaming the failure on 'imperialism and its lackeys', the more enlightened Iranian analysts *now* put some emphasis on the movement's lack of a positive programme. That is, they emphasise the fact that, in more than two and a half years of his government, Muṣaddiq did not carry out a major social reform. Yet, when it comes to the issue of the oil dispute, these same analysts proudly declare the government's failure to settle the problem as its greatest achievement, and the clearest evidence for Muṣaddiq's popular anti-imperialism! Romantic idealism is a very safe, but entirely unproductive, position. It is a disease which still bedevils the community of progressive intellectuals in Iran and elsewhere, and plays havoc with the hopes and prospects of the peoples in whose name they parade their arid piety.

It would have been impossible to carry out *any* serious reform prior to the settlement of the oil dispute: the oil revenues, both as the main source of government finance and as the main source of foreign exchange, had vanished; the economy was *in decline*, and this reduced other government revenues (from taxes and the like) even further; the government was so poor that it had to postpone salary payments to the state bureaucracy, borrow from the public, and print paper money; it simply lacked the finance which it needed for running the daily affairs of the country, let alone for meeting the costs of any major reform; and any such attempt would have resulted in a full-scale, countrywide confrontation with powerful domestic vested interests, backed by foreign powers, that – in the face of all the other outstanding problems – the movement would most probably lose.[17]

To say that there should have been a settlement of the oil dispute is by itself not a very original idea: there were many conservative elements (not necessarily 'imperialist lackeys') who from the very beginning urged Muṣaddiq to make a deal. But in so doing they missed the broader, much more important dimensions of the Iranian Popular Movement. For them, the whole question hinged on a better deal, and 'more money', for the Iranian political economy; while Muṣaddiq, and the people behind him, regarded the oil nationalisation as a first step towards the democratic transformation of Iranian society. That is why from the early 1940s Muṣaddiq himself had never ceased to emphasise the wider political significance of the oil issue, rather than its narrower economic implications (which he too, unfortunately, at times underrated). Indeed, there was a coincidence of opinion between these conservative 'realists' and the aforementioned romantic idealists which they themselves were unlikely to realise: both groups regarded the oil nationalisation as an end in itself, even though their motives for so doing were very different. For the conservatives, everything else had to be sacrificed for a quick settlement and 'more money'; for the romantics, everything else had to be sacrificed for a lack of settlement, for the empty boast that the movement and its leader did not yield an inch to the enemy on a strategic issue, even at the cost of the annihilation of the movement itself, and its devastating consequences for the Iranian people, their society and their political economy.

The oil nationalisation was only one strategy in a war for sovereignty and democracy: it was a major means to a greater end. For this reason, Muṣaddiq should have obtained the best *possible* terms from a position of strength, and settled the question, disregarding the reaction of romantic idealists, Stalinist slanderers, and the spineless demogogues in his own entourage, all of whom by their very nature would have come into line with the socio-political success which would have followed such a settlement: the British government would at least temporarily have suspended its operations against Muṣaddiq; the Shah and the conservatives would have been rendered defenceless; the inflow of oil revenues, used by an incorruptible and democratic government, would have increased the level *and* the spread of socio-economic prosperity; major social and economic reforms would have become both possible and irresistible; and, finally, all these developments would have made it easy to move towards a complete, even ideal, rectification of Iran's oil interests within a few years. We appeal to the intelligence and the social conscience of the most puritanical anti-imperialist Iranians to tell us whether or not this sequence of events would not have been preferable to the irreparable damage that the movement's failure caused to the Iranian political economy.

Khalīl Malekī was the only man – both then, and for a long time afterwards – who held this comprehensive vision of how things ought to move. But he held no public office – not even membership of the *Majlis*; he was constantly libelled by the Tūdeh Party as a British spy; he lacked systematic access to Muṣaddiq; and he was childishly envied for his brilliance by some lesser mortals who were closer to the great man. Therefore, Muṣaddiq had to rely on his own personal judgement, and the advice and information given to him by well-meaning men, most (though not all) of whom lacked either courage or judgement or ability – or all of these put together. This is not intended to clear Muṣaddiq himself of all responsibility for this fateful mistake. Rather, it is meant to analyse his position with realism and understanding, and, more significantly, to bring out the implications of this tragic lesson for the present position and the future prospects of Iran: after the lapse of twenty-five years of *un*history, and a great revolution that, at the time of writing (March 1979), has overthrown the Shah's despotism, *all* those forces that had led to the defeat of the Popular Movement are back in a state of flux: romantic idealism, traditionalist conservatism, left-wing modernism, *and* the battered, but surviving, institutions of despotism and foreign interventionism. It is to be hoped that for once, after centuries, the dialectic of Iranian history will yield a progressive synthesis.

Appendix: Some Notes on the Oil Dispute and the Economic Situation

A Note on the 'Economics' of the Oil Dispute

We have emphasised the *political* significance of the oil dispute from the viewpoint of the Popular Movement. Yet, not only was the economic aspect of the dispute important in its own right, but it was also the most tangible argument that could be used in defending the case of Iran. Table 9.1 is a

TABLE 9.1 AIOC income and expenditure, 1948

	£m.	*% of total*
Net income (gross of tax payments)	79	100.0
Taxes paid to the British Government	28	35.5
Capital investment, retained profits, etc.	34	43.1
Dividends, etc. (paid to British and other non-Iranian shareholders)	7	8.7
Revenues paid to the Iranian government	10	12.7

Source: based on the AIOC's published accounts, quoted by Muṣaddiq as chairman of the *Majlis* Special Commission for Oil, 17 Oct 1950.

rearrangement and extension of the AIOC's published accounts for 1948. After the failure of the Stokes mission, Muṣaddiq, in an official address to the nation, produced figures for the whole of the 1933–49 period consistent with the company's figures shown in Table 9.1 for 1948. However, from the text of Muṣaddiq's address, it looks as if not even he himself had quite realised how damning these data were for the AIOC. His basic figures have been rearranged and extended in Table 9.2, from which the following observations may be made.

TABLE 9.2 AIOC income and expenditure: total, 1933—49

	£m.	*% of total*	*% of net profit*
Net *income*	895	100.0	—
Taxes paid to the British Government	175	19.5	—
Net *profit* (net income minus taxes)	720	81.5	100.0
Capital investment, retained profits, etc.	500	55.8	69.4
Dividends, etc. (paid to British and other non-Iranian shareholders)	115	12.8	16.0
Revenues paid to the Iranian government	105	11.9	14.6

Source: based on the figures in Muṣaddiq's 'Message to the People of Iran', in *Iṭṭilā'āt*, 30 Aug 1951.

First, the revenues paid to Iran were only 11.9 per cent of the total net income (gross of tax payments) of the company. Secondly, this was appreciably less than the 19.5 per cent in *taxes* which the company paid to the British government, which itself had the controlling share in the company. Thirdly, it was also less than the 12.8 per cent in payments to the company's shareholders, of whom the British government was the biggest. Fourthly, 55.8 per cent of the total had been retained for investment and the like, or held as undistributed profits. Fifthly, Iran's share in the company's net *profits* (i.e. even excluding tax payments to the British government) was only 14.6 per cent, when even under the D'Arcy concession of 1903 the Iranians had been entitled to 16 per cent of the company's net profits.

Therefore, under the 1933 Agreement, which had extended the period of concession for another thirty-three years, the Iranians were receiving – from a British company, controlled by the British government, paying its taxes to the British government, financing its investment from the sales of *Iranian* oil, and paying dividends to British 'shareholders' – only 11.9 per cent of the proceeds of their own oil. In other words, the resource was Iranian, the capital investment and other costs (except the initial historical costs) were met from the sale of this Iranian resource, and over 88 per cent of the income was paid out to (or retained by) Britons.

A Note on the Economic Situation

The economic plight of the country – owing to the British oil blockade, the American refusal to grant financial aid, the Soviet government's refusal to repay its wartime debts to Iran, the political instability, and so forth – should by now be quite familiar to the reader. This is the sort of situation which would normally topple any government within a short period of time. Yet the reader may be surprised to learn (a) the realism and relative efficiency with which the government tried to meet the situation, and (b) the degree to which the people were prepared to put up with material hardship for the sake of greater social objectives. The government was especially successful in the field of foreign trade, managing to restrict imports without cutting them drastically, and, at the same time, mounting a great effort to boost the country's *non-oil* exports. As a result, Iran even managed to accumulate a trade surplus on its non-oil trade account, which, in the second and last year of Muṣaddiq's premiership, even became substantial. Table 9.3 presents the non-oil trade figures for the period 1948–53, enabling readers to compare figures for the country's performance prior to and under Muṣaddiq. In Chapter 10 it will be seen that the Shah's dictatorship turned Iran's balance of trade into a growing deficit, in spite of the rapidly growing oil revenues; and put her balance of payments, too, into deficit, in spite of substantial American and other grants, loans and investment.

The effort to boost non-oil exports was particularly successful in the field of carpets: in 1952 the value of exports of carpets was 1339 million rials, or twice what it had been two years before. Apart from that, the government resorted to the exportation of products, such as live sheep (to Saudi Arabia) and tobacco (to Russia), that were not usually exported in great quantities. This

TABLE 9.3 The non-oil balance of trade, 1948–53 (million rials)

Year	(1) *Exports (excluding oil)*	(2) *Imports*	(3) *Balance* (1) – (2)
1948	1867	5480	–3613
1949	1785	9320	–7535
1950	3563	7109	–3546
1951	4391	7405	–3014
1952	5832	5206	+626
1953	8426	5756	+2670

Source: based on Vizārat-i Iqtiṣād, *Āmār-i Bāzargānī-yi Khārijī Iran* (official foreign trade statistics from Ministry of the Economy) 1966.

meant that the Iranians themselves had to consume less of their own products than they were used to. But the game could be played both because the government was not corrupt, and because the people were ready to co-operate: for example, early in 1952 the government avoided the threat of a big increase in mutton prices by an efficient operation to distribute large amounts of fresh Caspian fish, the production of which had recently been taken out of Soviet hands (as their long-standing concession for exploiting Iranian Caspian fish had lapsed, and had not been renewed by the Iranian government). All this is evidence that a lot can be achieved in the right socio-political atmosphere, even in spite of great financial and economic scarcities and deprivations – just as later chapters will show how great damage can be caused, in the wrong socio-political system, even in spite of great financial and economic abundance and opportunities. However, it is clear that all these efforts could not possibly succeed *in the long run*, and the government itself knew (though, unfortunately, it did not act accordingly) that everything depended on an honourable settlement of the oil dispute. Yet, in 1953 Muṣaddiq decided to increase the money supply, in order to expand domestic economic activity, but withheld the information in order to prevent speculation in trade. This was a kind of 'Keynesian' policy and, in the special circumstances of the time, it even made 'pure' economic sense: aggregate demand had been artifically reduced to a significantly lower level than the country's domestic production capacity.There was, therefore, demand-deficiency unemployment of resources, which could be reduced by monetary expansion. It was this confidential printing of money which the *Majlis* opposition seized as a pretext for calling a censure motion against the government, and which resulted in Muṣaddiq's tactical mistake to hold a referendum for the closure of the *Majlis* in August 1953, two weeks before the coup.

NOTES

1. See further below for an analysis of the causes of the movement's failure.
2. For a single example, see *Nashrīyeh-yi Ta'līmātī. . .* (internal party publication) no.12 (1951).
3. Apart from the hostile attitude of Britain, Russia, the Tūdeh Party and the Iranian conservatives towards the movement, what would support such a hypothesis in this case (as it would not in Razmārā's) is the fact that (a) the Americans were not prepared to support Britain in the first year, and hesitated even afterwards; (b) the Soviet Union and the Tūdeh Party regarded Muṣaddiq as an 'American agent'; and (c) the Soviet Union, for strategic considerations and regardless of the implications for the Iranian people, preferred, of any two possible Iranian régimes, the one less dependent on American support. That is partly why it snubbed Muṣaddiq but came to an understanding with the Shah in the 1950s; and why it attacked Amīnī, but came to terms with the Shah in the 1960s (see Chs 10 and 11, below).
4. A casual survey of the British press as well as parliamentary debates in the period would quickly prove this point. For an elaborate discussion of the subject, see

Hamid Enayat, 'The British Public Opinion and the Persian Oil Crisis' (an extended and unpublished MA dissertation, University of London, 1958).

5. Malekī's originality of thought, and his critical realism in political analysis and application, cannot be exaggerated, and that is the main reason why he was so little understood (let alone appreciated) during his lifetime. For a few examples, see his *Du Ravish Barāy-i Yik Hadaf* (1948), *Barkhurd-i 'Aqāyed u Ārā* (1950), *Nīrūy-i Sevvum Chīst?* (1951), *Nīrūy-i Sevvum Pīrūz Mīshavad* (1951), *Sociālīsm va Kāpītālīsm-i Dawlatī* (1952). See further Chs 11 and 15, below.
6. Muṣaddiq dismissed General Zāhedī, the Minister of the Interior, as well as General Baqā'ī (the Prefect-General of the police), whom a military tribunal later 'cleared' of insubordination. Whether or not some elements in the Tūdeh Party leadership had been privy to a conspiracy, the party played right into the hands of the Shah and his supporters. Strangely enough, ten years later the Shah played a similar game in order to force the resignation of Ali Amīnī, and it is probable that this time some elements in the leadership of the Second National Front, which in any case played into the hands of the plotters, had previous knowledge of the plot. See further Ch.11, below.
7. See *Nuṭqhā va Maktūbāt-i Duktur Muṣaddiq . . .*, vol. II, book 1 (? Paris: Intishārāt-i Muṣaddiq, 1969) esp. pp 41–70.
8. Ibid.
9. Ibid., pp.64 and 69–70.
10. See, for example, Khalīl Malekī, *Nīrūy-i Sevvum Chīst?* (Teheran: Hizb-i Zaḥmatkishān, 1951).Muṣaddiq himself admitted this fact in a *Majlis* speech in April 1952.
11. See for example, *Nuṭqhā va Maktūbāt-i Duktur Muṣaddiq . . .* , vol. II, book 3 (? Paris; Intishārāt-i Muṣaddiq, 1972).
12. They included the well-intentioned Kāẓim Ḥasībī, who undoubtedly could not see the devastating politiconomic effect, for the Popular Movement, of his proud personal statement, 'We will seal off the oil wells!'.
13. Though their statements to the press, some members of Muṣaddiq's entourage, including Ḥasībī, gave the impression that the main bone of contention had been the World Bank's proposed sale price. No doubt there had been disagreements on such issues, which, in the circumstances, were matters of detail. However, in an address to a group of American journalists in Teheran, Muṣaddiq himself gave three reasons for the lack of agreement: (a) the World Bank's insistence on the return of 'the British technicians' – this is something that had been expressly acceptable to Muṣaddiq as long as it did not involve high-level British management; (b) the Bank's refusal of Iran's demand to declare itself to be 'acting on behalf of the Iranian government'; and (c) the Bank's proposal to apply the Persian Gulf price of $1.75 per barrel, as against the Mexican Gulf price of $2.75. But the Persian Gulf price too had already been accepted by Muṣaddiq in his earlier negotiations with Stokes. There can be no doubt at all, not only on the basis of this and other evidence, but according to the recollections of those closely involved (whose names I am not at liberty to divulge) that failure to reach an agreement with Bank was mainly due to point (b) above. See *Nutqhā va Maktūbāt*, vol. II, book 3, pp. 74–82.
14. Yet the most fatal part of that speech was probably the following: 'As weary as I am of demagogy in politics, I also loathe hypocrisy and duplicity in religious matters . . . . While I will respect the sacred teachings of Islam, I will keep religion apart from politics, and I will prevent the spread of superstition, and retrogressive ideas.' Kāshanī's response to this speech was suitably damning: 'Aḥmad Qavām must realise . . . that he should not officially threaten the stifling of thoughts and ideas,

and the mass execution of the people, I declare, unambiguously, that it is the duty of all Muslim brothers to set out for this great crusade (jahād-i akbar]. See *Kayhān* (daily newspaper), 18 July 1952, for the text of both statements.

15. Kāshānı (who was the *Majlis* president at the time) also wrote a letter of support to the Shah, in his own hand, declaring that the Shah's presence was much needed in the country. This was generally unknown, and it was revealed in Iran after this chapter had been finally drafted. See *Parkhāsh* (weekly newspaper), 4 July 1979.
16. A series of recent 'revelations' on this case in various issues of the weekly magazine *Umīd-i Irān* 1979 have typically led to greater confusion rather than the clarification of the problem.
17. It must be pointed out, however, that in the field of administrative, judicial, and other reforms, the record of the democratic government is (in spite of the difficulties it had to endure) impressive. For the detailed reports to the *Majlis* of the activities of various government departments (reports otherwise unparalleled in Iranian history), see *Nuṭqhā va Maktūbat-i Duktur Muṣaddiq* . . ., vol. II, book 2 (? Paris; Intishārāt-i Muṣaddiq, 1970). Furthermore, in 1953 Muṣaddiq enacted a law which compelled Iranian landlords to pay 10 per cent of *their* share of the agricultural output back to the peasantry, and a further 10 per cent into a public fund for rural development. This had had a precedent in Aḥmad Qavām (al-Salṭaneh)'s legislation during his 1946 government for a 15 per cent contribution from the landlords' share of output to the peasants' income. Muṣaddiq's act was, however, effectively destroyed by the post-coup régime (see 10 and 11, below). On the state of the economy and economic policy, see further 'A Note on the Economic Situation' in the appendix to this chapter.

10 Political Dictatorship and Economic 'Liberalism', 1953–61

The Tenuous Alliance

The *coup d'état* of August 1953 was won too easily: with the Shah on the run, the army loosely divided between 'pro-Shah' and 'pro-Muṣaddiq' factions, and with a well-organised and well-placed Tūdeh Party network inside it, the existence of relatively large political parties, the overall control of the administrative apparatus by the government, and so on, it is not only surprising that the insurgents gained control within a single day; it is even more strange that they succeeded in stabilising their position, and in normalising the political economy, in the course of a few months. How was this possible? This question may be tackled on two inter-related levels: (a) the role of groups, organisations and personalities; and (b) the socio-economic situation and its subtle impact on the attitude of the people, and their various social classes.

GROUPS, ORGANISATIONS, ETC.

Let us first examine the means and ends of the insurgents. The means are simple and well-known: the organisational technique was provided by the CIA; the finance, by the American government, through Roy Henderson, its ambassador in Iran; the forces, partly by the army and police factions loyal to the Shah, and partly by the *Lumpen* element within the community of ordinary people (though it must be emphasised that the Iranian *Lumpen* element is not simply a shapeless and transitory '*Lumpen* proletariat' *à la* Marx: it is, and has always been, an integral part of communal life among the urban masses, with significant social functions, for both good and evil).

The motives, aims and objectives of the coup-makers, however, varied according to the particular foreign and local forces they represented. The American and British stake is rather obvious; but it is likely that the American attitude was determined primarily by global political, rather than local economic, considerations, even though the latter must have added force to the former. The Shah and the hard-core pseudo-nationalist men around him are symbolic of the traditional despotic force, which at this time was extremely weak and largely dependent on other – foreign and Iranian – forces, both for finance and for manpower. In fact, the most powerful Iranian force behind the coup came from the ranks of conservative political and religious groups: without their active support, it would have been very difficult for the coup to succeed, and impossible for the succeeding régime to establish its power and authority without a major challenge. These conservative forces were principally made up of landlords, old-school politicians, a powerful faction among the *'ulamā*, their retainers, religious followers and personal adherents, and the enclave of big merchants, who had at least one foot out of the traditional *bāzār*, in the emerging modern import–export sector. There were also many individuals who would not exactly fall within any of the above social groups, but in general it was this combination which provided the active conservative support for the coup.

THE SOCIO-ECONOMIC ROOTS

The last chapter ended with an outline of the general economic situation of the country in the latter half of Muṣaddiq's premiership: the stoppage of oil extraction and refining had led, both directly and indirectly, to a drastic decline in public revenues and foreign exchange, which severely depressed the rest of the economy through the multiplier effect, and – with no prospects of a solution in sight – greatly reduced economic confidence among the business community. The First (seven-year) Plan – of which more below – had become no more than a dead letter; poverty, even begging in the streets, had increased, and the unemployment of school-leavers and university graduates was becoming a serious problem. Meanwhile, the country was shaking with political fever – ranging from daily street demonstrations and violence, to political conspiracies and organised agitation – which was both a cause and a consequence of economic instability and depression. This complex state of socio-economic depression and uncertainty rapidly persuaded the conservative forces to commit themselves to the overthrow of the government. The conservatives had never been happy with Muṣaddiq's democratic approach to politics; but Muṣaddiq had not taken any major step against their economic interests (which, without the prior settlement of the oil dispute, could have been counter-productive). In fact, in the earlier periods of the movement, the radical conservatives had supported Muṣaddiq, the moderate conservatives had vacillated, and only the diehard reactionaries had consistently opposed him. Therefore, the later consolidation of the conservative forces, and its alliance with the despotic nucleus and their foreign contacts, was the result not of Muṣaddiq's strength but of the growing weakness of his government. The conservatives were particularly scared that – with or without Soviet interference – the Tūdeh Party would seize power. It is not insignificant that Falsafī, an able and well-connected religious preacher, lost no opportunity, both before and after the coup, to claim that the Tūdeh Party rallies were beginning to attract larger crowds than those in support of Muṣaddiq. The three conservative factions described above may be identified, briefly and symbolically, in the following way: the radical, anti-imperialist conservatives, symbolised by religious leaders such as Āyatullah Kāshānī, and politicians such as Hāyerīzādeh and Makkī, had for some time actively supported the Popular Movement, but in the end either acquiesced in the coup, or remained indifferent towards it; the centrist conservatives, symbolised by some religious leaders in Qum, and such politicians as Ḥusain 'Alā, had been critical of, though not actively opposed, to Muṣaddiq until September 1951; and the authoritarian conservatives, symbolised by religious leaders such as Āyatullah Behbahānī, and politicians such as Jamāl Imāmī, had actively opposed Muṣaddiq by various means almost from the start. The latter two factions made up the main basis of conservative support for the coup and the régime which it established. It is unlikely that all or any of those involved in this conservative combination were paid agents of imperialism, in whose interests alone they were intervening; rather, it is much more probable that – especially in the circumstances of the Cold War – they saw no other option but to rely on either the East or the West, and it is hardly surprising that they chose the latter. Principally, however, they must have been spurred on by a determination to defend their economic, social, political and religious interests, and, perhaps, their very existence as social and cultural entities.

A note of qualification before concluding this section: there were still some radical religious leaders, preachers and activists who remained totally committed to the cause of the Iranian Popular Movement at all times: prominent among these were Āyatullah Zanjānī and Sayyed Maḥmūd (now Āyatullah) Ṭāliqānī. But it is certain that religious *power* as a whole either acquiesced or was directly involved in the coup and its aftermath.

THE IMMEDIATE CAUSES OF DEFEAT

The *long-term* causes of the failure of the Popular Movement have already been briefly discussed. It would now be appropriate to add a few comments on the *immediate* reasons for the rapid victory of the insurgents and the lack of a major challenge from the opposition, once they had had time to regain their composure. It is true that the second and final coup (of 19 August) came as a complete surprise to the government. Indeed, on the previous day, Muṣaddiq had personally asked the Popular Movement parties – the Third Force, the Iran Nation (a splinter faction of the Pān-Iranīst) and Iran parties – to keep their members and supporters off the streets on 19 August, because the government wished to reassure the ordinary public that it was still in command of the situation. Consequently, the headquarters of these parties were empty of most of their activists; and they were attacked and captured before they could organise resistance. It is just possible that these political parties – and especially the Third Force Party, which was by far the strongest in terms of membership and organisational ability – would otherwise have been able to put up serious resistance, and get the people out on the streets; something like the role which it had played in the 9 Isfand (28 February) conspiracy, although this time the enemy was much more powerful and better organised.

Muṣaddiq has sometimes been criticised for not distributing weapons among the public to rise against the insurgents. But anyone with some sense of realism will recognise that such a move would have been impossible: such a decision, and especially its implementation, had already been forestalled by the swift turn of fortunes. If there can be any such criticism, it must be referred to his earlier refusal – after the 9 Isfand Conspiracy – to help organise a popular militia, as had been suggested by Khalīl Malekī and the Third Force Party. But perhaps his reasons for this refusal are clear, even though some may disagree with them.

Another question is why there was no spontaneous uprising along the lines of the 30 Tīr (21 July) struggle over a year earlier. There are several reasons for this, of which the following are the most important: the 30 Tīr uprising took place at a time when the political economy was in a better state, and there were still great hopes for a successful settlement of the oil dispute; the *Majlis* was in session, and the Popular Movement deputies staged a sit-in inside it in protest against Qavām's appointment to the premiership, thereby providing a strong rallying point for the demonstrators; the political parties of the Popular Movement had had time to organise and lead the demonstrations; the radical conservatives – both religious and 'lay' – were still behind Muṣaddiq and the Popular Movement; and, finally, there was no direct and active foreign involvement in that episode, as there was in the 28 Murdād (19th August) coup.

There remains a puzzle which has not yet been resolved: why did the Tūdeh Party remain inactive in spite of its large and disciplined civilian organisation, and – especially – its strong and extensive secret military network, which included 600 of the most able and intelligent (both junior and senior) army officers? It too may have been caught napping, even though it had been crying wolf about an imminent coup almost daily since the 9 Isfand incident. But the Tūdeh leaders claim that on that fateful afternoon they contacted Muṣaddiq by telephone, and he told them that his house had been encircled and that they were free to take their own decisions.[1] It is not unlikely that the party leaders decided to watch the events of that day, and take a definite stand after they had carefully studied the emerging situation from the point of view of the party's own interests, which did not exactly coincide with the interests of the Popular Movement. After all, they had done this at least once before, in the case of the 30 Tīr uprising. Yet it is astonishing that for a long time afterwards they simply sat back and allowed the consolidation of the Shah–Zāhedī régime (as it was known at the time) and, what is more, the active destruction of their entire party apparatus in Iran at the hands of the new régime: their civilian and, later, military organisations, which had survived intact and in full operation, were torn apart – piece by piece – by a ruthless and savage oppression, and the party leaders did nothing but further demoralise their membership by talking about an 'imminent' uprising – at times, even giving dates, but cancelling them at the eleventh hour![2]

A full explanation of this bizarre behaviour is surely not as simple as both the party leadership and their critics (in and out of the party) have normally made it out to be. But the answer must be sought in a combination of the leadership's habitual ease in coming to terms with conservative, rather than democratic, forces; the attitude of the Soviet Union, especially once the Shah–Zāhedī régime had become established; and the character of the individuals in control of the party. Whatever else they may or may not have been, the leaders of the Tūdeh Party were no revolutionaries.

The Shah-Zāhedī Régime, 1953–5

THE NATURE OF THE RÉGIME

Ordinary people have, at times, an unerring instinct in recognising facts as they are. The régime that took over after the coup had emerged from a broad alliance which justified the common title of the 'Shah–Zāhedī régime'. This can be seen not only from the elements who supported the coup, but also from the resulting Cabinet, the composition of the Eighteenth Session of the *Majlis*, and the general attitude and policies of the Zāhedī government.

The cabinet was headed by Zāhedī himself, who was an able army officer, a conservative politician and, in general, the kind of person who may make a good ally but a bad servant: he had already been a prominent officer before Reżā Khān's enthronement; and he had played a leading role both in the arrest of Shaikh Khaz'al and in the defeat of the Kurdish rebel leader Ismā'il Āqā Simītqū before 1926. In 1941, as the military governor of Isfahan, he had been arrested and banished to Palestine by the British occupying forces, because of his secret contacts with German agents. He had even been Minister of the Interior in Muṣaddiq's first cabinet, although not for long. The Finance Minister in Zāhedī's cabinet was Dr Ali Amīnī, grandson of a Qajar king and a Qajar prime minister, a big landlord, and an able and strongly willed politician who had also served in one of Muṣaddiq's cabinets. Others were a mixture of old-school politicians and important army generals.

The election to the Eighteenth *Majlis* was, of course, not free. It was impossible for any of Muṣaddiq's supporters, let alone the Tūdeh Party, to be elected. It was not even open to political mavericks such as Dr Muẓaffar Baqā'ī, who was not content to be elected without protesting against the state control of the elections. Yet, men such as Hāyerīzādeh, and Muhammad Derakhshish (the anti-Tūdeh, but independent, leader of the teachers' union) were allowed to get into the *Majlis*. And, more significantly, the *Majlis* itself was dominated by influential landlords and other conservatives, primarily seeking their own personal and class interests rather than nurturing His Majesty's private aspirations to total power. This was also largely – though not entirely – true of the Nineteenth *Majlis*, in which individual deputies still carried a lot of weight and influence.

Thus, the 1953 coup did not impose a despotic system: it established a conservative–authoritarian régime. In fact, as we have seen in the foregoing chapters, Iranian despotism is incompatible both with power-sharing of whatever kind, and – at its worst – with any legal or traditional check or balance. It is significant that in their recantation letters the members of the Tūdeh Party, even including the party General Secretary, were made to declare their loyalties not only to the Shah, but also – at times even more emphatically – to the Islamic faith. It is also significant that Falsafī, the able religious preacher, was given a weekly programme on the state radio in which, for many years, he did not merely deliver religious sermons and counsel, but also engaged in biting polemics against 'materialists', Muṣaddiq and the Popular Movement.[3] It was only after the dismissal – and it was a dismissal – of Zāhedī early in 1955 that power began to become gradually concentrated in the hands of the Shah himself, until the chain was broken by the economic and political crisis of 1960–3.

Between 1953 and 1960, the régime that ruled in Iran evolved from a conservative plutocracy towards a more personal dictatorship. It was not despotic in the Iranian sense of that term.

POLITICAL PERSECUTIONS

The coup was followed by wholesale arrests. Muṣaddiq, his cabinet members, and the influential former deputies loyal to him were arrested and imprisoned. Leaders of the Popular Movement parties, such as Khalīl Malekī and Dārīyūsh Furūhar, were likewise thrown into gaol. The unconstitutional practice of trying political prisoners in military tribunals – which became notorious between 1964 and 1978 – dates back to this period. Muṣaddiq himself was tried in an open military court, where he conducted his case with great courage and dignity, as well as political skill: the great parliamentary opposition leader – unmatched in the whole of the *Majlis* history, except by Sayyed Ḥasan Mudarris – had been given a forum suited to his best capacities, and he made the most of it. He declared that he was still the constitutional Prime Minister; he produced documentary evidence that the régime itself regarded the 19 August putsch as a *coup d'état*, not a 'national uprising'; he defended the law and the cause of the popular democratic movement; and he openly attacked British and American imperialism for interfering in the destiny of the Iranian people. He wept, laughed, shouted, went on hunger strike, and – once or twice – fainted. And all that the British and American mass media saw in this heroic as well as skilful conduct by a man of seventy-two was, on the whole, the antics of a broken old fool. The Iranian people, however, saw it in an entirely different light: Muṣaddiq had lost some popular support before the coup, for reasons which we have broadly discussed. But his unfair and illegal trial, and, especially, his conduct both at the trial and in the appeal tribunal won him more support and admiration than he had ever enjoyed. The sentence of three years' solitary confinement was upheld by the military court of appeal. But – and this is once again significant in relation to the nature of the régime – the Supreme Court judges to whom the case was finally referred gave in to state pressure for confirming the conviction, without supporting their decision by legal argument: they gave the show away by declaring that they had reached their decision 'for special reasons'. Shortly afterwards, they lost their jobs.

Dr Ḥusain Fāṭemī – Muṣaddiq's foreign Minister – who held out in hiding for a few months, was found, arrested and attacked and seriously wounded while he was being escorted to gaol by the officers of the martial-law administration. This piece of open lawlessness had been officially contrived – indeed, it almost certainly originated with the Shah himself – and was carried out by the infamous Sha'bān the Brainless. Fāṭemī was later tried *in camera*, condemned to death, and executed by a firing squad. It is certain that his fate in particular had been sealed by the vindictiveness of the Shah, who still remembered Fāṭemī's fiery speeches and articles after his own escape from the country.

Others, such as Dr Shāigān, Dr Ṣadīqī, Kāẓim Ḥasībī and Dr Sanjābī, were given various sentences ranging from ten years (though they were commuted after the first three had been served) to a few months. Many of the partisans and activists of lower rank were also thrown into gaol, although as a rule they were not held for long.

Meanwhile, on 7 December 1953, in an indiscriminate firing on a few hundred demonstrators in the University of Teheran, three students were shot dead. The main centres of peaceful protest in Teheran were the *bāzār* and the University. The *bāzār* community was systematically dealt with, by intimidation and arrest of individual merchants, and indiscriminate sanctions against the lot. The University campus was under army occupation, but students did not stop their occasional hit-and-run (but peaceful) protests. The wanton killing of those three students was certainly premeditated in order to deter the others from further action. Since then, 7 December has been unofficially observed as University Day.

The attack on the Tūdeh Party cadres and members was savage and indiscriminate. There was no heroism from the top echelons of the party; in particular, Dr Bahrāmī, the party General Secretary, capitulated and was released shortly after arrest; and Dr Yazdī, a powerful and wholly cynical member of the leadership, later became a supporter of the Shah, though he spent nearly ten years in prison (the Shah agreed to spare his life largely because of the intervention of Sayyed Żīā Ṭabā-Ṭabā'ī). Many of the first and second ranks of the party leadership had already escaped to eastern Europe, and the few remaining managed to smuggle themselves out. The assault on the party cadres and members led to different reactions: a few of the cadres were quickly converted, joined the régime, and participated in the witch-hunt against their own former comrades; others resisted, suffered torture, were killed – with or without official ceremony – or ended up with long prison terms. Most of the ordinary party members usually wrote a recantation letter and, depending on their previous party positions and records, were released sooner or later. Meantime, the secret party arsenal, press, and so forth, were uncovered and destroyed, one after the other. The biggest blow was the *accidental* discovery and destruction of the party's powerful military network. The callousness of the civilian leadership immediately in charge – and especially Dr Jawdat – provided the best opportunity for the régime to take full advantage of the accidental arrest (in August 1954) of an officer, Captain 'Abbāsī, and uncover the whole of the network in its own good time![4] Only Colonel Khusru Rūzbeh, the able, determined and daring organiser and chief of the network – whose relations with the civilian leadership had been seldom friendly, and deteriorated even further after the coup – gave them the slip, until he was captured and executed, as a result of a betrayal, in 1959. Six hundred officers were arrested and put on trial: twenty-seven of them – including Colonel Mubashshirī, Colonel Sīyāmak and Major 'Aṭārud – were executed by firing squad, and others were given long prison sentences. A few of the latter group defected to the régime – either immediately or some time later – and became members of the SAVAK, the notorious secret police, when this was formally instituted in 1955.

In this period, the executive arm of persecutions and witchhunts was the martial-law administration, headed by Brigadier Taimūr Bakhtīyār and – to a lesser extent – army intelligence. When the SAVAK was formed, Bakhtīyār, – by then promoted a general – became its first chief, and a most powerful, ruthless and hated man in the country.

The Gradual Concentration of Power

THE FALL OF ZĀHEDĪ

In 1955, Zāhedī was politely but firmly dismissed by the Shah, and sent to Switzerland to treat a non-existent illness. There he died, without ever returning to Iran, in the early 1960s. Zāhedī had served the Shah, and the Americans, loyally; and his son Ardishīrrad recently married the Shah's daughter by his first marriage, Princess Shahnāz. The Shah's decision to force him out of office was intended to tighten his own personal grip over the country's affairs. When Zāhedī informed the Cabinet of his impending resignation, he emphasised that this was due to His Majesty's unwarranted anxiety about the state of his health. And, when – on the steps of the aeroplane which took him to Switzerland – he was saying his last farewell to a few personal friends, he ended by saying, 'Poor Dr. Muṣaddiq was right after all'!

Ḥusain 'Alā, the old conservative politician and Minister of the Imperial Court, succeeded Zāhedī for a short period. This was intended to pave the way for the appointment of a more permanent and subservient government, headed by Dr Manūchehr Iqbāl – the first Iranian Prime Minister since 1941 to declare himself publicly as no more than 'the house-born slave of His Majesty'. Zāhedī's 'mission' had been to consolidate the new régime's power, break the Popular Movement, destroy the Tūdeh Party, conclude a new oil agreement, and normalise the political economy. He fulfilled this mission relatively smoothly with the help of American financial and military assistance.

Before the oil began to flow out, and revenues flow in, the American financial injection played a crucial role in pacifying the general public, both by increasing the spending power of the state and by increasing incomes and demand, which was directly beneficial to army officers, bureaucrats and professionals, and indirectly helpful to landlords, merchants and artisans. It was not enough to enrich more than a few; but it was sufficient to restore the standard of living – even though unevenly – of a greater number of urban people, at least to their pre-1952 levels. Besides, it increased business confidence, and created social aspirations and expectations: within two years, the University of Teheran and a few smaller universities and further-education colleges – which for a long time had been partially unused – were full to capacity, so that they had to impose increasingly competitive conditions for entry.

All told, it was time for His Majesty to rid himself of a prime minister with strong army support who did not owe any of his positions entirely to the Shah, and put a 'house-born slave' in his place.

IQBĀL'S TERM OF OFFICE, 1956–60

Dr Manūchehr Iqbāl was a physician born in a 'middle-class' family in Mashhad. He had earned his French medical training by a state scholarship, and his rise to fame and fortune was mainly the result of his own entrepreneurial ability. In his younger days, he had been sufficiently attractive to enjoy a close friendship with Princess Ashraf, and sufficiently loyal and subservient to become a Shah's own man. He had been a minister in several cabinets in the 1940s, and at the time of his appointment he was holding several important positions, including the presidency of the University of Teheran and membership of the Iranian Senate. At the relatively young age of forty-nine, he combined academic titles and extensive foreign and domestic contacts, which – in addition to his own arrogance to his inferiors and subservience to the Shah – made him a perfect choice for His Majesty's designs. It is certain that the Shah had not been entirely happy with the domestic alliance that had put him back on the throne: he hated power-sharing, even with landlords, religious leaders and old-school politicians; he had been brought up by his father as a pseudo-modernist and pseudo-nationalist, estranged from Iranian culture, embarrassed by its 'backwardness', and impatient for self-glorification through superficial modernism; and he intended to keep his American friends and patrons happy by showing that he was not a 'traditional ruler' but a 'progressive monarch' – for, especially in the 1950s and 1960s, the Western (and, particularly, American) modernist attitude towards the underdeveloped countries was dominated by the idea of a 'land reform', 'parliamentary' government, 'liberal' economic policies, and the like. The Shah accomplished all of this, except a land reform, the reasons for which will be discussed more fully in the following chapters.

The Iranian government was already 'parliamentary', including a lower and an upper house. We know that elections were not free; but we also know that the deputies in the Eighteenth and Nineteenth *Majlis* were not simply the Shah's appointees, and for that reason they enjoyed some real power and influence. The length of the *Majlis* sessions had been increased from two to four years, mainly in order to reduce the frequency of elections, and the potential trouble which they involved. Thus, the Nineteenth *Majlis* sat between 1956 and 1960, when it was dissolved for elections to the Twentieth Session. Meantime, the Shah decided to score a few points by the single act of inaugurating a 'two-party' political system within the existing constitutional framework: to show his American patrons that he was in favour of 'liberal democracy'; to make it impossible to get into the National Assembly through any genuine political grouping, or as an independent candidate; and to let his own henchmen and cronies play the role of Tweedledum and Tweedledee. Two 'parties', Mellīyūn (intended to mean Nationalists) and Mardum (People), were invented out of thin air. The former was headed by Dr Iqbāl, the Prime Minister, and the latter by Asadullāh 'Alam – the Shah's childhood friend and loyal servant – the Minister of the Interior. These 'parties' were ignored by the people, and only attracted small bands of flatterers, self-seekers and ordinary thugs. In reality, they also left the *Majlis* deputies unaffected, who went on operating along their own traditional lines.

This is the period of the Shah's positive nationalism. Although it was never spelled out, the implication of this new royal 'ideology' was that, whereas Muṣaddiq's 'nationalism' was negative, His Majesty's was positive. Apart from the demagogic aspect of the show – which, however, deceived no one except the Shah himself – this slogan was to some extent a reflection of the shadow of Muṣaddiq and the Popular Movement. It was intended to prove that the Shah, too, belonged to the spirit of that movement, which, according to him, Muṣaddiq's 'negativism' (*Manfī-bāfī*) and the treachery of 'the men around him' had led astray.

Iqbāl's government survived for four years until the Shah was forced to sacrifice it in response to the crisis of 1960.

Foreign Relations

It is no wonder that the West in general, and the American and British governments in particular, welcomed and helped establish the new régime: it was, after all, partly of their own making. The two governments were both keen for a favourable settlement of the oil dispute; the British more for economic, and the Americans more for political, reasons. The Americans wanted not only to 'save Persia for the free world', but also to use her in their Cold War strategy of encircling the Soviet Union. That is why they did not simply stop at arming and training the Iranian army, but pressed on with the formation of a regional military pact, and the conclusion of a 'bilateral' Irano-American defence treaty which would enable the Americans to establish air-bases in Iran.

With Bayar and Mendres in Turkey, Nūrī al-sa'īd and 'Abdul'ilāh in Iraq, and Iskandar Mīrzā in Pakistan, the conclusion of the Baghdad Pact (in 1955) – to which these three countries, Iran, Britain and America were signatories – was not difficult. The real purpose of this pact was, unlike NATO, not so much to defend the member countries against an (unlikely) Soviet invasion, but to prevent 'communist subversion' – i.e. the rise of any power other than those acceptable to the West – from within. Yet, the *coup d'état* of 'Abdulkarīm Qāsim in Iraq in July 1958 failed to drive the lesson home to Britain and America. The Shah, however, took the matter seriously, if only because six months earlier no less than the chief of Iranian army intelligence, General Valīullah Qaranī, had been arrested and, *secretly*, charged with intending to topple the régime. Therefore, the Shah decided to strengthen his *domestic* position, by getting either more direct guarantees from the Soviet Union, or greater military and financial support from the Americans. Meanwhile, with Iraq having left the pact, the pact had to be rechristened, and that is how the Central Treaty Organisation (or CENTO) came into being.

The Soviet reaction to the 1953 coup puzzled – and may still puzzle – romantics and dogmatists, but not the realists. Russia, which had afforded no real support to the Iranian Popular Movement, and whose loyal fraternal Tūdeh Party had attacked and hindered it, acquiesced in the coup and established cordial relations with the Shah–Zāhedī regime: among other things (including the inaction of the Tūdeh leadership, which must have been related to the Soviet attitude), she repaid her wartime debt to Iran – which in the desperate economic situation under Muṣaddiq she had refused to do; indeed the Shah himself was received in the Soviet Union on a state visit with great pomp and circumstance; and the Soviet mass media, especially the Persian service of Moscow Radio, became increasingly complimentary to His Majesty and his government. The reason for this attitude must have been much simpler than complex and misleading 'ideological' analyses would make out: the Russians believed that the new régime – unlike Muṣaddiq's – was there to stay; they regarded the Shah not as a mere stooge and puppet of the Americans, but as first and foremost a self-seeking political animal; and they thought that, by reassuring His Majesty that they were not going to encourage opposition against him, they would be able to get the best possible terms in the circumstances.

This cordial and, later, friendly relationship, was abruptly turned into hostility and confrontation in 1959. And the reason for it was the Shah's double-cross in *nearly* concluding a Soviet–Iranian non-aggression treaty, and suddenly signing a 'mutual' defence pact with America! But, to try and understand these various manoeuvres, we should go back to the strange case of General Qaranī's attempted coup late in 1957.

Qaranī was arrested in January 1958 on obscure charges. It is certain, however, that the real charge, though never publicly announced, was his involvement in a planned *coup d'état*. He was tried *in camera*, before a military tribunal, and was sentenced to three years' imprisonment. This was the *minimum* mandatory sentence for any *civilian* convicted of 'acting to overthrow the constitutional monarchy', and was meted out, both before and after this episode, to any opposition leader or activist who was merely involved in systematic political activity. The fact that Qaranī's charge and trial was kept secret, *that he was not court-martialled and executed,* and that he was given such a relatively light sentence, make it certain that he had been in league with a foreign power; and that foreign power can only have been the United States. There was also the recent precedent of a Western-backed 'white coup' in neighbouring Pakistan, which had ousted Iskandar Mīrzā and supplanted him with Ayyūb Khān – together with his 'land reform programme' and his 'basic democracy'. It follows that Qaranī must have been moved by the Americans on behalf of a group of Iranian politicians.[5]

At this point we must rely on widespread (but, I am convinced, largely trustworthy) rumours among the political elite. These concern the very probable involvement of Dr Ali Amīnī in the plot: Amīnī was, by political conviction, a radical conservative, or – in not wholly accurate, Western jargon – a right-wing liberal; he was pro-Western in the sense that he believed that American financial support and strategic guarantees were indispensable for a *moderately reformist* régime in Iran, though I do not think – as some do – that he was 'a paid agent of American imperialism'; he was by nature an able, ambitious but self-respecting politician who would not be prepared to become a 'house-born slave' to His Majesty; he was not a liberal by any stretch of the imagination, but he was opposed to dictatorship and corruption; he had been Minister of Economic Affairs in one of Muṣaddiq's cabinets, and a Minister of Finance in Zāhedī's. Clearly, this combination of personal attributes and political tendencies was extremely unpalatable to the Shah; that is why he had honourably discharged Amīnī by sending him as Iranian ambassador to Washington. This, however, played into Amīnī's hands, who – given the weight of his personality as well as his pro-American credentials – managed to persuade the Americans that their long-term interests lay in dropping the Shah and betting on himself. Clearly, Amīnī cannot have gone so far without preparing the ground among some other influential politicians back in Iran. For example, it was further rumoured that the old Iranian statesman Sayyed Ḥasan Taqī-zādeh had acted as liaison for Amīnī in Teheran, although this may be less reliable than the rest of the story. Almost immediately after Qaranī's arrest, Amīnī was dismissed and recalled to Teheran; there, at the airport he met none of the crowd of well-wishers who had seen him off when he first left for Washington.

Since the army intelligence chief had wisely been nominated for engineering the coup, another source of mystery is how it was uncovered. No doubt the SAVAK was involved at some stage, but – according to rumours which may or may not be correct – it was Russian intelligence that smelt a rat and leaked it to SAVAK. This may not have been so; but, if true, it would make political sense. The Russians must have preferred the Shah to a moderately reformist régime led by a strong personality and brought to power directly by American support. Apart from that, the Soviet friendship with the Shah was then at its height.

Six months later the Qāsim coup in Iraq (in which no foreign power was involved) replaced a corrupt pro-Western régime with one that became increasingly pro-Soviet. No wonder that the Shah tried to play off one superpower against the other in order to obtain firmer guarantees for his own political survival. The Russians were eager to accommodate and, early in 1959, a high-level delegation arrived in Teheran to sign a non-aggression treaty with Iran; they were even ready to withdraw article 6 of the 1921 Irano-Soviet treaty, according to which Soviet troops could enter the country if Soviet security was threatened by a foreign power operating in Iran. Yet, at the last moment, the Iranians backed down and, instead, signed the 'mutual' defence pact with America in return for more military and financial aid. The Soviet Union was incensed and – much to the relief and joy of the Tūdeh leadership, who must have expected the last nail in their political coffin – retaliated by wholesale anti-Shah propaganda, which continued until the rapprochement of 1963.[6]

One last word of speculation against currently fashionable trends. It is likely that, without a great deal of pressure from conservative political and religious forces in the country, the Shah would have seen to the end of his gamble, and signed a non-aggression pact with the Soviet Union. But perhaps the future will expose all the facts and fictions concerning this, and many other episodes in modern Iranian history.

Economic Policy and the Political Economy

AN OVERVIEW

Economic policy and activity, especially in the first few years after the coup, was simply a normalisation of the post-abdication era: after Reżā-Shah's departure, pseudo-modernist economic strategy had vanished even before the parts of the steel plant imported from Germany began to rot away. During the war, the Iranian economy had been dislocated by the needs and requirements of the Allies. At the end of the war there was a year of Azerbijan followed by the oil workers' strike, and the political struggles against the Gass–Gulshā'īān oil agreement. This was the beginning of the campaign for the nationalisation of Iranian oil, and the Iranian Popular Movement. Nevertheless, Razmārā, who was a modernist type, intended to stimulate and expand the economy by extensive public investment. An *ad hoc* 'machinery' for state investment had already been created to implement a seven-year public expenditure project, euphemistically known as the seven-year plan. But, before any tangible move was made, the oil dispute, the British blockade, the lack of revenues from oil, and so forth, left no room either for public investment or for economic normality. Therefore, for the first time since 1941, the economy began to normalise along fairly traditional, unambitious and conservative lines after the coup: under Zāhedī, American aid and the oil revenues of 1954–5 were generally spent on consumption and brought the economy out of its acute depression. Later, however, oil revenues and further American aid were received at unprecedented levels and increasing rates. In 1955 the Plan Organisation came into being as a permanent body with extensive spending powers, of which more below.

Good evidence for the loose alliance which had brought the Shah–Zāhedī régime to power is that the system of land-holding and tenancy was left undisturbed. For a brief period, landed property became stronger than it had ever been since 1921; and the one new piece of legislation which concerned its fortunes was retrogressive: in 1953 Muṣaddiq had passed an act which obliged landlords to allocate 20 per cent of *their own* share of the output partly to supplement peasants' incomes, and partly to be paid into a rural development fund. In 1955 the new *Majlis* reduced this – in some cases to 7.5 percent.[7] In practice, however, if any landlord paid anything to anyone at all, then this must have been due to the soundness of his character! For good measure, the Shah himself, who had regained control of the so-called crown lands after the coup, hit several targets with one blow by beginning to 'redistribute' these lands: he rid himself of extensive immovable property which he knew he did not rightfully own; he realised its full value at the expense of the public treasury; and he sent his domestic and foreign heralds everywhere to show off His Majesty's 'distribution of his own lands' among the peasantry.

This traditionalist attitude to the indigenous economic sectors was accompanied by a relatively modernistic 'strategy' of state investment from 1955–6, when the state was in receipt of increasing oil revenues and foreign aid. And, true to the American politiconomic prescription for the entire universe, a policy of high private consumption expenditure was blended with low tariffs and, therefore, high imports: 'the policy of open doors', as Iqbāl used to call it. Corruption, embezzlement and incompetence aside, it was this policy more than any other which led to the squandering of the oil revenues and American aid, until the chickens came home to roost in 1960.

OIL, FOREIGN AID AND THE ECONOMY

The Consortium Oil Agreement of 1954 effectively destroyed the spirit of the oil nationalisation, even though it kept the appearance of it: a consortium made up of a number of British companies (with a 40 per cent share), American companies (also with a 40 per cent share) and French and Dutch companies (with a total share of 20 per cent) was set up to produce and market Iranian oil for twenty-five years, and pay 50 per cent of the net proceeds to the Iranian government. This was certainly less than Muṣaddiq could have settled for in every respect, as was forcefully demonstrated by a long and comprehensive critique that Khalīl Malekī wrote with technical help from Kāẓim Ḥasībī, and persuaded Muhammad Derakhshish to present to the *Majlis*.[8] Ali Amīnī, the Iranian *ex-officio* negotiator, gave the show away by replying that the agreement was far from ideal, but that they had had to consent to it in the country's special circumstances. Yet, without Muṣaddiq and the Popular Movement, nothing as much as this could have been achieved: looking back to the attitude of AIOC before nationalisation, it is impossible to believe that it would have agreed to reduce the 1933 concessionary period by so many years, and to increase the Iranian share to 50 per cent. The fact that, in addition, it paid for its arrogant follies by losing 60 per cent of Iranian oil to others contains a lesson which they did not learn, or they would have avoided the Suez disaster of 1956.

As mentioned earlier, in 1949 an *ad hoc* planning body had been set up which drafted a statement of state investment projects entitled the Seven-Year Plan (1949–56). The plan allocated a quarter of its proposed expenditures to agriculture, 32 per cent to social welfare and postal and telecommunications schemes, and 24 per cent to industrial and mining projects, including oil explorations outside the domain of the AIOC. However, since 69 per cent of the required funds for financing the projects were expected to come from oil revenues and World Bank loans, and a further 21 per cent from domestic credit creation, the Anglo-Iranian oil dispute left the First Plan as a dead letter.[9]

In 1955 the Plan Organisation was turned into a permanent and extensive body, and it was charged with the preparation and execution of the Second Plan (1955–62). This, too, was more a statement (albeit somewhat more precise) of the proposed state investment projects than a detailed blueprint for economic development, but the total projected expenditures were three and a half times as large as those laid down for the First Plan period. Table 10.1 summarises the projected and actual expenditures of the plan, showing that the actual expenditures (of 87,200 million rials) exceeded the projected expenditures (of 70,200 million). This, however, is doubtful, if only the official data for 'actual' expenditures in the last three years of the plan were themselves (rather optimistic) *estimates*. In general, the actual Second Plan expenditure was probably no more than the projected 70 milliard rials. The sectoral allocations of the Second Plan, however, give the flavour of the Western approach to economic development in the period: the development of the 'infrastructure' was given first priority, 'agriculture' came next, and industry last. It was thus in keeping with the blueprint which was later formalised in W. W. Rostow's *Stages of Economic Growth*, although by the time this book appeared the Iranian clients of America had already been

TABLE 10.1 The Second Plan (1955–62): projected and actual expenditures

	Projected expenditures		*Actual expenditures*	
	'000 m. rials	*% of total*	*'000 m. rials*	*% of total*
Infrastructure	41.3	59.0	42.1	48.0
(Transport and telecommunications)	(22.9)	(33.0)	(30.4)	(35.0)
(Public utilities and other services)	(18.4)	(26.0)	(11.7)	(13.0)
Agriculture (including dam construction)	18.3	26.0	18.9	22.0
Industries and mines	10.6	15.0	6.7	8.0
Regional programmes	–	–	12.2	14.0
Unanticipated costs	–	–	7.1	8.0
Total	70.2	100.0	87.2	100.0

Source: based on *Second Seven Year Development Plan of Iran* and *Review of the Second Seven Year Plan Programme of Iran* (Teheran: Plan Organisation, 1956 and 1960). See also P. B. Olsen and P. N. Rasmussen (economic consultants to the Plan Organisation), 'An Attempt at Planning in a Traditional State: Iran', in E. E. Hagen (ed.), *Planning Economic Development* (Homewood, Ill.: Irwin, 1963); and G. Baldwin, *Planning and Development in Iran* (Baltimore: Johns Hopkins, 1967).

disillusioned with 'the model' and were about to enter the realms of steel, import-substitution and comprehensive planning (on paper).

This standard recipe for economic development is, however, reflected more in the projected allocations than in the 'actual' expenditures. In particular, actual expenditures on public utilities and social services, as well as industry and mines, turned out to be significantly *less* than planned, even though the total plan expenditures are claimed to have been greater than projected. Assuming that estimates of actual expenditures are correct, we see, in Table 10.1, that the percentage share of agriculture in the total declined, although much of the investment in 'agriculture' was wasted in the construction of hydroelectric dams, none of which was completed in the plan period, or brought any benefit to agriculture when they were finished. Expenditures on transport and communications, apart from camouflaging expenditure on military logistics, included the extension of the Teheran–Mīyāneh railway to Tabriz, and the construction of the Teheran–Mashhad railway, which was a wasteful project intended mainly for travel services: the renovation of the existing road would have been much cheaper, and more beneficial to the towns and villages in and around this stretch of some 600 kilometres. Private modern manufacturing expanded mainly in such established areas as textiles, cooking oil, glass, carpentry and cabinet-making, and in connection with some new ventures, such as machine-produced carpets and shoes. Public investment in modern manufacturing was limited, and usually related to such senseless projects as the chemical-fertiliser plant founded in Shiraz, which, as late as 1972, was shut down for six months of the year for want of customers. In this case, the main 'mistake' was one of location, the Shah himself having for some obscure reason insisted on Shiraz. This, in fact, provided the last straw for Abulḥasan Ibtihāj, the able and unsubservient Plan Organisation chief, who resigned his post protesting against subversive interference by the Shah.

To finance the plan's projected expenditures, it had been decided to allocate an average 75 per cent of oil revenues for the period to the activities of the Plan Organisation. These revenues, however, turned out to be much greater than expected, and, in addition, the country received substantial sums in free foreign grants, loans and investment. Table 10.2 shows that between 1955 and 1962 the oil revenues amounted to $2129 million, which, together with $1278 million of additional foreign exchange in foreign aid and investment, made up the substantial sum of $3407 million. To illustrate the potential, for good and evil, of this sum, it is probably sufficient to say that it amounts to more than five times Iran's total foreign-exchange receipts (from oil and foreign loans put together) for the whole of the *previous twenty years*. Even if we were to put aside the $469 million worth of *free* military aid (which is not entirely legitimate, for at least some of the expenditure would have been met from the other sources), we should still have $2938 million left to set against His Majesty's 'achievements' in those years. Assuming that the official figure of 87,200 million rials ($1147 million) of actual expenditures for the Second Plan

TABLE 10.2 Available financial capital in foreign exchange (1955–62)

	$m.	*% of total*
Oil revenues	2129	62.5
Foreign aid and investment	1278	37.5
American non-military grants and loans	(681)	(20.0)
American military grants (non-repayable)	(469)	(13.8)
British aid	(28)	(0.8)
Foreign investment (until 1961)	(100)	(2.9)
Total excluding military grants	2938	86.2
Total	3407	100.0

Sources: based on Bank Markazi Iran, *National Income of Iran, 1959–72* (Teheran, 1974); USAID Mission to Iran, *Summary Highlights of A. I. D. . . . in Iran, 1950–1965* (Teheran, 1966); and Rahmatullah Muqaddam Marāgheh'ī, parliamentary address to the Twentieth *Majlis*, 23 April 1961, repr. from the official *Majlis* minutes (Teheran, n.d.) (in Persian).

is correct, in Table 10.3 we compare this figure with the amounts of financial capital, *in foreign exchange*, which were available over the period. Thus, taking the authorities at their own word, it turns out that the actual plan expenditures amounted to only 54 per cent of oil revenues, 39 per cent of the total available other than from military grants, and 34 per cent of total foreign-exchange receipts. In fact, the total actual plan expenditures were less than the amount of foreign aid alone, as if there had been no revenues from oil at all.

Between 1955 and 1962, Iran's receipts of foreign exchange *from oil and aid alone* were, on average, about 17 per cent of her national income per year. For

TABLE 10.3 Capital receipts and 'development' expenditures by the state:[a] a summary balance sheet, 1955–62

	Receipts ($m.)	*Expenditures*		*Excess of receipts over expenditure*	
		$m.	*As % of receipts*	*$m.*	*As % of receipts*
Total receipts	3407	1147	34.0	2260	66.0
Total receipts excluding military grants	2938	1147	39.0	1982	61.0
Oil revenues	2129	1147	54.0	982	46.0
Foreign aid and investment	1278	1147	90.0	131	10.0

[a] 'Receipts' refers to capital funds directly paid out (in foreign exchange) to the state. They exclude the whole of the state's tax, customs and other revenues. They also exclude the amount of foreign exchange available from exports of non-oil Iranian products.

Source: Tables 10.1 and 10.2.

development economists this must indicate the road to paradise on earth: they tell us that the main barrier to rapid economic progress is a shortage of domestic capital and foreign exchange; they believe that a saving and export earning of around 12 per cent of the national income should be adequate for steady economic growth and development; they teach (and preach) that the trouble is that underdeveloped countries are so poor as to be unable to accumulate at home, and sell abroad, a reasonable share of their national output, and this prevents sustained growth and progress; and they defend foreign aid and investment precisely on the basis of these arguments. Here, then, was a country where, if the private sector saved nothing at all from the proceeds of its own productive effort, the state could accumulate a maximum of 17 per cent of the country's national income, which rose from the earth and poured from the heavens. Yet by 1960 hardly anything permanent and useful had been achieved, and the country was bankrupt. However, as we shall see in the next part of this study, this was only the beginning.

This brings us to a brief review of Iran's balance of trade and payments in the period. It is clear from Table 10.4 that (a) imports of goods grew very rapidly (by 1959 they were over six times what they had been in 1954); (b) exports of *non-oil* goods declined and never regained their 1954 level; and (c) whereas in 1954 and 1955 both the non-oil *and* the oil-inclusive balances of trade were in surplus, a rapidly growing balance-of-trade deficit developed, even though oil revenues continued to grow fast. In fact, these figures alone

TABLE 10.4 The Balance of Trade 1954–62 ($m.)

Year	*Oil revenues*[a]	*Non-oil exports*	*Imports of goods*	*Balance excluding oil revenues*	*Balance including oil revenues*
1954	10	135	106	25	35
1955	88	106	143	−37	11
1956	146	104	345	−241	−95
1957	167	109	429	−320	−153
1958	291	104	610	−506	−215
1959	323	101	656	−555	−232
1960	364	110	693	−583	−219
1961	395	126	620	−494	−99
1962	443	113	551	−438	−5

[a] In official Iranian publications, entries in this column show the value of Iranian oil exports, as if the country received the full value of its exports of oil! This procedure has been uncritically adopted by some students of the Iranian economy (e.g. J. Bharier, in his *Economic Development in Iran 1900–1967*), with the result that, just like the original Iranian source, they provide the wrong picture for the overall Iranian balance of trade.

Sources: based on Vizārat-i Iqtiṣād, *Āmār-i Bāzargānī-yi Khārijī-yi Irān* (official foreign trade statistics by the Ministry of the Economy) 1966; Bank Markazi Iran, *National Income of Iran, 1959–72*, and *National Income of Iran 1962–67* (Teheran, 1969); and International Monetary Fund, *International Financial Statistics*, various dates. Figures originally quoted in rials have been converted at $1 = 76 rials.

provide a telling picture about the decline of Iran's traditional (non-oil) exports, the invasion of Iranian markets by foreign goods, the squandering of the oil revenues, the corruption of the state and its officials, and the enrichment of a small clientele of the state through the agency of oil revenues and foreign aid. The foreign-aid figures are apparently absent from the table, for they would normally appear in the capital accounts of the balance of payments. But it is clear that, without the receipt of $1278 million in aid, the import of goods would not have been as high as in the table. However, even such receipts could not save 'the open-door policy' from its fate, and that is how a chronic balance-of-payments (as distinct from balance-of-trade) deficit also began to develop, as certain proof of the bankruptcy of the régime.

SOCIAL AND ECONOMIC CHANGE

The socio-economic logic of the attitude of the state to the political economy was to try and create an urban 'middle class' as the social base for the régime. This would be consistent with the Western liberal blueprint by providing the presumed agents both for economic development and for liberal democracy. The real intention, however, was to create a degree of contentment among the educated and semi-educated urban community in order to forestall serious political opposition; to provide an alternative power base to the landlords, who were economically too independent, and politically too powerful, an ally for His Majesty (as well as being a source of embarrassment, both inside and outside the country); to show the Americans that their financial and military support was obtaining results in combating communism, by replacing 'backwardness' with imported refrigerators, motor-cars, and so on, and home-produced 'drive-in' cinemas.

This is the mechanism whereby the boom in import–export (but mainly *import*) business, and the related tide of consumption of modern products was created: at once, the country began simultaneously to display the signs of Rostow's stages of 'tradition', 'transition' *and* 'high mass consumption' – of course in different sectors, and for different social classes; there were, however, no signs of 'take off' and 'industrial maturity'. Towards the end of the period, little banks began to be added to the already extensive Bank Bāzargānī (which under Muṣaddiq had taken over the assets of the old British Imperial Bank), Bank Ṣāderat and Bank Pārs. Speculation in urban land became the most lucrative method of making money out of excess liquidity, at the expense of ordinary home-buyers and tenants. Bills of exchange began to circulate at a high velocity, often ending in default. In 1959, the market was shaking with fever.

Population had been growing since the war, probably at an average annual rate of 2 per cent. The 1956 census estimated the population at 18.5 million, 70 per cent of which was rural, and of the remaining 30 per cent one-third was located in Teheran. Rural–urban migration was still insignificant: the growing concentration in the capital was primarily due to the flow of migrants from other towns and cities because of better social and economic prospects, the concentration of bureaucracy in Teheran (to which any Iranian applying for a passport had to come, wherever his home), and modern attractions such as drive-in cinemas. The peasantry grew relatively poorer, but the urban 'middle class' increased in number, and enjoyed a significant rise in income and consumption. They began to buy refrigerators, television sets, and so on – all of which were imported – on hire purchase.

The emergence of *urban* dualism – of a complete sociological division within the urban population – is a product of this period: formerly, the old residential quarters had included families of *all* ranks. High officials, older families, merchants, ordinary artisans, and petty traders lived side by side in the same city quarters (or *Maḥallāt*). Clearly, rich and poor houses were very different in every respect; but, by and large, they were built on the basis of traditional Iranian architecture. More significantly, this ensured social contact between different classes: the rich were in daily contact with the ordinary, the poor and even the beggars. But all this began to change when new wealth led, in the case of Teheran, to an entirely unplanned movement towards the northern parts of the city, into new houses the building of which was facilitated by the state's free grants of urban land to army officers and the higher civil servants. The damage was completed when the poor immigrants began to settle in the declining districts; and the departure of the rich left no local influence for the environmental protection and renovation of the old districts by city authorities. In the southern parts of Teheran, many old houses with large tree-shaded gardens were levelled off by property speculators, who built new little hovels in their place – and no one cared. Meanwhile, tremendous social and psychological pressures were applied to those older families which had fallen behind in the race, to make them move out of their traditional districts at all costs. The sense of community which, in spite of class differentiation, had always been present in Iranian cities was lost – perhaps for ever.

The growth of state expenditure was most visible in the expansion of the military–bureaucratic network: the conscript army was 200,000 'strong'; the state bureaucracy included 260,000 men, a lot of whom were underemployed. Yet the unplanned expansion of secondary (and, to a much smaller extent, higher) education had given rise to an army of jobless school-leavers and graduates, who, because of the state strategy of investment, could not be accommodated in productive activities! Therefore, the state was obliged to provide them with disguised hand-outs by giving them a desk in an office and making life even more difficult for the unfortunate masses who did not have contacts in higher places. Meanwhile, unemployment among the unskilled urban labour force was rising fast.

In 1960, the cumulative balance-of-payments deficit, unemployment and a high rate of inflation, burst the bubble of the 'open-door policy', Rostovian 'economic growth' (before Rostow), hire-purchase consumerism, and positive nationalism all at once. This was followed by two years of economic depression, political instability, and a fierce power struggle, out of which the Shah's pseudo-modernist (petrolic) despotism was born to cause unprecedented damage and destruction to Iranian society.

NOTES

1. Dr Kīyānūrī claims to have telephoned Muṣaddiq, but Dr Firaidūn Kishāvarz, a former member of the party Central Committee, has recently cast doubt on the truth of this claim, because, he says, there are no witnesses to this but Kīyānūrī himself, whose testimony he does not trust. See Kishāvarz, *Man Muttaham Mīkunam* . . . . (Teheran: Ravāq, 1977).
2. A few months after the coup, the party Executive Committee published a pamphlet 'analysing' the coup, the Party's role, and so on. This blames the coup on the 'bourgeois leadership' of the Popular Movement, and has to be seen to be believed; see *Darbāreh-yi Bīst-u-hasht-i Murdād* (1954). However, the Executive Committee retracted some of its positions in the earlier pamphlet in a later one issued in December 1955 (i.e. two and a half years after the coup), which, apart from familiar 'theoretical analyses', says nothing about the party role during and immediately after the coup, and 'explains' the complete failure of its leadership in the intervening period in terms of which the following is a specimen:

   > In the first few months after 19 August [i.e. the coup], some relatively strong Blanquist tendencies dominated the Party. The Central Committee, instead of fighting against these incorrect tendencies, was itself taken by them, and followed them. In this period, we made a number of tactical mistakes. . . . The negative effect of such decisions was that the Party was not paying sufficient attention to the most important issue of the day, that is, the problem of protecting the Party organs from the enemy's offensives.

3. In addition to that, in 1954 – 5 Falsafī was given the task (through the state radio) of leading a sudden and, apparently, unprovoked attack on the Bahā'ī community, which ended with the official confiscation of the community's centre in Teheran (*Ḥazīrat al-quds*), and its use as the headquarters of the martial-law administration (which was later turned into the SAVAK); this is probably why in its issue of 3rd June 1955 *Nabard-i Mellat*, the conservative Islamic newspaper, compared the martial-law administration to a centre for Islamic propaganda. (In a recent interview with *Iṭṭilā'āt,* Kāẓim Ḥasībī has revealed that the campaign was launched on the request, to the Shah, of Āyatullah Burūjirdī, the then *Marja' al-taqlid* in Qum.)
4. After 'Abbāsī's arrest they literally sat back for days hoping that they would manage to obtain his release through the intervention of Sayyed Żīā Ṭabā Ṭabā'ī but in the meantime they took no security measures whatever in order to protect their military network and its documents. (The details of this catastrophe were known to many political activists. But they have now appeared in a series of articles in the weekly magazine *Umīd-i Irān*, April – May 1979.)
5. Qaranī had personally contacted a number of opposition leaders, including Khalīl Malekī, who told me that he had hesitated to believe that Qaranī was sincere in his strong criticisms of the régime. At the time of writing (March 1979), General Qaranī is the army chief of staff in Bāzargān's provisional government. (*Postscript.*

Just before his recent death by assassination Qaranī publicly affirmed that he had planned a *coup d'état* in 1957 – 8. But his claim that the Americans had not been involved cannot be believed, both because of the circumstances of his move – and his unusually mild treatment by the régime after its failure – and because of the circumstances in which he has now had to deny this. He has, however, confirmed that he had contacted 'the statesmen of the Popular Movement of Iran' in the process. See *Umīd-i Irān*, 30 Apr 1979.)

6. The Shah and his Prime Minister even refused, on shallow pretexts to see their Soviet guests. For various details see *Iṭṭilā'āt* and *Kayhān* (daily newspapers), various issues, Oct 1958 – Feb 1959. See also R. Sukhanvar, 'Darbāreh-yi Munāsibāt-i Kunūnī-yi Irān va Showravī' ('On the Present Relations of Iran and the Soviet Union'), *Dunyā* (theoretical organ of the Tūdeh Party), no. 2, 1960, which justifies all the previous Soviet demonstrations of goodwill towards unpopular régimes in Iran, and blames the hostility of Soviet–Iranian relations at the time on the Shah's treachery over his mutual defence pact with America. The party's position was, however, very drastically changed after the improvement of Soviet – Iranian relations three years later. See further Chs 10, 11 and 16, below.
7. See H. Katouzian, 'Land Reform in Iran: A Case Study in the Political Economy of Social Engineering', *Journal of Peasant Studies*, Jan 1974; and Chapter 15, below.
8. See *Nuṭq-i Jinābi Āqāy-i Muhammad Derakshish* . . . (Teheran, 1955).
9. See, Plan Organisation, *Second Seven Year Development Plan of Iran* (Teheran, 1956), and *Review of the Second Seven Year Plan Programme of Iran* (Teheran, 1960). See also, B. Olsen and P. N. Rasmussen 'An Attempt at Planning in a Traditional State', in E. E. Hagen (ed.), *Planning Economic Development* (Homewood, Ill.: Irwin, 1963) esp. pp. 224–5.

Part IV

Petrolic Despotism, 'Economic Development' and the People's Revolution, 1961–79

11 Economic Crisis, Political Instability and Power Struggles, 1961–3: Preludes to Petrolic Despotism

Amīnī's Premiership

In 1960 the economic crisis, the growing American awareness of the corruption and incompetence of the Shah's régime, and the open hostility of the Soviet Union forced the Shah to resort to his habitual tactic of 'liberalisation'. With the approach of the general elections, he said in a public speech that elections would be completely free, implicitly admitting that the previous elections had been controlled. This gave the signal to various shades of political opposition to surface once again. The Shah was hoping to ride over the events with a few empty promises, until economic recovery would help return the situation to the *status quo ante*. This might have been the case, had the Americans agreed to co-operate. But they did not: with the impending American presidential elections, a definite commitment could not be made, especially as leading Democrats, such as Senators John Kennedy and William Fulbright, were critical of the Republican attitude towards corrupt régimes in underdeveloped countries in general, and Iran in particular. The triumph of the Cuban Revolution had, at that time, been helpful to such critical views, even though its later developments helped harden the attitude of the future Kennedy administration. Eisenhower could no longer stand for the presidency, and his Republican heir-apparent, Vice-President Richard Nixon, may have thought it wiser to wait until after the elections before going to the assistance of a close friend.

Meantime, the farcical *Majlis* elections of summer 1960 were cancelled before completion – the Shah 'advised' those already elected to resign their seats, and they dutifully took his 'advice' – and in September Iqbāl 'resigned' as Prime Minister. The Shah appointed Ja'far Sharīf–Imāmī, the Minister for Industries and Mines (who until that time had not created much personal animosity among the opposition), hoping that his friend Nixon would become American president and pull his chestnuts out of the fire. He even (reportedly) contributed a few million dollars to the Nixon compaign fund. In November

1960 John Kennedy was elected President, and in January 1961 he moved into the White House.

During this time the main challenge to the Shah had come from the reconstituted National Front, and the group of politicians gathered around Ali Amīnī. The Front had a social base among the people which the Amīnī group lacked; the latter had declared a political programme, including a programme of land reform – which the former had not. In addition, the Amīnī group was better placed for attracting American support. The student movement was growing in strength, and, though it included many different shades of opinion, it solidly supported the National Front. The *bāzār* was the Front's other main popular power base. The second round of elections to the Twentieth *Majlis* was as unfree as the first. Indeed, in February 1961 the elections of Teheran deputies took place while 5000 students staged a sit-in in the Faculty of Letters at the University (a protest that, through the folly of a Front leader, Dr Shāpūr Bakhtīyār, was called off after a single night), and nearly all the National Front leaders were effectively imprisoned in the country's Senate building.[1] The only opposition leader who was given a fair chance at the polls was the respectable Allāhyār Ṣāleh, who was the natural representative of Kāshān, had been Iranian ambassador to Washington under Muṣaddiq, was not yet *officially* associated with the National Front, and – above all – was not *personally* despised by His Majesty.

The trend of events compelled the Shah to make a choice between the Front and Amīnī, and in April 1961 he opted for the latter. A serious change would, in any case, have been unavoidable; but what brought it about at that particular time was the strike of the teachers' union over pay – organised and led by Muhammad Derakhshish, an Amīnī supporter – which culminated in the violent death of a part-time teacher and theology postgraduate when a police colonel shot into the crowd of demonstrators outside the *Majlis*. The Shah both hated Amīnī – a hatred which became obsessive in years to come – and felt threatened by him. He would certainly have preferred Ṣāleh, or some other leading member of the National Front, to Amīnī. The reasons why he had to choose Amīnī were twofold: (a) Amīnī had greater American backing, mainly because the Front's position on a number of key issues (and, in particular, foreign relations, land reform and the Tūdeh Party) was not quite clear; and (b) the appointment of a Front leader would have opened a Pandora's box of old troubles for the Shah himself. In particular there was the ominous shadow of Muṣaddiq – the aged statesman who, as the most popular individual in the country, was the person the Shah most hated, envied, and feared – who had been illegally confined to his rural estate ever since the completion of his prison sentence in 1956. This does not, however, mean that the victory of Amīnī over the Front was inevitable: with better organisation and leadership (of which more below), the Front would have stood a good chance of imposing itself, both on the Shah and on the Americans, as the only sensible choice.

Amīnī took over office after some bargaining points had been struck: in particular, the Shah would dismiss the *Majlis,* largely in order to clear the way for Amīnī's proposed land reform; he would agree to a degree of press and other freedoms, even for the National Front; and he and his third wife, Queen Farah, who had recently borne him a son, would immediately leave the country for a visit to Norway. In return, the Shah would still control the army and the SAVAK, though it was agreed that the latter should act with restraint; nominate some of his own henchmen – such as 'Aṭā'ullah Khusruvānī, the Minister of Labour – to cabinet posts; and would be generally consulted on matters of policy. The new cabinet was a hotch-potch of the Shah's own men, Amīnī's own men, and compromise candidates. Ḥasan Arsanjānī (Agriculture), Nūral-Dīn Alamūtī (Justice), Muhammad Derakhshish (Education) and Ghulām-ali Farīvar (Industry) were Amīnī's own appointments. Arsanjānī was a trained lawyer, a journalist, and a former Tūdeh sympathiser who later in the 1940s had joined the entourage of Qavām al-Salṭaneh. Alamūtī was a high-ranking and highly respected judge who, as a member of the Marxist group of the Fifty-Three, had been arrested and gaoled in 1937, joined the Tūdeh party in 1941, and left it in 1945, never to engage in party politics again. Derakhshish was the independent political activist who had spoilt his chances with the régime by delivering Khalīl Malekī's comprehensive critique of the consortium oil agreement in a speech in the Eighteenth *Majlis.* Farīvar had been a founding member of the Iran Party, an ally of Muṣaddiq in the Fourteenth *Majlis*, and a respected figure by the leadership of the National Front.

Amīnī had already circulated his programme in an election manifesto in 1960, the most important item in which was a comprehensive reform of the land-tenure system involving distribution of land among peasants. Therefore, as soon as the new cabinet was formed, Dr Arsanjānī was charged with drafting the legal and administrative details of implementing the programme. This was met with considerable opposition, of which more below. Meanwhile, the economy was sliding further into depression, mainly as a result of emergency public-expenditure cuts, a credit squeeze and the import surcharge already imposed by Sharīf-Imāmī's government: the sharp decline in urban land prices hit the land speculators hard, a number of the little banks born out of the previous boom began to fail, import–export businessmen were on the verge of bankruptcy, and the *bāzār* community was in financial difficulty. There was general dissatisfaction and uncertainty about the future.

When Amīnī became Prime Minister, there was a change in the political atmosphere that had not been experienced since the 1953 coup: the *Majlis* was dismissed, the Shah departed, Teheran airport was temporarily closed, more press and other freedoms were granted to the opposition, and a number of notorious financial racketeers and political 'wheeler-dealers' (such as Asadullah Rashīdīyān and Fatḥullah Furūd) and some publicly despised individuals (for example, General Ḥusain Āzmūdeh, the chief military prosecutor, who had personally conducted the case against Muṣaddiq) were arrested. Indeed, in a press conference Alūmūtī, the Minister of Justice, compared Āzmūdeh with Adolf Eichmann, the Nazi war criminal, who had recently been on trial in Israel.[2]

Yet, within a few months the situation began to change: at home, the combined opposition of the Shah, the conservative forces and the National Front, and, abroad, the total hostility of the Soviet Union, increasingly weakened Amīnī's position and strengthened the Shah's hands against both Amīnī and the National Front. After fourteen turbulent months, Amīnī resigned his office, and was put under surveillance by the SAVAK. This was followed by His Majesty's 'Revolution of the Shah and the People' – or, more accurately, the revolution of the Shah *against* the people – the bloody uprising of June 1963, and the development of petrolic pseudo-modernist despotism.

Political Parties and Tendencies

THE SECOND NATIONAL FRONT

In August 1960 the new National Front was born in a small meeting which was hastily called by some of the former ministers and leading supporters of Dr Muṣaddiq – notably Bāquir Kāẓimī, Ghulām-Ḥusain Ṣadīqī, Karīm Sanjābī and Mehdī Bāzargān, and, among the younger and less prominent, Shāpūr Bakhtīyār and Dārīyūsh Furūhar – and a larger group of publicly unknown individuals who in various ways were associated with the popular leaders. The manner in which the second National Front came into being was a serious cause of its later mistakes and ineffectiveness: it alienated a number of leading figures, such as Ṣāleh and Rażavī, who for a few months refused to be identified with it; it created a large council of thirty-six men (of different views, characters, ability, popularity, and so on) which for a long time was the sole decision-making body of the Front, with the implicit assumption that all decisions – even the wording of a public statement - had to be unanimous; it purposefully excluded Khalīl Malekī and his group, of which more below; and it was neither in composition nor in conduct to the liking of some of its own members, especially Mehdī Bāzargān, Sayyed Maḥmūd (later, Āyatullah) Ṭāliqānī, Dr Yadullāh Saḥābī and Ḥasan Nazīh, who six months later formed an independent group, the Freedom Movement of Iran. The prominent leaders of the Front drew their popularity almost exclusively from their past association with Muṣaddiq, and their unknown colleagues drew theirs from their association with them. The Front eventually became dominated by Dr Muhammad Ali Khunjī – a prominent intellectual who had been a very close associate of Khalīl Malekī before leading an apparently senseless crusade against him when, after the 1953 coup, Malekī was in prison – and Dr Shāpūr Bakhtīyār, a strong-willed lesser light of the Muṣaddiq era. In effect,

Khunjī became the theoretical strategist, and Bakhtīyār the practical operator of the 'line' which finally led the Front, and the Iranian people who gave them loyal support, straight into a complete political catastrophe, although this should not mean that the others – and, especially, the prominent leaders – can be absolved of their own responsibilities. The history of this second National Front would make a serious and enlightening subject of study in its own right. Here, however, we must restrict ourselves to the more analytical aspects of its emergence, defeat and disappearance.

THE TŪDEH PARTY

The Tūdeh Party organisation had been virtually destroyed inside the country. But, in spite of its disastrous 'mistakes' before and after the 1953 coup, the Central Committee still enjoyed a wide measure of support among its former members and sympathisers, although many of them remained relatively inactive. Among the reasons for this irrational attitude of the broad membership, the following must have played a decisive role: the Soviet Union was popular in Iran because of (a) its open hostility to the régime, (b) its recent successes in space engineering, (c) the apparent (though not real) unity of the socialist countries as the only legitimate anti-imperialist camp among the party's supporters, and (d) the Soviet public stance against imperialist interventions in Cuba and the Belgian Congo; apart from that, the Central Committee kept playing martyr by hammering in the impressive record of the devoted party members' persecution, imprisonment, torture and death at the hands of the régime, and the rank and file wished to be identified with this legacy. However, although the party played an independent role through its daily Persian broadcasts from East Germany, on Paik-i Irān (Iran Messenger) radio, its publications and its student sympathisers in Europe, it did not, and could not, assert itself independently, or influence events *directly*, inside the country. By and large, its active supporters (mainly among the younger generations) joined various organs of the National Front, and followed its lead. It was about this time that some critical Tūdeh sympathisers among the university students – notably Bīzhan Jazanī, and Ḥasan Żiā-Ẓarīfī – formed an undeclared nucleus for a future independent Marxist movement which, as a result of later events, led to the formation of the Marxist guerrilla group Fadā'īan-i Khalq, or Selfless Devotees of the People, and their own wanton assassination in gaol (in 1975).

THE SOCIALIST LEAGUE

The National Front had, at first, included all the political parties which had supported Muṣaddiq and the Iranian Popular Movement – the Iran Party, its splinter group the People of Iran Party, and the Iran Nation (the splinter group of the Pan Iranist) Party. The one exception was the Zaḥmatkishān,

Nīrūy-i Sevvum (or Third Force) Party, which had been reorganised under the name of the Socialist League of the Popular Movement of Iran (SLPMI). In fact, as early as 1958 Khalīl Malekī had arranged a meeting with some leading personalities of the Popular Movement – including Ṣāleh and Sanjābī – and suggested that they should begin to prepare themselves for 'the next round of the struggle' by forming a broad socialist alliance, to be called the League of Iranian Socialists, which would include all the existing socialist tendencies, from right-wing social-democrats to *independent* Marxists. Those approached, however, had shied away, mainly on the grounds that it would be a very long time before any serious opportunity for action would arise, though Malekī had tried to prove that this was incorrect. But, when the Shah's free-elections speech took them by surprise, and encouraged them to rush into the 'formation' of the National Front, Malekī and the remainder of the Third Force activists formed the SLPMI: the 'Popular Movement' was added to the title of the organisation mainly in order to keep its claims in line with its actual strength and resources – in the circumstances, the 'Socialist League of Iran' would sound like an empty boast.

The League was not invited to join the National Front, the sole object of this being to keep Malekī out: by then, he had been thoroughly painted as an agent of the régime (even of the SAVAK!) by Tūdeh Party propaganda, as well as by his own former comrade-in-arms, Dr Muhammad Ali Khunjī; but, since he was relatively unknown among the masses of the Front's supporters, this cannot have been the real reason for his exclusion. The leading personalities of the Front had no doubts about Malekī's complete sincerity, and they knew that his inclusion in the Front's leadership would be sufficient to sweep away all those groundless accusations. Instead, they took advantage of the mud slung at Malekī for a combination of the following reasons: all the Front leaders recognised Malekī's superior analytical powers and organisational abilities, and all except one or two of them were afraid that he would naturally dominate the Front if he were admitted into its council. In addition, some of them – notably Shāpūr Bakhtīyār – suffered from the illusion that direct association with Malekī would lose them the 'Tūdeh Party vote' during the next election. In fact the Khunjī–Bakhtīyār strategy of dissolving all the affiliated political groups and parties into a mass individual membership had originated as an expedient to keep the Socialist League out, although eventually it served to estrange other political groupings, and divide the Front itself. The Socialist League went on giving critical support to the Front, especially in all its meetings and demonstrations; but by first privately, and later publicly, warning the Front against some of its gross tactical and strategic mistakes, it irritated the Front's leading personalities instead of influencing them. The Socialist League was a well-organised political body composed of an exceptionally able band of older intellectuals, writers and students. But it did not have, nor did it seek, a popular base, mainly because it was hoping for a National Front victory in the next round of the struggle.[3]

In 1960 there had existed a number of Iranian student unions and societies in Europe and America, and in general these did not *overtly* indulge in political activities. The student organisations in western Europe had already formed themselves into the Confederation of Iranian Students in Europe. In Paris in January 1962, the third annual congress of the Confederation (which had already been explicitly politicised) produced a split in its ranks, ostensibly on the terms of the affiliation of the Iranian students' union in America, but in fact because student members and sympathisers of the Tūdeh Party were afraid of the domination of the student movement by National Front members and supporters. In the next year, passions and energies were largely wasted on factional in-fighting, rather than utilised in concerted action against the régime, until the next congress (in Lausanne) belatedly healed the breach. Expatriate National Front organisations came into being late in 1961. But, a few years earlier, some former members and sympathisers of the Third Force Party and the Tūdeh Party had formed the League of Iranian Socialists in Europe, which remained independent from, although close to, the Socialist League that was later formed in Iran. Tūdeh Party members and sympathisers in western Europe received their instructions directly from the party leadership in East Germany.

THE SHAH AND THE ESTABLISHMENT

The loose 'coalition' of domestic forces behind the 1953 coup was composed of the Shah and his despotic nucleus of powerful elements within the army and the bureaucracy, and three – traditionalist, moderate, and radical – conservative groups. Amīnī was a representative of radical conservatism, even though he himself was a large landowner. He could easily have rallied the other conservative groups behind him, and created a solid conservative power, against the Shah, the National Front and the Left. But this would have run counter to his belief that, outside communism, Iran's long-term salvation lay with the creation of an independent peasantry, as a solid economic and political base on which to nurture a mixed capitalist economy and promote modern manufacturing. He was therefore quickly confronted by landlords as a class, and by some influential members of the religious leadership.

The Shah, who by then was in complete control of the army and the SAVAK, had no love for the landlords, nor for any of the religious leaders, for, in spite of incredible political naïveté of fashionable 'analyses', he was not – and had never been – the *representative* of landed interests, merely their increasingly uneasy *ally* since 1952. His ideal was to monopolise political power both for its own sake and in order to pursue his superficial nationalist and modernist dreams, neither of which was consistent with a strong landlord class or an autonomous religious authority. Yet, in the beginning he gave the landlords and other conservatives the impression that their former alliance was still valid. It is illuminating that early in 1961 Fatḥullah Furūd, one of the

Shah's own cronies, who was mayor-designate of Teheran, organised a band of thugs, led by 'Abbās Shāhandeh – the 'journalist' and political dealer – and Ṭayyeb, a powerful protection racketeer in the Teheran vegetable market, to attack and break up a peaceful and authorised National Front meeting held within the walls of their headquarters.[4] This same Furūd, together with similar characters, such as Asadullah Rashīdīyān and even General Ḥusain Āzmūdeh, later began to agitate against Amīnī when he became Prime Minister; and Ṭayyeb was killed by the Shah's apparatus on the charge of complicity in organising the popular uprising of June 1963. For by that time His Majesty had turned a complete political somersault.[5]

The Shah's Triumph: An Analysis of the Power Struggle

THE ROLE OF THE NATIONAL FRONT

At the end of spring 1961, there were hopes of a new and better season for life and labour in Iranian society. The Shah's position was in a delicate balance: Amīnī was Prime Minister, the National Front was strong and popular, the Americans had shifted their exclusive support, the Soviet attitude was belligerent, and, to add insult to injury, General Taimūr Bakhtīyār, the powerful SAVAK chief, had begun to discover the virtues of 'freedom' and 'constitutional monarchy', and had been replaced in March 1961. Two years later, His Majesty had rid himself of Amīnī, broken the National Front, defeated the moderate and traditionalist conservative opposition, drowned thousands of men and women in a river of blood, and driven the remnants of all opposition into silence, prison cells, banishment, or underground activity. How did this change come about?

Amīnī had hoped to succeed in fulfilling his programme, and putting the Shah permanently in his place, with the tacit co-operation of the National Front. For this reason, a few days before or after his appointment to the premiership he had even arranged a small private meeting with the Front's leading members and put some of his cards on the table: that he had no personal quarrel with the Front; that he was serious about his land-reform programme, and for that reason had made it a condition of his premiership that the Shah should dismiss the newly elected *Majlis*; that he could not hold a *Majlis* election before his land reform, because the landlords and the Shah's men would once again dominate it; that the economy was in a desperate plight, and its further deterioration would *now* play into the Shah's hands; and that if, in any case, the Shah managed to sink his boat, the Front would also go down with him. It is likely, though not certain, that he also offered a couple of cabinet posts to be filled by the Front's candidates, though not in a formal coalition. The front leaders responded with sympathy, although no definite (formal or informal) agreement was reached.

Amīnī's strategy for his own success was simple and sound: he was prepared to grant important concessions to the National Front – on the condition that they did not enter a life-and-death struggle against his own government – so that he could tacitly use their power and presence against the Shah and the landlords. When the Shah departed for his trip to Norway, the National Front was allowed, for the first time since 1953, to hold an open-air meeting, which attracted an estimated crowd of over 80,000. Meanwhile, the national press, which had hitherto been forbidden even to acknowledge the existence of the Front, was engaged in a competition for publicising its views and meetings.

Yet within a couple of months the Front had turned all its guns directly against Amīnī's government. The main slogan of its supporters at the University of Teheran, in their frequent campus demonstrations, was 'Amīnī, resign!' ('Amīnī, isti'fā!'). Its own slogan, tactic, strategy, aim and objective was 'immediate general elections'. It began a bizarre courtship – both directly and indirectly – with the anti-Amīnī elements (other than the Shah), to the extent that, in return for the donation of 200,000 rials ($2500) to its funds, it co-opted Amīr Taimūr (Kalālī), a conservative large landowner, to its High Council. In public it maintained absolute silence about Amīnī's proposed land reform (until after his dismissal), and in private declared it to be a total lie; it concentrated instead on personal attacks on Amīnī for his role in the consortium oil agreement, and Arsanjānī, for his previous ties with Qavām al-Salṭaneh. If the Shah himself had been in charge of its operations, he could not have used the Front more skilfully in his own favour and against his *entire* opposition (including the Front itself)! Why did this National Front – in whose hands the fate of a nation, and the trust of a large body of its political public had been put – embark on such an unmitigated suicide mission? The short answer is, because of a combination of analytical feebleness, political misjudgement, absence of a decisive leadership, lack of internal democracy, and organizational chaos. The political body which had inherited the great legacy of Muṣaddiq and the Popular Movement was thus an empty bluff which led another popular movement to a perfectly avoidable defeat, and paved the way for the predictable disaster of the Shah's personal despotism.

This was predictable, and it was predicted in detail, and with precision, by Khalīl Malekī and the Socialist League: from the very beginning they pointed out that the defeat of Amīnī by the Shah would not only spell doom for the democratic opposition, but also result in a 'fascist dictatorship' the like of which had not been seen in the country; they emphasised that, by offering a progressive programme – including a genuine land reform, political democracy, international non-alignment, reorganisation of the state bureaucracy, reduction of military expenditure, and so on – the Front should turn itself into an alternative (shadow) government; they criticised the organisational chaos of the Front, and suggested ways of turning it into an effective political force; they argued, with realism, that, even if an immediate general election were held, the Front would only be able to send a few deputies to the

Majlis, owing to its lack of organisation (even lack of a sufficient number of candidates), its internal feuds, and the interference of both the army and the provincial conservative powers; they suggested that therefore the Front should remain in opposition, but avoid a total war with Amīnī's government. Leaving aside private counsel to the more prominent members of the Front's leadership, there is overwhelming published evidence of the League's correct analysis of this situation. Yet the National Front publicly ignored all these warnings and suggestions, and privately responded by demagogic insinuations, especially against the person of Khalīl Malekī. A few days before Amīnī's fall, the Socialist League issued a long public communiqué containing an acute analysis of the Front's mistakes, offering intelligent suggestions for the immediate future, and including the following prophetic statement:

> If things go on in the same way, the National Front as a political force will be destroyed, and, instead of being the headquarters of those who struggle in the Iranian Popular Movement, it will be turned into a disused temple for its most faithful believers alone to attend each other's funeral services, and nod their heads to one another as a sign of recognition and regret.[6]

Amīnī's government was dismissed in July 1962, fourteen months after its inception. Yet even that was not the end of the lesson for the National Front. On the contrary, it gave the impression of believing that its own turn was round the corner.

Apart from disorganisation, political naïveté, intractable personal ambitions, and a certain degree of internal sabotage by dubious characters, the 'logic' of the National Front's attitude and conduct may be summarised as follows. It refused to present even a minimal political programme, because, as it argued openly, *any* programme – other, that is, than calls for free elections, a neutral foreign policy, democratic (*mellī*) government, and so forth – would be 'divisive'. Apart from anything else, this says something about the kind of incompatibilities gathered in the Front's High Council. By extension, the Front was genuinely fearful of even declaring general support for the *idea* of a land reform, because of the opposition of the conservative forces to it. Indeed, in a belated little pamphlet published in autumn 1962 – the only one of its kind ever produced by the Front – it effectively argued that since feudalism had never existed in Iran, there was, therefore, no need for a land reform![7] It is true, as we have argued in Chapter 2 above, that Iran was not a feudal state, but this hardly constitutes grounds for leaving the existing landlords – who, incidentally, had had their property rights greatly strengthened since 1941, and particularly since the 1953 coup – to continue exploiting 70 per cent of the Iranian people. Indeed, Arsanjānī, the minister in charge of land reform, had already used this argument in order to defend the land-distribution programme from the charge of attacking private property, which is sacred in Islam.[8]

There was also the Soviet Union and the Tūdeh Party. Although Soviet hostility – dating back to 1959 – was systematically directed against the Shah and Amīnī alike, the Persian programmes of Moscow Radio gave the distinct impression that the main object of attack was Amīnī and his government. For example, in defending Iranian political prisoners, they specifically named the infamous racketeers Rashīdīyān and Furūd, who had been locked up by Amīnī both because of their record of corruption and because they were busy plotting on behalf of the Shah. We have already discussed the 'rationale' behind this attitude in various contexts: Amīnī was regarded as the American candidate *par excellence*, and so had to bear the brunt of Soviet hostility until such time as he had managed to establish his position – in which he failed. The Tūdeh leadership abroad was not well informed about the situation; it was still busy *mis*applying Marxist–Leninist theories in its assessment of the political situation in Iran; given that it did not foresee the consequence of Amīnī's failure, both for itself and for others, it had no interest in his fate; and, finally, it is very unlikely that its attitude could have been significantly different from the Soviet Union's.

This combination of the Soviet and Tūdeh strategies helped harden the 'line' of the National Front in its groundless fear of losing the propaganda game to the Tūdeh Party, alienating its own members, and perhaps even losing some of them to the Tūdeh Party.

THE SHAH AND HIS 'WHITE REVOLUTION'

The Shah had pulled off a number of domestic and international tricks to get rid of Amīnī. As we have seen, he had first given landlords and their allies the impression that land reform was an American plot in which he had no role or interest. At the same time, he mobilised the SAVAK and well-known racketeers and thugs both against the National Front and against Amīnī's government. In addition, he had gathered a band of ambitious, ideologically *déclassé* and politically unprincipled younger technocrats in a private club, calling itself the Progressive Centre, as his own alternative government. This contained a nucleus of men such as Amir 'Abbās Hovaidā, who later became agents and administrators of the Shah's despotic rule for fifteen years. However, within a few months of Amīnī's government, His Majesty concluded that he could not obtain American support for himself as long as he maintained his critical attitude towards the land reform, and that Amīnī and Arsanjānī would implement their programme, steal his show, and push him aside in the hierarchy of power. Therefore, he invited himself to Washington, where, whatever other horses were traded, he must have promised Kennedy full support for the land reform, and obtained some reassurances for himself.

A few weeks after his return, the Shah engaged in a conspiracy to force Amīnī's resignation by laying a large trap for the National Front, which predictably fell into it: on 21 January 1962, the army's crack troops raided the University of Teheran in full force, broke up a large campus demonstration, savagely attacked, beat and maimed many young men and women, entered, the faculty buildings, smashed doors, windows and laboratory equipment, and threw students, chairs and library books out of the upper-storey windows. The raid had been planned well beforehand for a dual purpose: to teach a very hard lesson to the students, and – more significantly – to bring down the government. The demonstration's specific purpose was to protest against the reported expulsion of one or two secondary-school pupils for political activity. The case had not been properly investigated; there was no great urgency about it; and it was not necessary to use a mallet to crack a nut – i.e. to organise such a large political demonstration over such a relatively small issue. Furthermore, some information about the Shah's plot had leaked out the day before, and was entirely ignored by the National Front leaders in charge of student activities. In fact, it is very likely that – for reasons which are not yet wholly clear – a couple of National Front leaders had insisted on that day's demonstration with some previous knowledge of the conspiracy. Therefore, unless they were the Shah's agents (which is improbable), they must have believed that Amīnī's fall in those circumstances would somehow be useful to themselves.[9] The commando raid was so indiscriminately barbaric that the University president and senate resigned, declaring that it had had no precedent since the Mongol invasion of Iran. However, Amīnī was more stubborn than even the Shah can have believed: he responded by making a public statement in which he said that he had had no knowledge of the attack until after the event. It was implicit who had! What he told the Shah in private is not known.

Amīnī's resignation in July 1962 was probably due to a miscalculation, although circumstances had already made his fall inevitable: he took issue with the Shah over the size of military expenditure, and, when His Majesty insisted on his own, higher figure, Amīnī resigned, perhaps hoping that the Americans would come to his support. But the Shah had already made his deal, and the Americans had realised that Amīnī could not establish his political authority in the country: he lacked a popular, even a social base; and *all* the political forces – the Shah and his civil and military henchmen, the National Front, the landlords, and so on – were opposed to his government.

The Shah ordered Asadullah 'Alam – his most loyal servant, and the leader of the Mardum 'party' – to form a caretaker cabinet, and personally took over the direction of events. But, to keep up appearances both at home and abroad, Ḥasan Arsanjānī, the Minister of Agriculture who was most closely identified with the land-reform programme was kept in his post for another year. The screws were tightened against all opposition, including Ali Amīnī, the Shah's obsessive hatred of whom was now second only to his hatred of Muṣaddiq. But an olive branch was privately offered to the National Front leaders: at first, they were offered a deal including a few cabinet posts, which fell through apparently because of an indirect intervention by Muṣaddiq; next, the Front leaders were asked to nominate two independent elder statesmen, one of whom the Shah would appoint to the premiership. They suggested the old-school politician Najm al-Mulk, who was unacceptable to the Shah because of his forceful character and bluntness, of which the Shah had already had an unpleasant taste; and Muhammad Surūrī, the respected Chief Justice, who, although acceptable to both parties, was too intelligent to take on a completely thankless task.[10] Thus, the sherbet parties were soon over, and attitudes hardened.

Having chased Amīnī out of office and secured American support for himself, the Shah was aware that his espousal of the land-reform programme still involved a serious risk to his position: landlords and other conservative forces would not give up without a struggle; the economy, although showing signs of recovery, was still in poor shape; political dissatisfaction and opposition were still strong, even in spite of the feebleness of the National Front's leadership; and Ali Amīnī, who had gained some popularity immediately after his resignation, had not yet given up the fight. The Shah therefore planned the greatest manouevre of his life: a deal with the Russians abroad, and a 'revolution' at home.

The rapprochement with the Soviet Union would, *and did*, stop its damaging propaganda and other agitations; demoralise the naïve and forgetful Iranian public, who, in their despair against internal oppression, have always regarded the tactical hostility of a foreign country towards their régimes as being due to that country's innate goodness, as well as good-will towards themselves; and effectively discredit the Tūdeh Party leadership. The 'revolution', would, *and did*, present him as a powerful and progressive leader to the outside world; rally the (apolitical) Iranian peasantry to his side, at least for a crucial period; eliminate the landlords, together with their power base, as a class; restrict traditionally autonomous and potentially dangerous communities such as the *bāzār* and, especially, the religious leaders; and throw into confusion the broadly democratic and, particularly, left-wing opposition, most of whom accepted a simple and mechanistic analysis according to which the Shah was the representative of the feudal class and a puppet of American imperialism.

The programme of the Revolution of the Shah and the People (or 'White Revolution') contained six points of principle, with no details: distribution of arable land (the first stage of which had already begun under Amīnī); nationalisation of woods and forests; electoral reform, including the granting to women of the right to vote, and to be elected to the *Majlis*; de-nationalisation of state monopolies in order to finance the land-reform programme; company profit-sharing for industrial workers; creation of a 'literacy corps' by sending educated conscripts to 'campaign against illiteracy' in rural areas.[11] On 26 January 1963, this programme was put – *in toto*, in De Gaulle's style – to a plebiscite entitled 'the National Approval', and, as usual, 90 per cent of the entire electorate (including the abstainers!) voted for it. Over the next fifteen years, a number of other 'principles' – the establishment of a health corps, the nationalisation of pastures, and so forth – were arbitrarily added to this list, until now, when the revolution of the people against the Shah has finally got rid of the Shah's revolution against the people.

THE MASSACRE OF JUNE 1963

The National Front and the Tūdeh Party were thoroughly confused by the event, for their theoretical apparatus was incapable of a clear analysis of the situation. The Front could not even formulate a sensible tactic in order to cope with the Shah's *coup de grâce* against it. Up to then, it had not only offered no programme for action, but it had even emasculated two of its three basic principles: it had changed its demand for democratic (*mellī*) to one for legal (*qānūnī*) government; and it had reduced the clear principle of international non-alignment to the ambiguous slogan of 'an independent national attitude' to foreign relations (the Shah was soon to adopt this meaningless phrase as his own principle of foreign policy!). During the months of preparation for His Majesty's Revolution, the Front had passed no comment at all on the various 'principles', except that in its earlier little pamphlet it had implied that, since there had been no feudalism in Iran, a land reform would be meaningless.

Having been caught with their political trousers down, on the eve of the plebiscite the Front leaders issued a public statement most of which discussed the absence of freedom in the country, ending with the advice to the public to respond to the plebiscite by saying, 'Land reform, etc. – yes, I agree; dictatorship – no, I disagree'.[12] This was typical of a leadership which had seldom been able to give a clear direction even to its own supporters, for they knew very well that the plebiscite involved a straight positive or negative answer. It is, in any case, unlikely that more than a few hundred voters ever saw their public statement. Clear evidence for the Front leaders' total confusion is provided by their Council meeting of October 1963 – nearly five months after the June massacre – at which a leading figure of the Front summed up the situation as follows:

> The régime's position, which is supported by both East and West, has become stronger, such that it regards itself thoroughly successful. . . . And, besides, the régime is apparently claiming to have done those things which we have always had in mind, the reforms which we intended to carry out: those apparently progressive ideas which are acceptable to everyone. The question which still remains is [the principle] that the Shah must reign not rule; and the other task which we can still point out – and which it cannot claim to have done – is the establishment of freedom. . . .[13]

Apart from the mood of total despair which is betrayed by these words, one wonders when, where and how the Front's leadership had intended to carry out *any* programme at all. However, the second National Front was already undergoing a process of dissolution, and it was soon to wither away.

Other social and political forces, which did not suffer either from intellectual feebleness or from practical indecision, saw the situation differently, and clearly. The landlords realised that the White Revolution would spell doom for themselves not only in pure economic terms, but also in the broader sociological sense: that is, it would eliminate them as a powerful socio-economic class. Their old-school political allies – men such as Ḥusain 'Alā and Ḥāj Āqā Reżā Rafī' – were also unhappy. But the most important challenge to His Majesty's White Revolution came from the religious community.

The attitude of the religious leadership and the faithful requires a careful assessment. At the politico-sociological level, three distinct tendencies among the religious leaders may be identified. First, there was the traditionalist conservative tendency (whose leading representatives were the Āyatullahs Khomainī, Behbahānī, and Chelsutūnī), which was against both land reform and 'women's rights', and against the potential hegemony of the Shah, which – with uncanny instinct – all the religious leaders saw coming as a result of the 'revolution'.[14] Secondly, there was the anti-despotic tendency, symbolised by the Āyatullahs Milanī and Shari'atmadārī, whose main concern was the threat of the return of despotism in the style of Reżā Shah; they were not, however, opposed to the *spirit* of the Shah's reforms as such. Thirdly, there was the radical democratic tendency – best identified with the Āyatullahs Zanjānī and Ṭāliqānī – which had always identified itself with Muṣaddiq and the Popular Movement; its advocates were opposed both to the 1953 coup and its resulting dictatorship, and to the threat of despotism.

The movement was led by the Āyatullahs Khomainī, Shari'atmadārī and Mīlanī, the three *Marāji'al-taqlid* in Qum and Mashhad, and – more covertly – by the Āyatullahs Behbahānī and Chelsutūnī, the powerful *'Ulamā* of Teheran. Āyatullah Zanjānī and Sayyed Mahmūd (later Āyatullah) Ṭāliqānī, had already been active against the régime since the 1953 coup. The most forceful and outspoken challenge, however, came from Āyatullah Khomainī, who thus began to lead and symbolise the whole movement.

The Shah was in a powerful position to meet the challenge, both politically and militarily. And its propagandist position was further strengthened by the traditionalist religious tendency's spoken, and occasionally printed, statements specifically directed against the land reform and 'women's rights' (in fact, even men did not enjoy any political rights, let alone women!). It thus identified the whole movement with 'black reaction', 'feudal conspiracy', and so on – a viewpoint that for a long period of time had a lot of naïve and biased consumers, especially in the foreign academia and mass media.

The movement gathered momentum in the holy month of Muḥarram, when religious leaders and preachers were openly comparing the Shah with Yazīd, the Ummayid caliph on whose orders Imām Ḥusain and his family were massacred in the plain of Karbila, thirteen centuries ago. On 6 June 1963 (15 Khurdād 1342 AH), massive riots erupted all over the country. The Shah withdrew to the Sa'ad-Ābād Palace, in the northern suburbs of Teheran, and, as the *Daily Telegraph*'s headline triumphantly put it, ordered his troops to 'shoot to kill'. The massacre continued for three days, until the people decided that they had offered enough sacrifice for that round. There exists no proper estimate of the number of those killed and wounded, if only because – *dead or alive* – they were quickly cleared off the streets, buried in hastily dug mass graves, or dumped, from the air, into the inaccessible salt lake of Hawż-i Sulṭān, between Teheran and Qum. The official estimates put the number of casualties below ninety (!) – as against unofficial estimates of 5000 to 6000. For the country as a whole, the figure must have been at least a couple of thousand.

This was neither a purely religious, nor a purely conservative, nor a purely radical and democratic, uprising: it was an insurrection of *the people* against *the state*, and it included *all* of those tendencies among its participants. It was led by religious leaders, particularly Khomainī, and it was manned by the *bāzār* community, small traders, shopkeepers and artisans, students, workers, the unemployed, and political activists. Religion was its overall cloak, and anti-despotism its common denominator. The leadership was passed on to the religious community because of the traditional role and significance of Shī'ism and its leaders as a powerful autonomous social force; because of the clarity of mind of religious leaders and the faithful regarding the nature of the events – a clarity that was in total contrast to the confusion of the National Front leaders (and the Tūdeh Party leadership); and the historical, moral and physical courage of leading religious figures, most notably Āyatullah Khomainī's.

The only honest *and* intelligent summary evaluation of the events from outside the country (indeed, perhaps from anywhere) in the period immediately following them appeared in a little-known article by A. K. S. Lambton:

> The disturbances were subsequently alleged to have been stirred up by the opponents of land reform and women's suffrage. They no doubt had a finger in the pie, but it would be an oversimplification of the issue to attribute the disturbances . . . to them. . . . Unless there had been a feeling that injustice (*Ẓulm*) had passed all reasonable bounds, it is unlikely that the protest would have taken the form it did. . . . What is interesting is the extent to which political opposition still tends to manifest itself in religious guise.[15]

An Economic Round-up

Between 1960 and 1963 the Iranian economic situation was conditioned by the political conflict and power struggles which it had helped to actualise and intensify. The previous boom, inflation and balance-of-payments deficit had forced the state to tighten credit, impose import surcharges, reduce public expenditure, and go begging abroad. These policies radiated through to the business sector, and led to a number of bankruptcies and bank failures; in addition, the general atmosphere of political uncertainty and poor economic prospects reduced domestic saving and investment. It is likely that the tight monetary control played the most effective role in the circumstances: unofficial interest rates in the urban business sector rose to 30 per cent; and urban land values, which at the time were almost the only speculative assets, fell sharply by 500 per cent. In general, monetary policy tends to be an effective short-term instrument in underdeveloped countries because of the relative insignificance of speculative balances in the total demand for money.

The economy was depressed but not stagnant: the oil revenues were increasing fast because of increasing exports; and American aid provided helpful short-term relief. For the period 1960–2, the percentage annual average rate of growth of GNP per capita was 1.6, of oil revenues 10.0, of manufacturing and construction 5.6, of services 0.8, and of agriculture 1.6. The low average growth rate of services is partly due to the effect of Amīnī's reduction of military–bureaucratic expenditures in his first budget. The very poor performance of agriculture was, directly, because nearly all the oil revenues and foreign loans were spent in the urban sector, and, indirectly, because of the campaign for land reform. The much faster growth of manufacturing and construction, especially in 1962, was also due to the expenditure of oil revenues and foreign aid in the urban sector. The future pattern of the impact of oil revenues on the economy is already evident from these simple observations.

The size and pattern of saving and investment provide a glimpse of what was yet to come. From Table 11.1 the following observations may be made: first, two-thirds of total gross investment went to 'construction', and only one-third was spent on machinery; secondly, most of the *state* investment was in construction; thirdly, private investment was almost twice state investment,

TABLE 11.1 Percentage distribution of gross domestic fixed-capital formation, 1960–2

	1960	*1961*	*1962*	*Average 1960–2*
Construction	60.8	67.2	71.8	66.6
Private sector	(34.8)	(39.6)	(41.4)	(38.6)
State	(26.0)	(27.6)	(30.4)	(28.0)
Machinery, etc.	39.2	32.8	28.2	33.4
Private sector	(32.0)	(22.5)	(21.3)	(25.3)
State	(7.2)	(10.3)	(6.9)	(8.1)
Total	100.0	100.0	100.0	100.0

Source: based on Bank Markazi Iran, *National Income of Iran, 1959–72* (Teheran, 1974) table 86, p. 89.

even though the oil revenues and foreign loans were directly received by the state.

Table 11.2 provides us with a telling picture about many things: the net inflow of foreign capital, which was about 3.5 per cent of GNP in 1960, became insignificant in 1961 and increased to 3.0 per cent in 1962; gross saving out of non-oil output was generally negligible, and net saving was negative; the state, receiving the entire oil revenues plus direct and indirect taxes (which, for lack of complete data, have not been separately shown), invested appreciably less than the private sector: in 1960, the oil revenues plus foreign credit amount to a total of 41,200 million rials, yet the state invested only 18,400 million rials even though it had collected 20,700 million in indirect taxes and x amount from direct taxation! The depression of the following years has modified this picture, although the pattern remains the same: in each of these years *domestic* addition to capital stock – that is, *the sum of national and foreign investment* (or disinvestment) – was, on average, 9.9 per cent per annum. Yet on the face of it, the average annual rate of 'saving' and 'investment' was 17.2 per cent!

During these years a team of foreign consultants was busy trying to draft a *comprehensive* plan for the period 1962–7. By then, comprehensive planning had become both respectable among Western technicians and fashionable among Iranian (and similar) technocrats. The plan frame was based on

TABLE 11.2 Composition of national output and expenditure, 1960–2 ('000m. rials)

	1960–1	*1961–2*	*1962–3*
1. Aggregate non-oil output (at market prices)	268.0	273.4	284.2
2. Oil revenue	31.0	35.2	40.0
3. Net inflow of foreign capital	10.2	1.3	9.5
4. GNP, at market prices: (1 + 2)	299.0	308.6	324.2
5. GDP, at market prices: (3 + 4)	309.2	309.9	333.7
6. Aggregate consumption	253.7	254.9	265.3
7. Gross national saving (excluding oil revenues) (1 – 6)	14.3	18.5	18.9
8. Replacement of capital stocks	20.9	21.6	22.7
9. Net national saving (excluding oil revenues) (7 – 8)	–6.6	–3.1	–3.8
10. Gross domestic investment	55.5	55.0	49.4
private investment	(37.1)	(34.2)	(31.0)
state investment	(18.4)	(20.8)	(18.4)
11. Net domestic investment (10 – 8)	24.6	33.4	26.7
12. Net national investment (11 – 3)	14.4	32.1	34.2

Source: Bank Markazi Iran, *National Income of Iran, 1959–72*, various tables. For the theoretical and technical basis of the tabulation see Ch. 12, Appendix.

assumptions a lot of which bore little resemblance to reality: there was, for example, no reference to an imminent land reform! The régime's intention was not serious; its main purpose was to keep up with the Joneses of comprehensive planning. And the plan was never adhered to, either in the letter or in spirit. The interested reader may consult the works of Baldwin, and Olsen and Rasmussen, who, as members of the advisory group, present a fairly clear account of the saga, and the socio-bureaucratic frame of mind which betrayed the reality of the game.[16]

NOTES

1. I was myself an eye-witness of the sit-in at Teheran University, its consequences and its inglorious ending. This and the later critical references to the role and position of Dr Shāpūr Bakhtīyār in the events of 1961–3 are entirely unrelated to his attitude and behaviour towards the end of the recent revolution, when he became Prime Minister in extremely difficult circumstances; nor should they be used in an attempt to confuse the issues over this recent episode. See further Ch. 17, below.
2. The Shah fell into a rage at the implications of this analogy for himself, but failed to obtain Alamūtī's dismissal. Four years later, he was strong enough to take his childish revenge by denying the sick Alamūtī a trip to Europe which might have saved his life. It is enlightening about His Majesty's character (and, in this sense, useful for the understanding of many important events when this man held total power over the destinies of an entire nation) that when, in 1965, Alamūtī died, he fell into another rage because the Ministry of Justice was effectively closed while the judges attended Alamūtī's funeral, which had been announced and led by Amīnī; and, a few months later, he publicly rebuked his own subservient Minister of Justice for 'representing' those judges who, to quote the Shah's own words, had 'attended the funeral of a corrupt traitor, at the invitation of another corrupt traitor'.
3. For a more detailed study of the League's position, see my introduction to *Khāṭirāt-i Sīlyāsī-yi Khalīl Malekī* (Teheran: Ravāq, 1980); see further, the Leagues' various publications, especially its quarterly periodical *'Ilm u Zingidī* ('Science and Life') and its weekly journal of the same name, between 1960 and 1962. These formal publications were officially banned afterwards, but the League went on issuing statements, communiqués and pamphlets until 1965, when its leaders were arrested.
4. I was an eye-witness of this attack, which had been intended both to terrorise the opposition and to obtain a pretext for an official ban on political meetings (even in private grounds), in the name of public peace and order.
5. Ṭayyeb (Hāj Reżā'ī), prompted and paid by the two most powerful religious leaders in Teheran, Behbahānī and Chelsutūnī, had been a leading organiser of the anti-Muṣaddiq street demonstrations on the day of 1953 coup.
6. Socialist League of the Popular Movement of Iran, public communiqué, July 1962; repr. in *Socialīsm* (quarterly periodical of the League of Iranian Socialists in Europe), I, no. 5 (Nov 1962). In a long private letter written to Dr Muṣaddiq in March 1963, Khalīl Malekī presented a frank and clear analysis of the reasons for the Front's failure, which must now be regarded an important political document

of the period. (This has now been posthumously published by Murtiżā Muẓaffarī, although the published version is slightly at variance with a copy of the original in my possession. See Khalīl Malekī, *Du Nāmeh* ('Two Letters') (Teheran: Murvārīd, 1979).

7. The argument about Iran not being a feudal society was extremely loose, lacking both theory and historical evidence, except for some broad references mainly to the fact that many landlords had been persecuted under Reżā Shah. See *Mashy-i Aṣlī-yi Jibhi-yi Mellī* ('The Basic Line of the National Front') (Teheran, 1962).
8. In fact, it could be argued that only personal possessions and *merchant* capital are sacred in Islam – not productive property, and especially not landed property.
9. There were strong rumours in the higher circles of the opposition (emanating from the High Council of the National Front itself) that, the night before the event, General Taimūr Bakhtīyār had sent a message to the Front saying that, if Amīnī's government fell, and he was helped to replace him, he would both be sympathetic to the Front and 'personally apologise to Dr Muṣaddiq' for his own past misdeeds!
10. High Council (on foreign affairs), although he was not a member of the Front, and his special relationship with it was not publicly known. The Shah's dislike for him dated back particularly to 1955, when Najm, turning down his invitation to replace Ḥusain 'Alā as Minister of the Imperial Court, said that he would make a 'good counsellor but a bad lackey'. Both this information and that concerning the search for a compromise candidate, ending with Surūrī's declinature of the premiership, come from one of these two statesmen themselves.
11. The implementation and consequences of these 'principles' will be discussed in the following chapters.
12. The statement was published on 22 January, but it was poorly circulated even in Teheran itself.
13. See *Mukātibāt-i Muṣaddiq* ('Muṣaddiq's Correspondence') (?Paris: Intishārāt-i Muṣaddiq, 1975) document no. 59, pp. 126–34, esp. p. 128
14. I myself saw a printed public statement signed by Āyatullah Khomainī in 1963 which advised the faithful to oppose the land reform and 'womens' rights' as well as the Shah's dictatorship, etc. See further Chs 16, 17 and 18, below.
15. See her 'On the Position of the *Marja'al-taqlīd*', in *Studia Islamica*, 1964. See further her *The Persian Land Reform* (London: Oxford University Press, 1970). Ten years later, when I suggested the following assessment of the June 1963 revolt (which I had held for a long time), it was gibed at by Western liberals and Iranian radicals alike, although for very different theoretical and ideological reasons:

> The reform did not take place without considerable political turmoil. The National Front were still demanding free elections. Some landlords felt that they had been betrayed by their own people. The *'ulamā* were disenchanted for a number of different – reactionary and libertarian – reasons. But one thing is quite clear. All these forces felt that the events of 1962–3, if allowed to succeed, would lead to a complete loss of what autonomy they had, since 1941, enjoyed. There can be no doubt that, on the whole, the opposition viewed the matter as one of life and death. The revolt was 'ideologically' heterogeneous. Incoherent and otherwise incompatible as they were, the participants were brought together by a last desperate attempt to prevent the re-emergence of the traditional total power in Persia.

See M. A. H. Katouzian, 'Land Reform in Iran: A Case Study in the Political

Economy of Social Engineering', *Journal of Peasant Studies*, (Jan 1974) pp. 220–39.

16. G. Baldwin, *Planning and Development in Iran* (Baltimore, Md.: Johns Hopkins, 1967); P. B. Olsen and P. N. Rasmussen, 'An Attempt at Planning in a Traditional State: Iran', in E. E. Hagen (ed.), *Planning Economic Development* (Homewood, Ill.: Irwin, 1963).

12 Petrolic Despotism (1): Oil and the Political Economy

The Road to the Revolution of 1977–79

The revolution of 1977–79 marked the end of two socio-historical cycles: the *long cycle* which began with the 1921 coup and led to the rise and fall of Reżā Shah's pseudo-modernist despotism, the twelve years of interregnum and dual sovereignty (1941–53), the decade of dictatorship (1953–63), and the fifteen years of petrolic pseudo-modernist despotism; and, the *short cycle* which rose with the Shah's bloody counter-revolution of 1963, reached its peak with the 'oil-price revolution' of 1973–4, and ended with one of the greatest revolutions in human history. The explosion was volcanic in its duration and impact precisely because it marked the end of both these cycles.

There is some truth in the American saying that 'nothing succeeds like success'; that 'success' tends to be self-sustaining and cumulative. But there is also some (perhaps even greater) truth in the old Persian expression that 'when the (water) jet rises too high, it topples' ('what goes up must come down'); that too much 'success' leads to failure. The mechanisms of natural and social change are likely to be different; yet they are both dialectical in the above simple sense. The main difference is that human consciousness can help or hinder – perhaps even alter and redirect – the process of social dialectics. In this case, the cycle of petrolic despotism (which was *not* inevitable) produced its own downturn, and the will of the Iranian people finished it off. That, however, does not mean that the historical institution of Iranian despotism has been totally uprooted. The Shah's 'success' was clearly not for, but against, Iranian society, and that is why it ended in his failure – even though those journalists and academics who merely understand and respect the language of power saw it differently at the time.

Having fulfilled its caretaking mission, the 'Alam cabinet was replaced by the band of intellectual and technocratic mercenaries whom the Shah had been nurturing in the Progressive Centre club – individuals who would be ready to sell their services, sometimes even their souls, to the founts of power, regardless of their constitution, ideology, economic strategy, political attitude, and so forth: Ḥasan Ali Manṣūr, a man of very average ability, and the son of a one-time prime minister; Amīr 'Abbās Hovaidā, brought up in Beirūt, later educated in Paris, one-time affiliate of the French Communist

Party, who had a few years earlier returned to Iran, about which he knew next to nothing; Hūshang Nahāvandī, one-time sympathiser of the Tūdeh Party, later supporter of the National Front, with a doctoral degree in economics from France which cannot have taught him much about the subject; 'Abdul'alī Valīyān, the SAVAK colonel put in civilian offices, the obscurity of whose origin was consistent with his resemblance to Sha'bān the Brainless, both in thought and in action; Hūshang Anṣarī, a shrewd operator with an elementary education who had pushed his way in through speculative activities; Manūchehr Āzmūn, who made a deal with the régime while he was still a prominent member of the Tūdeh Party; Manṣūr Rūḥānī, a former member of the opposition Iran Party, who – apart from his notorious corruption – divided labour with Valīyān in destroying Iranian agriculture and rural society; Bāhirī, a former Tūdeh Party functionary who had reputedly abused party funds in order to study law in Switzerland, as a passport to political 'success'; and so on.

These are a few of the leading individuals who, as no more than servants and lackeys, ran the techno-bureaucratic apparatus of despotism between 1963 and 1968. The reader need only use his imagination to guess what kind of characters were running the SAVAK, the uniformed police, the gendarmerie and the army. The list, even of prominent administrative officials, is too long to complete. Not all the individuals involved, however, would answer to the above descriptions: more specifically, there were a number of officials (mainly at the secondary level) who were not necessarily corrupt, incompetent, or blatantly opportunistic; but these were relatively few and, whatever they may have told their consciences, they acquiesced in the general corruption, injustice and evil.

The new *Majlis* elections, in autumn 1963, were – for the first time since Reżā Shah – *totally* controlled by the state. And the composition of the deputies was yet another sign of the great events to come: they were hand-picked from among all those who would be ready to act as no more than soulless puppets, regardless of social rank and class, profession, political experience, and so forth. Most of them had never been heard of before; a few were well-known wrestlers, weight-lifters, comic actors, and the like. This was sold as evidence for the 'abolition of feudalism' and the emergence of 'political democracy'. In fact, it was the 'legislative' counterpart to the executive cabinet it nominally voted into office.

This was accompanied by the establishment of a new official 'party': of the twin imperial parties of Mellīyūn and Mardum, the former vanished almost overnight, and a new 'party' – the Irān Nuvīn (or Modern Iran) Party – suddenly appeared under the leadership of Manṣūr, Hovaidā and their like. Even the name of this 'party' – though this has gone universally unnoticed – was symbolic: Reżā Shah had once intended to invent a political party by his name, but he had later abandoned the idea.[1] The 'oil-price revolution' of 1973 resulted in, among many other things, His Majesty's discovery that – in spite of his own (wholly dishonest) earlier preachings – Western democracy and a multi-party political system were all decadent (even in Western society). That is how the farce of the Iran Nuvīn and Mardum parties gave way to the black comedy of the Rastākhīz-i Mellī (or National Resurgence) Party.

As the year 1963 drew to a close, the Shah could review his achievements with appropriate pride and self-satisfaction. He had led his White Revolution; held a series of theatrical performances in the name of the Peasants' Congress, the Congress of Free Men and Women, and so on; beaten the drum of 'abolishing feudalism' all over the globe, and even obliterated the term *ra'āiyat* ('landless peasant') from the Persian dictionary; emasculated the National Front; drowned the people's revolt in a pool of blood; purchased the support of both superpowers; put rootless and dependent men – his own men – in the cabinet, the *Majlis* and the army (which had still included a few relatively independent, though not necessarily honest and competent, generals); driven the meddlesome General Bakhtīyār – the former SAVAK chief – out of the country, and purged the SAVAK of anyone who had owed his appointment and promotion specifically to that individual. It was now time to press on with pseudo-modernistic policies in the name of growth and development.

The 1963 'Alam budget had already reflated the economy by running an explicit deficit – explicit because, as Table 11.2 has shown, there already was an annual state deficit, once the accounts were demystified. Between 1963 and 1973, oil revenues began to increase rapidly – at first because of the rapid growth in the volume of oil exports, and later also because of relatively moderate price increases. In addition, there was still some American government credit (mainly for arms purchases) in the earlier years, and an increasing amount of foreign investment later in the period. The period of permanent boom began in 1964.

1964 was also a year of fundamental strategic rethinking, or – as far as the Shah was concerned – reconstruction of Iranian despotism. Dictatorship, plutocracy, oligarchy and similar undemocratic systems are consistent with the existence of some social classes, groups and communities with a degree of autonomy from the state, by virtue of property, income, educational and other status, religious affiliation, ethnic identity, and so forth, so long as they do not overstep the mark. Despotism – that is, the monopoly of both absolute and arbitrary power – is, by contrast, the very antithesis of any such autonomy. That is how, as argued in Chapter 2 of this book, despotism destroys any *functional* distinction between the social classes, even though these classes do exist in the empirical sense of differences in wealth, income, and the like. It turns everyone into a subject – or, rather, object – regardless of his station, if only because his station itself is either owing to the state, or the state can change it for better or worse at a moment's notice. Exploitation, even private exploitation, can and does go on, but the private exploiters themselves can be exploited by the state; and, more important, they have no *right* to exploit, but merely a *privilege* for exploiting; and this privilege may be passed on to anyone else at the state's pleasure.

The Amīnī group had intended to distribute land among the 65 per cent of the existing peasant households which had a traditional right to cultivation (i.e. the *nasaq*-holders); finance the reform by compensating the landlords mainly through the sale of state property; and promote private industry in the urban sector both by encouraging the landlords – who had always constituted an *urban* class – to invest in the urban sector (or at least finance others who were ready to borrow and invest), and by providing direct grants and other support for the same purpose. Theoretically, this would have created a large class of peasant proprietors; perhaps expanded traditional rural manufacturing by the greater employment of landless peasant households, and encouraged their surplus labour to move to towns; led to the expansion of urban modern manufacturing, financed by the state and former landlords, manned by peasant immigrant labour, and controlled by the private sector; and created a social base, both in towns and in villages, for a stable polycentric political system. In practice, it could have led to the emergence of a 'mixed' political economy of its own type. Whether or not these developments would have been workable and/or desirable is another matter (though they would have been infinitely more desirable than the reconstruction of despotism), but this was, or appears to have been, their vision.

The Shah's inclusion of the sale of state property in his White Revolution plebiscite was the result of this immediate legacy, especially as Arsanjānī, the architect of the land reform, was retained as Minister of Agriculture for a year after the fall of Amīnī. When the Shah's own breed of men were ordered to office, the idea of denationalisation of state monopolies in favour of the private sector was still on the agenda: they were calling it 'leaving the business of the people to the people'[2] or, as Khalīl Malekī put it in an article shortly before his arrest and trial, 'to the non-people [*nā-mardum*]'[3] – it was their translation of *laissez-faire* into Persian.

Things, however, changed rapidly. Private shares from a few state monopolies were issued and given to landlords. But the increasing oil revenues and the rising boom led to the growth of existing and the setting-up of new state industries, which, as usual, were run along perfectly bureaucratic lines: from this point of view, there is not much difference between a state bank and the Ministry of the Interior! At the same time, the land-reform programme was quickly overturned in its spirit, and this opened the way to the growing concentration and bureaucratisation of ownership, life and labour in rural society (see further Ch. 15). The combination in the Shah of the contemporary pseudo-modernist and pseudo-nationalist and the Iranian despot gave him the following dream, which the oil revenues helped him realise, to the detriment of the Iranian people and, eventually, himself: to 'modernise' the Iranian political economy by means of investing in heavy industry, creating a consumer boom through import-substitution consumer durables, which would keep the well-to-do and the educated classes quiet, destroying traditional forms of agriculture and the nomadic life, which were both difficult to control politically and a sign of social 'backwardness', and importing the latest and most sophisticated tecnology so that all the world would admit (as a lot of commentators, honestly or dishonestly, did) that Iran was on the road to becoming 'the Japan of the Middle East'; to build up the Iranian army, airforce and navy, partly for his own internal security, but mainly as a practical tool for his chauvinistic boasts (and, probably, designs); to create a police state to crack down on any and all of those who so much as dared to think outside the rules of his new 'mission for his country'; and to do whatever was necessary to purchase and maintain the support and/or friendship of the superpowers and other existing and emerging big powers, both in order to be free of destabilising foreign agitation, and – at the same time – to confuse the bulk of the radical opposition thanks to their simplemindedness in identifying truth, justice, radical ideologies or whatever – at any moment – with this or that foreign state.

Naturally, His Majesty's dream took time to realise in full. Besides, the dictates of foreign policy, the needs and requirements of his Western allies – for example, for policing the Persian Gulf area after the British withdrawal in 1968 – were also very important. He was certainly not independent from foreign powers – especially America; few countries are, in this age of CIA, or KGB, 'diplomacy'. But it would be theoretically ahistorical and factually incorrect to attribute the Shah's petrolic pseudo-modernist despotism wholly, or even mainly, to a grand imperialist design which he had simply been ordered to carry out. In fact, with the rapid growth, and later explosion, of the oil revenues (in which he himself had a direct hand), the Shah gradually became *less* dependent on the Americans; that is why he himself saw little in the great revolution of 1977–9 except an American conspiracy to punish him for his self-assertiveness towards them. He was neither a pure agent of imperialism, nor did imperialism conspire to invent a revolution in Iran. But, of course, old ideas – like old habits – die hard.[4]

Between 1964 and 1966, remnants of the old opposition were still trying to keep the torch alive. The second National Front leadership was about to die of natural causes when Muṣaddiq – the Old Man of Aḥmad-Ābād, who, even in confinement, could see matters more clearly than the entire High Council of the Front – delivered it the *coup de grâce* by his direct interventions through (smuggled) correspondence: the Front leaders resigned *en masse*, and Muṣaddiq gave the lead for the creation of the third National Front, consisting of the Freedom Movement, the Socialist League, the Iran Nation and the People of Iran parties.[5] It was too late. The régime had already begun a savage crack-down on all those opposition leaders who were not ready to withdraw silently.

From the Freedom Movement, Mehdi Bāzargān, Sayyed Maḥmūd Ṭāliqānī, Yadullah Sahābī and others had been 'tried' (in a military tribunal) and imprisoned; shortly afterwards, even their military counsels, appointed by the 'court', were to suffer persecution, on account of their honest defence of the victims! Of the Socialist League, Khalīl Malekī, 'Abbās 'Āqilīzādeh, 'Alījān Shānsī, Reżā Shāyān and others had suffered exactly the same fate. This was also true of Dārīyūsh Furūhar, leader of the Iran Nation Party, and Kāẓim Sāmī, a leading member of the People of Iran Party. There were many others from the rank and file of these parties, student activists, and the like, who were crowded into gaols – with or without trial – and/or conscripted, against all regulations, as ordinary privates, and posted to the back of beyond.

Meanwhile, the general defeat of the opposition, and the Soviet rapprochement with the Shah's régime, which was fully and uncritically endorsed by the Tūdeh Party press, opened up the old internal party wounds;[6] and, at the same time, the coming into the open of the very old and deep-rooted Sino-Soviet hostility provided both a power base and a psychological escape route for a growing number of Tūdeh Party members, first in Europe, and later in Iran itself. There was a pro-Chinese split within the party, which in the course of a few years fragmented into a number of rival groups. But the turn of later events, and in particular Sino-Iranian friendship on the diplomatic level, was to halt this new road to mass conversion. Early in 1965, a few young former Tūdeh members with pro-Chinese sympathies, together with some other oppositionist young men with whom they were in contact, were arrested and charged with conspiracy to assassinate the Shah: a young conscript in the Imperial Guard had already been killed during an unsuccessful attempt on the Shah's life in the grounds of his administrative office, the Marble Palace.

The charge was absolutely false: it is very likely that the conscript, a former National Front supporter, had acted entirely on his own initiative; but, in any case, none of the other young men who were apprehended had been involved in such a conspiracy. What they *had* been involved in were *discussions* concerning the possibility of launching a rural guerrilla campaign against the régime. The idea had originated in a series of informal talks between five twenty to twenty-six year olds in England; three of these young men were not in the country when the arrests were made. The plans were discovered, *at the time of the arrests*, through captured letters and discussion papers; and, afterwards, by the application of torture. It led to charges of conspiring to overthrow the 'constitutional' monarchy, and the like. There was a show trial, in which Parvīsz Nīkk̲h̲āh, a leading member of the group, turned himself into a people's hero by displaying tactless and impulsive courage and defiance, only to become a people's bogyman five years later when he recanted and joined the régime. He was sentenced to ten years' imprisonment; others were sentenced to serve from three years to life imprisonment, though most of them were released sooner. In the *Observer*, Amnesty International's legal observer at the trials, Louis Blom-Cooper, summed up the show by saying that 'the prosecution has no case'.

But an important political assassination had already taken place for reasons which were much closer to the hearts of the ordinary people. Because of a number of previous incidents involving American servicemen and other personnel in Iran, the American government – true to the universal rules of great-power arrogance – had made the further supply of such technical advisers conditional on their immunity from trial by Iranian courts. The Shah obliged by telling his Prime Minister, Manṣūr, to submit the appropriate bill to the *Majlis*. This had had a hateful precedent when, after the Russian defeat of Iran in 1828, the Russians had imposed such a provision in favour of their own subjects, until it was abolished by the 1921 Irano-Soviet treaty of friendship. It is a great measure of the people's feelings against this blatant attack on Iranian sovereignty and the Iranian judiciary, that even the otherwise blank-faced and servile *Majlis* deputies kicked up a row against it and, eventually, passed it only under extreme pressure.[7] But its impact was much greater than a constitutional violation, injury to the national pride of the people, or a naked demonstration of imperialist presence: it hurt the moral and religious feelings of the people, who felt that even their personal lives, privacy and dignity were now on pawn to blue-eyed aliens. It would be impossible to convey the depth of this feeling to anyone who does not thoroughly understand the social and cultural complexities of the land. The religious community became restless, leaflets were circulated, and denunciations were delivered from the pulpit. But, most important of all, Āyatullah Khomainī – who since the uprising of July 1963 had been confined and, later, put under close surveillance – broke his public silence, and delivered a stinging speech against the bill. He was promptly arrested and exiled to Turkey; and, later – as a result of pressures brought by other leading *Marājī'*, such as Āyatullah Sharī'atmadārī – he was allowed to go to the holy city of Najaf in Iraq, whence he was forced to fly to Paris in September 1978.[8]

Manṣūr was assassinated in front of the *Majlis* gates by Muhammad Bukhārā'ī, a young Muslim Iranian who had been incensed by the capitulation of Iranian jurisdiction in cases involving American nationals. It was followed by wholesale arrests of active Muslims, counterfeit trials, and the execution of four people, three of whom had not been directly involved in the assassination. Beginning in 1966, conventional opposition disappeared from the surface, providing the regime with a false sense of total security. That is why the régime, always eager to please a politically inactive intelligentsia, began to distribute posts and privileges even at lower levels, to allow the publication and circulation of such books as the classic Marxian texts (in foreign languages), and – contrary to the 1953–63 period – to race with the intellectuals themselves in uncritical propaganda for such unorthodox literary personages as the modern Iranian writer Ṣādiq Hedāyat, and poet Nīmā Yūshīj, who, in any case, were safely dead. Anything was possible so long as it was not used in defiance of, or even autonomously from, the state. For example, in 1968 the state television cameras were rushed to a literary gathering in Teheran University's Faculty of Letters, where, among others,

Jalāl Āli Aḥmad – the oppositionist Iranian writer and essayist, whom the authorities did not feel strong enough to intern – was talking about Nīmā's life and works.

Yet, the defeat of conventional opposition opened the way to unconventional views and methods. The pathetic failure of the second National Front had already divided its former supporters between those who developed greater commitments to Shī'ism and other Iranian traditions, and those who – encouraged by events in Vietnam and Palestine – began to develop Marxist tendencies. The clandestine group led by Bīzhan Jazanī developed a Marxist tendency critical of the Tūdeh Party, but its members were arrested and locked up before they could move into action; however, they had already sown the seeds of the urban guerrilla movement known as the Fadā'īān-i Khalq (Selfless Devotees of the People) which began its operations in 1970. Another independent Marxist group, the Gurūh-i Filistīn (the Palestine Group) – led by Pāknezhād, a former National Front affiliate – was also uncovered before action. At the same time, Dr Ali Sharī'atī, a sociologist and former member of the Freedom Movement organisation, began to publish his revolutionary interpretations of Islam and Shī'ism. He, too, was first arrested (late in 1971), then released and banished (in 1974), finally escaping to London in 1977 to meet his untimely death. By that time, a radical Muslim urban guerrilla movement, the Mujāhidīn-i Khalq (Holy Warriors of the People) had already been fighting side by side with the Marxist guerrilla group for some years. That is how His Imperial Majesty, now self-titled the Light of the Aryans, became both incensed and obsessed with the 'shit-tellectuals', as he called the Iranian intellectuals in intimate conversations. And that is how the torture machine conquered Iran more thoroughly even than the Holy Inquisition conquered Spain. We shall discuss some of these developments in Chapter 17.

The assassination of Manṣūr had led to the premiership of Amīr 'Abbās Hovaidā. In the nearly thirteen years of his premiership, he caused more harm to Iranian society than any single individual, except his master: he was an intelligent, ambitious and amoral cynic who, like many others like him, cannot have had much self-respect; but who knew better than most of his kind how to please the master, to (mis-)inform him with the 'information' he himself expected, and to help him remain a victim of his own propaganda.

The oil-revenue explosion of October 1973 removed nearly all that was left of a sense of realism and propriety in the Shah and his henchmen. In March 1974, having rid himself from the last remaining foreign outpost of hostility towards his régime by making peace with the Iraqis (through the intervention of President Boumédienne in an 'Islamic' summit in Algiers, thus plunging his knife into the back of the Iraqi Kurdish guerrillas whom he was commited to support) he suddenly launched his new gimmick: the one-party state *via* the invention of the National Resurgence Party. This time, however, the Light of the Aryans was not to be snubbed by the people: he told all those who held an Iranian birth certificate to join 'the all-embracing party', remain silent but 'expect nothing from us' or get their passports and leave the country, for the country was not in need of 'traitors'. A flatteringly euphoric *Majlis* deputy declared the last month of the Persian year (the month of Isfānd, roughly corresponding to March) as 'the month of destiny'; and a British journalist and former Labour minister of disarmament, Lord Chalfont, recorded this nauseating piece in his pro-régime article in *The Times*. The irony of history would soon catch them both on the wing, by proving them right for the wrong reason. Nothing, however, came out of the party: most people signed the book and went on cursing the Shah and his machine; some did not sign, received 'nothing from them', and put up with various degrees of harassment; the party itself became another channel for useless employment, bureaucratic self-advancement, and financial corruption.

The crisis of 1976–7 finally persuaded the Shah to give his government a facelift (as he already had himself) by appointing a new prime minister: the wheeler-dealer Hūshang Anṣārī almost got the job, but in the end the arrogant technocrat Jamshīd Āmūzegār – oil spokesman and Minister of the Interior – was appointed. Hovaidā was retained, perhaps even promoted, as the new Minister of the Imperial Court, and the loyal 'Alam, who was mortally ill with cancer, was dropped without ceremony. The new cabinet (though still retaining Hūshang Anṣārī, who was soon to become Chairman of the NIOC, on the death of Dr Iqbāl) was a better team, even including two or three men of integrity. This was August 1977; they were removed by the revolutionary tide exactly a year later. And six months after that, the Light of the Aryans himself was an international fugitive (see further Ch. 17).

The following theoretical model of the oil countries presents the mechanisms through which the receipt of oil revenues by the state tend to make their indivisible impact on the economics, politics and sociology of these countries, in ways that cannot be completely understood by means of existing theories. The reason for producing a simplified and abridged version of this model here is that it provides the frame of reference for our discussion, in subsequent chapters of the Iranian political economy and its developments. Furthermore, it will enable the reader to see the significance of the oil revenues in reinforcing the historical features of the Iranian political economy in the past fifteen years, and gain an insight into its future prospects. The model is preceded by a brief summary of the politiconomic trends of the twentieth century, which is helpful both in recapitulating the main features of our previous discussions, and in underlining the relevance of the model itself.

Oil and the Political Economy: A Theoretical Framework

THE HISTORICAL PERSPECTIVES

Traditional Iranian despotism drew its strength from the weakness of private property in land – and, by extension, merchant capital as well – on the basis of extensive state property, its direct contribution to state revenues, and the indirect revenues obtained from the varieties of taxes imposed on the output of non-state land. These various sources of income and wealth enabled the state to finance its relatively considerable administrative, military and social expenditures, and at the same time reward and punish the bureaucratic and propertied classes by the assignment of land and grant of privileges, and their withdrawal at will. Social classes – landlords, peasants, merchants, and so forth – had always existed . But there was no guarantee that their members would remain in the same social class for the duration of their own life time, let alone that their descendants would. Therefore, other things remaining equal, the Iranian state was – at least internally – powerful and safe in periods when, for economic reasons, it enjoyed large revenues with which to maintain and even tighten its authority over all the social classes.

When, for reasons which we have briefly discussed in Chapter 3, the financial position of the state began to weaken in the nineteenth century, it tried to supplement it by the receipt of financial grants and loans from, and sales of concession to, foreign sources. This policy, however, proved to be counterproductive, for it effectively weakened the domestic economy further, hence reducing the state's own domestic revenues, and fuelling discontent among merchants and landlords. The *Mashrūṭeh* Revolution was the culmination of responsive movements that had their origins in the unsuccessful urban uprisings of 1848–50 against the state, within the ideological context of religious heresy.

The main reason for the failure of these earlier, and fundamentally political, revolts was – I believe – precisely their formal ideological framework: in this way, they alienated the bulk of the religious leadership and community, and made it easier for the state to suppress them. For the attitude of the religious leadership and community *as a whole* has nearly always played a significant – sometimes decisive – role in the outcome of struggles against the state: this was so in the Tobacco-Régie incident of 1890–1; in the *Mashrūṭeh* Revolution itself; in the successful opposition to the 1919 Agreement; even in the final accession of Reżā Khān to the throne (for, through private talks and public conduct, he managed to get the '*ulamā* to accept assurances that in the event he soon withdrew);[9] in the rise and fall of Muṣaddiq and the Popular Movement – though in this case, as we have seen, matters were more complex; and in the unsuccessful, but dramatic, revolt of June 1963. This, too, seems to be a generally unlearned lesson, even in spite of the recent revolution in Iran and the role of the religious community in shaping it. 'Analyses' based on the role of the 'petty bourgeoisie', and the like, are still proliferating.[10]

The oil revenues had been a relatively reliable source of state finance since 1921, and particularly since 1933. Their total value and share in Iranian exports and output also began to rise from these dates. This, combined with the pseudo-modernist and pseudo-nationalist ideas personified by Reżā Shah, helped in the restoration of despotism in its modern guise, as discussed in Chapters 6 and 7 above. These three factors, however – oil revenues (in addition to traditional sources of state income and wealth), pseudo-modernism and pseudo-nationalism – resulted in the extension of the despotic system to the one (urban) social entity which had usually enjoyed, and jealously guarded, a large degree of autonomy from the state: that is, the religious leadership and community. This autonomy had had many historical and ideological facets; but its economic base was the religious leadership and institutions' financial independence from the state through the existence of (usually inviolable) public endowments (the *owqāf-i ām*) in landed and other property, and the payment of religious dues by the well-to-do *directly* to the *'ulamā*.

The growth of oil revenues added to the quantity and quality of the financial independence and political power of the state relatively to the propertied classes and religious institutions; the growth of state bureaucracy (on which it was partly dependent) increased the demand and supply for European-type education, which became the most important channel for higher bureaucratic positions; and the interdependence of these changes with other material and ideological factors pushed religion, and the religious community, to the periphery of the socio-economic complex. It is anybody's guess what would have been the consequence of these developments had the Second World War not intervened and forced Reżā Shah to leave the throne, and the country. But, once this had happened, the series of events discussed in previous chapters involved the reassertion of power and autonomy by various social groups and institutions – albeit in different degrees, and in various, sometimes conflicting, political forms – until 1963. In this year, the conservative and conventional radical opposition were defeated, landlords lost their economic *power base*, and the people's revolt (organised and led by the religious community) was crushed; soon afterwards, the religious endowments began to be 'administered' by the state. At the same time, the Treasury began to experience a rapid increase in the oil revenues flowing into it. Therein lay the main cause of the rise and the specific features of petrolic despotism, which – as we shall see later – also contained the seeds of its own destruction.

A THEORETICAL FRAMEWORK

What follows is a basic, simple and abstract theoretical framework to elucidate the pure mechanisms of an otherwise complex political economy. It is based on a similar model that was developed for the political economy of development in the oil-exporting countries in general, and those which have a relatively large population – and, commensurately, an extensive rural society – in particular.[11] The model would certainly need appropriate re-adjustments for meaningful application and adaptations to each of the relevant countries: the purely mechanistic application of *any* theory *any*where can result in serious mistakes and – sometimes – catastrophic misapprehensions of present and future events and tendencies.

(i) *Oil, the state and the social classes.* Oil is a scarce and efficient source of energy, capable of diverse use both in generating energy and in producing countless industrial products (such as petrochemicals), and largely concentrated in the Middle East. These are well-known facts which are helpful to the analysis of various regional and international issues of a technical and economic, as well as political, nature. Yet, from the point of view of the producing countries, the most distinctive feature of oil production, export and income is that – except in the initial stages – they require hardly any contribution from the domestic means of production. In particular, the involvement of the national labour force in the production of oil is all but negligible. This provides the most important contrast between oil production and the production of other important minerals, such as coal, copper, diamonds and even gold itself. In the case of all these other minerals, the proceeds are shared by private and public capital and labour; the share of the state in the income (other than the return on its own investment) would, as usual, arise from the indirect taxes imposed on the product, and the income tax paid by the owners of all the means of production. By contrast, oil revenues accrue to the state directly as a large and *independent* source of finance: the state does not even have to depend on the domestic means of production for this revenue, and does not have to return a large percentage of it in terms of wages and other costs, as in the productive enterprises under public ownership.

Therefore, oil revenues are in the nature of a pure collective economic rent (in the technical sense of this term) which is directly paid out to the state. Once these revenues rise to a high level, making up at least 10 per cent of the national output, they begin to afford the state an unusual degree of economic and political autonomy from the productive forces and the social classes of the country. For society at large, these revenues become an invisible (almost mysterious) source of growing 'welfare' through the state, until they begin to appreciate its hidden mechanism (this cannot, of course, be true of those oil countries which are almost exclusively dependent on oil production). However, given the technical and sociological features of oil revenues, they also afford the state a great deal of flexibility in its disbursements: in a word, these do not constitute 'taxpayers' money' for which the state may be held accountable.

To the extent that the oil revenues make the state independent of the domestic means of production and the social classes, the latter become dependent on the state for employment, direct hand-outs and privileges, borrowed capital for investment, booming domestic markets for high profits in production, trade and speculation, as well as general welfare schemes ranging from education and health to food subsidies. Therefore, as the fount of economic and political power which it would like to maintain and enhance, state expenditure affects the fortunes of various social classes. In a larger, agricultural oil country – where the oil revenues *per head of the population* are not large enough to ensure a reasonable living standard for literally everyone – this type of relationship gives rise to a new, petrolic system of social stratification: the state has to be selective in affording even the minimum standard of comfort to individuals, and those who benefit constitute only a small percentage of the urban population.

The expanding military–bureaucratic complex, the professional and other educated groups and even the business class together make up the *clientele of the state*. Clearly, both as groups and as individuals, the increasing numbers belonging to the clientele will benefit from the state in different ways and in varying degrees; what justifies their inclusion in a single category is that they all depend on the state for a level of income and wealth which is compatible with their growing aspirations, and their membership of various privileged social groups makes them perhaps the greatest potential challenge to the state monopoly of power. Next in line are the masses of the urban population, who will look up to the state for actual employment opportunities, a guaranteed minimum wage, food subsidies, public health and educational schemes, and so forth, as well as the chance of rising to join the clientele. This, too, is a heterogeneous social category, some of whose expectations are likely to be frustrated, producing dissatisfaction and bitterness. Last come the vast majority of the rural society, the peasantry, who are too numerous and too poor to count among the beneficiaries of the oil revenues, and in some cases, such as that of Iran, politically too weak (for a variety of socio-economic and historical reasons) to threaten direct retaliation. They are more likely to retaliate with their feet, by marching on the cities and, at their gates, swelling the ranks of those urban masses whom the state would like to keep reasonably happy. This is the first dialectial dichotomy arising from the system itself; but, as we shall see, there will be others. In a word, the petrolic system of stratification turns the state into the *patron* of a growing *clientele*; the *patrimonial guardian* of life and labour for the urban masses; and the *agent of social excommunication* for the peasantry. If, as in the case of Iran, there already exist historical forces and institutions of despotism, and a traditional domination of urban over rural society, the petrolic system merely serves to reshape and reinforce the already existing, or surviving, relations and tendencies.

(ii) *State expenditure: patterns and implications.* The entire system – economic, social and political, together with their various elements – depends on the size and strategy of state expenditure. The state's *consumption* expenditure will rapidly expand its own military–bureaucratic network, both in the size of its membership and in earnings; and bureaucratic earnings set the floor for earnings in other, alternative activities. These effectively unearned increases in the clientele's income lead to a high rate of consumption expenditure, which begins with better food and housing accommodation (even private palaces), motor-cars, modern home appliances, and so on, and ends with higher expenditure on private services, ranging from legal and medical services to restaurants, entertainments, hotels, holidays, and so forth. Therefore, the increase in state consumption expenditure, results – both directly and indirectly – in the expansion of, in particular, bureaucratic and modern services, and also of construction and modern durable consumer goods. On the other hand, members of the clientele are either employers or employed in these very activities: bureaucrats, army officers, import traders, members of the professions, modern hotel and restaurant owners, building contractors, assembly-plant owners, and the like. Thus, both on the demand and on the supply side, the clientele benefits from this change in the economic structure, which becomes circular and cumulative. The only break in the process comes with the increasing shortage of, especially, high-quality food, which can be met through higher investment and productivity in domestic agriculture and/or imports. As we shall see in a moment, the former will not materialise, and the latter will not relieve the pressure.

State *investment* expenditure places great emphasis on the urban sector; it emphasises construction, modern service activities, such as banking and insurance, and heavy industries (steel, machine tools, and so on); and it employs the latest – capital-intensive as well as skill-intensive – modern technology. This is the usual pattern of the pseudo-modernist approach to economic development, with or without oil, the complex reasons for which cannot be discussed here.[12] The difference is in the degree and duration of its applicability: the pseudo-modernist oil country feels able to invest in the capital, to import the machinery, to hire a lot of foreign experts, to expand urban consumption of domestic and foreign products, to remedy the domestic food deficit *via* imports, and to let agriculture die a natural death without worrying about a balance-of-payments deficit. The fact that this strategy does not work quite so easily, even in the 'purely' economic sphere, is something it has to learn from hard experience.

Therefore, the investment strategy of the state also promotes construction, services, and so on, and discriminates against agriculture. This results in agricultural stagnation, a more rapid widening of the urban–rural gulf, a shortage of food and agricultural products from the supply side, and the growth of peasant migration to towns and cities.

(iii) *Modern technology and skilled labour.* The 'rationale' – in fact, the pretext – for the use of high modern technology, and more capital (i.e. machinery) than labour in manufacturing and service industries, is that an oil country has an 'abundance' of financial capital and foreign exchange, and, therefore, both can and should use more capital-intensive techniques of production. There are, however, a number of serious flaws in this argument which may even have escaped the attention of many development economists and experts.

First, an economic resource can be abundant if and only if it cannot be *gainfully* employed: for example, when a certain percentage of the labour force is not gainfully employed anywhere, there is an abundance (or surplus) of labour in the economy, or one of its sectors. But there can be no abundance of foreign exchange in this sense; for its 'surplus' can be either *invested* – i.e. gainfully put to use – abroad, or *prevented*, by exporting less oil, or there may be a combination of the two. Secondly, the blanket term 'capital-intensive technology' itself is misleading: it makes a lot of difference where the capital (i.e. machinery) comes from, and what technology it embodies. Domestically developed equipment will have different financial and technological implications from imported foreign equipment; and foreign equipment itself may have various specifications in cost and technological characteristics. To choose 'capital-intensive' methods is one thing; to use imported and highly technological machinery is something else. Lastly, the oil countries may have an 'abundance' of foreign exchange, but what about their shortage of skilled workers?

The problem of 'the skill constraint' is of course recognised by 'experts'. Some of them may even admit that, to seek to relieve the shortage mainly through hiring foreign skilled lanour of the required types and levels, will be technically impossible, economically too expensive, and socio-culturally troublesome. Yet, they may argue that the problem can be exaggerated: these countries can make large amounts of 'investment in human capital' – a relatively recent terminological mystification for higher and technical eduction – in order to increase their supply of skilled labour. This, however, is too simple and mechanistic a view: it would take too long; its planning and execution would require the kind of administrative machinery which does not and, in the circumstances, cannot exist; it would require a great deal of correct information on present *and* future requirements in various fields; and so forth. Besides, a rapid *quantitative* increase does not gurantee the maintenance of *quality*; and, in any case, conclusions on the social effectiveness – the serviceability – of the results are too readily reached without reference to the social context: if the social system is such that 'skilled labour' prefers to be concentrated in one or two large cities, and, worse still, occupy bureaucratic desks, and in general follow no professional code of conduct except the maximisation of its income *at all costs*, it is anyone's guess what the net social benefit to the society will be.

The 'experts', however, have overlooked one other important issue which they could even use in procuring a few more mathematical 'models': unless a country – with or without oil – has literally just arrived on the world stage, it will have its own traditionally developed techniques of production, and the related skilled labour force – weavers, spinners, dyers, cobblers, smiths, tailors, and so forth. Therefore, the 'shortage of skilled labour' refers to *modern* skilled workers; that is, to those who, at least in theory, can run *imported high technology*. It follows that the application of this kind of technology at once multiplies the import bill, creates an acute shortage of *modern* skilled labour – bidding up their wages and leading to slack capacity – and results in the wastage of *traditional* skilled labour, diluting their skills and incomes, and even turning them into (probably unemployed) unskilled workers. This is the simple economics of the problem; its social implications are even simpler to envisage. Yet, all this is to assume that the economy which applies this kind of capital-intensive technology would otherwise suffer from a long-term shortage of unskilled labour; for, if this were not the case, the country would, sooner rather than later, face an unemployment problem on top of all its other 'achievements'. So much for this one aspect of experts' modernism, and the pseudo-modernism of their clients in the underdeveloped countries – oil or no oil.

(iv) *Money, inflation and the balance of payments*. There is a great family dispute between the monetarists and the 'Keynesians' about whether or not – regardless of the economic, social and cultural context – monetary expansion is inflationary. I incline to leave them to determine their own Universal Truth, while believing that in underdeveloped countries in general, and the oil countries in particular, monetary expansion will tend to be inflationary, although for reasons which are outside the homogeneous universe of the two groups of theorists. In a society where ostentation is a most important determinant of social status (even recognition as a *person*), and incomes, consumption and ownership of household possessions are generally low, people will tend to spend their excess liquidity on goods; and when, for this and other reasons, inflation becomes a feature of everyday life, even those with a great deal of cash to dispose of will buy a lot of durable goods – especially urban land and property – in order both to defend and to improve the value of their liquid assets. Further, because of the general atmosphere of insecurity arising from the politiconomic system, as a whole, they will speculate, but their speculation, the type of assets which they purchase, will itself fan the inflationary fire, and *official* interest-rate charges are unlikely to have much influence in their decisions.

This does *not* mean that money is the cause, or the primary cause, of inflation. Structural inflation – resulting from both monetary expansion *and* real income increases (at different rates in different sectors) – is probably the most important 'cause' of the problem: in the laboratory case of an oil economy in which demand for food – especially high-quality food of all kinds – is rising fast, agriculture is stagnant, and the physical capacity to import (ports, roads, transport facilities, storage capacity, the distribution network, and so forth) is being stretched to its limits by the incoming tide of machines, manufactured goods, raw materials, food, and so on, no amount of foreign exchange will be capable of relieving the bottlenecks at the right time and by the right amount.

This, therefore, is the net result of the state's strategy of expenditure and choice of technology: the creation of excess liquidity; high aggregate consumption; emphasis on imported high industrial technology – which not only jams the ports but also, more significantly, inflates the purse of modern skilled labour out of all proportion; and a feverish race for higher incomes, increased consumption, greater ostentation, and the rest. Unearned private money and income is not only 'morally' wrong; it is – more importantly – economically corrosive, socially destructive, and psychologically destabilising. The case of 'successful' gamblers and even lottery winners has demonstrated this simple fact without any need for mathematical models and econometric tests.

What happens to the balance of payments in such an oil country will depend on the relative size and growth of oil revenues. But, even allowing that there still remains a foreign-exchange 'surplus' – which is by no means true in every case – waste is waste even if the society (or the country) can 'afford' it. And, of course, there is such a thing as the future, near or distant.

(v) *A concluding note.* To recapitulate, the above is the summary outline of a simple model, developed a long time ago – even before the oil-revenue explosion of 1973 – in order to predict the impact of oil revenues on the political economy of, especially, the larger, agricultural oil-exporting countries, with some regard for realism, and with the intention of solving problems. It can be tested, improved, or refuted in specific cases, as long as all the relevant qualitative and quantitative politiconomic factors are carefully taken into consideration. History has proved it right in the case of the Iranian political economy in ways which we shall investigate in the following chapters.

Figure 12.1 portrays a diagrammatic sketch of the socio-economic structure and relations in an 'agricultural' oil-exporting country. In this diagram, relative proximity to the position of oil and state reflects the *level* of linkages, as well as the significance of each sector within the national economy. In addition, the relative thickness of the connecting lines shows the relative *degree* of interdependence. It summarises our brief analytical framework for the political economy of development in the 'agricultural' oil-exporting country. It may be noticed that once the bottom part of the diagram is removed, the remainder may still be relevant to the smaller, desert-type oil economies.

Appendix: A Technical Note

The following is intended to express, in simple technical terms, some of the implications of our model for saving, investment, growth, inflation, and so on.

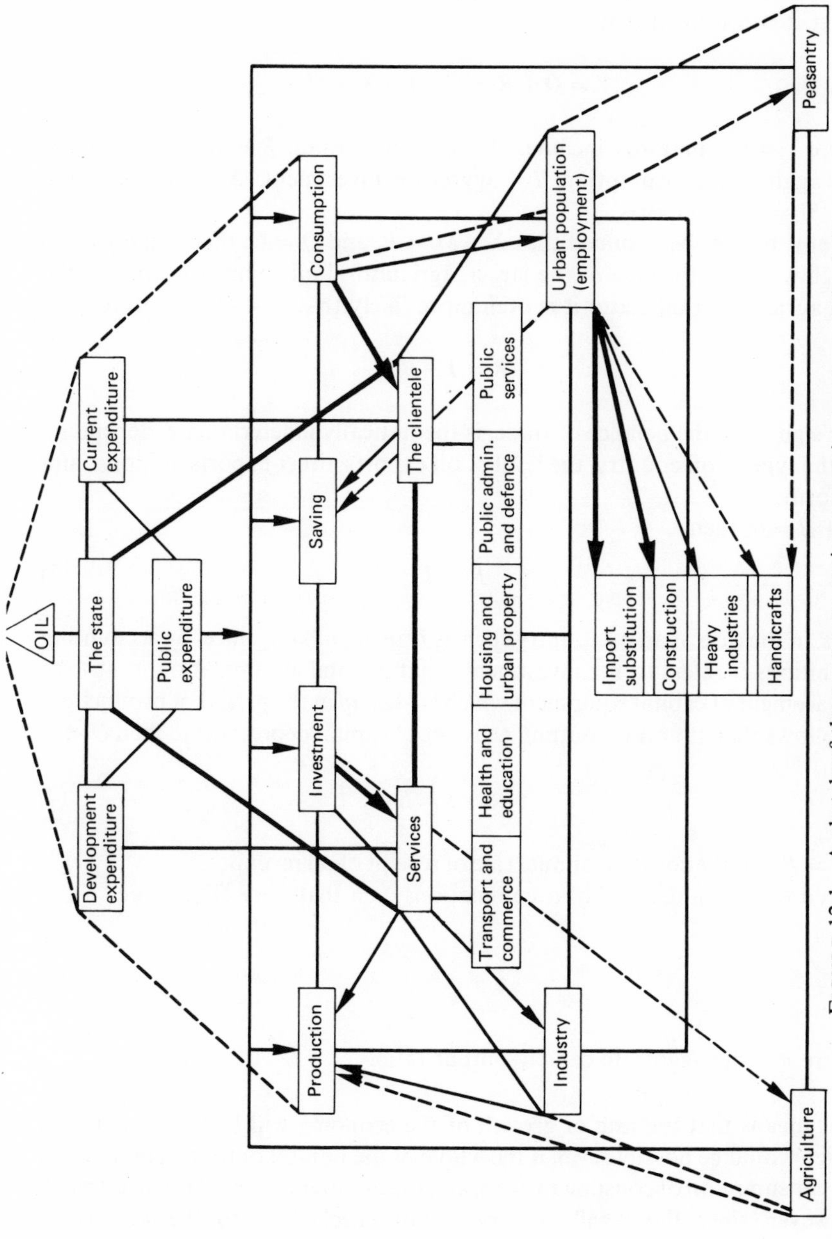

FIGURE 12.1 A sketch of the aggregate socio-economic structure and relations

It would not be difficult to build up complicated mathematical and econometric models on this simple basis, but I do not believe that these would add much to our knowledge of the relevant problems.

Let it be assumed that

$$Y = O + R = C + I + X - M \quad (1)$$

where Y = the national income; O = non-oil output; R = the oil revenues; C = aggregate consumption; I = aggregate investment; X = total exports; and M = total imports.

Let it further be assumed that $X - M = B$; and $O = C$: this is likely to be roughly true in the case of the larger, agricultural oil countries, while in the non-agricultural oil states it is even more likely that $O < C$. Therefore,

$$R = I + B \quad (2)$$

The sign of B, the balance of trade, is theoretically indeterminate, depending on the type of oil country, the level of oil exports, other exports, imports, and so forth.

If $B = 0$, then

$$R = I \quad (3)$$

This, in the case of an oil country such as Iran is unlikely, since, by accounting definitions, I refers to net investment – that is, total accumulation minus the replacement of capital equipment which is *used up* in the period of production. It follows that, if non-oil output, O, is net of capital depreciation, then $O < C$ and

$$R > I = S \quad (4)$$

If $r = R/Y$ is the constant annual rate of receipt of oil revenues, then $s = S/Y$ is the constant annual rate of accumulation, such that $s < r$. Therefore

$$g = \frac{s}{v} < \frac{r}{v} \quad (5)$$

where v = the aggregate capital–output ratio.

This means that the rate of growth of the economy will be lower than that which would be possible even if the whole of the non-oil output were spent on the consumption of consumer goods, and the oil revenues spent on investment. However, since there will be serious bottlenecks due to the scarcity of domestic, non-importable inputs ranging from modern skilled labour to physical facilities for importing, there will be both under-capacity production and sectoral wage inflation. That is, the rate of growth of modern skilled labour will be lower than it would be compatible with the potential rate of growth permitted by the rate of capital accumulation, so that there is both a lower actual growth rate and a high rate of inflation.

To sum up, even if the country has an absolute surplus of oil revenues over national expenditure, it can grow only at the rate permitted by its non-importable domestic input constraints, which themselves may be different for different choices of techniques. Further expansion would be lost in wasted capacity, high inflation, and a worsening income distribution for the less privileged.

NOTES

1. Reżā Khān had intended to convert his Pahlavi Club into a political ('Irān Nuvīn') party, after succeeding to the throne. In this, he had been much influenced by the example of Atatürk, and encouraged by his own entourage. But Reżā Shah abandoned the idea, probably because he was afraid that it might become a partially autonomous political body. See Muṣṭafā Fāteḥ, *Panjāh Sāl Naft-i Irān* (Teheran, 1956); 'Ibrāhīm Khājeh Nūrī, *Bāzīgarān-i 'Aṣr-i Ṭalā'ī* (Teheran, 1942–4); and Ḥusain Makkī, *Tārīkh-i Bīst Sāleh-yi Irān* vols 1–3 (Teheran: 'Ilmī, 1945–7).
2. *Iṭṭilā'āt* and *Kayhān* (daily newspapers), 1963–4, various issues.
3. In his unsigned articles in *Sociālīsm* (monthly newspaper of the League of Iranian Socialists in Europe), 1963–4.
4. See further Chs 16, 17 and 18, below.
5. See *Mukātibāt-i Muṣaddiq* ('Muṣaddiq's Correspondence') (?Paris: Intishārāt-i Muṣaddiq, 1975) Appendix, Part II.
6. This defensive strategy was opened with an offensive campaign under the slogan 'Long live the Irano-Soviet Friendship'. See *Mardum* (organ of the Tūdeh Party), 1963–5, various issues. For a serious appraisal of the Tūdeh Party's systematic justification of the Irano-Soviet relations under all circumstances, see 'A Study of the Views of the Tūdeh Party Leadership concerning Irano–Soviet Relations' *Sociālīsm* (quarterly periodical of the League of Iranian Socialists in Europe), II no. 5 (1965) 4–14.
7. The bill was passed in November 1964, and Manṣūr was assassinated in February 1965. Bukhārā'ī and his three associates were executed in July 1965.
8. Khomainī was threatened with arrest and possible prosecution, but the intervention of Mīlānī and Sharī'atmadārī (who wrote a testimonial to the effect that Khomainī, too, was a *Marja'al-taqlīd*) compelled the régime to exile him to Turkey. Sharī'atmadārī's later intervention enabled Khomainī to go to the holy city of Najaf in Iraq. See interview with Sharī'atmadārī in *Umīd-i Irān* (weekly magazine) June 1979.
9. See Ch. 5, above, for the acquiescence of the '*ulamā* in Reżā Khān's rise to power.
10. As recently as June 1979, Iraj Iskandarī, a founder member and veteran leader of the Tūdeh Party, produced the following analysis of the dominant political forces in Iran: 'The government [of Mehdī Bāzargān] is the representative of the national bourgeoisie, and the Imām [i.e. Khomainī] is the representative of the urban and rural petty bourgeoisie. . . . We do not support the national bourgeois position as represented by the [Bāzargān] government. . . . We defend the people, and,

therefore, we support the correct positions of the petty bourgeoisie against the bourgeoisie.' See the interview with Iraj Iskandari, *Tehrān Muṣavvar* (weekly magazine) XXXVII, no. 21 (15 June 1979) 35–9. See further the interview with Dr Kīyānūrī, General Secretary of the Tūdeh Party, *Irānshahr* (fortnightly magazine) no. 30 (15 June 1979) 17–19. Such superficial 'analyses' (which are *direct reproductions* of the excellent studies by Marx and others of the French Revolution, the *coup d'état* of Louis Bonaparte, and so forth) are, among other things, very convenient, because they make it unnecessary to spend time and effort in learning the *methods* of analysis used by past European scholars, study Iranian history and sociology, and apply relevant theories and methods for a realistic assessment of social and political events in Iran. They are, however, not exclusive to the leaders of the Tūdeh Party. See Chs 17 and 18, below.

11. For the complete version of the model, see H. Katouzian, 'The Political Economy of Development in Oil Exporting Countries', *Peuples Mediterranéens*, Sep 1979, pp 3–22. The first draft of this model was produced ten years ago, and I used it as the theoretical framework for my earlier studies of the Iranian economy and its agricultural sector, published in *Taḥqiqat-e Eqtesadi* (1972), *Quarterly Journal of Economic Research* (1972), and *Journal of Peasant Studies* (1974 and 1978).
12. See H. Katouzian, 'Peasant Societies and Industrialisation: A Critique of Modernism and Pseudo-Modernism in Economic Development', paper presented to the international symposium 'Three Worlds or One?', Berlin Institute for Comparative Social Research, June 1979. A German translation of this paper will appear in the Symposium's proceedings in 1980.

13 Petrolic Despotism (2): the Quantity and Quality of Economic Change

The most important factor influencing the quantity and quality of life and labour from 1964 was the growth, and later explosion, of the oil revenues. Other factors were also at work; but, independently from oil, they would have led to significantly different results. Without the growing oil revenues – and the spurious economic growth which they promoted – the attempt to restore Iranian despotism would not have succeeded – at least, not completely: there would not have been sufficient funds to purchase the co-operation, acquiescence, complicity (or, simply, desperate silence) of various social groups, and individuals; or to finance the pseudo-modernist strategy of economic development. Apart from that, the régime would have been more dependent on Western powers, especially America, because of its military and financial requirements; and less able to establish friendly relations with the Soviet Union, China, and similar countries. By contrast, there would have been less foreign trade and less economic *presence* of foreign capital and labour. In a word, the state would have been much less powerful, and the political economy much more independent of it. Oil was *the* independent variable of the whole socio-economic fabric. Its abuse led to an uneven growth of purchasing power among the urban community; radically changed the structure of the economy; effectively destroyed Iranian agriculture and rural society; rapidly increased social and geographical mobility; resulted in urban regional and environmental problems of unimaginable proportions; brought the traditional, and lower, social strata into the sphere of pseudo-modernist mass consumption; destroyed or diluted some skills and industries, and promoted or inflated others; raised social and material expectations which could not be possibly fulfilled; undermined cultural traditions and communal relations without replacing them with functional substitutes; led to acute bottlenecks and imbalances, both between and within various economic sectors and entities; separated the state from society so much so that it would be difficult to find parallels anywhere in human history; greatly increased death and disability through accidents, cardiac arrests, and cerebral haemorrhages; brought about widespread mental disorder, depression and suicide. These were the main costs of Iran's march towards the Shah's entirely hallucinatory goals of 'the fifth most industrial state in the world', and the 'Great Civilisation'.

Economic Change

We shall postpone a discussion of individual economic sectors to the next three chapters. What follows here is a description and analysis of overall economic change in its various aspects.

ECONOMIC GROWTH AND STRUCTURAL SHIFTS

The oil revenues exploded late in 1973. The preceding decade covered the period of the Third and the Fourth (five-year) Plans; and, the succeeding quinquennium was the Fifth Plan period. It would be wasteful to produce a summary of the sources, allocations and expenditures of these 'plans', partly because they exist in numerous official publications and have been reproduced elsewhere;[1] but mainly because they will not add to one's knowledge of the causes and consequences of economic decisions and events, independently from the basic factors and issues which we have already discussed, and will be discussing further below: in a despotic political economy 'economic plans' are little more than formalisations of whims and propaganda, which are themselves subject to violent fluctuations.

According to different methods of calculation, between 1963 and 1972 the average annual growth rate of GNP was around 8 to 9 per cent, and GNP per capita 5 to 6 per cent: manufacturing, construction and non-oil mining – which later included growing revenues from the sale of gas to the Soviet Union – increased at an average annual rate of around 10–11 per cent per year; services by 8–9 per cent; agriculture by 2–3 per cent; and *oil revenues by 20 per cent*. The oil-revenue explosion of October 1973 makes it very difficult to attach any significance to GNP growth rates in the following years; what is much more important in this period is the *differential* rates of expansion among the domestic non-oil sectors: 'services' rocketed; construction would have grown even faster than it did had there not been a serious shortage of cement, bricks, builders, plumbers, and so forth; manufacturing and mining grew less rapidly, even though a higher price for natural gas was negotiated with the Soviet Union; and agriculture remained the permanent observer of the great fever.

Table 13.1 gives some indications of quantitative change, and structural shift in the economy over the three five-year 'plan' periods. Figures in row 5 of this table show that GNP (which indicates the level of the national income) increased by over tenfold during the fifteen-year period: assuming a *constant* rate of exchange of 75 rials per dollar, this means that GNP rose from $4323 million in 1963 to $49,365 million in 1978; in *per capita* terms, the figures are,

TABLE 13.1 Sectoral distribution of gross national product 1963–78, selected years ('000m. rials, constant prices)

	1962–63		*1967–8*		*1972–3*		*1977–8*	
	Amount	*% of GNP*	*Amount*	*% of GNP*	*Amount*	*% of GNP*	*Amount*	*% of GNP*
1. Agriculture	88.8	27.4	111.1	21.6	271.0	10.3	339.0	9.2
2. Industry	57.8	17.8	106.3	20.7	333.0	12.6	684.3	18.5
manufactures and mines	(41.5)	(12.8)	(72.5)	(14.2)	(224.4)	(8.5)	(468.2)	(12.6)
construction	(14.1)	(4.3)	(24.9)	(4.8)	(91.4)	(3.5)	(179.5)	(4.8)
water and power	(2.2)	(0.7)	(8.9)	(1.7)	(17.2)	(0.6)	(36.6)	(1.1)
3. Services	119.8	40.0	187.0	36.4	629.4	23.9	1281.3	34.6
state services	(24.7)	(7.6)	(48.6)	(9.4)	(207.8)	(7.9)	(402.3)	(10.9)
4. Oil	40.0	12.3	92.4	18.0	1333.3	50.6	1284.9	34.7
5. GNP at market prices[a]	324.2	–	513.8	–	2635.7	–	3702.4	–

[a] This is not the exact sum of rows 1–4, because it includes indirect taxes, and non-oil net factor income from abroad.

Source: based on Bank Markazī Iran, Annual Report, various years, and other official publications.

respectively, $188, and $1410. However, the *actual* dollar figures would be higher for 1978, because of the appreciation of the Iranian currency after 1973.

Oil revenues, which in 1963 were 40,000 million rials, or over 12 per cent of GNP, increased at a high rate (rising to over a quarter of GNP in 1971–2), and suddenly exploded to 133,3300 million rials (nearly $18,000 million) in 1973. The clearest evidence of spurious economic growth is seen in the year 1973, when the share of oil revenues rose to 50 per cent of GNP because of the fourfold increase in oil prices. But, once it had had a chance to permeate through to the economy, this share fell to 34 per cent in 1978; that is, over one-third of GNP was *directly* supplied by the providence of the oil revenues.

Services have made up a large proportion of GNP since the initial period. The question, though, is why 'economic development' should involve the growth of this heterogeneous group of activities at the same rapid pace as the national income itself.[2] Expenditure on education and housing grew fast, although a lot of this was of on wasteful and expensive projects. Transport and trade expanded, but road construction and the like must have been included in the figures for 'construction'. Communications and air services increased at a rapid rate, but their *share* of total services was still very small. This is also true of banking and insurance activities, most of which were, in any case, no more than disguised methods of handing out oil revenues to influential people and privileged social groups. A real clue to the fast growth and high share of services is provided by the item 'state services': this grew faster than any other category of GNP except for oil revenues; *in 1963, it was less than one-fifth of total service expenditure (119.8 thousand million rials), and in 1978, it was almost one-third of total service expenditure (of 1,281.3 thousand million rials); in fact, at the latter date, its total value was almost equal to the entire manufacturing output of the country* (see the 1977–8 figures for manufactures and mines, and state services, in Table 13.1). Yet, it is certain that the figure of state services, especially for later periods, is a deliberate underestimate: a consequence of camouflaging much of the SAVAK budget, and a part of other bureaucratic and military expenditures, under other items. It would not even be surprising if some of the ever-increasing costs of buying sophisticated military equipment are included in the data for state investment in 'machinery and equipment'. There are other reasons for the general inflation of the service group which a mechanistic application of econometric technology is unlikely to reveal: the high rates of earnings of the rentier class of modern skilled personnel involved in their production; and the high levels of consumption by them, and their like, of expensive luxury services such as hotels, restaurants, holidays, and modern educational and medical services. In general, the service sector provides the meeting point of the strong links between oil revenues, the state and its clientele.

On the face of it, 'industry' also grew fast; it contributed 18.7 per cent of GNP in 1977–8. But (a) construction had a permanently large share of this, and it generally grew faster, in later years much faster, than manufacturing output – in fact, the construction fever created by the oil-revenue explosion was so intense that between 1974 and 1977 (not shown in Table 13.1) the share of construction in GNP almost caught up with manufacturing itself (see the sources); (b) figures for manufacturing and mining output include everything from gas and other non-oil minerals, traditional arts, crafts and industries, to motor-car and steel production; and (c) the total contribution of manufacturing and mining output to GNP was – as we saw above – not much more than the official figure for state services in 1977–8.

The position of agriculture speaks for itself, and it will be discussed in some detail in Chapter 15. To sum up, *at the very 'gates of the Great Civilisation', the output of all agricultural and industrial goods put together was only about one-fifth of the entire national output of the 'Japan of the Middle East'.*

POPULATION AND THE LABOUR FORCE

Between 1963 and 1978, total population grew – at an average annual rate of 2.9 per cent – from 23 to 35 million. However, the average annual rate of population growth in the *rural sector* was as (relatively) low as 1.2, and, in the *urban sector* as (absolutely) high as 4.6 per cent. The difference of 3.4 per cent is almost entirely due to the high rates of rural–urban migration, in consequence of the economic decline of agriculture and the social excommunication of peasant society: in 1963, peasant population was 65 per cent of the total; in 1978, it had been reduced to 53 per cent. Clearly, the Shah's boast in early 1973, even before the oil-revenue explosion, that by 1980 the peasant population would have declined to 2 million – i.e. 5 or 6 per cent of the total – was an unrealisable nightmare; but things were bad enough.[3]

The regional and environmental problems – concerning employment, housing, urban transport and other public utilities, and so on – created by the high population growth in towns and cities can be easily imagined, especially given the bureaucratic, corrupt, callous, cynical and wholly inefficient state machine that was supposed to cope with it.

The labour-force statistics lack comprehensive detail, mainly in order to save official embarrassment. But even aggregate figures lack consistency, because of the mystifying tactics used by official technicians and technocrats – the products of 'investment in human capital' – in order to cover up the truth. For example, there are some discrepancies in the data given by the same official source which, according to the source's own explanation, are due to statutory changes in the minimum employment age. That may be so. But, even after allowing for the 'statutory readjustment', the figure for the *employed* labour force in 1973, quoted in one of the source's publications, is more than the figure it quotes for the *total* labour force in 1973 in a later publication! Altogether, it looks as if 'human capital' was doing its best to hide the unemployment of human labour. However, according to the last annual report of the Central Bank, in 1977–8, the number of 'potential employees' was 9.9 million, and that of 'actual employees' was only 9.0 million; in plain language, 900,000 workers, i.e. 9.1 per cent of the labour force, were unemployed.[4]

For these and other reasons it is difficult to have a clear picture of the sectoral distribution of the labour force (employed or no). Table 13.2 shows that the oil sector – which was responsible for up to one-third of the national income – employed a negligible proportion (i.e. around 0.6 per cent) of the

TABLE 13.2 Sectoral distribution of total labour force (thousands), 1963–78

	1962–3		*1967–8*		*1972–3*		*1977–8*	
	No.	*% of total*	*No.*	*% of total*	*No.*	*% of total*	*No.*	*% of total*
Agriculture	3672	55.1	3861	49.0	3600	40.9	3200	32.2
Industry	1372	20.6	1947	24.7	2550	29.0	3300	33.2
Services	1584	23.8	2020	25.7	2600	29.5	3379	34.0
Oil	36	0.5	46	0.6	50	0.6	60	0.6
Total	6664	100.0	7874	100.0	8800	100.0	9939	100.0

Source: as in Table 13.1.

total labour force: hence the collective economic rent, and its various implications, which we discussed in Chapter 12. The labour force engaged in *agricultural* activities declined both relatively and absolutely. However, the *rural* labour force is not exclusively engaged in *agricultural* activities: in 1977–8 the *rural* labour force (not shown in the table) was over 5.5 million, while the *agricultural* labour force was 3.2 million (see Table 13.2: the surplus of 2.3 million cannot all have been engaged in rural handicrafts and trade; therefore, this provides us with a clue about the size of *rural* unemployment). Predictably, however, there was a rapid increase in the level and the percentage share of labour involved in industry and services. But employment in services was lower, and grew more slowly, than could be justified by its share of the national output.

Take the year 1977–8. In that year, the share of services in the national output (excluding oil revenues, which are not *produced* by the national labour force) was 55.6 per cent, while its share in the employed non-oil labour force was 35.6 per cent; the share of industry in the output was 29.7 per cent, and its share in employment 31.1 per cent; and the share of agriculture in total output was 14.7 per cent, while its share in the labour force was 33.3 per cent. These and other figures have been tabulated in Table 13.3.

The question is, why? Suppose we believed that the great discrepancy between the share of agricultural output and employment was entirely due to lower productivity, because – perhaps – of the more limited use of capital machinery in that sector. But why should the share of services in national output be so much more than its share of the labour force; and how can this be explained in a comparison with industry? It is normally believed, though not necessarily correctly, that the productivity of services is lower than industry; what is certain, however, is that it cannot be much *higher*.

The problem may be analysed with the aid of Table 13.4. In this table, figures in columns (1) and (3) measure the value of product per worker (or 'labour productivity') for the three sectors, in 1962–3 and 1977–8; and those in columns (2) and (4) show the *relative* product per worker in these sectors –

TABLE 13.3 Contribution of the Non-Oil Economic Sectors to Output and Employment, 1977–8

	Output		*Employment (excluding official unemployment)*	
	'000m. rials	*% of total*	*m.*	*% of total*
Agriculture	339.0	14.7	3.0	33.3
Industry	684.3	29.7	2.8	31.3
Services	1281.3	55.6	3.2	35.6
Total	2304.6	100.0	9.0	100.0

Source: as in Tables 13.1 and 13.2.

TABLE 13.4 Absolute and relative product per worker in various economic sectors

	1962–3		*1977–8*	
	Product per worker ('000 rials)	*Relative product per worker*	*Product per worker ('000 rials)*	*Relative product per worker*
	(1)	(2)	(3)	(4)
Agriculture	24.2	0.60	105.9	0.45
Industry	42.1	1.00	267.3	0.88
Services	75.6	1.90	380.3	1.62
Total non-oil output per worker	40.2	1.00	233.6	1.00

Sources: Based on Tables 13.1 and 13.2.

that is, they show the ratio of each figure in columns (1) and (3) to the corresponding total figures. A comparison of the figures in columns (2) and (4) shows that (a) relative product per worker, in both years, is appreciably lower for agriculture and higher for services; and (b) in 1977–8 the position of agriculture had worsened, because relative product per worker had declined relatively more in agriculture than in the other sectors.

Suppose, once again, that the case of agriculture is entirely explained by lower labour productivity due to lower investment in machinery, which must be *partially* true, and evidence for the abandonment of the agricultural sector by the oil state. But why should 'labour productivity' in services have been almost twice that in industry? It is true that *modern* services use a lot of new machinery, but surely not relatively more than modern industry, especially in what was to become 'the fifth most industrial state'. Besides, in Iran perhaps more than elsewhere, state services, as well as the lower end of the service tail, which employs most of its labour force – petty traders, shop assistants, and so forth – must involve a lot of disguised unemployment; that is, overemployment of labour. What, then, could account for the enormously higher product per worker in services than in industry? There can be only one answer to this question: *income* per worker was much higher in this sector because of high monopolistic rents enjoyed by employers and employees in *modern* services and the state bureaucracy – modern skilled 'workers', professionals, bureaucrats and technocrats, bankers, insurance brokers, hoteliers, restaurateurs, cinema owners, and so on; that is, much of the state's clientele and the country's 'human capital'.

The above discussions give us some idea of the pattern of income distribution between the urban and rural sectors, and within the urban sector itself.

CONSUMPTION, SAVING AND CAPITAL ACCUMULATION

In the previous chapter it was postulated that, given an undemocratic – and, especially, despotic – politiconomic framework, oil revenues make the state a big spender, both directly and through its patronage of the privileged minority: its clientele.

In general, this is the likely pattern of consumption behaviour by individuals, social classes and other social entities when a large proportion of their income is not due to their own productive effort. That is why the European feudal class was in fact – and, therefore, by theoretical assumption – not a social agent for capital accumulation. That is also why successful gamblers and lottery winners tend to waste a lot of their income and wealth. This simple generalisation has some important lessons, too, for the likely impact of foreign aid and credit to underdeveloped countries. The problem is more complicated when we remember that, although habits, norms and behavioural patterns have social and material roots, they do not easily change when their material basis is removed: even in the soulless mechanical world, moving objects do not immediately stop when their motive force is withdrawn, and this is even less the case in the conscious world of the human individual and society. This applies to both actual and expected levels of consumption. Compare rows 1 and 4 in Table 13.5. In all the years between 1963 and 1968 (including those for which figures are not presented in the table), the Iranian

TABLE 13.5 National output and expenditure by origin and use (constant prices), selected years ('000 m. rials)

	1962–3	*1967–8*	*1972–3*	*1977–8*
1. Non-oil output	284.2	421.4	1302.4	2417.5
2. Oil revenues	40.0	92.4	1333.3	1284.9
3. GNP (at market prices) (1 + 2)	324.2	513.8	2635.7	3702.4
4. Aggregate consumption	265.3	404.2	1234.5	2208.5
5. Replacement of capital	22.7	36.0	86.4	161.3
6. Gross *non-oil* saving (1 – 4)	18.9	17.2	67.9	209
7. Net *non-oil* saving (6 – 5)	–3.8	16.8	–18.5	47.7
8. Gross *domestic* investment	49.4	113.1	410.5	1152.6
private	(31.0)	(58.0)	(198.9)	(505.4)
state	(18.4)	(55.1)	(211.6)	(647.2)
9. Net *domestic* investment (8 – 5)	26.7	77.1	324.1	991.3
10. Net inflow of foreign capital	9.5	3.5	–923.8	–129.8
11. Net *national* investment (9 – 10)	17.2	73.6	1247.9	1121.1
12. 'Statistical discrepancies'	–	–	66.9	211.5

Source: as in Table 13.1

economy consumed (the equivalent of) nearly all that it *produced*; that is, the output of agriculture, industry and services (all of which include indirect taxes) was almost equal to the consumption of these goods and services. Two points are worth emphasising. First, this observation is independent of the explosion in the country's material fortunes in 1973; for example, in the year before (not shown in the table), both aggregate consumption and non-oil output had been only a half of the corresponding amounts in 1972–3, and, likewise, total consumption and output in 1977–8 were almost twice what they had been in 1972–3. Therefore, those 'experts' who have belatedly discovered that the Shah's 'mistake' was to accelerate *growth* at a very high rate may have to revise their views once again: the oil-revenue *consumption* super-boom must have been a real culprit. Secondly, a look at rows 6 and 7 of the table will show that, except in 1977–8, genuine 'saving' (i.e. *produced* output minus *total* consumption) has been consistently *negative*. *Gross* saving (row 6) includes the necessary sums for the maintenance of *existing* capital stocks, which is an indirect consumption category. It is *net* saving which is the relevant figure in this case: if I 'save up' to buy a new pair of shoes, this will add to my existing stock of shoes so long as it is not merely replacing a pair which has been worn out.

The figures in Table 13.6 help further clarify these observations. Row 2 shows that only in 1977–8 was the net rate of saving out of *produced* output positive;[5] and then it was only 2.0 per cent! In order to have some idea of the rate of capital accumulation – i.e. the rate at which the economy was adding to its capital stock – the relevant concept is net domestic investment: that is, all investment in *additional* capital stock, both by Iranians and by foreign creditors and investors. It can be seen from row 4 that net domestic investment was low in 1962–3, fair in 1967–8 and 1972–3, and high only in 1977–8. The fact that the rate of net *national* investment has been very high since the oil-

TABLE 13.6 Saving and investment rates, per cent (constant prices), selected years

	1962–3	*1967–8*	*1972–3*	*1977–8*
1. Gross *non-oil* saving rate (as % of non-oil GNP)	6.6	4.3	5.2	8.7
2. Net *non-oil* saving rate (as % of non-oil GDP)	−1.3	−4.2	−1.4	2.0
3. Gross *domestic* investment rate (as % of GDP)	14.5	20.3	15.4	32.1
4. Net *domestic* investment rate (as % of NDP)	8.4	14.8	12.5	27.9
5. Net *national* investment rate (as % of NNP)	5.7	15.4	48.9	31.7

Source: Based on Table 13.5.

revenue explosion of 1973 contains no real mystery: it shows that a lot of capital has been exported from the country in the form of Iran's investment abroad.

Aggregate consumption was greater than net, and almost equal to gross, non-oil output. The question is, *who* consumed how much? It is impossible to answer this question with any precision; but the available figures provide some information about its broader aspects. First, let us consider the case of state consumption in row 4 of Table 13.7: it was 31.5 thousand million rials in 1962–3, and it had risen to 786 thousand million rials by1977–8. Moreover, at the end of each of the five-year periods state consumption expenditure had more than doubled; and in 1973, the year of the oil-revenue explosion, it had jumped by more than 220 per cent over the previous year. Private consumption also increased very fast, but at an appreciably slower rate: in 1977–8, private consumption was *seven times*, and state consumption *twenty-six times*, what they had been in 1962–3 (cf. rows 4 and 3 of Table3.7). Yet all this is to assume that the official figures for *state* consumption are true, when in fact they are likely to exclude some of the state's expenditure on the army and the SAVAK, which may have been included in the figures for 'public investment'.

A comparison of rural and urban private consumption is also revealing. In the year before the oil-revenue explosion, the rural population was about 60 per cent of the total; but rural consumption was only 35 per cent of total *private* consumption. What is more important, however, is that about 80 per cent of *state* consumption must also have been confined to the urban sector. These two points taken together give us some impression of the great gulf in real (both direct and indirect) consumption per capita between rural and urban areas. All of these observations are, nevertheless, too aggregative: they

TABLE 13.7 Distribution of consumption expenditure among various categories ('000m. rials), selected years

	1962–3	*1967–8*	*1971–2*	*1972–3*	*1977–8*
1. Urban consumption	122.9	187.2	293.0	590.3[a]	1052.5[a]
2. Rural consumption	110.5	143.4	158.4	290.0[a]	370.0[a]
3. Total *private* consumption (1+2)	233.4	330.6	451.4	880.3	1422.5
4. State consumption	31.5	73.6	159.3	354.2	786.0
5. Aggregate consumption (3+4)	264.9	404.2	610.7	1234.5	2208.5

[a] Estimates.

Source: based on data published by Bank Markazi Iran (Annual Report, various years) and the Statistical Centre of Iran.

reveal nothing about the concentration of both private and state consumption expenditure in Teheran, and a few other large cities; they say nothing about the very different shares of per capita consumption of the (urban) clientele and the urban masses; and they show nothing about similar regional and functional variations in the consumption of the rural society itself. We shall return to some of these issues in the next two chapters. (See, however, the appendix to this chapter on the state of poverty in Iran.)

What is particularly important for understanding the 'logic' of such a petrolic political economy is, however, the persistently high consumption rates *before* the oil-revenue explosion of 1973. This was a period in which all the oil-exporting countries were fiercely competing to export *higher quantities* of crude oil in order to increase their revenues. The situation was such that the international operating oil companies were constantly in fear of the development of a crude oil *surplus*, not shortage, in the international market, and were trying hard to moderate the enormous appetites of the oil states for higher annual revenues by the sale of greater *volumes* of crude oil. In the case of Iran, a delegation of the National Iranian Oil Company, led by its inimitable Chairman, Dr Iqbāl, would meet the representatives of the Consortium every year, usually in London, pressing His Majesty's demand for a large percentage increase in the *quantity* of Iranian oil exports. They would bring with them glossy official Iranian publications containing estimates of investment funds required for the Shah's development designs. This would entail long sessions of horse-trading, in which feelings would sometimes run high over 2 or 3 per cent more or less than the two sides were prepared to settle for. Occasionally (as in 1965–6) the Light of the Aryans would even go so far as to order his public mouthpieces, the press and other mass media, to begin threatening the other side with the possible reaction of 'the Iranian People' – a reminder to the foreign companies of Muṣaddiq and the Popular Movement! Until 1970 there had been no significant oil-price increases; and there certainly was no hope, let alone expectation, of a price explosion so dramatic and so soon.

To conclude this particular point, the Shah was determined to sell as much of the country's exhaustible resource as soon as he could – at the existing unfair prices – in order to raise as much revenue as possible, ostensibly for the sake of rapid economic development. In addition, he was frantically busy borrowing abroad, attracting foreign investments, and so forth. Yet, between 1963 and 1972 the Iranian balance of payments was almost permanently in deficit, and large funds were wasted on ostentatious consumption and injudicious investment projects.

Was this sacrifice of Iranian social wealth really for the sake of rapid economic development? Yes – if 'economic development' means the growing instant consumption of motor-cars and home appliances, holidays abroad, the entertainments offered by restaurants and gambling clubs, palatial housing, and so on and so forth, by a privileged minority; rocketing military –

bureaucratic expenditures; and shameless squandering of money in a belated Coronation party (1968), a grotesque international party for the hallucinatory 2500 years of the Persian Empire (1971), the Tenth Anniversary party of the Shah's bloody counter-revolution (1973), and his wife's annual escapades in Shiraz, where, in the name of an 'art festival', funds would be wasted, local life would be made impossible, modernist Western music would be played in the old Shiraz *b̄az̄ar* (and merchants threatened with reprisals if they would not keep their doors open so as to provide the necessary guinea pigs), and the ruins of Persepolis would provide a stage for the modern international court jesters and their pseudo-modernist Iranian audiences. The social impact and implications of this madness will be discussed in a later chapter.

Meanwhile, those who would describe this combination of despotic tradition, petrolic novelty, and pseudo-modernist and pseudo-nationalist dreams as private *or* state capitalist development may like to think again unless their understanding of capitalism (private or otherwise) is something very different from the socio-economic sense of this concept rendered familiar by the historical experience of other countries. Let us examine the distribution of investment between private investors and the state: row 8 of Table 13.5 shows that before 1973 'private' investment was more, and after 1973 not much less, than state investment. What would this indicate: 'private capitalism', 'state capitalism', or even both? These are serious questions which cannot be resolved by the use of simple figures; yet, even the use of such figures within their proper social context would not support either of those descriptions: the relatively high 'private' investment, especially from 1973 onwards, is the result of the state's policy of passing on large portions of the oil revenues to its clientele, through grants and low-interest credit. The recipients 'invested' the funds and enjoyed a high income from them, and those of them who were already in business simply replaced their own capital (using it in land and property speculation, and/or investment abroad in order to avoid the high socio-political risks) with the gifts of oil revenues from the state. In short, *the traditional institution of direct land assignment to the State clientele had been replaced by the novel policy of indirect capital (i.e. oil revenue) assignment to them: the state was still the monopolist of economic and financial resources, from which it granted privileges to (and withdrew them from) whoever it pleased.* Apart from that, the state 'investment' is itself likely to camouflage many other things, including construction for military purposes, and the purchase of 'machinery and equipment' for the armed forces. *This was 'capitalism' in no sense whatsoever; it was pseudo-modernist petrolic despotism.*

Capital accumulation takes place *via* additions to the stock of physical ('fixed') capital; that is, the stock of machinery and other fixed equipment. The ratio of gross domestic fixed-capital formation to total output can tell us how much, on the average, must be spent on physical capital – i.e. how much fixed investment is required – in order to produce a unit value of output. Given that the share of the oil sector in fixed capital formation is insignificant, in the case of Iran we must take the ratio of fixed investment to *non-oil* output as a first approximation.

Columns (2) of Tables 13.8 and 13.9 show the amount of investment per unit value of non-oil output produced, over the period 1963–78. For 1963–72, the average value of the investment–output ratio is 2.7, and deviations from the mean are not very significant; for 1973–8, the average rises to 4.1, which is significantly higher than the expected ratio of around 3.0. However, it is clear from Table 13.9 that this increase is entirely due to the years 1975–8 when

TABLE 13.8 The relation between fixed-capital formation, output and employment, 1963–72

(1) *Year*	(2) $I/\Delta X_1$	(3) $I/\Delta X_2$	(4) $In/\Delta L$ *('000 rials per worker)*
1963–4	3.3	3.9	91.0
1964–5	2.8	3.4	209.7
1965–6	2.1	2.8	298.9
1966–7	2.7	3.6	174.1
1967–8	2.8	3.9	438.1
1968–9	2.5	3.3	372.4
1969–70	3.2	3.8	356.0
1970–1	2.5	3.0	334.0
1971–2	2.6	2.6	513.6

Notes: I = *gross* domestic fixed-capital formation; ΔX_1 = change in non-oil GDP; ΔX_2 = Change in non-oil GDP, *excluding the agricultural output*; In = *net* domestic fixed capital formation; ΔL = change in total labour force.

Source: as in Table 13.1 and 13.2.

TABLE 13.9 The relation between fixed-capital formation, output and employment, 1973–8

(1) *Year*	(2) $I/\Delta X_1$	(3) $I/\Delta X_2$	(4) $In/\Delta L$
1973–4	2.4	2.6	Average 1973–8: 1.50 million rials (= $21,633.0)
1974–5	2.7	3.0	
1975–6	3.6	3.9	
1976–7	4.3	4.6	
1977–8	7.3	7.1	

Notes: I, ΔX_1 and ΔX_2 the same as in Table 3.8. However, the total figure for In has been reduced by the amount of Iranian investment abroad, in order to obtain a realistic figure for investment in physical capital *at home*, because only this would affect domestic employment.

Source: as Table 13.8.

investment was increasing very fast owing to the sudden doubling of the Fifth Plan targets; a part of this high, and rising, investment–output ratio must have been owing to greater investments in large-scale projects with highly sophisticated technology and long gestation periods (for instance, nuclear power stations), and the rest must have been because of the pressure on the supply of highly specialised personnel, which normally results in the underutilisation – i.e. waste – of productive capacity. Columns (3) of the two tables show the ratio of investment to non-agricultural as well as non-oil output – that is, the total output of industrial and service activities taken together. Since, especially in the later years, most of the investment was made in these two groups, the exclusion of agriculture may give a better impression of the investment–output ratio in the urban (mainly modern) sector. The means of the ratio are 3.4 for 1963–72, and 4.3 for 1973–8. It is not surprising that these are higher than when agricultural output was included, but it is interesting that deviations from the mean are now comparatively less. Theoretically, one would expect a lower investment–output ratio for more capital-intensive techniques of production. This is not borne out by our observations – mainly, it would seem, because of the growing shortage of 'skilled labour', which results in under-capacity production.

What, however, is of much more significance is the investment–labour ratios in columns (4) of the two tables. The investment figures used in this case are those of *net* domestic investment, in order to prevent an overestimation of the ratios. Yet these ratios are extremely high even for the period 1963–72: the average investment–labour ratio for these years was 300,000 rials, or about $4000 ($1 = 75 rials). This could mean that, on average, $4000 worth of capital investment had to be made in order to employ one more member of the labour force. The average figure for 1973–8 – shown in column (4) – is much higher; 1,514,317.3 rials, or $21,633.0 ($1 = 70) – i.e. in these latter years over $20,000 worth of capital investment resulted in the employment of a single new worker.[6] It should be emphasised that the figures of net domestic investment for 1973–8 have been reduced by the full amount of Iranian investment abroad, in order to prevent an overestimation of the ratio.

Yet the average ratios are so high that, no matter what other modifications are applied, they cannot alter their basic implications: in 1963–72, when the annual GNP per head (even including oil) was always less than $500, the Development Strategy, and the techniques of production chosen and encouraged by the state, led to an average expenditure of $4000 in order to employ one more worker; in 1973–8 this figure rose to over $20,000 but it would make little difference even if it were only half that figure. In fact, there is a grotesque consistency between the two average figures of $4000 and $20,000: in each of the periods (before and after the oil-revenue explosion) the average investment–labour ratio was about twelve times the average annual GNP per head! And this was in a country with a 2.9 per cent average annual rate of population growth, a declining agriculture, a high rate of rural–urban migration, and a limited supply of modern skilled labour.

There were two mechanisms for this abnormally low labour absorption of new investment: the state itself applied capital-intensive techniques in its own (usually) large-scale investment projects; and it encouraged the private sector to do the same (even in smaller-scale investments) by supplying cheap money capital to it. When we consider the fact that a high proportion of total investment went to construction projects (i.e. projects which are relatively labour-intensive), we may form an impression of how much lower the employment creation of new investment must have been in industrial and other production plants.[7] Nevertheless, the whole of this low employment creation of new plants cannot be explained by the high capital-intensity of production techniques alone. It is partly the result of its further consequence that limited modern–administrative as well as technical–skilled labour leads to underutilisation of capacity, which in turn results in the employment of even fewer ordinary workers than would otherwise be possible. Finally, the sociological aspects – the bureaucratic and highly centralised system of administering state enterprises, lack of commitment of both management and workers, and so on – certainly provide further explanations for the total phenomenon, even though they cannot be expressed with precision. Let us take a single important case which the state and its agents found impossible to cover up by their usual camouflage tactics: the failure of the newly created countrywide electricity supply system in the summer of 1977, when household supplies in Teheran (which, for political reasons, had priority over supplies to many other, including industrial, customers) were cut off for an average of four hours per day. The state produced many conflicting 'explanations' for this, but perhaps the most important reason was the incorrect specification of the electricity system itself. How much output was lost due to this long period of electricity shortage is not known. Yet, the Japan of the Middle East, which was evidently incapable of running a simple electricity system it had been able to pay for, was still going ahead with the installation of gigantic nuclear power stations. The Shah was determined to prove – at all costs – that Iran was no longer 'backward'!

In the following chapters we will discuss some of these issues in greater detail, by examining the urban, rural and foreign-trade sectors of the political economy.

Appendix: A Note on Poverty in Iran

A serious analysis of variations in the standard of living, or the 'distribution of income' among various social classes or different sectors of the population, is usually difficult and in the case of a country such as Iran next to impossible: apart from the forbidding inadequacy and unreliability of the basic data, there are the problems of defining social classes (for instance, who is to be identified as an industrial worker); the variations in the cost of living in different regions; the differences in the nature, security, and so forth, of employment; the consumption of some of their own products by the peasantry; and so on. It is always possible to produce some crude indicators of, say, what percentage of the working population earns what level of the national income, but it is difficult to draw any meaningful conclusions from such 'studies', except the obvious fact that there exists some kind of inequality of incomes.

Poverty, however, is, or can be, both a more precise and a less difficult concept to quantify and discuss, with the purpose of obtaining meaningful and significant results. The abstract concept of poverty itself is, of course, not very helpful, for poverty is a politiconomic phenomenon which can only be defined in the given social context, and for a particular stage of development: as early as two centuries ago, Adam Smith realised that the notion of subsistence in England was likely to be different from in China. It may look as if an index of biological subsistence – that is, the amount of material welfare necessary for survival – is more objective and less ambiguous. Yet, even such an index must imply other specific assumptions concerning the nature of a person's occupation; the length of his working day, week and year; and the expected length of his life; and so forth. For example, what may be 'biologically' sufficient to keep a working person alive and active over twenty years may be insufficient for life and activity over forty years.

The following observations are based entirely on Ḥusain 'Aẓīmī's extensive, as well as intensive, study of poverty in Iran.[8] 'Aẓīmī identifies three levels of calorie intake, which in the specific conditions of Iran indicate three distinct 'poverty lines'. Using an index of minimum calorie requirement consistent with normal well-being in Iran, he defines Line A for calorie intakes of between 90 and 99 per cent of the minimum requirement; Line B, for calorie intakes of between 75 and 90 per cent of the mimimum requirement; and Line C, for intakes at 75 per cent, or less, of the minimum requirement. Applying these concepts to a countrywide sample of expenditure groups, 'Aẓīmī has

TABLE 13.10 Undernourishment in Iran, 1972–3: countrywide figures, millions of people

	Line A	*Line B*	*Total (A + B)*
Urban areas	5.4	3.3	8.7
Rural areas	6.6	0.7	7.3
Total	12.0	4.0	16.0

Source: based on Ḥusain 'Aẓīmī's study of poverty in Iran, Ch. 4, table 3.

TABLE 13.11 Undernourishment in Iran, 1972–3: countrywide figures, percentage of population

	Line A	*Line B*	*Total*
Urban population	39	25	64
Rural population	38	4	42
Total population	39	13	52

Source: Table 13.10, and the population data sources cited in the text above.

obtained some revealing results, on which Tables 13.10 and 13.11 have been based. The figures in these tables speak for themselves: in 1972–3, the calorie intake of 16 million people (i.e. 52 per cent of the population) was less than the minimum requirement; 4 million of these people (i.e. 13 per cent of the population) were *severely* undernourished (see 'Line B' in Tables 13.10 and 13.11). It is also interesting to note that (a) undernourishment in the rural sector seems to be both relatively and absolutely less than in towns, and (b) this difference is particularly pronounced in the case of *severe* (i.e. Line B) undernourishment. We shall briefly discuss the possible causes and implications of these sectoral differences later.

These results, based as they are on *countrywide* data, do not take into account the great degree of *regional* variation in a country such as Iran. Therefore, 'Aẓīmī has extended his research by conducting similar separate analyses for every single one of the twenty-three Iranian provinces, which are then aggregated for the whole country. Tables 13.12 and 13.13 are based on these aggregated figures of the original provincial results. According to these tables (whose figures are more reliable than those of Tables 13.10 and 13.11) it appears that the *total* undernourished population is 13.5 million (or 44 per cent of the population), which is less than the 16 million obtained from the countrywide analysis. However, these latter tables show that (a) there are about a million people (i.e. 3 per cent of the population) who are in Line C – that is, dangerously undernourished – most of whom are in the rural areas; (b) there are 6 million people (or 20 per cent of the population) in Line B, as compared with the 4 million (13 per cent) shown by the countrywide analysis.

TABLE 13.12 Undernourishment in Iran, 1972–3: aggregated provincial figures, millions of people

	Line A	*Line B*	*Line C*	*Total (A+B+C)*
Urban areas	4.5	3.7	0.3	8.5
Rural areas	2.0	2.3	0.7	5.0
Total	6.5	6.0	1.0	13.5

Source: based on 'Aẓīmī, table 8.

TABLE 13.13 Undernourishment in Iran, 1972–3: aggregated provincial figures, percentage of population

	Line A	*Line B*	*Line C*	*Total*
Urban population	34	28	2	64
Rural population	12	13	4	29
Total population	21	20	3	44

Source: Table 13.12, and population data, as in Table 13.1 above.

Altogether, the latter results show that 21 per cent of the population (most of them in towns) are undernourished, 20 per cent (also mostly in towns) are *severely* undernourished, and 3 per cent (mostly in villages) are *dangerously* undernourished.

The reasons for the differences between urban and rural results may be manifold, and we have no scope here to engage in a thorough discussion of the subject. Briefly, the cultivating peasants can at least partially feed themselves from their own produce; their other subsistence requirements (housing, clothing, bedding material, and so on) are normally supplied by their own household labour, thus enabling them to spend a larger proportion of their income on food; and, while the unemployed landless peasants are more likely to fall into Line C than are unemployed workers in towns, most of those in Lines A and B in the urban centres must themselves be recent immigrants from rural areas, living on the edge of towns, where they are at least partially unemployed and no longer are able to supply some of their own food.

Apart from that, Aẓīmī's individual results from each province bring out the desperate plight of some particularly deprived regions of the country: in the rural areas of Kurdistan, for example, virtually every expenditure group – that is, almost the entire Kurdish peasantry – was found to suffer from undernourishment; and results for Khūzistan, Kirman, Bakhtīyārī, and so on – i.e. the main areas of ethnic–tribal concentrations – were significantly worse than for other parts of the country.

According to 'Aẓīmī's calculations, it would require a 10 per cent annual average growth rate of *real expenditure by undernourished households* in order to eradicate this kind of *nutritional* poverty within eight years in the rural sector, and six years in the urban sector.[9] Those who have some idea of the magnitudes involved, the policies required, and the efficiency demanded in carrying out such a task, would conclude that in the present situation the problem is more likely to be aggravated than relieved: each year, the undernourished population must be increasing at a high rate, and it is very doubtful that the present (post-revolutionary) politiconomic atmosphere, consciousness, commitment and machinery are up to mounting a serious assault on such problems.

NOTES

1. For a sample of studies on the Iranian economy and its recent development, see, Robert E. Looney, *The Economic Development of Iran, a Recent Survey with Projections to 1981* (London: Praeger, 1973), *A Development Strategy for Iran through the 1980s* (New York: Praeger, 1977), *Iran at the End of the Century* (New York: Praeger, 1977); Jahangir Amuzegar, *Technical Assistance in Theory and Practice: the Case of Iran* (New York: Praeger, 1966); Jahangir Amuzegar and M. Ali Fekrat, *Iran, Economic Development under Dualistic Conditions* (Chicago, Ill.: University of Chicago Press, 1971); Jahangir Amuzegar, *Iran: an Economic Profile* (Washington: The Middle East Institute, 1977). See also articles published in specialised journals, e.g. *The Middle East Journal*, in the past fifteen years. The analyses and predictions of these and similar studies may now be more readily compared with the realities of the Iranian political economy.
2. For a general examination of the nature and significance of the service sector, see H. Katouzian, 'The Development of the Service Sector: a New Approach', *Oxford Economic Papers*, November 1970, pp. 362–82, and 'Services in International Trade: a Theoretical Interpretation' in, Herbert Giersch (ed.), *International Economic Development and Resource Transfer* (Kiel: Institut für Weltwirtschaft, 1978).
3. See Bank Markazi Iran, *National Income of Iran 1959–72*, Table 57, and *Guzārish-i Iqtiṣādī . . . 2534* (Annual Report 1975), Appendix Table 86.
4. See Bank Markazi Iran, *National Income of Iran 1959–72*, Tables 43–46, *Guzārish . . .*, op. cit., Appendix Table 87, and *Annual Report and Balance Sheet 1356* (1977), Appendix table on p. 162.
5. A similar operation, showing the ratio of changes in capital stock to changes in non-oil output, that is the 'capital-output' ratio, would further reveal that this has been abnormally high, or, what is statistically the same thing, that 'capital productivity' has been unusually low. This contradicts the predictions of development economics, since it is assumed that 'capital deepening' will increase the productivity of capital, both directly and because of 'technical progress'. See the text below for a brief discussion of the reasons why in this case such a general prediction may not be supported by the evidence.
6. In order to prevent confusion, it should be emphasised that this does not necessarily mean that no saving was actually made out of the non-oil, or *produced*, part of output (which is the same thing as the *earned* part of income). It means that total aggregate consumption, from both the non-oil and oil parts of output (i.e. both *earned* income and the oil *rent*), was greater than the non-oil, or *produced*, part of output. This, as far as it goes, is a descriptive, statistical statement; its analytical significance lies in the fact that if the oil revenues disappear, or are drastically reduced, then in order to maintain the present level of aggregate consumption, the whole of currently *produced* output must be spent on present consumption, and there would be little or no capital accumulation.
7. Construction, even road construction (which can utilise a great deal of cheap underemployed and unemployed *rural* labour), was nevertheless highly capital-intensive, making it difficult even for the unskilled labour force which it employs to work with the advanced equipment used, and bidding up the wage rate of the skilled personnel required in handling them. See G. W. Irvin, *Roads and Redistribution . . . in Iran* (Geneva: International Labour Office, 1973); and my review of Irvin's book in the *International Journal of Middle Eastern Studies*, 1978.
8. Ḥussain 'Aẓīmī is at present a research student at the University of Oxford. The data used in this Appendix are extracts from chapter 4 of his D Phil thesis (about to be presented), which he generously put at my disposal.
9. See further ibid., ch. 4, table 9.

14 Urbanism, Industry and Services

The politiconomic policies of the state resulted in a very rapid growth of towns, cities and urban activities: the growth of urban incomes and consumption, and the demise of agriculture and the peasantry, resulted in a cumulative exodus from villages into towns; the expansion of the state bureaucracy, and the further – in fact, phenomenal – concentration of administrative decisions, led to a torrent of immigrants from smaller towns into larger cities.

In November 1972 the state summit meeting for the finalisation of the Fifth Plan (1973–8), was held in the prosperous city of Shiraz, and, as a result, the daily cabinet meetings were also held in that city. The local radio reported that Manūcheh Pīrūz (a former member of the Tūdeh Party, and the governor of the Fars province, of which Shiraz is the capital city), having been invited to report to a cabinet meeting on the provincial problems, had brought the difficulties of the city bus services to the attention of the council of ministers, and the cabinet had promised to take appropriate decisions for improving the bus services of the city of Shiraz. This is what the overconcentration of state bureaucracy meant for the daily affairs of a large, historic, prosperous *and* non-industrial city which, for propagandist reasons, was a favourite city of the Shah and his spouse.

I happened to be in Shiraz at the time. In the week before the arrival of the Light of the Aryans himself, the whole of the city's life became chaotic – state offices ceased to function, traffic was thrown into total confusion, and so forth – in the process of 'beautifying' the city, patching-up and repainting all the central streets, and washing down the leaves of their trees individually with soap powder. Yet, apart from its extensive slum areas, the city where the annual 'art' festivals were held each year had two large 'shanty towns', very well hidden from sight, and closely watched by SAVAK agents. I managed, with the aid of two guides, to visit these areas, and the hovel of a representative family. This hovel was entirely made of tin plating (from large unwanted oil cans); it had an estimated total space of 15 cubic metres; it 'housed' a family of eight – six children between the ages of six months and twelve years, together with their parents. The father of the family (Bābā Ṣafar) was seasonally unemployed: his regular employment was to empty – bucket by bucket – the toilet pits of the city slums, which lacked a sewerage system. He was an opium addict, because, he explained, it would otherwise have been physically impossible for him to go down the toilet pits, and he had passed on his addiction to his wife, who had passed it on to their youngest child. There was evidence of trachoma in the eyes of the five older children. There was no furniture, except for large pieces of cardboard material made from unwanted trade boxes, a few pieces of worn-out 'bedding', and an open charcoal container (*manqal*) for heating. It was a bitterly cold winter, and there was snow on the ground. There were no private or public baths and lavatories anywhere in the whole of the area. There was one small NIOC kiosk, which sold paraffin oil; a large banner was stuck on its roof which read, 'Long Live His Highness Prince Reżā Pahlavi, our beloved Crown Prince.'

What took place in Iran was not social and economic progress, not modernisation, but pseudo-modernism fuelled by the oil revenues; likewise, the structural shifts of the economy were due not to urbanisation, but to urbanism. When the country was at 'the gates of the Great Civilisation', the share of all (including rural and traditional) manufacturing in *non-oil* GDP was 20 per cent, while the share of 'services' was 56 per cent. Yet urban transport everywhere, and especially in Teheran, was so bad that it would be impossible to describe; housing conditions, except for the state's clientele and the trading community, were either terrible or terrifying; most towns and cities, including Teheran, lacked a workable sewerage system; medical and hospital facilities for the rich were extremely expensive and hazardous, and, for the poor, were expensive and dangerous.

Industry

Let us begin with a brief examination of the structure and growth of the industrial sector. According to the Iranian statistical conventions, this sector consists of all manufacturing and non-oil mining activities, construction works of all kinds, and water and electrical power. Table14.1 shows that the value of total industrial output rose by nearly twelvefold, from 57.8 thousand million rials in 1962–3 to 684.3 thousand million rials in 1977–8, and the highest rate of increase was experienced after the oil-revenue explosion of 1973. For the whole period of 1963–78, water and power, beginning with a very low supply base, had the fastest increase; but in 1978 their total share of the industrial output was still 5.5 per cent. Construction claimed a consistently high share, around a quarter of the total industrial output, throughout the period, while manufacturing and mining, though increasing fast, reduced its share from less than 72 per cent in 1963 to over 68 per cent in 1978.

In spite of their relatively small share of the total, water and power have claimed a sizable portion of state investment in these years: expensive hydroelectric dams mushroomed in many parts of the country; conventional power stations were imported, and put into operation; and, finally, large

TABLE 14.1 Sectoral distribution of industrial output, 1963–8

	1962–3		*1967–8*		*1972–3*		*1977–8*	
	'000 m. rials	*% share*	*'000 m. rials*	*% share*	*'000 m. rials*	*% share*	*'000 m. rials*	*% share*
Manufacturing and mining	41.5	71.8	72.5	68.2	224.8	67.5	468.2	68.3
Construction	14.1	24.4	24.9	23.4	91.4	27.4	179.5	26.2
Water and power	2.2	3.8	8.9	8.4	17.2	5.1	36.6	5.5
Total	57.8	100.0	106.3	100.0	333.4	100.0	684.3	100.0

Source: based on Bank Markazi Iran, Annual Report, various years.

nuclear power stations were ordered and, in part, installed, but – perhaps luckily – never reached the stage of utilisation.

In times of rapid economic growth, construction is bound to have a relatively high share in total industrial output: roads, railways, and other national and regional networks of transport and communications, schools, hospitals and other public and private services of this kind, factories and office accommodation; public buildings and housing schemes, private house-building and property development – the expansion of all of these results in more construction. Therefore, it is usually difficult to know the relative significance of investment in construction without a great deal of detailed information. We saw in the previous chapter that construction consistently had a very high share in total fixed investment; in fact, its share in state investment was higher than 'machinery and equipment'. Figures for a thorough analysis of the growth and distribution of construction activities are not available; it can only be pointed out that a high share of construction must have been claimed by unproductive state projects (especially for military purposes), palatial and luxury private housing, modern hotels, restaurants, holiday resorts and similar investments. At any rate, this sector provided a good source of urban employment, both because of its continuous boom, and because of its relative labour-intensity.[1] Indeed, with the explosion of construction activities after 1973, this was the most reliable sector for the maintenance and growth of urban employment. That is also why between 1974 and 1978 the general index of the wages of construction workers rose (from 100) to 275.6. Many workers with traditional (or ordinary mechanical) skills left their jobs to become building workers, van drivers, and the like.

This brings us to a more detailed discussion of manufacturing industry, as the most important industrial sector. In this respect, the industrialisation strategy of the state – its industrialism – may already be familiar to the reader: investment in some heavy industrial plants, such as steel and machine tools, and promotion of import-substitution modern consumer durables, such as motor-cars and home appliances, were its main priorities; at later stages, feeble attempts at creating a petrochemical industry and providing some encouragement for the promotion of traditional arts and crafts – though not traditional *industries* – were added to the list. There was, of course, no strategy worthy of the name: these were the results of haphazard pseudo-modernistic whims and aspiration which emerged and accumulated in step with the growth and explosion of the oil revenues.

'Going for steel' was the highest priority: it would be the best single evidence of 'economic progress'; it would meet the criticisms of oppositionist intellectuals, who had seldom lost an opportunity to point out that the country still lacked a 'metal-smelting factory' (i.e. a steel plant); it would, they hoped, lay the foundations of an Iranian heavy industrial and engineering sector. The above general considerations apart, the Shah, in his arrangements for the establishment of an Iranian 'metal-smelting factory', once again managed to hit several targets at a single blow. When, in 1963, discussions were in progress for the new, and long-lasting, honeymoon between the Shah and the Soviet Union, the question of the Soviet supply of a steel plant (as well as a small machine-tool plant) in exchange for Iranian natural gas began to appear on the agenda: it would supply the Russians with cheap natural gas, and to some extent compensate them for their historical 'grievance' of not having a share in Iranian oil; it would provide a material basis for good political relations, and their survival in the longer run; it would also realise the dreams of the Iranian pseudo-modernists of all varieties, and at the same time pre-empt the likely charge of oppositionist intellectuals in general (and their pro-Soviet wing, in particular) that Western imperialism had imposed the cost of a 'certified lemon' on the poor Iranian people. 'Certified lemon' is a common North American term for decrepit and almost unusable second-hand (or 'used') cars. As it happens, this is how the more outspoken Iranian officials described the Soviet steel plant after its delivery and instalment. Whether or not it is a fair description, I am not qualified to judge.[2]

The final deal committed the Iranians to the construction of a gas pipeline from the source – the gas-heads in the west of the country – to the Soviet border. Perhaps it will never be known exactly how much this cost the country. It was probably in the region of $700 million, and certainly much more than the original estimate.[3] The pattern became typical of this kind of grandiose, and often worthless, state project: when in 1972 he attended the Fifth Plan summit meeting in Shiraz, the Light of the Aryans was much annoyed on learning that the recently completed Dārīyūsh dam, in Fars province, had cost $300 million instead of the original $100 million estimate.[4] However, the steel plant, which had been expected to earn the country $600 million worth of exports by 1969–70, earned only $4 million in that year! At the present time, that and similar plants are high-cost liabilities rather than useful capital assets for the country, irrespective of the economic 'policies' of the post-revolutionary provisional government.

The provision of import-substitution consumer durables was left mainly to the 'private' sector, with large amounts of financial aid as well as indirect support from the state. This was not a private sector; and the people who enjoyed its fruits were not industrial capitalists. Typified by such individuals as the Khayyāmmī brothers, these were people who, often with relatively little capital of their own, acted as little more than agents of the state empowered to use public funds, and other privileges, for supplying assembled motor-cars, and the like, in order to demonstrate Iranian economic progress and so keep the growing state clientele happy. In return, they enjoyed substantial profits, most of which they had not really earned by the use of their own capital, or even managerial labour.

In the middle of the 1960s, the National Iranian Oil Company and the official technocracy began to entertain thoughts about creating a reasonable export sector for the distant future. What could be more appropriate than the foundation of a petrochemical industry? These men, who had little or no knowledge of the technological basis for such an industry, the existing and future world markets for its various products, the relative production costs of their major suppliers to the international market, and so on, simply believed that, because of the country's oil resources, it would be able to become a serious contender in the world petrochemical market. The idea of developing a petrochemical industry in an oil-exporting country is, by itself, not unsound; for it can provide a technical linkage between the oil sector and the rest of the economy, supply not only neighbouring markets but also the home market, where it would at least have an advantage in transport costs and at the same time increase employment. What was typically grotesque was the belief that, within a reasonable period of time, such an industry could become a major contributor to the country's exports and, therefore, foreign-exchange earnings.[5] In 1977–8, the total value of exports of *all* industrial and agricultural goods was no more than *2 per cent* of the total value of Iranian exports (see Ch. 16).

The machine-tool plant purchased from Czeckoslovakia in 1970 and installed in the city of Tabriz, in Azerbijan, was producing at no more than 10 per cent of its total capacity: the existing domestic market was certainly limited, but the main reasons for this showpiece of public waste were (a) the *relative* shortage of technical and managerial staff, both because of the absolute general shortage, and because of the further difficulty in persuading such people to live and work in one of the largest Iranian cities, rather than in the capital itself – clear evidence for the impact of the concentration of everything in Teheran; (b) the highly bureaucratic nature of decisions and relations in state enterprises, as already mentioned and (c) the high cost of production, which was in part a consequence of the first two problems. Yet, Iran now had a modern machine-tool plant, and a socialist country had earned its own share of Iranian oil revenues.

Another relatively new venture of the state was investment in the production of vegetable oil, which had its beginnings in the private sector late in the 1950s. Apart from supplying the expanding home market, the idea was to promote greater technical linkages between modern manufacturing and domestic agricultural raw materials than already existed *via* the textile and sugar industries. There can be no objection to the principle. The problem, however, was that, given the general attitude of the state towards the agricultural sector (discussed in the next chapter), this policy brought no benefit to peasant smallholders, most of whom were not involved in the production of relatively capital-intensive, and land-extensive, products of this kind. Hence, it mainly benefited large estates and, once again, 'prestige' played a more important role than costs and other technical considerations: for example, it was regarded as prestigious to develop and use sunflowers, rather than other vegetable-oil plants that are better suited to the growing conditions and therefore less costly to cultivate.

Romania provided most of the experts and advisers for this project.[6]

There were other, relatively new industrial products which grew fast because of the direct and indirect state support they received. A good example of such a product is cement, the suppliers of which had privileged access to state funds and enjoyed a permanent, as well as permanently rising, boom because of the state's overall policies. Indeed, in the years following the oil-revenue explosion, cement and other building materials became so scarce that their prices rose beyond all reason, domestic black markets developed, and official buyers and privileged private customers were given priority over all the rest. The state's attempt to relieve the shortage by importing cement, both from regular international suppliers and from shady international dealers (at high costs), was not successful, partly because of the general world shortage (induced by the sudden increase in demand from *all* the petrolic countries), partly because of the slow pace of delivering such a bulky and heavy product at the Iranian ports, partly because of the jamming of all sorts of imports at these ports, and the relative shortage of internal transport facilities, and, finally, partly as a result of corrupt and speculative practices by middlemen – dealers, contractors and state officials – aimed at lining their own pockets. In the end, the situation got so bad that, from time to time, the state would ban *private* housing construction for a period. This is just one piece of evidence for the kind of contradiction involved in the petrolic pseudo-modernist 'strategy', which – incidentally – goes beyond 'purely' economic considerations: the very privileged beneficiaries of the oil revenues – that is, the bulk of the state's clientele – who were in effect being paid off in return for blind obedience, became increasingly frustrated, because land speculation had increased urban land prices between five and tenfold, and – even after acquiring a piece of urban land at extortionate rates – they found themselves forced to postpone the construction of their new homes, or mini-palaces, which they were otherwise able and willing to build at astronomic costs. At any rate, this provides some idea of the phenomenal increase in the cost of housing accommodation, which hit the urban masses very hard indeed.

Yet, in spite of the pseudo-modernist 'strategy' of industrialisation, Iranian industry was dominated by textiles, which – although they had been increasingly using modern equipment for several decades – were a traditional Iranian industry. It was not until some time after the oil-revenue explosion that pride of place began to pass to the motor-vehicle assembly plants. Likewise, it was only after the oil-revenue explosion that the sugar and tobacco industries, which had had decades of experience in production and enjoyed an expanding market, began to suffer a reduction in their *share* of the market for manufactured products.

Table 14.2 enables us to make some useful observations about the level and composition of modern manufacturing output. The table refers to twenty-one modern, or modernised, manufacturing industries for which individual data are available for the period 1971–6. These are certainly the most important

TABLE 14.2 Output of twenty-one selected industries ('000 m. rials), 1971–6 (at 1969–1970 prices)

	1971–2	*1972–3*	*1973–4*	*1974–5*	*1975–6*
1. Textiles	19.7	22.2	25.0	26.8	28.0
2. Motor-vehicles	16.2	20.6	26.3	35.0	44.8
3. Sugar	11.3	11.4	11.9	12.9	13.2
4. Basic metals	9.8	12.8	14.1	16.0	19.5
5. Tobacco products	9.6	9.5	9.9	10.9	12.0
6. Home appliances	7.0	8.7	11.4	13.5	17.3
7. Vegetable oil	7.0	7.6	7.8	9.7	10.7
8. Cement	4.0	4.8	5.0	6.6	7.8
9. Radio, television and telephone	3.8	4.8	6.4	9.2	10.0
10. Petrochemicals	3.6	4.8	5.9	5.7	5.9
11. Toiletries	3.3	3.9	4.3	5.3	5.8
12. Others[a]	15.5	19.3	24.2	27.6	32.8
Total	110.8	130.4	152.2	179.2	207.8

[a] This item consists of ten more industries taken together. These are (in descending order of the value of their outputs in 1971–2): shoes, tyres, electrical accessories, drugs, paint, leather products, non-alcoholic beverages; alcoholic beverages, and glassware. Shoes dominated this group, accounting for 2.2 per cent of the total output of the whole sample both in 1971–2 and in 1975–6.

Source: based on Bank Markazi Iran, Annual Report 1975–6 (Persian edition) table 50.

industries which have been established or developed since 1964, and they thus provide a fairly authentic picture of the direct and indirect industrialisation strategy of the state. First, in 1975–6 the total value of the output of these industries (at 1969–70 prices) was about 208 thousand million rials, or less than $2900 million, and 57 per cent of the total manufacturing and non-oil mining output – which includes revenues from the sale of gas – in the same year. It follows that roughly about 35 per cent of total industrial output must have been made up of small-scale traditional urban and rural industries, including carpets; and the remaining 8 per cent by non-oil mining. Secondly, it shows that the output of the entire modern and modernised, private and state, manufacturing sector was still only about 14.5 per cent of the contribution of oil revenues to GNP. Thirdly, it can be seen from the table that modern manufactures were dominated by a mixture of new (import-substitution) consumer durables, older (but modernised) Iranian industries, and modern heavy industries: vehicles, home appliances, textiles, basic metals, and so forth.

The changing composition of this group of industries may best be examined with reference to Table 14.3. This table shows that in 1971–2 textiles still had the largest single share of total output (17.8 per cent) in the group of modern, though not necessarily recent, manufacturing industries. Similar industries, such as sugar and tobacco, also had relatively large shares in total modern manufacturing output. By 1975–6 the oil-revenue explosion of 1973–4 had already altered the picture significantly: in particular, the share of motor-vehicles had increased very rapidly to 21.6 per cent, while textiles had lost their dominant position, with their share declining to 13.5 per cent of the total. The shares of sugar, tobacco, and so on, had also declined, while those of metals, home appliances, radio, television and telephone had all increased. This is a reflection of the petrolic impact on the level and consumption of home demand and, connected with this, pseudo-modernist priorities in investment and supply. Yet, even in spite of the oil-revenue explosion, the share of all the old and new modern manufactures was still no more than one-quarter of the whole of manufacturing and mining output. However, it is important to note that most of the new industries have very little export potential and few prospects, and their expansion – even survival – is completely at the mercy of

TABLE 14.3 Distribution of output among twenty-one selected industries (per cent), 1971–6

	1971–2	*1972–3*	*1973–4*	*1974–5*	*1975–6*
1. Textiles	17.8	17.0	16.4	15.0	13.5 (3)
2. Motor-vehicles	14.6	15.8	17.3	19.5	21.6 (1)
3. Sugar	10.2	8.7	7.8	7.2	6.3 (6)
4. Basic metals	8.8	9.8	9.3	8.8	9.4 (4)
5. Tobacco products	8.6	7.3	6.5	6.1	5.8 (7)
6. Home appliances	6.4	6.7	7.5	7.5	8.3 (5)
7. Vegetable oil	6.4	5.8	5.1	5.4	5.1 (8)
8. Cement	3.6	3.7	3.3	3.7	3.8 (10)
9. Radio, television and telephone	3.5	3.7	4.2	5.1	4.8 (9)
10. Petrochemicals	3.2	3.7	3.9	3.2	2.8 (11)
11. Toiletries	2.9	3.0	2.8	3.0	2.8 (12)
12. Others	14.0	14.8	15.9	15.4	15.8 (2)
Total	100.0	100.0	100.0	100.0	100.0

Source and note: as Table 14.2.

the domestic market, which in turn depends on the providence of oil revenues, *and* the strategy of the state in disbursing them. That is also partly the reason why, a few months after the final collapse of the Shah's petrolic despotism, they are already in difficulties.

The total workforce in all of the above sample of twenty-one modern industries, grew from less than 129,000 persons in 1971–2 to over 170,000 employees in 1975–6.[7] This is worth a moment's pause: the total number of industrial workforce (employed in construction as well as manufacturing and mining) has been around 2.5 million average – since 1971. Modern manufactures (claiming 57 per cent of total manufacturing and mining output) employed an average of only 150,000, or 6 per cent, of the whole industrial labour force. This observation shows that (a) modern, and especially new, industries were significantly capital-intensive; (b) traditional and semi-traditional (urban and rural) industries – contributing 35 per cent of manufacturing and mining output – must have employed about 65 per cent of the total industrial workforce (the rest being employed in construction); and (c) therefore there must have been a certain amount of disguised unemployment (what in polite circles they now call 'overmanning') in the traditional and semi-traditional manufacturing sector.

When the ratio of machines to men is high, it follows normally that the ratio of output to labour employed is also relatively high. This is a simple statistical index of labour productivity, which is usually taken as an indicator of relative efficiency in an industry – although, as far as it goes, it may be no more than a tautology: efficiency will be higher only when labour productivity rises with the *existing* stock (and technical characteristics) of other means of production – machines, management, and so on; otherwise, figures for output per worker cannot tell us much about relative performance and efficiency. However, figures are available not only for the size of the workforce, but also for their total annual earnings, in the above sample of industries; these have provided the basis for Table 14.4, which will give us some idea about other

TABLE 14.4 Output per worker and earnings per worker in modern manufacturing, dollars ($1 = 72 rials), 1971–6

	(1) *Annual output per worker*	(2) *Annual earnings per worker*	(3) *Weekly earnings per worker*	(4) *(2) : (1) × 100*
1971–2	11944.4	1222.2	23.5	10.3
1972–3	13100.0	1416.6	27.2	10.8
1973–4	14113.2	1667.0	32.1	11.8
1974–5	15453.4	2066.3	39.7	13.4
1975–6	16943.9	2763.2	53.1	16.3

Source: based on Table 14.2, and Bank Markazi Iran's Annual Report, 1975–56, appendix tables 52 and 53.

aspects of modern manufacturing, as well as other industries.

Column (1) of Table 14.4 shows the annual output per worker – or 'labour productivity' – for the years 1971–6; columns (2) and (3) respectively refer to the annual, and weekly, earnings of the workforce. Let us discuss column (3) first, for on the face of it, it may look rather impressive: it looks as if the average earnings of workers in these industries increased from \$23.5 to \$53.1 – i.e. by 225 per cent – within the course of five years. But appearances are deceptive: first, the data for the workers' earnings have not been adjusted for the high inflation rate of this period, which cannot have been less than 150 per cent for all the five years taken together; secondly, the rate of inflation for food and accommodation – on which most of the workers' incomes are spent – was much higher than the general rate (for example, between 1971 and 1976 the price of working-class accommodation must have risen at least by 400 per cent); thirdly, the figures refer to the average earnings of all the employees, beginning with the directors and ending with the door-keepers – thus, given the abnormal monopolistic salary earnings of the managerial, administrative and technical staff, the average earnings of the ordinary workers must have been appreciably lower than the figures in column (3) of Table 14.4, especially in later years when the greater scarcity of modern skilled personnel further strengthened their bargaining position; and, fourthly, the figures explicitly refer not to average weekly wages and overtime pay, but to total wages, salaries and all other benefits, which must include bonuses as well as the so-called workers' share in the firms' profits.

Having considered all the above points, let us now see what it meant to earn \$53 a week in 1975–6 in terms of everyday living, always remembering that the mass of the ordinary workers of these modern industrial showpieces must have earned appreciably less than this amount. This was equal to the weekly rent of a small five-room house in a declining district of Teheran; the cost of an average meal for five in a more modern (though not fashionable) restaurant, in the same city; the price of an ordinary man's jacket; the cost of 12 kilograms of fresh Iranian mutton, or 23 kilograms of white cheese, or 47 kilograms of imported rice (Iranian rice itself is scarce, of an exceptionally high quality, and much more expensive). What these figures tell us about the life of those employed in traditional industries and services, the unemployed, and the peasant immigrants encircling the cities, in their dwellings sunk into the ground it is best to leave to the reader's imagination. As for the mass of the peasantry, more will be said in the next chapter.

The impossibility of presenting a comprehensive and precise discussion of the distribution of income, across the country, among and within geographical regions and economic sectors, or among and within social classes, has already been indicated. But we can learn something from Table 14.4 about the distribution of the product between capital (both state and 'private') and labour in the modern manufacturing industries. Column (4) of this table shows the workers' annual earnings as a percentage of annual output. Thus, the workers' share was 10.3 per cent of total modern manufacturing output in 1971–2; and it *apparently* increased to 16.3 per cent in 1975–6. However, we should emphasise that, since the output figures are reckoned in terms of constant (1969–70) prices, and the earnings figures reflect their purchasing power in each individual year, the increase of 6 per cent in the workers' share over the period is likely to reflect no more than the rate of inflation; indeed, the figure of 10.3 per cent for 1971–2 must itself be an overestimate. To sum up, it looks as if, in real terms, the average annual share of the workers was about 10 per cent of output. Yet, these were the most privileged, and the fastest growing, industries; the earnings, as we have said, refer to all the benefits, and include payments to the modern skilled personnel; and the mass of the workers employed in these industries were some of the most highly paid within the industrial sector. No further comment.

To summarise, petrolic industrialism emphasised the expansion of modern capital-intensive manufacturing industry, as well as construction, both from the demand and from the supply side of the market. Nevertheless, at the end of the period, only one-quarter of the total industrial output was contributed by this sector, another quarter was contributed by construction, and the remaining 50 per cent was shared out between traditional and semi-traditional (urban and rural) manufactures, non-oil mining, and water and power. The labour-absorptive capacity of the new industries was extremely low, the share of their workforce was also low, and the case must have been much worse in other industrial sectors, except construction.

Services

As a group of economic activities, services are in some ways comparable to construction: they, too, expand in the process of economic development; they, too, are difficult to analyse in relation to the contributions which they make, or do not make, to the development process. This is clear enough if only because a lot of construction activities are themselves the first steps towards the provision of a variety of public or private services. However, the case of services is even more complicated than that of construction: to mention only one important problem, in the underdeveloped countries the share of services in GNP and (sometimes) in employment is usually high, but past experience of advanced countries would suggest that the service sector grows fast only after industrial maturity has been achieved. I have discussed some of these issues in a general framework elsewhere, to which the interested reader may wish to refer.[8]

However, as argued in Chapter 11 of this book, in the specific case of the oil-exporting countries the petrolic mechanism will encourage the use and provision of different kinds of services, so that the service sector has a large share of both total and non-oil GNP, though not necessarily of the labour force: *modern* services are intensive in the use of capital equipment and modern skills; therefore, their labour-absorption capacity will be low, while the skilled personnel involved in their provision will be paid monopolistic salaries. We have seen already that both of these predictions – a large share of services in total output, and a relatively small share of employment – have been confirmed in the case of Iran: in 1978, the share of services was 34.6 per cent in GNP, 55.6 per cent in non-oil output, and 34 per cent in the labour force. The value of service 'output' – measured by the *income* received by this sector – is certainly an overestimate, since it includes monopolistic rent enjoyed by both capital and skilled labour engaged in their provision: in 1978, the *bare* annual salary of the managing directors of private banks and insurance companies varied between $50,000 and $170,000, depending on the size and importance of the firm, and the background of the person employed. On the other hand, the size of employment in this sector is also an overestimate, because many of those employed in traditional as well as state services – i.e.the group of services which employ most of the sector's labour force – are partially redundant in spite of their apparent full-time occupation: this, as we have seen, is the case of disguised unemployment or overmanning.

Yet, it must be emphasised that, whereas services alone had a significantly larger share in output than agriculture, manufacturing, construction, mining, water and power put together, their share of the labour force was only half that of the latter group of industries. In particular, since the oil-revenue explosion of 1973, services as a whole have grown faster than any other economic activity in the country. Therefore, to cut a long story short, the functional linkage between oil and services and their social agents (i.e.the state and its clientele) is almost self-evident. I have few doubts that similar politiconomic patterns could be found in many of the oil-exporting countries.

Chapter 13 included some general observations on the size and growth of some service categories. In particular, we noted that between 1963 and 1978 the state services grew faster than any other socio-economic activity in the country. The bureaucracy, the army, the SAVAK, the uniformed police and the gendarmerie had pride of place in this phenomenal expansion, and it would be too easy to emphasise these groups of state 'services' at the expense of other services in the provision of which the state played an increasingly important role, especially after the oil-revenue explosion of 1973. Education and health would be much better, more difficult and, therefore, more convincing candidates for an exposition of the 'logic' of petrolic pseudo-modernism.

Education and health are rightly regarded as important areas for public investment, especially in underdeveloped countries, where the existing social and economic 'infrastructure' is too weak for the foundation of an industrial political economy. Apart from their intrinsic values, greater facilities for education and health could increase the rate of literacy and numeracy, raise the level of public consciousness, increase the stock of skilled manpower, maintain a reasonable standard of health for the working population, and so forth – all of which would contribute to higher productivity, innovation and/or absorption of new techniques and values, and the extension of social citizenship and political participation. These and many other theoretical and qualitative arguments for the importance of education and health in the development process are all unexceptionable. What is highly exceptionable – and, unfortunately, standard practice among professional social scientists of all denominations – is to use numbers (as they come, or after the addition of a few mystifications) and little else in order to analyse the performance of a given – especially, underdeveloped – country, in these as in many other areas.

On the face of it, the Iranian strategy for the expansion of education and health looks very reasonable, even though it is unlikely that the state conceived it in quite the following way: to raise the general standards of literacy and well-being among the masses of the peasantry, by posting young conscripts to serve in the Literacy and Health corps in villages; and to invest in modern technical and academic education, as well as hospital services, in order to increase the supply of modern skilled personnel and the more sophisticated medical and hospital facilities. The main questions, however, are: *how* were these policies pursued; *what* did they involve in the process of their implementation; *how much* was spent for *what* quantitative achievements; *who* benefited from them; and, most difficult *and* most important of all, *what was the quality* – the social effectiveness – of the various numbers involved?

Let us begin with a few numbers. Between 1962 and 1972, the number of total secondary-school students increased at an average annual rate of over 14 per cent, from 260,000 to 1.4 million. By 1978, this figure had increased almost by a million, to 2.3 million.[9] Likewise, the number of students in colleges of further education, polytechnics and universities increased by over 250 per cent, from 59,000 in 1968 to 154,000 in 1978.[10] The growth of primary education, including the Literacy Corps classes, was less spectacular, but still very considerable: the number of registered students rose from 3.2 million in 1973 to 4.8 million in 1978. Nursery schools, teacher-training institutions, and industrial training centres also grew fast (especially from 1973), although they make up a smaller part of the education sector.[11] All these figures refer to both state and private education: except for universities and teacher training colleges, in which there is a state monopoly, and nursery education, which is almost completely supplied by private investers, the rest of the education sector involves both state and private participation. However, the state has a dominant share even in these other areas of the education sector, although the quality of education in the private sector is generally better. Apart from that, it is certain that the state schools and colleges increased more rapidly than the private ones, even though this was undoubtedly a lucrative area of private investment for the state's clientele.

The state expenditure on education began to increase with the oil revenues, and was given priority over all the rest of social services. In the Fifth Plan budget of 1972–3, prior to the oil-revenue explosion, current expenditure on education was over 8 per cent of total current expenditure; development expenditure on education was 10 per cent of total development expenditure; and total educational expenditure was 9 per cent of the total plan budget.[12] These percentage shares, and the absolute values to which they refer, are not to be lightly dismissed, even though they may not have been entirely realised. When the oil revenues exploded, educational expenditures were among those which were earnestly – and foolishly – doubled. This brings us to some discussion about the less easily quantifiable aspects of the problem.

First, a lot of the expenditure was channelled through expensive educational networks, at a time when the country lacked a basic standard of literacy and numeracy. Notwithstanding the Literacy Corps, by 1978 only 65.6 per cent of the age-specific population between six and twenty-nine years old could read and write: this was made up of 81.9 per cent of the urban, and only 48.0 per cent of the rural, population in that age group.[13] It follows that, on the basis of these and other offical figures, about 65 per cent of the total population and 80 per cent of the rural population (above the age of six), must still be illiterate. Since the Literacy Corps was exclusively concerned with the promotion of literacy in rural areas, the credit side of the balance sheet of the fifteen years of its development looks extremely poor. On the debit side must be put the considerable, and increasing, sums which were ostensibly spent on this almost wholly propagandist venture, which was valuable chiefly to domestic and, especially, foreign apologists of the régime. Apart from that, both this and the Health Corps venture caused a tremendous amount of social hardship and dislocation in villages and rural townships owing to the total contempt with which many of the young, 'educated', 'modern' conscripts treated the rural people; the exploitation of different kinds to which they subjected their 'pupils' and 'patients'; their institution of prostitution among simple peasant folk; the rapes they committed with complete impunity; and so on. Indeed, some of the eye-witness accounts bring one close to tears: in 1965 a Health Corps officer, a doctor of medicine, together with a sergeant, his assistant, respectively *purchased* a nine-year old and a six-year old peasant girl for sexual comfort. In this case, their immediate superior was a young man of conscience, and upon discovering what had happened – a few months after the event – he had them arrested and committed for trial. They got away with it, none the less![14] There was, however, one important, and wholly unintended, outcome of these White Revolutionary ventures: they put the educated young men of conscience in touch with the realities of life and social relations in their country; it taught *them* a great deal, even if they did not manage to teach much to others.

Secondly, a lot of the expenditure on education was concentrated in urban areas, especially the larger cities; and in 1973–4, bedazzled by the oil-revenue explosion, one of the first spectacular political bribes that the state paid to the wider circle of its clientele was to declare *all* primary and secondary education – even in 'private' schools – free of charge: that is, the state began to pay all the expensive fees, hitherto paid by middle and higher income groups, to these educational firms. The impact of this move alone on the rate of inflation could have been predicted by any intelligent member of the political public, except the Shah, his henchmen, and their paid domestic and foreign propagandists. But this is only by the way. This considerable increase in educational expenditure clearly did not increase the number of schools, pupils, and so on: it was merely a more blatant hand-out to the well-to-do families. However, other, less lucrative and more comprehensive 'educational' bribes were also given, by the sudden provision of free school milk and other 'goodies' for schoolchildren, until the Japan of the Middle East discovered that the country's supply of milk could not nearly support such 'benevolent' projects. Soon enough, hard financial and material economic facts made the régime beat a retreat on all these counts, in spite of its original earnestness in advancing these idiotic policies.

Thirdly, the rate of expansion in the number of schools and their pupils, colleges of higher education, universities, and their students, was certainly very considerable. But, whereas the limitations on the supply of milk and similar products can in time be understood even by such as the Light of the Aryans, the non-financial constraints on the sudden expansion of schools and universities may be overlooked even by more reasonable people: their buildings and equipment may be provided at growing costs, if there is no serious financial problem; but what about the teaching, academic and administrative staff, without whom there will be no education? Consequently, standards fell, and educational institutions began to turn out graduates who were even less qualified than their predecessors used to be. All this is not to mention the problems arising from the typical overconcentration of the education bureaucracy, with the Ministry of Education and the Ministry of Science and Higher Education in Teheran grotesquely involved in the problems of educational institutes in distant places; or the pressures brought by the SAVAK on university staff to show administrative and academic leniency to the students, in the hope of preventing political discontent.[15] According to a sample survey conducted by the Ministry of Science, and published in June 1973, 48 per cent of the (responding) students in universities and colleges of higher education came from bureaucratic families, 35 per cent from the industrial and commercial classes, 7 per cent from the families of landlords and independent farmers, 2 per cent from the urban working class, and 1 per cent from the peasantry.[16] It will be useful to add that in 1973 the last two classes made up around 85 per cent of the country's population.

Fourthly, it had already been a part of state policy, both as an indirect reward to its own henchmen and well-wishers, and as a means of paying off some politically and, sometimes, academically select students, to finance their studies abroad. The former usually received lavish grants from the Pahlavi Foundation, and the latter from the relevant state departments: the

Ministry of Education (later Science), the central bank, the National Iranian Oil Company, and even CENTO. The numbers, though growing, were still limited, until the oil revenues exploded: within a few months, all the Iranian students anywhere outside the country became entitled to receive 'partial' state grants – in Britain, £210 per quarter – upon the production of some certificate of registration at an institute of higher education; and those registered at universities could claim a full grant of £750 per quarter, in addition to fees and 'other expenses'. At first, they were required to sign some sort of declaration to the effect that they would return to their country and serve in a state department for some time; later, the state began to tighten up this condition, and try to ensure that the students fulfilled their promise. By 1976–7, this line of political bribery, too, had to face the hard financial facts. Apart from these largely unnecessary hand-outs to those who had already left the country to study through 'private' (but still petrolic) finance, large numbers of grants and scholarships were given to Iranian university graduates, schoolteachers, younger civil servants, university instructors without doctoral degrees, and so on, to go abroad, in order to increase the country's 'stock of human capital'. Young men and women, drawn from various – now predominantly traditional – social classes, often without any knowledge of the relevant foreign language, with relatively weak educational foundations (though through no fault of their own), already confused with the psychological and sociological impact of petrolic pseudo-modernist despotism in all its aspects, frequently with the sole objective of returning home with a higher degree (the higher, the better) in any subject whatever, arriving in strange lands with hardly any knowledge of them, their ways, their educational systems, and so on, without prior guidance, even without educational placement, trailed by at least an equal number of SAVAK informers and *agents provocateurs* – how can all this be described in a book on political economy?

Education is valuable in itself, and the logic of Iranian history – with its lack of an established aristocracy and a relatively high degree of social mobility through the service of the state – had always put a high premium on education, especially among the less privileged, as a passport to success in this world. Petrolic despotism emphasised this historical tendency beyond reason: it made people above the age of forty try to get a higher degree, perhaps a doctorate, from somewhere, in order to do better in society, especially by getting an important official post; the rest may simply be guessed. Therefore – and especially with regard to higher degrees – a great deal of caution must be used in assessing the quality of the resulting large increase in 'human capital'. In plain language, some of the degrees are fake, some were obtained from dubious institutions, some are the result of the 'benevolence' of respectable academic institutions in the face of actual despair and potential suicide. Yet a lot of them are genuine, and their owners would be useful, qualified citizens in a reasonable social environment. But, in the petrolic state of social and mental disorder, even most of these became a net social liability, through their frantic and feverish race for official desks, social recognition and unlimited wealth.

So much for education. The provision of health services by the state and through the private sector also expanded rapidly in this period. The quality and social effectiveness of hospital and medical care were, however, quite comparable with those of education: private medical practice became little more than a lucrative channel for accumulating wealth and investing it elsewhere, even in orange groves and vineyards; investment in private hospitals was a most profitable line of business activity, and exhorbitant fees (certainly much more than in, say, Britain) had to be paid for usually unsatisfactory, and sometimes dangerous – even fatal – 'services'. The latter considerations – of unconscientious care and application – are much more serious than the mercenary and entirely materialistic attitude of many doctors and hospitals towards their profession; yet, it is clear that the one cannot be isolated from the other. Frequently, reports on important laboratory tests were confused, the report on one patient being given for that on another; and occasionally laboratory reports were simply filled in without even carrying out the required test. Many a time patients suffering from neuroses and nervous depression were treated for stomach and heart diseases, even hospitalised and operated upon, only to find out – usually by a relatively cheap trip abroad – that they were sound in body but frail in spirit. The import, production and distribution of medicinal drugs were no less than a racket, involving import licensees, traders, chemical firms and, most of all, officials in the Ministry of Health. Furthermore, genuine and highly expensive drugs were often left out in the blazing sun for days, and even weeks, in their wooden boxes at the ports of entry. That is why Iranian travellers to the West took large supplies of ordinary aspirin back home, because the same brands sold in Iran were ineffective, or inferior in their effect.[17]

The state's expenditure on health care took the same pseudo-modernistic form as all other state expenditure: the emphasis was on large and general hospital building in the main urban centres, rather than the widespread provision of elementary medical care, clinical services, and smaller hospitals needed for the treatment of common afflictions. State hospitals were divided into two groups: those which were free of charge, and almost devoid of any real services; and those which cared for low-income people, on the basis of a fixed annual insurance contribution. The latter group was smaller in number, and concentrated in a few cities; and only those who have had a chance to observe their workings at first hand will be able to appreciate the extent of gratuitous contempt and hardship to which their patients were subjected. To cite just one example from my own experience: in the summer of 1977 a working-class couple were returned home from the hospital where the woman's pregnancy had been 'under observation', having been told to come back a few days later; but on arrival at home the woman went into labour, and the baby was delivered in a taxi on the way back to the hospital! This was in the privileged Shemīrān district of Teheran, in a hospital which required private insurance contributions.

The Fifth Plan allocated 127 milliard rials – or 4.4 per cent – of the state's current expenditures, and 191 milliard rials – or 5.7 per cent – of the development expenditures to public health, social security and public welfare, including 'nutrition', which must mean indiscriminate state food subsidies in order to offset some of the effects of the rapid inflation of staple food prices. These items of social expenditure amounted to 6.2 per cent of the total Fifth Plan budget.[18] These sums, and their percentage shares of the total budget, look derisory when we consider the fact that the figure for 'defence' and 'security' funds – which is bound to be an understimate – was 1,969 thousand million rials, or 31.5 per cent of the total.[19] Yet it is more important to emphasise the relative ineffectiveness of these expenditures, regardless of the absolute sums involved. In 1974, after doubling the Fifth Plan budget in the Gājerēh conference of experts, and its confirmation in the following Rāmsar conference of the Shah and his ministers, the Central Bureau of State Hospitals – led by its chairman, Dr Ḥusain Khaṭībī, a one-time promising professor of Persian literature – began to consider the crazy scheme of founding twenty new *general* hospitals, each of them containing 1000 beds, in different parts of the country. This was the bureaucrats' idiotic way of taking public health facilities to the regions. They were thinking of employing foreign medical staff – consultants, general medical and nursing staff, and so on – on contract, with exorbitant salaries and 'perks'. Realising that they had to create the right 'social environment' for attracting foreign medical personnel of this type, they even envisaged the creation of exclusive entertainment centres in the palatial estates which they would construct to house them. If the whole of this imbecilic 'project' foundered at the exploratory stage, this was not due to any sudden flash of common-sense; it was the consequence of bureaucratic incompetence, and the reductions in state expenditure forced by the 1976 balance-of-payments deficit, of this 'capital surplus' country – a phenomenon which puzzled domestic and foreign 'experts' alike.[20]

In 1976, there was – according to official figures – one doctor of medicine for every 3,000, one dentist for every 19,000, and one hospital bed for every 711 Iranians.[21] These are average countrywide figures; half of the doctors, dentists and hospital beds must have been concentrated in Teheran alone.

Finally, transport and communications, banking and insurance, housing and urban property, and various private modern services all experienced rapid growth, both before and (especially) after the oil-revenue explosion of 1973.[22] Most of the transport and communications expenditure was on road and port construction (and reconstruction), a good part of which was dictated by military considerations. The very rapid growth of banking and insurance was partly the result of the general urban economic expansion, but mainly because these activities were extremely lucrative channels for the upper reaches of the state's clientele to make a lot of money from the state's effective handouts of oil revenues to them, and benefit from the grant of further credit facilities. Private services – hotels, restaurants, exclusive clubs and holiday resorts, and so forth, in the provision of which the Shah and his relatives had a large share – we have already mentioned. Likewise foreign trade – that is, the import business – was thriving and expanding.

There is one group of services which deserves special note, because of the social and political implications of its growth and prosperity: the domestic wholesale and retail trade. This was the only major group of urban economic activities from which riches were made *incidentally* – that is, without being a part of the pseudo-modernist designs of the state, and despite the fact that many of those involved in it did not belong to the state's clientele. In politiconomic terms, the effect of this event was nothing short of tremendous: it enriched the merchant and petty trading community, which was both economically and sociologically outside the framework of despotic pseudo-modernism, and opposed to all its practices, values and aspirations. The increased wealth of these merchants and traders was the inevitable result of a system to which they owed no allegiance, and against whose political and cultural norms their growing opposition was also inevitable.

Thus, the communal autonomy which the state had done its best to destroy by wholesale bribery, repression, violence and lawlessness was being quietly restored, and reinforced, by the incidental growth of the wealth of the merchant and trading communities and – mainly as a result – the religious leadership. If 'God moves in mysterious ways', so must history.

NOTES

1. We have seen however, that even this sector was much more capital-intensive than it could have been. See Ch. 13, n. 6.
2. The agreement concerning the exchange of natural gas for a steel plant was concluded in June 1966: see *Iṭṭilāʿāt* and *Kayhān* (daily newspapers). There were other important Irano-Soviet trade and political agreements over the period. See further Ch.16, below.
3. This was to be entirely financed by a Soviet loan of $286 million at an interest rate of 2.5 per cent. Therefore, the total cost of the gas-pipeline construction must have been originally estimated at around $300 million. The fact that a high Iranian official has confirmed the figure of $700 million for the final costs of the construction (although he says nothing about its damning implications for the régime he was serving) makes it virtually certain that this must be a realistic estimate. See Jahangir Amuzegar, *Iran: An Economic Profile* (Washington, DC: Middle East Institute, 1977).
4. Private information obtained by this writer, who happened to be in Shiraz at the time. The dam had been built by Israeli technicians.
5. In 1965 the NIOC was charged to set up a petrochemical subsidiary company as a joint venture with foreign capital. Between then and 1978, the National Iranian Petrochemical Company established five plants in different parts of the country, three of them joint ventures with American oil and petrochemical firms; a sixth

plant was scheduled for construction in 1978–9, with the participation of Japanese capital.

6. In an official conference on the subject held in Shiraz in November 1972, this issue was extensively debated, but the Romanian technical advisers present generally toed the official Iranian line, probably against their own better judgement. By chance, I happened to be a witness to the continuation of the debate in the lobbies. A professor of agriculture at the University of Shiraz (Dr Quaraishī) was almost the only technical expert who had the courage (because it required courage!) to criticise the official strategy with persistence.
7. See Bank Markazi Iran, Annual Report 1975–76, appendix table 52.
8. See Ch. 13, n. 2.
9. See Bank Markazi Iran, Annual Report 1977–8, table on p. 163.
10. See Ministry of Education, Conference Report, various years (in Persian); and Bank Markazi, Annual Report 1977–8, table on p. 165.
11. Bank Markazi Iran, Annual Report, and Ministry of Education, Conference Report, various years.
12. See Plan and Budget Organisation, *The Fifth Plan, 1973–8* (Teheran: Plan Organisation, 1973).
13. See Bank Markazi Iran, Annual Report 1977–8, table on p. 166.
14. The event was related to me by Dr M. Rassa, now a consultant radiologist in London, who, as their superior officer, had had the culprits arrested.
15. In 1972, a series of such pressures (in which the University President fully concurred) led to the resignations of the Dean and Sub-Dean of the Faculty of Economics, University of Teheran.
16. See their statistical report.
17. These facts are common knowledge among educated Iranians through a large number of direct and indirect experiences. However, they have been confirmed for me by Dr M. R. 'Amīdī-Nūrī, who has witnessed a range of specific cases. It must be emphasised, however, that the description presented here provides a general picture, and does not apply to all Iranian doctors and medical personnel.
18. See Plan and Budget Organisation, *Fifth Plan*. Note, however, that the absolute sums were substantially increased in the summer of 1974, after the Gājereh conference for the revision of the Fifth Plan, in view of the oil-revenue explosion. It was out of this considerable upward revision that the idea of building twenty new general hospitals was born. See further below.
19. Note that this gives the share of 'defence affairs' in the total – i.e. both current and development – expenditure budget. But, since the entire 'defence affairs' expenditure was a part of *current* expenditures, it follows that (according to the official data) the share of 'defence' in the ordinary budget was 69 per cent!
20. See further Ch. 16, below.
21. Based on Bank Markazi Iran, Annual Report 1975–6, appendix table 93.
22. For extensive numerical descriptions, see the references cited in Ch.13, n.1, above, or the official Iranian data which they use.

15 The Rural Society: Land Reform and the Plight of Agriculture

A Prefatory Note

In the history of economic development, agriculture has been a source of capital accumulation as well as cheap labour supply for the industrialisation of the urban sector: in England, the Enclosure Movement and technical progress in agriculture in the seventeenth and eighteenth centuries further weakened the foundations of feudalism, contributed to the accumulation of capital in industry, and drove landless peasants to the industrial towns, thus providing a continuous flow of cheap wage labour for modern factory production; in Japan, after the Meiji Restoration, agriculture made a significant contribution to industrialisation by releasing considerable saving funds which were invested in industry, providing an adequate supply of food for industrial workers, significantly helping the country's balance of trade (mainly through exports of silk and tea), and generally *retaining* its labour force, because in the Japanese conditions (up to 1914), a high rate of peasant migration into towns would *not* have been helpful; in the Soviet Union, agriculture was forced to make important contributions to industrial expansion *within a short space of time* (by releasing both capital and labour), mainly because the country was seriously threatened from without, and (although it had tried) it had not managed to obtain foreign credit for further industrialisation. Most of the models and theories concerning the primary accumulation of industrial capital that have been put forward in the past two centuries are based on these and similar experiences of the present industrial countries.[1]

In general, the problem with these theories (and their more detailed offspring) is that, when they are translated into national or international policies for economic development, they are usually applied everywhere without a sufficient and meaningful examination of their potential relevance to individual cases, and, therefore, without appropriate adjustments to the resources, needs and requirements of specific political economies. At any rate, rural reforms and agricultural strategies in many underdeveloped countries have provided the most evident, significant and painful examples of the failure of what this book has described as universalism in theory and method, and pseudo-modernism in policy and application. Yet, as Tolstoy once wrote, 'every unhappy family is unhappy in its own peculiar way', and the tale of land reformism and agricultural strategy in Iran has had its own specific politiconomic features, which we shall now briefly evaluate.

Historical Background and Preceding Developments

BEFORE THE LAND REFORM

Iran has never been a feudal political economy: private property ownership (especially in land) was weak and tenuous, based on various land-assignment systems as a military–bureaucratic privilege rather than an aristocratic right, and, both for these and other reasons, it could neither perpetuate itself nor concentrate; the state itself had a significant share of the agricultural land; there was no manorial system, landlords characteristically made up an *urban* social class, there was no serfdom, and no traditional system of peasant obligations other than the payment of crop shares (or, occasionally, rents) and taxes to the relevant agents of exploitation; towns and cities were relatively large and numerous, commerce was extensive and elaborate, and money played a significant role both as a medium of exchange and as a store of value, in the urban sector; consequently, politiconomic power was historically concentrated in cities, not the other way about: political power was both absolute and arbitrary (at all 'administrative' levels, regardless of whether or not there existed a large centralised bureaucracy), social mobility was high, and there existed neither an aristocracy nor bourgeois citizenship, in time or space. This theme has been developed at greater length in Chapter 2, and will be developed further in the next section.

The *Mashrūṭeh* Revolution against traditional despotism, which was led by merchants, landlords and their various social and intellectual allies, was bound to diffuse political power and strengthen private property (both in land and in merchant capital). The abolition of land assignment by the first *Majlis* was symbolic not only of the landlords' interests, but also of the merchants', who (together with their intellectual allies) in fact commanded a majority in the Assembly. The Act created a constitutional sanction for the existing ownership of land, turning the landlords' traditional *privilege* into a contractual *right* of ownership, which also served the merchants' interests in the following ways: it reduced the politiconomic power of the state, as all the social classes who backed the revolution desired; it actually served the interests of those relatively big merchants (many of whom had increased their fortunes through international trade) who had purchased land from the impoverished state, as well as some title-holders; and it potentially served the interests of the aspiring merchants who wished to do the same. In Europe, the feudal system had been responsible for the political strength and the economic monopoly of landed property, and the relative weakness of bourgeois property; therefore, the bourgeoisie had to break that monopoly as well as strengthen its own property rights by fighting the feudal system. In Iran, the despotic system was the cause of the strength and monopoly of state property, and the relative weakness of *all* private property; therefore, the propertied classes had to break that monopoly as well as strengthen their own property rights by fighting the despotic system. The two cases are thus quite comparable in basic mechanism, even though they are entirely dissimilar in terms of historical reality (see further Ch. 4, above).

It is therefore not surprising that Reżā Khān's rise to power was generally resisted by a combined landlord and merchant opposition, but helped by rootless modernist army officers, bureaucrats and intellectuals who were either actual or potential clients of the state. In spite of Reżā Shah's modern administrative reforms concerning land registration, and the like, the landlords (as a class) lost a great deal, through the increase in land tax, the state monopoly of trade in the main agricultural products (which kept the price of agricultural goods at an artificially low level), and the loss of political power and, hence, security of ownership; the merchants lost because of the state monopoly of international (as well as some domestic) trade, loss of political power and, hence, security of ownership. It was for these as well as other, related reasons that in 1941 both merchants and landlords (as social classes) welcomed the inglorious flight of His Most Powerful Majesty.

Between 1941 and 1950, both these social classes managed to strengthen their positions, the landlords being politically more influential because of their social power bases (the 'rotten boroughs' from which they went to the *Majlis* as deputies), and because of their generally more sophisticated educational background. After the first few months of Muṣaddiq's government, the landlords were almost completely alienated from it, because (a) they became frightened by the radicalism of the Popular Movement, which potentially threatened their politiconomic position; (b) the economic weakness of the country not only lost them money indirectly by reducing demand, but, more significantly, threatened a Tūdeh Party takeover; and (c) by trying to ensure genuine freedom of elections (as opposed to the 'natural' return of the landlords or their nominees from their power bases) Muṣaddiq was effectively destroying their newly acquired political domination. That is why they entered into an alliance with the Shah, the conservative religious leaders and the Anglo-American powers to overthrow Muṣaddiq and destroy the Tūdeh Party.

After the 1953 coup, the landlords enjoyed a brief period of politiconomic power (although the Shah's share of power was his own, as an ally, not an agent, of the landlords) during which they even managed to dismantle the partial tenancy 'reforms' which had been successively enacted by Qavām and Muṣaddiq.[2] But the inflow of substantial oil revenues and American aid increased the Shah's economic, military and, hence, political power at their expense, and there was a brief confrontation in 1960, when, on the Shah's orders, Iqbāl introduced into the *Majlis* a meek and mild tenancy-reform bill, which had been simply intended for American consumption: this was the first and last state bill which the deputies initially threw out, although eventually they passed it under great pressure (and on the strength of private reassurances). Meanwhile, they had obtained a public statement from Āyatullah Burūjirdī, the then *Marja 'al-taqlīd* in Qum, that the 'reform' would contravene religious principles.[3] It became a dead letter. Two years later, the Amīnī group took over the government intending to carry out a comprehensive land reform. At first the Shah allied himself firmly with the landlords and other conservatives merely in order to defeat Amīnī; but later he managed to defeat Amīnī by switching sides on the issue. That is how he became a White Revolutionary (see Ch. 11, above).

STRUCTURE AND RELATIONS: THE 'ARIDISOLATIC SOCIETY'

In general, the village provided the social boundary, as well as the production unit of peasant life and labour. It was normally made up of households with a traditional right of cultivation (the *nasaq*-holders), households without such rights (the *khushnishīn*), and a number of traders and moneylenders, who supplied small amounts of credit in cash or in kind at high implicit interest rates by advanced purchases of a part of the crop. In many villages, some *nasaq*-holding and/or *khushnishīn* peasants (known as the *gāvband*) 'rented' one or two pairs of oxen to other cultivators against a share of the crop. In more recent times, the development of *ijāreh kārī* (a form of small-scale tenant farming) in some parts of the country, had encouraged the use of wage labour, which was usually supplied by the *khushnishīn* community.

The traditional mode and method of production was communal. The Iranian village 'commune' is described by various terms in different regions, of which *buneh* and *ṣahrā* are the most common; there are also some differences in their strength of communality, the *buneh* being the strongest of all the regional varieties. This does bear comparison with the old Russian village commune, the *mir*, though it has its own peculiar features and, in any case, is a looser and less comprehensive institution; purely linguistically, *mir* means 'world' (in Russian), while *buneh* simply refers to a person's base, as well as his roots.

The *buneh* must owe its origins to the fact that water is the country's most scarce agricultural resource, except in one or two small pockets of land: the scarcity of water encouraged communal co-operation for the construction and upkeep of underground water channels (*qanār* or *kārīz*), as well as the distribution of water among the cultivators; hence also the peasant ranks of the *ābyār* (*owyār*), or 'water assistant'. Therefore, the climatic aridity did not turn Iran into a 'hydraulic society' (as defined by Wittfogel), because the village community itself, as one unit, organised the supply and distribution of water. Once the *buneh* came into existence, however, it developed other socio-economic functions, such as decisions concerning crop rotation and leaving fields fallow. One (though not universal) consequence of this institution was that peasant holdings were usually open and scattered, in order to ensure an average equality of fertility for the holdings of all the cultivators, but there were also cases of consolidated holdings: in general, the more arid the location, the stronger the *buneh*, and the greater the likelihood of scattered holdings. The landlord (who could be a land assignee, the state itself, or the trustees of a charitable endowment), was generally an outsider and, in any case, not a part of the *buneh*, but his local agent (the *mubāshir*) provided the necessary link between the two.

The traditional mode and method of distribution (of output) was crop-sharing (or 'sharecropping'), theoretically based on the 'five-inputs' rule, the inputs being land, water, seeds, oxen and labour: the landlord would take the two shares of 'land' (i.e. land and water), the peasant would take the share of labour, and the two shares of capital (seeds and oxen) would go to their respective suppliers: the landlord, the peasant or a *gāvband* ('ox-tier'). In practice, the mode of distribution varied from this theoretical rule, though not so far as to make it irrelevant; besides, in a very few cases a 'system' of rent payment was also practised. However, the share of the peasant was further subject to the state tax, the payment of religious dues, and the settlement of debt obligations to creditors. This happened at harvest time; hence the Persian expression 'promises for harvest time' (i.e. empty promises): occasionally the peasants could not meet all these obligations, and not infrequently they hid a part of the crop, in order to reduce the actual share of the exploiters.

Therefore, both the *internal* socio-economic structure and relations and the *external* (geographical as well as politiconomic) conditions made the Iranian village an independent unit of life and labour, with few links with other (usually distant) villages, and little interest in the urban outsiders who came and left at the right time taking their appointed shares of the village output. As mentioned earlier, Iranian agriculture and the Iranian peasantry were *not* dependent on the state for the provision and regulation of water supplies, or for anything else. It was the state that depended on scattered and isolated village units for the agricultural surplus which it either directly requisitioned, or assigned to landlords and tax-farmers. This is the likely origin of the despotic state, which, basing itself on urban centres and military outposts linked together by a countrywide transport system, dominated the scattered village *units* of agricultural production. In this way, the peasantry, being isolated from the organised urban state, and divided into small units which were independent from each other, served its two major (social and historical) functions: it was exploited by the cities through the despotic state and its dependants; and it helped preserve the basic cultural continuity of the land, in spite of periodic internal upheavals (which are a part of the 'logic' of despotism), as well as external invasions and raids. At least the latter function is still being served by those peasants who have remained on the land. That is, they care little for what goes on 'outside', even if it is a popular revolution: they have seen it all for millennia, and they have few illusions about any of the 'outsiders', whoever they may be, whatever they may promise; they would simply agree with all of them in their presence, and go on hiding their possessions.

To sum up and conclude, aridity did play a basic role in shaping the structure of the Iranian political economy, but in its own peculiar way: it served to create autonomous village units of production, none of which could produce a sufficiently large surplus to provide a feudal power base, but all of which taken together produced a collective surplus so large that, once appropriated by an organised external (regional or countrywide) force, it could be used to prevent the fragmentation of politiconomic power. This martial force was originally provided by invading *nomadic* tribes, and thereafter both by the existing and by further incoming nomads, who succeeded in setting up various urban states at different stages of history. The size of the direct and indirect collective agricultural surplus was so large as to enable these despotic states to spend on transport, communications, military and bureaucratic organisations, and so on, which both maintained their hold on the land and prevented the later emergence of feudal autonomy in agriculture, or bourgeois citizenship in towns. If this amounts to the rudiments of a 'model', and it must have a name to be taken seriously, then we may define it as Persian despotism, based on the 'aridisolatic' society.

The Land Reform

Prior to the Land Reform Law of 1962, there had only been one incident of relatively large-scale 'distribution' of land: this was the Shah's sale of the lands *usurped* by his despotic father which had been confiscated by the government after his abdication, put in the Shah's 'care' in 1948, taken back from him before the coup, in 1953, and retaken by him afterwards: he sold the land at his own prices to the peasantry by instalments, cashed in their value from the coffers of the state, and put the funds into very good use both inside and outside the country, thus increasing his wealth, ridding himself of dangerous immovable property, and boasting to the whole world that he was giving 'his own' lands back to the peasants. (See Chs 9 and 10, above.)

Amīnī and Arsanjānī seriously intended to carry out a comprehensive programme of land distribution: to divide the land among the *nasaq*-holding peasantry (roughly about 65 per cent of the peasant population), who would compensate the landlords by annual instalments. Their original method of evaluation, using the taxes paid by the landlords in the immediately preceding years, added insult to the landlords' injury, for everyone knew that they had been evading taxes at shameful rates. It is clear that the government had not thought through the whole of its scheme (as perhaps in the circumstances it could not), but, by making the receipt of land conditional on the peasant households' membership of rural co-operatives (to be set up concurrently with the land distribution) Arsanjānī must have hoped to preserve something of the old communal system of production. The proposed programme did betray some elements of pseudo-modernist naïveté – as for example, when certain junior technocrats began to talk about there being 35 per cent 'disguised unemployment' in the Iranian rural sector, i.e. the entire *khushnishīn* village community, on account of the simple fact that *theoretically* they did not have a traditional right of cultivation (*nasaq*)! Yet, in so far as it would keep the politiconomic boundaries of the Iranian village intact, it was still something more realistic and relevant than a simple blueprint imported from abroad. However, the Amīnī–Arsanjānī reform programme was seriously opposed by landlords and the conservative religious leaders (other religious leaders, including Āyatullah Sharī'atmadārī, did *not* oppose the principle); the Shah too, opposed it – until he himself took over the idea as something he had been dreaming of since his childhood; and it was publicly ignored and privately denounced as a 'lie' by the second National Front. The Tūdeh Party merely issued slogans from Eastern Europe in favour of land for the peasantry, and, of course, maintained that the Amīnī group were *bound* to be lying (how could a leading 'feudal' – i.e. Amīnī – betray his own 'class'?)

There was only one alternative programme put forward as a serious rival to Arsanjānī's: Khalīl Malekī's proposal for the democratisation or popularisation (*mellī kardan*) of land *and* water. This does not mean, and was not intended to mean, *nationalisation*, which in the Iranian conditions would mean *state* ownership as opposed to *public* ownership. Malekī's programme was as follows: to transfer the title of ownership from the landlords to the peasant community as a whole, which would dispossess the landlords at a stroke and without complicated legal and other wrangles; avoid the collossal administrative task of defining every single peasant-holding in every village; prevent the emergence of scattered and small *individual* holdings, which by division through inheritance could be reduced to plots so small as to have to be sold to a few large holders, resulting in the consolidation this time of private capitalist ownership of land; and bypass the immediate problem of dispossessing the *khushnishīn* community, with all the social and economic implications of such an act. What would the country do with so many dispossessed peasants being released from the land, and so many more to be released in future as a result of fragmentation through inheritance?[4] Malekī did not develop the further, momentous implications of his scheme, although he may have had them in mind; the fact that the scheme would preserve *in their entirety* the communal mode of production and the 'egalitarian' modes of land-holding and distribution in the village community, while simply getting rid of the outside exploiters. The idea was too advanced and too radical for it to be understood by *any* political force in the country: Amīnī and Arsanjānī would not, and could not, take it on (and Malekī did not expect *them* to so do); the leadership of the second National Front would not touch it even with gloves on; the Tūdeh Party and similar 'Marxists' would not understand it, and, in any case, would describe any and all ideas coming from Malekī as dictated by the SAVAK and various foreign demons and ogres. That aside, Malekī's programme would work only as part of the construction of a broader and genuinely democratic society; it was part of his vision of *Iranian* socialism.

The original Land Reform Law, described as the First Stage, eventually affected about 20 per cent of peasant households, although, once the Shah himself had taken over its operation, various amendments in favour of the landlords pulled out a few of its sharper teeth.[5] The Second Stage (1964–6) – affecting most of the remaining *nasaq*-holders – was mainly a tenancy-reform act, although it also tried to encourage the establishment of large-scale farm corporations, without success. The Third Stage (1966–78) was almost exclusively intended to create large numbers of such farm corporations, and the Fourth Stage was simply a state agricultural policy for the creation of 'agri-businesses', or giant capitalistic farms. The Third and Fourth Stages (of which more below) were in fact no part of a land reform, but a despotic pseudo-modernist strategy which *de*formed Iranian agriculture.

The politiconomy of the emergence and implications of each of these stages needs more detailed discussion. By turning the programme into his own show, the Shah had to reckon with the combined opposition of his conservative political and religious allies, whom he had abandoned. The amendments to the First Stage law were intended to dilute the opposition of the landlords. The religious opposition was, however, much more comprehensive and deep-rooted: first, the conservative religious leaders were opposed both to land reform and to the Shah's counterfeit 'feminism'; secondly, both the conservative *and* the enlightened religious leaders were anxious about the prospects for the charitable endowments in landed property (the *owqāf-i 'ām*), which had been traditionally the only relatively secure form of property, and a significant source of the financial autonomy of the religious community; thirdly, they *all* smelt the rat of an emerging despotism which, *contrary to traditional Iranian despotism*, intended to destroy the autonomy of the Shī'ite leadership in much the same way as Reżā Shah had previously attempted to do. That is also why the people's revolt of June 1963 had the support of all the anti-despotic forces: the Shī'ite leadership and community (not the Church), the merchant community (not the national bourgeoisie), the landlords (not the feudals) and the ordinary urban people (not the petty bourgeoisie and the proletariat). It was crushed by the military–bureaucratic apparatus of the state, while the educated, intellectual, and professional groups (which made up the leadership and cadres of modern opposition parties) were looking on with bewilderment, trying to use their books to make sense of the situation as they saw it: the Church, feudalism, the national bourgeoisie and the rest were all fighting against the land reform and other apparently progressive measures. It is true that in their own slogans they regarded these measures as inadequate and half-hearted, especially as they had all been 'designed by American imperialism'. Yet the puzzle was serious and demoralising.[6]

After he had further accommodated the landlords by turning the Second Stage into a tenancy reform, the rapid growth of the oil revenues increased the Shah's financial and military power, turned the politically battered landlords (as a class) into the most privileged clients of the oil state, and enabled the Shah to play pseudo-modernist games with the political economy, including agriculture. The Third Stage thus inaugurated the period of agricultural *de*formation: the 'voluntary' establishment of farm corporations, which would turn peasant property into paper shares of the large corporations, lead to the concentration of ownership (through the sale of paper shares by smallholders to big proprietors, thus creating absentee capitalist farmers as well as peasant wage labourers) and result in the state management of farm corporations by officials sent from Teheran or the provincial capital. Yet, the most damaging effect of this policy was to destroy the historic boundaries of the Iranian village as an autonomous unit of social life and labour.

By the time the Fourth Stage, the agri-business venture, came into being, despotic pseudo-modernism was in full swing. The programme was to set up huge capitalistic agricultural factories, a hybrid form of the Latin American latifundia and the Russian *sovkhozi*, by setting up joint-stock companies through the use of state as well as domestic and foreign private capital, in order to dispossess peasants in hundreds of villages in the most fertile areas of the country, and use them as migrant wage labourers: the companies put their own price on the peasants' lands, from which they also deducted the peasant's debt obligations to various state agencies, and charged them for the cost of the inhuman cinder-block hovels that were built for them. But no sooner than they had begun the operation than they also began to go bankrupt! (See further the chapter appendix on agri-businesses and farm corporations.[7]) So much for a brief analysis of the 'land reform'.

The Plight of Agriculture

OIL AND AGRICULTURE

Historically, the *collective* agricultural surplus had been the main source of the financial autonomy and despotic power of the Iranian state. This was a collective economic (i.e. monopolistic) rent, received by the state and its urban clientele (landlords, tax officials, and so on) from *outside* their own politiconomic domain, for use *inside* it. That was the basic logic of the 'aridisolatic' society. The basic logic of the petrolic society is, in a curious way, very similar to that: oil revenues are a collective economic rent, received from *outside* the political economy (i.e. the oil sector) for use *inside* the urban sector. The difference is, first, that revenues from oil are not due to the productive effort of *any* part of the political economy; secondly, that the revenues are received totally by the state, which instead of directly 'assigning' a part of the oil *resources* to some of its clientele, indirectly hands out a share of the *revenues* to them; and, thirdly, that, in the case of Iran, the revenues became so large (even in the late 1960s and early 1970s) that the state could widen its circle of clientele much beyond the growing military–bureaucratic complex, to other segments of the urban population, and for the first time in history could begin to extend its despotic hegemony over social life and labour even to the Iranian village. Historically, the state had been an agent of exploitation, taking the village surplus, but otherwise leaving the village community undisturbed; but the petrolic pseudo-modernist state (being economically independent of agriculture) entered the village either to destroy it or to stay and run the lives of its inhabitants.

The psychology was that a large traditional agriculture is shameful, and evidence of backwardness; the sociology was that of the despotic state stretched to its limits, in that despotism as an urban system wanted – for the first time – to internalise the historical 'outsiders', the peasants; the economics was that the state was no longer dependent on the agricultural surplus as a source of finance, food and exports, because the oil revenues more than compensated for all these agricultural contributions; and the politics was despotism. It followed that (a) the state had no interest in developing the agricultural sector, and (b) it had every interest in creating a small 'modern' agriculture through the disastrous means of agri-businesses and farm corporations, and turning the majority of the peasant population into urban wage labour. It was the Shah himself who, early in 1973 (even before the oil-revenue explosion), *boasted* that by 1980 there will be no more than 2 million people (that is 300,000 *workers*) on the land.

THE PERFORMANCE OF AGRICULTURE

Some macro-economic observations on the agricultural sector have already been presented in the previous chapters: for example, the fact that between 1963 and 1978 the share of agriculture in both the total and the non-oil GNP fell; that there was a very high rate of migration from villages into towns; and that relative output per worker was much lower in agriculture than in industry and (especially) services; and so on (see Chs 13 and 14).

Throughout the period, the average annual rate of growth of agricultural *output* was probably 2.5 per cent, and certainly less than 3 per cent; therefore, even assuming the latter rate of growth, the average annual rate of growth of agricultural *productivity* would be zero. Yet this observation itself is significant: this was a period in which the high rate of output and 'productivity' growth in the urban sector was exclusively due to the continuously increasing oil revenues; and, as both the previous chapter and the next should make clear, pseudo-modernist investments in industry and services cost the country very dear and paid it very little. Yet agriculture, enjoying no privileges of any kind, being institutionally and technologically devastated all the time, containing the poorest and socially most oppressed people in the country, may have grown at a rate of between 2.5 and 3 per cent per annum, as well as contributing over one-half of the total industrial and agricultural exports of the country, even as late as 1978.[8] In the circumstances, this performance is quite good, especially when we realise that it was almost entirely due to the traditional sector of agriculture, which received very little financial and other help from outside.

Output per head refers to 'labour productivity', but in agriculture another, sometimes more significant, index of performance is output per hectare, or 'land productivity', and its growth. The evidence indicates that in the period 1963–78 the growth of land productivity in Iranian agriculture was also zero or negative – that is to say, land reclamation did not proportionately add to total output, and probably even 'led' to its decline: naturally, the use of more land cannot by itself *reduce* output, so that, if the rate of growth of output per hectare was negative, this must have been due to factors countervailing the effects of land reclamation. Furthermore, the rapidly expanding application of technical inputs and capital equipment – for instance, chemical fertilisers and tractors – does not seem to have helped at all, there being no correlation between the growing use of such inputs and the agricultural outputs.[9] The reasons for these observations are as follows: (a) nearly all the state and private credit was injected into the disastrous twins, the farm corporations and the agri-businesses, and – for both politiconomic and institutional reasons – these 'modern' sectors performed extremely badly; and (b) the traditional sector was starved of funds, and pushed around by the gendarmerie and other state officials, including those involved in the 'co-operatives' (of which more below). Therefore, the 'modern' sector failed miserably, while the traditional sector, which was almost positively persecuted, could not do so well as to compensate entirely for the failure of the former (see further the appendix).

Iranian agriculture consists of both arable and livestock farming: arable farming is dominated by wheat and barley, which make up the staple food crops of the country, rice being the only other main food item; the rest of arable farming consists of the production of cash-crops, mainly cotton, fruits and tobacco, of which the first two make up the whole of Iranian agricultural exports. Iran has been a net importer of grain since the end of the last century, and the main reason for this is the reallocation that took place in that century in favour of cash-crop production for exports. As late as 1968, the agricultural balance of trade – that is, the value of agricultural exports minus imports – was *positive*. This meant that the country was still completely independent of oil revenues for its food and agricultural requirements, and that agriculture was still a net receiver of foreign exchange,[10] in spite of rapidly growing food deficits, which were caused both by the perpetual increases in demand and by the petrolic approach to agriculture, which prevented a commensurate growth of domestic supply. However, the picture radically altered when, on the one hand, the oil-revenue explosion exploded the demand for food, revalued the rate of exchange of the rial, increased domestic demand for agricultural exports, and emphasised, on the other hand, the adventurous strategy of the state *vis-à-vis* the agricultural sector.

Iranian livestock farming has been dominated by sheep, goats, cattle and poultry. Of these, sheep have always been the main item, supplying the best Iranian red-meat products. Meat, and dairy products (supplied by cattle-keepers) are the main luxury food items; therefore, the growth of incomes would increase the demand for them more rapidly than the demand for ordinary food products. That is why the earliest signs of a large food deficit, from the demand side, showed up in this range of products. But, on the supply side, the main reason for their earlier, and greater, scarcity was the despotic strategy towards their major producers: the nomadic population. For the pseudo-modernists, nomads must be bad, because they are the worst evidence of backwardness. But, more importantly, both tradition and the facts of nomadic life had turned them into a semi-autonomous martial entity whom the Shah would not tolerate, because they were independent from the state and could stir up trouble for it, as shown throughout Iranian history. The confrontation with the large and powerful Qashqā'ī nomads in the southern province of Fars was the test case. The Qashqā'īs had had a continuous record of bad relations with the Shah and his father, and that is why they provided the test case for the more general policy of statising all the country's nomads. The uprising began at the end of 1964, and it was defeated sixteen months later, because of the continuous pounding of the Qashqā'ī mountainous retreats by napalm and other bombs; their young military leader, Bahman Qashqā'ī, voluntarily gave himself up, on the official promise of being spared, only to be betrayed and put before the firing squad. Once the Qashqā'īs had been defeated, and the petrolic state had become more powerful, the fate of the other nomads was sealed. Many of the Iranian nomads, especially in the south and west of the country, were treated with a harshness that, in the view of Nāsser Pākdāman (an Iranian political economist), not even the Red Indians in America had suffered.[11]

This was probably the most important cause of the relative decline of livestock breeding. But, apart from that, the country's limited pastures were also nationalised – i.e. monopolised by the state – and guarded by gendarmes and other agents of despotism, as a further 'principle' of the White Revolution. This increased the cost of production to meat and dairy producers in settled agriculture, and exacerbated the problem. The food shortages became cumulative; liberal imports could not, and did not, relieve them, for reasons which we have already seen; and the state urban subsidies for bread and similar food items did not generally counteract the inflationary pressures, and were of no help to the peasantry.

THE STATE AND THE PEASANTRY

The policies of creating farm corporations and agri-businesses have already been mentioned. But it was the traditional sector of Iranian agriculture that still housed the Iranian peasantry, who make up 55 per cent of the whole population. The departure of landlords had created a number of institutional and economic gaps; for they had generally acted as a link between the peasantry and the military–bureaucratic agents of the state, and as a source of credit at least for investment in water supplies, from which they themselves also benefited. The Arsanjānī scheme for the creation of rural co-operatives had been intended to close the latter gap, by the supply of state credit to self-governing co-operative societies. Later developments reduced these co-operative societies to collective clients of the bureaucratic co-operative unions, which were themselves clients of the Central Organisation of Rural Co-operatives, which was, in turn, attached to the Ministry of Co-operatives and Rural Affairs! The reader must know something about the country in order to understand the full implications of all this for the distribution of the meagre credit facilities extended to the traditional sector: the real criteria for selection, the wholesale corruption at every level, the bureaucratic tyranny and blackmail, and so forth.

In 1971–2 (for which all the relevant data are available) the value of aggregate *agricultural output* amounted to 172.3 thousand million rials, while aggregate *peasant consumption* was 179.6 thousand million rials. That is, total peasant consumption was 7.3 thousand million rials *more* than total agricultural output. Now, total agricultural output includes not only the output of the *modern* agricultural sector, but also the output of forestry, fishing and such like, which are state monopolies. Apart from that, agricultural output includes the value of seeds and other capital replacements, as well as profits, rents, and so on, paid out by the peasantry to outsiders. Therefore, aggregate net peasant *income* from this output must have been much less than 172.3, say 120, thousand million rials, which was supplemented by rural handicraft and service production of a certain amount. Whatever this latter amount, it could not have been so large as to fill the gap of 52.3 thousand million rials between income and consumption, and aggregate peasant saving must have been negative.[12] Yet, the peasants' debts to private and state creditors were accumulating, while, at the same time, a proportion of the peasantry were undernourished (see Ch. 13, appendix on poverty).

Table 15.1 shows that the urban output of $1830 per capita is about seven times the agricultural output per capita of $251, *not including* the oil revenues which were received by the state and spent in the urban sector. As we have seen above, the agricultural output per capita is a good indicator of income per

TABLE 15.1 Distribution of GNP, output per capita and population by sector, 1976

	Share in GNP (per cent)	*Share in population (per cent)*	*Output per capita ($)*	
Rural	9.4	56.0	251	
Urban	53.6	44.0	1830	3079
Oil	37.0	–	–	

Source: H. Katouzian, 'Oil *versus* Agriculture: a Case of Dual Resource Depletion in Iran', *Journal of Peasant Studies*, Apr 1978, table 3.

head in rural society, while the urban income per head must be considerably more than the urban output per capita, because most of the oil revenues are spent in the urban sector. Therefore, figures in Table 15.1 indicate that the level of *income* per head in the urban sector must have been around $2500 per annum, which is ten times higher than the rural income per head. These average figures merely give us an idea of the difference between towns and villages in the general standard of living, but they tell us nothing about the differences between regions, or within each of the two sectors, which must also be very considerable.

To summarise, the original land reform had been intended to distribute land among the majority of peasant households, but this policy was first diluted in order to reduce the landlords' opposition, and then effectively reversed, for the sake of creating farm corporations and agri-businesses. At the same time, the growth and explosion of the oil revenues (a) encouraged the state to pursue its strategy of urban 'industrial expansion'; (b) made it independent from the agricultural (food, financial and export) surpluses; (c) diverted state and other credit and capital to agri-businesses and farm corporations; and (d) led to a cumulative growth of demand for food and other agricultural products. The combination and interaction of these policies and events resulted in (a) zero growth of agricultural productivity, which was mainly due to the 'modern' agricultural sector, in spite of its monopoly of agricultural finance and other state privileges; (b) poverty and insecurity among the peasantry, which led to a high rate of migration to towns and cities; and (c) a growing food deficit which could not be relieved by imports, and which led to a high rate of food inflation. In a word, it was a case of total and unmitigated failure.

The agrarian question in Iran is much too large a subject to be fully discussed within the limits of this study. For further information, the reader may consult some of the works cited in the notes to this chapter, as well as my own more comprehensive study of the subject.[13] Meanwhile, the following appendix presents a short investigation of a few outstanding issues concerning the relative performance of the traditional and the 'modern' sectors of Iranian agriculture in the past decade.

Appendix: A Note on Peasant Agriculture, Farm Corporations and Agri-business Units

An investigation of the relative position and performance of these different systems of agricultural production is useful both for an understanding of past events and for the formulation of future policies. It has already been stated that the basic reason for the poor performance of Iranian agriculture *as a whole* was that the policy-makers treated it as an unwanted sector of the political economy, and that an important contributory factor was the 'modern' modes or systems of agricultural production which developed at the initiative, and with the help and support, of the state. This appendix presents some evidence for these assertions, and then proceeds to discuss the politiconomic reasons behind them.

In a previous study, I have calculated from official data that (a) the number of peasant households in the traditional sector of agriculture is 98.8 per cent of the total, with the remaining 1.2 per cent accounted for by peasant shareholders of farm corporations (which cover about 1.7 per cent of total cultivable land); and (b) the value of capital stock per household is 20 times greater in farm corporations than in the traditional peasant sector.[14] This astronomic difference is almost completely due to the highly discriminatory policy of the state in distributing credit and grants between the two sectors. Table 15.2 contains data on both the total and the average annual credit (per

TABLE 15.2 Distribution of agricultural grants and credits by sector, 1968–75 (rials per hectare)

	Total 1968–75	*Per annum 1968–75*
Peasant co-operatives loans	6,470	808
Farm corporations	122,383	15,297
loans	(26,839)	(3,354)
grants	(95,544)	(11,943)

Source: based on Fatemeh Etemad Moghadam, 'The Effects of Farm Size and Management System on Agricultural Production in Iran' (unpublished D Phil thesis, University of Oxford, 1978).

hectare) extended to peasant co-operative societies and farm corporations over the period 1968–75. The table shows that the state's average annual financial loans and grants to farm corporations was nineteen times the credit extended to peasant co-operatives. But it must be added that (a) 78 per cent of the financial help given to farm corporations was in the form of grants: the remainder consisted of low-interest loans, and the corporations were allowed to reinvest most of the annual interest charges in the farm itself; and (b) whereas the grants and loans paid to the corporations were both long-term and systematic, the meagre credit advanced to the peasant co-operatives was short-term and haphazard. This is not to mention the real toil and trouble involved for a peasant who asks for a small loan.

Now, there does not exist a general study of the comparative performance of farm corporations and traditional agriculture, but nearly all the piecemeal and partial evidence indicates that the performance of traditional agriculture, even in spite of its gross disadvantages, has been appreciably better. For example, the Garmsār corporation, which is officially held up as a case (and probably the only case) of success, has performed no better, and probably worse, than the neighbouring traditional village of Rīsān, while a study of the Shams-Ābād farm corporation in Khūzistan has shown that its output is below the 1960 level (when the corporation did not exist) and its general performance is appreciably worse than that of the neighbouring traditional village units of production.[15]

Agri-businesses were yet another, much more extensive, capitalistic and technological group of farms, or better, agricultural factories. Published official information on agri-businesses is limited, and there has been no general study of their performance. There is no doubt, however, that this was the most disastrous gamble in the Shah's agricultural policy, and that provides the main reason for the paucity of published official information and research on the subject. Apart from that, a large proportion of foreign capital invested in agri-businesses has been withdrawn, and this indicates that these shareholders have been disappointed with the venture. But a recent micro-economic study of relative performance of farms of different sizes and modes of production has demonstrated, as clearly and rigorously as possible, that the agri-business farms have been performing worse than all other production types and categories in almost every respect.

The study in question is an elaborate statistical study of productive performance based on a carefully selected sample of five Iranian villages in different regions, as well as four agri-businesses, covering 50 per cent of the total land cultivated by this group. The study includes a number of detailed results on farms of various sizes, which, though they are important in their own right, cannot be summarised here. For our present purpose, however, the study's most important result is that the *total* productivity performance of medium-sized peasant holdings has been significantly better than that of larger independent capitalist farms, which in turn have performed significantly better than agri-businesses. This means that the productivity performance of the traditional mode of production has been appreciably better than the 'modern' grain factories not only relatively but also absolutely; not only in relation to their much lower resource endowments, but, more significantly, regardless of the differences in water, land, financial and technological resources available to them.[16]

The reasons behind these various, apparently astonishing observations can be discussed at great length. Put briefly, the traditional mode of production has (in spite of all the odds) performed better than the 'modern' systems because both farm corporations and agri-businesses are (at different levels) purely uninstitutional and ahistorical inventions, transplanted into a given social framework from the air. Both these 'modern' systems destroyed the technical characteristics and politiconomic relations of Iranian agriculture, and replaced them with completely alien and ill-adapted technological and institutional forms. Like all pseudo-modernistic strategies in Iran and elsewhere, they brought no *progress*, because any progress is by definition rooted in the existing history of the relevant entity: progress is a natural, sometimes even violent, extension of what there is already; it is not, and cannot be, the arbitrary superimposition of irrelevant blueprints. The farm corporations were set up normally against the will of the affected peasantry, and they were run by state bureaucrats. Agri-businesses were founded on the expropriation and eviction of thousands of peasants, in various villages, who then supplied the migrant wage labour for these factories; and they were managed by foreign technocrats who did not even understand the language of their employees, let alone know anything about the history, politiconomy or technology of Iranian agriculture. If it is clear why an attempt to create traditional Iranian-type village units of production in California would fail absolutely, then it should be equally clear why the uncritical application of Californian institutions and technology to Iranian agriculture failed so miserably.

NOTES

1. See, for example, M. H. Dobb, *Soviet Economic Development Since 1917* (London: Routledge, 1960); Paul Mantoux, *The Industrial Revolution* (London: Cape, 1961); Alexander Gerschenkron, *Economic Backwardness in Historical Perspectives* (Cambridge, Mass.: Harvard University Press, 1961); and W. W. Lockwood, *The Economic Development of Japan . . . 1868–1938* (Princeton, NJ: Princeton University Press, 1969).
2. See Chs 9 to 11 above.
3. The most important traditional authority invoked in the argument was the following *ḥadith* quoted from the Prophet: 'Annāsu musallaṭūna 'alā amwalihim wa'alā anfusihim' ('People have dominion over their persons and possessions'). Yet it is difficult to know why this perfectly reasonable statement should be used against the distribution of land among the peasantry. The word *amwāl* can mean

both 'possessions' and 'property', though in its social and historical context it in fact means 'possessions' or 'belongings'. We saw in Chapter 2, above, that even European feudal property was not a possession, but a contractual right founded on usurpation; and the case is similar for Iranian landed 'property', which was acquired through state usurpation and assignment. It follows that, if land was anybody's 'possession', it was the peasants' and no one else's; apart from that, it is not clear why such arguments had not been previously invoked to prevent the state from taxing people's incomes, which are certainly a possession.

4. See his various articles in issues of '*Ilm u Zindigi* (monthly periodical) 1959 – 62, and *Firdowsī* (weekly magazine) 1962.
5. All these amendments were effected during 1963, *after* the 'White Revolution', and Arsanjānī (who had been retained as Minister of Agriculture after Amīnī's dismissal) went along with them, thus proving that, in general, power and possessions are more important than principles. For the details and dates of the amendments, see H. Katouzian, 'Land Reform in Iran: A Case Study in the Political Economy of Social Engineering', *Journal of Peasant Studies*, Jan 1974, pp. 220–39.
6. This excludes a small minority, of whom Khalīl Malekī is the best example. See further Ch. 11, above.
7. See further A. K. S. Lambton, *The Persian Land Reform* (London: Oxford University Press, 1970); H. Katouzian, 'Land Reform in Iran' in *Journal of Peasant Studies*, Jan 1974, and 'Oil *versus* Agriculture: a Case of Dual Resource Depletion in Iran', ibid., April 1978, pp. 347 – 69 (and the references therein); Nikki Keddie, 'Stratification, Social Control . . . and Capitalism in Iranian Villages Before and After Land Reform', in R. Antoun and I. Havik (eds), *Politics and Social Change in the Middle East* (Bloomington, Ind.: Indiana University Press, 1972) pp. 364–401.
8. See H. Katouzian, 'Bakhsh-i Kishāvarzī dar Iqtiṣād-irān', *Tahqīqāt-e-Eqtesadī*, Dec 1972, pp. 211–46, and 'Oil *versus* Agriculture', *Journal of Peasant Studies*, Apr 1978. Ch. 16, below.
9. For the evidence, see Katouzian, 'Oil *versus* Agriculture', *Journal of Peasant Studies*, Apr 1978.
10. See Katouzian, in *Tahqīqāt-e-Eqtesadī*, Dec 1972.
11. This was said in a discussion group in Teheran in August 1977.
12. The original figures are all official data published in various reports of Bank Markazi Iran.
13. 'The Agrarian Question in Iran', International Labour Organisation paper (1980).
14. See Katouzian 'Oil *versus* Agriculture', *Journal of Peasant Studies*, Apr 1978, tables 4 and 5, p. 360.
15. See Fatemeh Etemad Moghaddam, 'The Effects of Farm Size and Management System on Agricultural Production in Iran' (unpublished D Phil thesis, University of Oxford, 1979) esp. pp. 78 – 82.
16. See ibid. In 'Oil *versus* Agriculture (*Journal of Peasant Studies*, Apr 1978) I cited the preliminary results of Etemad Moghaddam's works. In a more recent article, Nikki Keddie has found it difficult to believe that the *absolute* performance of traditional agriculture has been better than that of the agri-businesses, and has wondered whether it has not done better in terms of *relative* performance only. That is why it is emphasised here that the former have performed better than the latter regardless of the large differences in their resource endowments. See Nikki Keddie, 'The Midas Touch: Black Gold, Economics and Politics in Iran Today', *Iranian Studies*, x, no. 4 (Aug 1977) 243–66, esp. pp. 264–5.

16 Foreign Trade and Relations

Oil, despotism and 'economic development' were bound to have a profound effect on Iran's politiconomic relations with the outside world. As long as the petrolic expenditure strategy described in Chapter 12 – that is, the rapid expansion of the military–bureaucratic network, the consumption boom, and the industrialism of the despotic system – was in operation, certain effects were inevitable: internally, the growth and explosion of oil revenues and the cumulative inflow of foreign credit and capital attracted by their existence and prospects inflated the value and changed the composition of the country's foreign trade; and, externally, the increase in Iran's financial wealth made the Shah less dependent on Western finance, more powerful in the region, and able to use oil, its price and its revenues as diplomatic levers, while, at the same time, foreign (Western as well as Eastern) countries adjusted their methods and attitudes to such significant changes in his politiconomic position. This chapter, like many of the foregoing, is intended to present a general analytical appraisal of the problem. Attention will be focused on two main aspects of the topic: (a) the Shah's politiconomic relations with industrial Western and Eastern powers; and (b) the changing value and composition of the country's foreign trade and balance of payments.

The Situation before 1963

In 1963 the international political atmosphere and international relations were appreciably different from at present. In 1960, when Khrushchev publicly repudiated Stalin, and confidently promised the world that by 1980 the Soviet people would live in a society free of economic scarcity and political restraint (i.e. in a Communist Society), the Chinese Prime Minister laid a wreath on Stalin's grave, describing him as 'the great Marxist–Leninist of our country'.[1] Three years later, China had already made public her long-standing differences with 'certain comrades' when the Cuban missiles crisis and the Sino-Indian border war simultaneously broke out. In the same year, shortly before the assassination of President Kennedy, the Americans overthrew Diem in South Vietnam, and committed their troops to a long and bloody war against 'the agents of Chinese Communist aggression' (i.e. Ho Chi

Minh and the Vietcong) in that country. Meanwhile, the British Empire, having already granted independence to Kuwait, was beginning to experience the full force of the 'wind of change' in Aden (later South Yemen). This was in the Middle East, where there had been a lull in the confrontation between Israel and the Arab states, especially Egypt, while, Nasser, then at the height of his popularity among Arab as well as Iranian radicals, was virtually fighting a war in Yemen (now North Yemen).

In Chapter 11 we saw that, between 1960 and 1962, the Shah's external (as well as internal) position was very precarious: the Americans were unhappy with his disastrous misuse of their massive aid programme; the Russians had been incensed by his earlier treachery, though they were even less happy at the prospect of Amīnī's triumph against the Shah; Irano-Egyptian diplomatic relations had already been severed, and Nasser was describing the Shah as an agent of Western imperialism. The British position was, however, more complex. Although documentary evidence is not available, it is likely that Britain was not sympathetic to Amīnī for the following reasons: first, until the Shah managed to remove Amīnī, he had given the impression to landlords and other conservative forces that he was on their side, and there was therefore an anti-Amīnī front made up of the Shah and his conservative allies of the 1953 coup; secondly, this was the sort of coalition of Iranian political forces to which Britain had been closest since the war; thirdly, although there is no reason why British diplomacy should have been opposed to a land reform in principle, it would not have supported one (such as Amīnī's) which would have eliminated the landlords as a class *and* pushed His Majesty aside;[2] fourthly, the British must have been especially fearful of a takeover by the second National Front, because the experience of the oil dispute had created such an irrational British prejudice, even hysteria, against anyone and anything associated with the name of Dr Muṣaddiq (the old ogre who had tried to 'rob' them of 'their property') that they were simply incapable of a balanced judgement in this connection;[3] and, fifthly, individuals such as Abadullah Rashīdīyān – the combination of a Mafia-type operator and a cloak-and-dagger conspirator who himself had spread the rumour of being a British agent – were actively plotting against Amīnī, and this may have reflected the attitude of the British embassy in Teheran.[4]

To sum up, by early 1962 the *pattern* of the attitude of foreign powers towards Muṣaddiq seems to have repeated itself, even though there were many important differences in the details: while the Americans were still keeping their options open, the British and the Russians were less favourable to the two reformist tendencies; the British were particularly frightened of the second National Front, and the Russians especially worrried of a stabilisation by Amīnī, because, even in spite of their anger with the Shah, they still preferred him to a reformist politician imposed on the Shah *by the Americans*. For the same reason, they could not have hoped for the success of the National Front, because this, too, would have required American support.[5]

Politiconomic Relations with Foreign Powers

Once the Shah had rid himself of Amīnī, betrayed his conservative allies by launching his White Revolution, thrown the opposition into a state of confusion and demoralisation, drowned the people's revolt of June 1963 in a sea of blood, appointed his own deputies to the new and 'classless' *Majlis*, and so forth, he could easily establish close or friendly relations with all the major powers: the Americans must have been thrilled with the White Revolution; the Russians must have been happy that the Shah had defeated the actual or potential *American* candidates for reformism, as well as the forces of 'feudalism'; and the British must have heaved a sigh of relief that the 'traditional ruler' was still at the helm, the oil would keep flowing, and the evil of the Muṣaddiqites had abated. None of the above powers changed its friendly attitude towards the Shah (albeit that they were not all equally friendly) until late in 1978, although this does not mean that perennial tensions did not arise to strain relations for short periods of time.

For example, the issue of Bahrain, over which Iran had long claimed sovereignty, became topical when in 1967 Britain decided to give independence to the Persian Gulf states. It is incredible that the Shah should not have seen Bahrain as a great prize: his longings to become the Cyrus of the twentieth century were obsessive; his appetite for oil revenues (and any other unearned income) to spend, especially before the oil-revenue explosion, was insatiable; and his longing for popularity among the Iranian people was so strong as to make him a permanent victim of self-deception. Yet, whatever else he was, in his foreign relations the Shah was a realist to the point of cynicism. He knew that the real costs of a long 'battle for Bahrain' were likely to be much greater than its imaginary benefits. Therefore, he traded Bahrain for the small desert islands of Ṭunb and 'Abū Mūsā, on the condition that he should have a free hand to 'rule the waves' in the Persian Gulf and the Sea of Oman (for which the Americans would supply his arms requirements). The latter condition was, of course, also suitable to the Western powers, who were worried about the 'power vacuum' created by the British departure from the area.

Another case of a serious clash of interests between the Shah and the West was his active role in raising oil prices. Before October 1973, he had already played the hawk in conferences held in Teheran for pushing up oil prices; but in 1973 his double-edged manoeuvre in not joining the Arab oil strike, while auctioning off non-Consortium Iranian oil at prices of up to $17 per barrel, played a decisive role in the fourfold price increase that almost immediately followed. He was to maintain this attitude until November 1977, when he declared that he would not push for an oil-price increase in the forthcoming OPEC conference. There must have been two reasons for this change of attitude: (a) he had realised, very belatedly, that increasing expenditures were causing him more harm than good inside the country; (b) whether or not he genuinely believed that the Iranian Revolution was no more than an American plot in response to his oilmanship, he must have thought that, in the circumstances, the offer of an olive branch to the West would be helpful. In any case, unless they are masochists, the Western powers must have been annoyed by the Shah's behaviour over oil prices, which, apart from its obvious economic effects, harmed them indirectly by boosting the financial and bargaining power of the Arab countries in their dealings with the West over Israel. Yet, the Shah was the anti-communist policeman in the Persian Gulf, a big spender who would (willy rather than nilly) purchase the latest tanks, aircrafts, battleships, atomic power stations, computers, and so on, from them; and, in any case, there was really not much that they could do in the situation.

There were also occasional clashes with Soviet interests: in the protracted Kurdish uprising in Iraq, the Russians, who had once supported Mullā Muṣṭafā Bārezānī, were firmly behind the Iraqi régime, while the Shah was providing Bārezānī with financial, military and logistic support in various forms. The Russians must have been intelligent enough to know that the Shah's attitude had not been determined by the West, or, in other words, he was not simply getting 'orders from his American masters' to back the Kurds. In fact, the origin of the Shah's involvement was in the Irano-Iraqi border disputes in Khūzistan, which had once (in 1968) nearly led to an armed conflict; and the border dispute itself was deeply embedded in the more serious rivalry between Iran and Iraq in the Persian Gulf. That was also why the Iraqis had provided a home for the Shah's ruthless rival, General Bakhtīyār, to plot against his own former master, and resorted to massive persecutions and expulsions of Iraqi Shī'ites of Iranian origin in 1971–2. Therefore, the upsurge of a tribal war in Iraqi Kurdistan provided the Shah with an excellent opportunity to revenge himself on the Iraqis, as well as bring them to heel, one way or another. With the intervention of Boumédienne in the 'Islamic Summit' in Algiers, the Iraqis effectively capitulated, and overnight the Shah (presumably without consulting his American masters!) stabbed his Kurdish allies firmly in the back. This happened five months after the oil-revenue explosion, in March 1973, which (for both these reasons) a *Majlis* deputy described as 'the month of destiny' – a description euphorically repeated by Lord Chalfont in his column in *The Times*. It was certainly a month of destiny. However, another – this time economic – clash with Soviet interests was over the price of Iran's gas supplies to that country. When in 1974 negotiations dragged on without a solution in sight, a main gas pipeline 'inexplicably' exploded, disrupting supplies. Within a couple of weeks, a settlement was reached, and the pipeline somehow healed itself.

The same cynical hard-headedness was the main reason for the Shah's attitude towards the Arab–Israeli conflict: before the June War in 1967, partly because of his dependence on American financial and, especially, military aid, partly because of longstanding bad relations with Nasser (which was the main reason for the latter's popularity among the Shah's opposition), and partly because of his own basic anti-Arabism (which is shared by many Iranian pseudo-modernists of Right and Left alike), he maintained friendly relations with Israel, although with some degree of cautiousness. The military victory of Israel in June 1967 'proved' his policy right, and in fact led to a rapprochement with Egypt, for which a battered and isolated Nasser himself took the initiative. Meanwhile, the Israelis were training his SAVAK agents (as well as providing technical personnel, especially in dam construction), while the Palestinians began to train Iranian urban guerrillas who voluntarily made contact with them. By the time this position had been reached (in the 1970s), the Shah was no longer financially dependent on America, Egypt was effectively suing for peace with Israel (in which the Yom Kippur offensive of 1973 had played a major part), Saudi Arabia, Egypt, and Jordan did not object to the Shah's private relations with Israel, and Iraq, Syria and Libya had their own serious differences among themselves. Yet, the Shah managed to endear himself to Boumédienne of Algeria, and early in 1976 he even played host to Assad of Syria, whom – together with a large retinue – he received with great pomp and ceremony.

Even the adventure in the sultanate of Oman eventually paid off. His decision to intervene in the guerrilla war in Dhoffar, where a group of nationalists using Marxist–Leninist jargon were fighting the archaic régime of King Qābūs, involved the following elements: he had to prove both to his Western allies and to the sheiks of the Persian Gulf that he would fulfil his obligations as the policeman and Big Brother; he had to prove to the Chinese and others, who provided some material support for the guerrillas, that he would not tolerate 'subversion' in his zone of influence; and he had to ensure that the guerrillas would not win, or he would have had to reckon with a new base of both external and internal trouble for himself. It paid off, because the guerrillas, being weak and isolated both in quantity and quality, simply could not win the war with the support of South Yemen (it is significant that not even the Iraqis lifted a finger for them),[6] and the Chinese had already reached the conclusion that their best bet would be to compete with Soviet diplomacy in Iran with, rather than against, the Shah: when in 1973 the Kissinger–Leduc horse-trading in Paris was still in progress, the Chinese accorded the Shah's wife a lavish welcome on her state visit to China; they had already ceremoniously received his sister Ashraf as his 'good-will ambassador'.

This was an important diplomatic triumph: it reduced the attractiveness of China – which had once been great – for the internal Marxist (even non-Marxist) opposition; it removed China as a possible base for training Iranian cadres and guerrillas (which had had some precedent in the 1960s); it was good moral propaganda for the Shah inside the country; and it was a useful new card in his diplomatic game with the Russians. Between 1973 and 1978, Sino-Iranian relations steadily improved, and there is every reason to believe that Hua Kuo Feng's state visit to Iran in 1978 would have led to closer relations if the Shah himself had not had to run away from the country a few months later.

RELATIONS WITH AMERICA

The Shah had owed his return to the Iranian throne (with greater power than he had ever had before) to the *coup d'état* of 1953, which had been due partly to the active involvement of the CIA, and partly to the support of the domestic conservative political and religious forces. Apart from that, he had immediately afterwards been blessed with generous American financial and military aid, which in the 1950s helped him stabilise his position, push his conservative allies into the background, and squander a lot of money without results. Yet in 1958 these same Americans tried, without success, to bring him down, or at least bring him down to earth; and, again, between 1960 and 1962 they looked hard for a credible alternative (i.e. an alternative broadly acceptable both to themselves and to the Iranian people, with the will and ability to carry out basic reforms), and gave up when they failed to find one. They then settled for the Shah himself *with* his White Revolution, which, as usual, they uncritically bought as the right product.

The most important (though not the only) lever that they could and did use both for and against the Shah was financial: in the 1953 coup, $10 million or so had been sufficient to buy a few generals, and pay the boys and girls called out by the Āyatullahs to overthrow Muṣaddiq; between 1953 and 1959, they paid out nearly $900 million worth of aid (about $700 million of which were non-returnable grants) only to discover that it had all been squandered without any results. Between 1960 and 1962, they made the extension of further support (which the Shah then desperately needed for survival) conditional on political and economic reforms in the country. These well-known facts should be sufficient to show that the Shah was not inherently a paid agent of American imperialism, permanently echoing his master's voice, and that neither are the Americans an omnipotent power who can hire and fire everyone, everywhere, in all situations. The Shah was first and foremost his own agent, who would do whatever necessary to promote his own interest. Therefore, as his financial strength grew with the oil revenues, he could rightly feel a greater degree of freedom in his relations not only with domestic political forces, but also with external powers.

He was, nevertheless, acceptable to the Americans (more in the period 1963–73, and less afterwards) because of his White Revolution (which they no doubt regarded as evidence for non-communist 'economic development'), his anti-communism, for which he was in need of no order or advice from them, and his real success in foreign relations, including relations with the socialist countries. They were naturally very pleased with his ever-increasing arms purchases, mainly from America, but also from other countries, including Britain and the Soviet Union. But it would be naïve to think that he had been under orders from them to buy these toys (which occasionally, for example in the case of the AWAKS system, they were obliged to refuse to supply), if only because His Majesty simply did not need any persuasion in this field at all; or to believe that they would (or could) overthrow him, merely because of a reduction in his arms purchases from American firms. In any case, who would want to tell his own agent to play a decisive role in quadrupling oil prices, so that he would then spend a portion of it on their weapons and other products?

In 1977–8, the Americans ranked third (after West Germany and Japan, as they had done for a number of years) in their share of Iran's 'non-classified' imports: this amounted to $2200 million worth of goods, or 15.6 per cent of Iran's total imports. However, Iran's total 'classified' imports in that year were worth $4300 million, in which America must have had the largest share (see Table 16.1, below).

RELATIONS WITH THE SOVIET UNION AND EAST EUROPEAN COUNTRIES

The normalisation of relations with the Soviet Union in 1963 was followed by greater co-operation in the 1960s and 1970s. The Shah's interest in establishing good relations with Russia was purely political: it would emasculate the Tūdeh Party, confuse the Iranian Left in general, destroy the attractiveness of the Soviet Union for the masses of the people (who dearly loved any power, big and small, that poured abuse on the Shah through its Persian broadcasts, as well as by other means) and minimise the risk of subversion by Soviet agents infiltrated across the long frontier; in addition, and perhaps more significantly, it would free his hands to move his armies to the south and west of the country, which he badly needed to do in order to enforce his growing ambitions in the Persian Gulf area. In this respect, it is significant that, as early as the mid-1960s, he moved no fewer than nine divisions from the north to the south and south-west of the country, and most of his later military ventures also took place in that direction. Apart from that, even his interest in getting a steel plant from the Russians was more political in intention: he could have got a better plant at lower costs from elsewhere, but it would make an important *political* difference, inside the country, to get a 'metal-smelting factory' from the Soviet Union.

The Russians were in favour of good relations for both political and economic reasons: they needed Iranian gas, which they got on very favourable terms; they wanted a share of Iran's rapidly growing market, especially in view of their general foreign-exchange requirements for purchases outside the socialist countries; they were interested in importing certain other products (mainly agricultural raw materials and basic consumer products) from Iran; and, in view of their deteriorating relations with China, they were looking for as many allies, such as Iraq and Afghanistan, and friends, such as Iran, as they could find in that region. This does not mean that the Shah was the Russians' ideal man for Iran; it simply means that they accepted him as the real power in the country, and tried to come to terms with that reality as they saw it. And if this contradicts some theoretical models according to which the Soviet Union, *or any other country*, ought to base its international relations on criteria other than, or in conflict with, its own ordinary strategic and commerical interests, then either the models are wrong, or they refer to situations not yet experienced in the real world. History, experience and common-sense have all demonstrated that no country would voluntarily sacrifice its own interests for another, unless the 'sacrifice' itself genuinely promised a greater political or economic return in the near future. It is not so much puzzling that all great powers pursue their own self-interest in their foreign relations, as it is astonishing that they make so many *obvious* blunders in so doing. And, in this latter respect, the Nobel prize must surely go to the Americans.

The ice began to break when, in July 1963, an Irano-Soviet agreement for technical and economic co-operation in the construction of hydroelectric dams was concluded in Teheran. There followed a series of other protocols concerning air transport, aerial photography, and so on, until three years later, when the agreement for the exchange of a Soviet steel plant for Iranian gas was concluded in Moscow. This agreement involved the presence of Soviet steel technicians in Iran, as well as training of Iranian personnel in the Soviet Union. A year later, Iran purchased $110 million worth of arms from the Soviet Union, which, in the economic and political circumstances, was a considerable order.[7] Later co-operations included a series of agreements for mutual exchange of goods both between Iran and the Soviet Union, and between Iran and other east European countries. In addition, Iran placed a number of import orders with these countries (for instance, Czechoslovakia), which were paid for with foreign exchange. It must be emphasised, however, that the *share* of Iran's trade with the socialist countries was still very limited, and this was partly because of the Shah's much closer relations with the West, partly because of his need for Western *advanced* technology, which even the Russians are anxious to obtain, partly because of Iran's food requirements, which (with their own deficit) the Russians are not able to supply, and partly because Western (especially Japanese, German and American) *consumer* products – ranging from motor-cars and electronic equipment to cookers and refrigerators – are better in quality and lower in price. Yet, the Shah's growing economic co-operation with the East was politically symbolic, and promised better prospects for future commercial relations with those countries.

RELATIONS WITH WESTERN EUROPE AND JAPAN

In the 1950s Britain was quickly replaced by America as the dominant Western power and influence in Iran: the British lost their monopoly of south Iranian oil, the Americans could afford to spend, and, of course, America had left her pre-war 'isolationism' to play a full global role in the 'free world'. Yet, Britain's influence was greater than her actual position warranted, partly because she was still a military power in the region, and partly because of the old relations and contacts in the country. If Britain rapidly lost her substantial share of the Iranian market, it was purely and simply because she failed to compete, not so much with the Americans as with, especially, the West Germans first, and the Japanese later, while in between she also lost some ground to the French and Italians. To give but one example, in the early 1950s the streets of Teheran were crowded with Vauxhalls and English Fords, but by 1960 they were full of Mercedeses and Volkswagens. Nevertheless, later in the 1960s Britain managed to obtain a large share of the Iranian assembly-plant car production, in which the Americans and the French were the other, less significant suppliers.

When the rapid growth of oil revenues began the *absolute amount* of Britain's exports to Iran also grew. The single most lucrative British export was Chieftain tanks, which the Shah eagerly bought because these are the most advanced armoured weapons of their type; but in addition Britain annually exported to Iran a variety of manufacturing and agricultural products, the total value of which (other than services) amounted to no less than $971 million in 1977–8. Besides, Britain had a sizable share of the Iranian market in financial and other services, in which she still competes successfully in the international maket. Apart from that, she has benefited from large official and private Iranian deposits and investments since the oil-revenue explosion; these were particularly helpful to her international payments position before her own oil revenues began to help her balance of payments.

Yet, in the field of Iranian economic relations, no country, not even America, was as successful as Germany and Japan. The conclusion of the war had reduced Germany's previously large share of Iran's trade to negligible proportions; but she quickly began to recover the lost ground in the 1950s, increased her share in the 1960s, and ended by supplying about 20 per cent of Iran's 'non-classified' (as well as a large share of her 'classified') imports in the 1970s. In addition, she supplied a lot of financial and technical services to Iran, and benefited from a large share of Iranian deposits and foreign investment. The official investment in the Krupp heavy-industrial complex must be regarded as one of His Majesty's greatest follies in the field of foreign investment: he paid about $800 million of the country's capital for just over 25 per cent of the shares of this famous company and its subsidiaries, which mainly produce declining products, such as steel, and suffer from high running costs!

Japan's share of the Iranian market had never been significant. But the Japanese entered this field, in which they were strangers, with characteristic drive and acumen. They not only invaded with photographic equipment, watches, electronic instruments, and so forth; they also innovated in consumer products especially designed for the Iranian and neighbouring markets. Furthermore, they participated in the official joint-venture investments (replacing American firms in petrochemicals), and began to compete in the insurance and financial markets. In 1977–8, their exports of 'non-classified' goods to Iran amounted to over $2200 million, or 15.7 per cent of the total. (See Table 16.1).

TABLE 16.1 Distribution of non-classified imports by countries of origin 1977–8

	$m.	*% of total*
EEC	5,968	42.3
West Germany	(2,747)	(19.5)
Other EEC countries	(3,221)	(22.8)
Japan	2,215	15.7
USA	2,205	15.6
Other west European countries (i.e. non-EEC)	1,025	7.3
Rest of the world	2,687	19.1
Total	14,100	100.0

Source: based on Vizārat-i Bāzargānī, *Āmār-i Bāzargānī-yi Khārijī-yi Irān* (official foreign-trade statistics) 1977–8.

Table 16.1 summarises the distribution of Iran's imports of 'non-classified' goods by source. It can be seen that the countries of the European Economic Community have had the highest share (over 42 per cent) of the market, with Germany dominating, and Britain, Italy, France, Holland and Belgium, in that order, supplying the rest of EEC exports.[8] Other west European countries, mainly Switzerland, Sweden, Austria, Spain and Finland, supplied another 7.3 per cent of Iran's imports, so that, altogether, non-socialist Europe took 50 per cent of the total. Therefore, with Japan's 15.7 per cent and America's 15.6 per cent the rest of the world – that is, the socialist countries and the Third World – supplied just under 20 per cent of Iran's imports. This account excludes the distribution of $4300 million of 'classified' goods, and $4800 million of service imports, on which detailed information is not available, though America, Britain, Germany, France and Japan must have been the main suppliers on both accounts.

A BRIEF APPRAISAL

The Shah's politiconomic relations with the superpowers, as well as other global and regional powers, was determined by his despotic pseudo-modernism within, and cynical realism outside, the country: he monopolised absolute and arbitrary power inside the country, dreamed of turning Iran into a major industrial and military power, needed as much money as he could think of for realising his obsessive desires, and wanted peace with foreign (especially super-) powers so as to be able to follow his obsessive aims without any major external or internal disturbance. His cynical realism in foreign diplomacy completely paid off; it was his psychopathic designs inside the country which *alone* spelled his final and complete doom, both economically and politically.

Foreign powers, each according to their relative positions, do interfere in the affairs of other countries. The actual and aspiring superpowers do so both for economic and for strategic reasons. The primacy of one of these considerations over the other is determined by the specific situation at a specific time, and it therefore changes both in time and in space. Both the Americans and the Russians wish to maintain and improve their political and economic power; but, in a given situation, they will not sacrifice a major strategic position for a few hundred million dollars' worth of exports, nor will they sacrifice grave economic interests for the sake of ideological purity. Take the case of Iran: between 1953 and 1960, the Americans paid the Shah *$700 million in non-repayable (i.e. free) grants alone*, though the only American economic interest in the country worth talking about was the 40 per cent share of American oil companies in the Consortium, which paid those companies *$700 million including their capital and other costs.* Would it therefore make sense to say that the Americans' involvement in Iran during this period (when they in fact had a greater hold over the Shah than after 1963) was purely determined by a capitalist imperialist conspiracy to rob Iran of her economic wealth? On the other hand, when, in the 1960s, the Shah's coffers began to be inflated with growing oil revenues, the Americans had less of a financial hold over him, and little political (or economic) motivation for interfering with His Majesty's despotism and pseudo-modernism. The Shah's active role in pushing up oil prices must have annoyed as well as worried them, but they would not risk creating instability in the region (involving not only strategic but much greater economic, oil interests) by confronting their most dependable voluntary policeman in the area. In their turn, the Shah's militarism, pseudo-modernism and anti-communism automatically ensured that a great deal of the revenues would be spent on weapons, food, consumer products, and technological equipment, in Western markets.

The Soviet efforts in the 1950s to establish friendly relations with the Shah had been frustrated mainly because of pressures from the Americans as well as the Shah's own domestic conservative allies. In 1963, these pressures had begun to disappear both because of the Shah's betrayal and defeat of his domestic conservative allies, and because of the change in the world political atmosphere: this was the period of 'peaceful co-existence' between Russia and America, to be followed by 'détente'; apart from that, advances in military technology, especially the proliferation of long-range nuclear missiles, had rendered the establishment of American air and other bases around the Soviet Union unnecessary. Therefore, the Shah could respond to Soviet gestures, and later extend friendly relations to other east European countries, as well as to

China. In their turn, the Soviet Union and other socialist countries regarded the Shah as safely established in Iran; they realised that, although he was (for his own reasons) pro-Western, he had many familiar Eastern qualities, and he was unlikely to be a mere stooge or paid agent of the Americans; and they valued friendship with him, because of his growing military and financial power, both for strategic and for economic reasons. Indeed, his active role in pushing up oil prices must have received a round of applause in the Soviet Union (though not in China), because it automatically increased the international value of Soviet oil and other energy sources supplied to eastern Europe, threw the international monetary system into greater disorder, and increased costs of production and living in Western countries.

When the Shah fell in early 1979, all the major powers knew they stood to lose: the Americans mainly because of the loss of his policing role in the oil region, as well as a lack of certainty regarding the prospects inside Iran itself; the Japanese and west Europeans mainly because of the inevitable loss of substantial export orders; the Russians mainly because the new régime was likely to be even less friendly towards them. They were all proved right.[9]

Pseudo-Modernism and Foreign Trade

The Shah's strategy of 'economic development' automatically involved galloping imports of food, consumer durables, modern capital equipment, Western advanced technology, and financial, transport and tourist services, while his despotism and pseudo-nationalism led to cumulative imports of military hardware. From his point of view, the pseudo-modernist economic strategy was necessary for turning the country into 'the fifth most industrial state' in the world. The main question was, where and in what sectors would this millennarian paradise begin to replace oil as the dominant export product, on which everything else was so far dependent? Apart from completely groundless *boasts*, the Shah and his henchmen never supplied a clear answer to this crucial question even in their propaganda: as early as 1964, Amīr 'Abbās Hovaidā boasted that 'in fifteen years' time' Iran would have caught up with the advanced industrial countries – not, he emphasised, as they were in 1964, but as they would be in 1979.[10] This empty, cynical and dangerous boast (to be followed by many more both by his master and himself) was made when the country's oil revenues were no more than $600 million; by 1979, when the Shah lost his throne and Hovaidā his life, they had risen to $20,000 million (a level no one could have dreamed of even in 1970). What did they achieve in those fifteen years?

Tables 16.2 and 16.3 provide an overview of the moving picture. In 1963 Iran's total exports of goods were just over $600 million; by 1972, the year before the oil-revenue explosion, they had increased fivefold; and in 1978, the year of 'destiny', they were forty times their 1963 dollar value. Likewise,

TABLE 16.2 Exports and imports of goods ($m.), selected years

	1963	*1972*	*1978*
Oil and gas	471	2,600	23,500
All other goods	137	440	520
Total exports	608	3,040	24,020
Total imports	561	3,161	18,400

Source: based on Vizārat-i Bāzargānī, *Āmār-i Bāzargānī-yi Khārijī-yi Irān* (from the Foreign Trade Statistics of Iran, various dates).

TABLE 16.3 Composition of exported goods (per cent), selected years

	1963	*1972*	*1978*
Oil and gas	77	85	98
All other goods	23	15	2
Total	100	100	100

Source: Table 16.2

imports grew from $560 million in 1963, to over $3000 million in 1972, to $18,400 million in 1978 (see Table 16.2). The rapid growth of oil revenues in the 1960s led to a fall in the share of non-oil exports, from 23 per cent of the total in 1963 to 15 per cent in 1972, and the later oil-revenue explosion reduced it to no more than 2 per cent (see Table 16.3). At 'the gates of the Great Civilisation', exports of Iranian industrial and agricultural goods amounted to only 2 per cent of the country's total exports. This means that, if the country were to rely on her own *production* and exportation of goods, without the bonus of oil and gas revenues, she could only purchase less than 3 per cent of the goods which she is now buying.

Remembering that this is the period of pseudo-modernist economic development – of forward industries such as steel, petrochemicals, motor-cars, machine tools, and so on, as opposed to backward embarrassments such as agriculture and traditional manufacturing – it is important to know the relative contribution of these various industries to the country's non-oil exports: this, as we have seen, was no more than 2 per cent of total exports of goods, but it would be interesting to know where this 2 per cent came from. Tables 16.4 and 16.5 provide an answer: agriculture contributed 51 per cent of total non-oil exports, traditional (both handicraft and machine-made) products, contributed a further 28 per cent, and pseudo-modernist industries made up the remaining 21 per cent (see Table 16.4). Putting it differently, traditional Iranian products were still responsible for nearly four-fifths of total non-oil exports, while the pseudo-modernist industries of the emerging

TABLE 16.4 Composition of exported goods (excluding oil and gas), 1977–8

	$m.	% of total
Agriculture	264	51.0
Cotton	(93)	(18.0)
Fruits (mainly dried)	(90)	(17.5)
All other	(81)	(15.5)
Traditional industry	148	28.0
Carpets	(115)	(21.8)
Textiles	(24)	(4.5)
Shoes	(8)	(1.5)
Mineral ores	(1)	(0.2)
Pseudo-modernist industry	111	21.0
Detergents and soap	(16)	(3.0)
Other chemicals	(12)	(2.3)
Sweets and biscuits	(11)	(2.1)
Motor-vehicles	(10)	(1.9)
All others	(62)	(11.7)
Total export of goods (excluding oil and gas)	523	100.0

Source: as Table 16.1.

'fifth most industrial state' contributed only $111 million – that is, one-fifth of the total (see Table 16.5). Apart from that, it is most significant that the pattern of Iran's non-oil exports is still fundamentally the same as it was at the beginning of the century: carpets, cotton and (mainly dried) fruits still make up somewhat less than 60 per cent of the total. Considering that the total emphasis on pseudo-modernist industries was detrimental to the development of the traditional sector, and the related overvaluation of the rial drastically reduced their competitive position in the international market, it is both impressive and significant that this should be so: it shows that, despite all, experience, know-how and history still matter a lot.

The value and distribution of Iranian imported goods is in some sense a mirror image of the export pattern. In 1977–8, $18,400 million worth of goods were imported, about a quarter of which were 'classified' (i.e. military and

TABLE 16.5 A classification of exported goods (excluding oil and gas), 1977–8

	$m.	% of total
Traditional exports	412	79
Pseudo-modernist exports	111	21
Total	523	100

Source: Table 16.4.

TABLE 16.6 Distribution of imported goods by type of product, 1977–8

	$m.	% of total
Non-classified	14,100	76
Machinery, vehicles, locomotives, etc.	(6,100)	(33)
Steel, chemicals, paper and pulp, fibres, etc.	(5,300)	(29)
Food	(2,200)	(12)
All other	(500)	(2)
Classified	4300	24
Total	18,400	100

Source: as Table 16.1.

related) items, and the rest industrial and food products. In Table 16.6, we observe that the country still imported $5300 million worth of steel, chemical and other products, and spent $2200 million – that is, more than four times her non-oil exports – on food imports alone. Imports and exports of *goods*, however, make up only the 'visible' items of a country's current trade. The 'invisibles' consist of all the services (banking, insurance, tourism, and so on) which the country 'buys' or 'sells' in the international market. Iran has nearly always had a deficit on this account, but the crucial questions are the dimensions and composition of such a deficit. Table 16.7 shows that in 1977–8 the country's net import (deficit) of services was no less than $2632 million (that is, five times her total non-oil exports), of which nearly half was due to travel and tourism: the familiar petrolic pattern – reinforced by the over-valuation of the rial, and its free convertibility into foreign exchange – of a widespread *fever* for visiting Europe and the USA, and, among the state's clientele, for gambling in Western casinos.

TABLE 16.7 Net service transactions (exports minus imports) 1977–8

	$m.	% of total
Travel and tourism	–1316	–48.4
'Government and other services'	– 816	–30.0
Freight and insurance	– 375	–13.7
Miscellaneous	– 125	– 4.6
Net factor income from abroad	89	3.3
Total deficit	–2632	–96.7

Source: as Table 16.1

The balance of payments consists of two parts: the balance of current transactions of both goods and services; and the balance of long-term capital movements into and out of the country. In the case of the capital account, exports of financial capital from a country are shown as a debit, because they immediately reduce the country's foreign reserves, and imports of such capital into the country are shown as a credit, because they increase the reserves. Foreign aid and investment are of this type: they would normally have to be repaid (together with interest, etc.) in the longer run; but they immediately increase the country's financial capacity to buy more goods abroad, and the gradual repayments (usually called debt-servicing) will show up in the country's future current accounts. For example, in Table 16.7 a large portion of the $816 million deficit described as being due to 'government and other services' transactions must consist of such debt-servicing of past official borrowings – of international credit obtained by the state. When politicians speak of 'the balance-of-payments deficit', they usually refer to the deficit of exports over imports of *goods and services* – that is, of the current account.

In 1963–4 Iran's current account had turned into a surplus, mainly because of the drastic measures taken in the previous two years to reduce imports; her capital account showed a deficit mainly because the flight of foreign capital was greater than its inflow, but the two accounts put together still afforded a small surplus to the country. Between 1965 and 1971, the country's current account was persistently in deficit, because she bought more goods and services than she sold in spite of the rapid growth in her oil revenues; her capital account was persistently in surplus, because of the Shah's success in borrowing abroad and attracting foreign investment into the country; and, yet, the overall balance of payments (i.e. the current and capital accounts put together) was in deficit in every single year except 1967. This means that His Majesty's zeal to spend was so great that considerable increases in the country's oil revenues and substantial foreign credits were incapable of offsetting it. Meanwhile, the country went on accumulating debts. In 1972, when oil prices had already increased, though not yet exploded, the current account was still in deficit, but, on the strength of further foreign credit and investment, the overall balance moved into surplus.

The oil-revenue explosion of 1973 inevitably reversed this pattern for the following years: there was so much foreign exchange that even the huge increase in the country's imports could not outstrip it, because this increase itself resulted in an acute shortage of port, transport and distribution facilities, causing merchant ships to queue up to unload their cargoes, perishable material to rot and be dumped into the sea, inland deliveries to be delayed, market shortages to become a part of everyday experience, and so on; therefore, there was no longer a *net* dependency on long-term foreign capital, but even a 'surplus' of Iranian financial capital which could be lent and invested abroad. Between 1973 and 1978, the Iranian current account was persistently in surplus, and the capital account persistently in deficit. The overall balance was generally in surplus except in 1975–6, when the net export of capital had been so great as to be $1100 million more than the current-account surplus.[11]

In principle, if a country has too much financial capital to invest in its own economy, it would make sense to lend or invest it abroad, in order to maintain or increase its value and receive additional income from its earnings. However, in the specific case of Iranian export of capital since 1973–4, a number of points must be considered: first, it would have been better to reduce the size of this 'surplus' capital by reducing the rate of oil output, *which would have been possible without creating an oil shortage in the international market*; secondly, the official overvaluation of the rial (apart from its other consequences) made it artificially more attractive for the private sector to export capital; thirdly, the state of socio-economic insecurity created by the Shah and his henchmen became such that in 1975 a galloping *flight* of private capital (not only a number of large sums, but, more significantly, a large number of small sums) became a feature of the political economy; finally, the pattern of official state investment abroad – even when political factors were not its main determinants – was inefficient and wasteful, because they were determined not by market considerations, but by the Shah, his despotic decisions and his psychopathic whims.

The explosion of state expenditure combined with the pseudo-modernist strategy for 'economic development', created acute physical bottlenecks, of which the shortage of skilled and professional labour (that is, 'human capital') was one of the greatest. But the problem had its own specific implications: it not only inflated the earnings of the existing skilled personnel, but also reduced their productivity per unit of time worked, because they often found additional employments which they were physically able to manage only by reducing effort in their other occupations; it increased social pressures among the professionals themselves, and intensified the sense of envy and frustration of ordinary workers; it led to a bizarre market reallocation of skilled labour such that highly skilled workers such as those involved in printing and tailoring would leave their occupations and become drivers (therefore exacerbating labour shortages in those industries) because, as a result of a greater short-term scarcity of drivers, their incomes had increased disproportionately. Apart from that, the employment of foreign skilled personnel created its own social problems, not least because they were invariably paid significantly more than their Iranian equivalents: despite development economics, the 'skill constraint' was not alleviated by hiring foreign technicians, and the employment of large numbers of foreign workers created serious politiconomic problems: ordinary Iranian workers put the *absolutely* high level of earnings of foreign technicians down to an imperialist conspiracy; Iranian technicians put the *relatively* higher earnings of foreign technicians down to the country's lack of independence; and the Iranian people at large viewed the sudden massive increase in the number of blue-eyed people in the country as evidence that 'America' was about to take over their personal and private lives.

All of these interrelated consequences of the disappearance of the 'foreign-exchange constraint', and attempts to alleviate the 'skill constraint' made a significant contribution to the People's Revolution of 1977–9.

NOTES

1. These references are to the proceedings and events of the famous Twenty-second Congress of the Soviet Communist Party. Khrushchev immediately retaliated against Chou's gesture (which had been intended more against himself than in favour of Stalin) by removing Stalin's body from Lenin's shrine in Moscow.
2. In this respect, the views of their conservative Iranian *contacts* (though not agents), such as Ḥusain 'Alā, must have carried a lot of weight. As for the role of their possible agents, see the text below.
3. It is almost hilarious that, while the *Daily Telegraph* was putting down the people's revolt of June 1963 to the machinations of 'the National Front and Communist Tūdeh', these organisations were themselves at a loss to know how it had come about, and what attitude they should adopt towards it.
4. It is important to note that, while conservative politicians such as 'Alā were opposed to the land reform in principle, even when this was carried out by their own former ally, the Shah, individuals such as Rashīdīyān conveniently went along with the White Revolution, and continued to amass fabulous riches as high-ranking members of the state's clientele.
5. As mentioned earlier, the Persian service of Moscow Radio was supporting the likes of Rashīdīyān and Furūd when they had been interned by Amīnī.
6. The Iraqis were at that time very close to the Soviet Union, and the Soviet Union cannot have been enthusiastic about the Dhoffar revolution, with its Chinese sympathies and connections.
7. See Peter Mansfield, *Middle East: A Political and Economic Survey* (London: Oxford University Press, 1973); for details of various agreements and protocols, see the official *Iran Foreign Policy Series*, various issues.
8. These further breakdowns are not shown in Table 16.1. For these as well as other details, see the source of this table.
9. The Soviet Union must have thought that she was going to be the greatest loser. That is presumably why she delayed any vocal support for the revolution (indeed, the Soviet press had been pretty unsympathetic to it for a good part of the year). There was not a single major political tendency in the revolution, including Marxists and radicals, which was favourably inclined towards the Soviet Union (the Tūdeh Party was not even represented in the revolution, let alone forming one of its major political tendencies); the *conservative* religious tendency was bound to be unfriendly towards the Russians; the broader communal–religious character of the movement could provide a model for the Soviet Muslim republics next door; there was an Islamic revolt already in progress in 'communist' Afghanistan; it is generally more difficult to deal with a temperamental revolutionary régime than a sober and cynical establishment; and prospects for commercial relations were not good, both for these reasons, and because of the inevitable change of direction, as well as instability, of the Iranian economy. Therefore, the Russians' sudden diplomatic somersault at the eleventh hour in warning the Americans not to intervene in the Iranian situation was a thinly disguised method of throwing in

their lot with the inevitable victors in the hope of minimising their losses.

10. See the Iranian daily press.
11. For figures and details of the movements in the balance of payments, see Vizārat-i Bāzargānī, *Āmār-i Bāzaragānī-yi Khārijī-yi Irān* (Foreign Trade Statistics of Iran), as well as Bank Markazi Iran, Annual Report, various issues.

17 The People's Revolution, 1977–9

In a famous verse of the Qur'ān, 'the hour approaches, and the moon is split into halves';[1] and, according to a well-known prediction in Marx's *Capital*, 'the death-knell of bourgeois property tolls'. When the former happens, sinners will face their final judgement; when the latter happens, 'the expropriaters will be expropriated!'. The recent Iranian revolution was, *metaphorically*, no less momentous than the splitting of the moon, and, *terrestrially*, as perfect a response to total injustice as a celestial judgement. The death-knell tolled not for bourgeois property–which, in its rigorous Marxian sense, was not significant–but for petrolic despotism, and pseudo-modernism; it was not so much the private expropriators who were expropriated, as the bureaucratic usurpers of the people's collective wealth and socio-political rights. 'From their palace rooms, they went into their tombs.'[2]

The process was truly dialectical: petrolic despotism and pseudo-modernism nurtured the seeds of their own destruction by the very means which they had used for the propagation of their roots and branches: their selective social bribery alienated many more souls than they managed to purchase; their vicious intolerance of *any* form of personal or communal autonomy led to a degree of official violence that would inevitably legitimise violence itself, and develop new forms of political resistance; their permissive attitude towards *any* activity which did not imply an assertion of independence from the state was such that it resulted in wholesale financial, moral and cultural corruption–there was complete 'freedom' with the state, and none without it; and their mindless expenditure of the oil revenues created serious economic bottlenecks, unlimited expectations, unrestricted demonstrations of consumption and wealth, social envy and frustration, mental disorder, and so forth. *Total* triumph must end in *total* defeat; *total* repression must result in *total* revolution; the *complete* absence of rights must mean the *complete* absence of responsibilities: these are the simple rules both of science and of society.

The Immediate Causes of the Revolution

The long-and short-term politiconomic factors leading up to the revolution of

1977–9 have been discussed throughout the preceding chapters. Here, the aim is simply to try and explain *how* the various routes to that volcanic eruption crossed *when* they did. In fact, allusion has already been made to some of the more immediate causes of the revolution. For example, the complete destruction of all conventional organisations and methods of political opposition led to two important developments: first, a change of tactics from organised public criticism to organised underground political activity and, therefore, urban guerrilla warfare; secondly, widespread disillusionment with conventional ideologies – National Front constitutionalism, Tūdeh Party (pro-Soviet) communism, and traditional (anti-despotic) religious conservatism – which led to new ideological forms and attitudes: democratic Islamic radicalism, pro-Chinese and independent Marxism of various descriptions, and traditionalist Pan-Islamism. These tendencies are clearly different from their previous counterparts, which still survive as less powerful ideological forces; but, in a broader sense, they are the inheritors both of those traditions and of the social categories to which they had appealed.

The first two tendencies were symbolised by the two urban guerrilla groups: the Mujāhidīn-i Khalq, or Holy Warriors of the People, and the Fadā'ıān-i Khalq, or Selfless Devotees of the People. The third tendency did not resort to urban guerrilla tactics; it organised the masses of the urban religious people on a greater scale, though much less visibly, by the use of religious dues paid directly to religious leaders. For, what the usurpation of charitable endowments (or *owqāfi'ām*) had taken away from the religious authorities was being returned to them, several hundred times over, through payments of annual religious dues and other financial contributions by merchants, traders and other religious practitioners, who, thanks to the oil revenues and the state's methods of disbursing them, were increasing both in numbers and in fortune! This is the tendency which is now mainly identified with Āyatullah Khomainī and the men around him.

These political forces had all been present before the oil-revenue explosion of 1973. In fact, that event managed, for a brief period of two years, to force them into social and psychological retreat: the sudden and substantial growth of wealth, and the resultant direct and indirect hand-outs numbed the socio-political senses of many for a while; the school milk went down well while it lasted; the new owners of ordinary motor-cars, who were now able to visit London and Paris, were as pleasantly surprised as were those who began to buy Jaguars and gamble in Monte Carlo. At the same time, and by the same logic, the instruments of comprehensive violence and repression – ranging from forced membership of the Resurgence Party to the proliferation of SAVAK informers and *agents provocateurs* – seemed so overwhelming that various groups and classes of the people (each relatively to their station) exercised greater self-control and political caution than ever before. In July 1974, less than a year after the oil-revenue explosion, and four months after the 'month of destiny', I spent three weeks in Teheran: my private residence was constantly watched by three SAVAK agents, every day, from dawn to dusk, and an agent followed me everywhere I went in the city – in both cases with the express purpose of making it known to me that I was under surveillance. As a final reminder, my passport was inexplicably confiscated before departure for London, so that I had to resort to various personal acquaintainces in higher officialdom in order to be able to leave the country. If the SAVAK had had any evidence of my involvement in organised political activity, things would have been very different. For, from their point of view, all this was merely a response to the continuing personal – financial and political – independence from the state of someone with a background of political opposition.

By 1975, however, economic and social realities had begun to assert themselves. The high rate of inflation of food and accommodation prices forced the state to take short-term tactical measures, which did nothing to solve the problem but created others for itself. The SAVAK told the Shah that food inflation was mainly the result of speculative practices by ordinary traders and shopkeepers. The state-run Chamber of the Guilds, Consumers' Association and National Resurgence Party were all mobilised to fight against 'the speculators'. Young men – mainly students – carrying special party cards were regularly sent round to ordinary retail shops for 'inspections', which in reality involved harassment and persecution. Some shops were summarily closed down without any hearings or appeal procedures. 'Shock troops' – a term which some of the Shah's henchmen must have remembered from their readings about the Russian Civil War, when they had been members of the Tūdeh Party – were 'organised' to deal with the economic 'bottlenecks', but merely created greater chaos and confusion.

The prices of urban land and property, and thus rents for accommodation, soared so fast that the highly paid younger state officials had to pay 50 per cent of their salaries for the rental of a five-room apartment. Large numbers of people were simply homeless. Apart from the growing population of subterranean hovel-dwellers, and ordinary working people, even semi-skilled workers were hit very hard by the housing problem. In Teheran, numerous 'housing' communities began to mushroom up outside the official city boundaries – drawn up by the office of the Mayor of Teheran, who was appointed by the Shah himself – where no electricity, water, transport or other public services were provided. In order to 'cope' with all these problems, the agents of petrolic despotism took a series of basic decisions. First, they took some legal measures to fight speculation in urban land, but this made the large-scale professional land speculators use bribery and influence to prevent short-term losses, while switching their speculative activities to housing and urban property. It was only the large number of middle-income people, who had put their savings in urban land as a protective measure against inflation, who sustained a real loss and became discontented. Secondly, they tightened up the rules of rent control and tenancy rights, which benefited only the *sitting* tenants, hit the petty rentier who had invested his money in a flat or a small house, and created a greater shortage of vacant accommodation, because those who had not yet let their property did not put it on the market. The state retaliated by threatening to send undercover agents to discover vacant property, force the owners to let it, and penalise them for not having done so already. This, of course, was impossible to do in practice. But the threat was taken seriously, so people with an empty flat began to 'furnish' them with pieces of decrepit furniture, keep a light or two burning all the day round, and send a member of the family to spend a night or two in the vacant property every week!

It is perhaps worth mentioning that the position of the owners of those 'private' properties – often a large old house – which had been let to a department of state was simply hopeless: the rents which they received could be as low as 5 or 10 per cent of the market rate; any idea of reclaiming their property – even genuinely for their own use – was, of course, out of the question; they had to bear the costs of all – internal as well as external – repairs which their 'tenants' asked them to carry out, or they would receive no rent; and, in order to obtain a revision of their rent they had to go to the law courts – at the Ministry of Justice – incurring high costs in a case which would take at least a couple of years to be concluded, frequently against them. But, even when they won their case, there would be no question of the defrayment of their legal expenses; the increase 'ordered' by the court would be derisory; and – most important of all – the court 'order' would not be binding, because, according to a general 'law' enacted in the despotic period, law-court decisions against departments of state could only be regarded as recommendations. If this was a capitalist political economy, then so be it!

However, the socio-politically most significant measure taken by the state affected the large number of working-class and lower-income families who had built one or two rooms outside the official city boundaries. When the agents of despotism realised that lack of public services was not a deterrent against such 'developments', they went into direct action. City officials, in collaboration with SAVAK agents, the uniformed police and the gendarmerie, began to invade these communities with means of demolition, including bulldozers, and level them off. On a few occasions, some residents were buried under the rubble.[3] Once the word had gone round, however, residents of these communities began to organise themselves and resist the invaders. The agents of injustice (of *ẓulm*, pure and simple) 'improved' their tactics, began to send in undercover inspectors and surveyors, drew up plans of the condemned 'estates', and employed paramilitary methods, such as nightly raids, in order to be more effective. Yet, the residents quickly learned *these* tactics too, and innovated appropriate defensive – and, increasingly, counter-offensive – measures.

In a vivid, detailed, sober and authentic description of a whole series of unsuccessful raids against one such community, a resident – married, with two children, living in a single room – summed up the last battle (which led to the defeat and final withdrawal of the invaders) in the following words: 'We sent the little kids to puncture the tyres of the bulldozers which led their whole army, thus bringing it to a halt and forcing their infantry to invade the area in a disorderly fashion; our women then began to bombard them from the roofs with stones and cobbles which we had already stored up; having thus created disorder, confusion and dismay among the enemy, and inflicted some casualties upon it, we then launched an offensive, and took on the bastards in a pitched hand-to-hand battle. The sons-of-a-whore finally had to run away, leaving some of their machinery and equipment behind. I swear to God, sir, it was really like a Vietcong operation.'

The reporter was Mr Muṭlaq, a thirty-eight-year old senior driver of a state company whose total annual earnings (wages, overtime pay, bonuses, etc.) amounted to the relatively large sum of $8000. He had been given a state home loan of $35,000, but nowhere in the city could he find a couple of rooms with a private yard at that price. He had finally decided to buy a house jointly with his brother in the town of Karaj, some 40 kilometres west of Teheran. He was a practising, but not fanatical, Muslim. He related his great story to me – a story on the full version of which a good realistic novella could be based – in July 1977. The final 'battle' had been fought in the previous April, between 2 a.m. and 4 a.m. on a weekday. Mr Muṭlaq had had to report as usual for duty at 6.30 a.m.

Apart from the central and provincial state departments, the SAVAK, the Special Bureau (the Shah's own extensive and powerful private office) and the various departments of military intelligence, there had already existed an Imperial Inspectorate, led by a few retired senior generals, ostensibly to look into special cases of official corruption, complaints against the bureaucracy, and so forth. Now a new Imperial Commission was created to monitor the work of state departments, discover their weaknesses and inefficiencies, and summon high officials, even cabinet ministers, to answer for their administrative mistakes and failures. In practice, the commission became another channel for personal rivalries and smear campaigns within the despotic apparatus itself: those who know something of Iranian history, and of the logic of despotism anywhere, will know that campaigns of personal vilification, and conscious attempts by one henchman even to undo the useful work of another, form an inalienable part of that history and this logic. The Imperial Commission added to existing headaches, confusions, anxieties and corruptions, and achieved nothing.

However, no basic development had a more devastating consequence for the state than the enrichment and numerical growth of merchants and petty traders, on the one hand, and the growth of ordinary urban workers, on the other – both of which were socio-economic by-products of the state's own pseudo-modernist strategy of urbanism and industrialism. The practical significance of the growth of domestic trade had already been mentioned. It may be useful to add that, whereas the ever-growing circle of the state's clientele had effectively emasculated – turned into unpersons – the vast majority of state officials, intellectuals, professionals, and other educated people, it had led to a greater sense of social importance, and relative autonomy, among the traditional trading community. They had a lot of money without owing any allegiance to the state, and they were openly proud of the fact that they were not agents of injustice (*dallāl-i maẓlameh*), i.e. state employees above a certain level. However, it was no less significant that an urban working class had also emerged who were by and large literate, broadly informed and conscious of domestic and international events, and much less subservient than their predecessors. Finally, peasant immigration had rapidly increased the size of the country's political public. Up to now, the Iranian peasantry has shunned all forms of political participation; they did not even make much contribution, as a class, to the country's recent revolution. The reasons for this state of affairs are complex and manifold, and it is certainly not 'hereditary' (see Ch. 15, above). On the contrary, once the peasant has arrived in a town or city, he can become politically conscious even within a few weeks. In fact, many of these immigrant peasants participated in this revolution.

All the above social classes – merchants, petty traders, workers, immigrant peasants (as well as those remaining on the land) – have one thing in common, in spite of the vast differences in their wealth, incomes, social status, lifestyles, and so forth: they make up those Iranian social classes the majority of whose members are practising Shī'ite Muslims. This is part of the country's cultural tradition, which – as social classes – they alone have fully inherited, or, at least, have not had a chance of being alienated from; for they have been brought up that way, and it influences every aspect of their lives – birth, death, marriage, community relations, methods of settling disputes and differences, and so on. They do not suffer from an inferiority complex towards modern European and American culture; and, as a result, they have no superiority complex about the facts and fictions of pre-Islamic Iranian glories.

Preludes to the Revolution

Social discontent had never ceased to exist, and political activity, in various forms, had continued through the 1960s. Up to 1970, the public expression of dissent mainly took the typically Iranian forms of spreading rumours (normally false), such as the rumour spread during the Shah's belated Coronation party (in 1968) that his mother had just died, and her body was being kept in a mortuary in order not to spoil the official merrymaking; or public jokes, such as the subtle and meaningful story about a man who, finding his wife and her lover in bed together, asked the lover who the hell he was, and, upon being told that his name was Cyrus, replied, 'Well, in that case sleep happily, for we are awake.' The joke alluded to the Shah's pseudo-nationalist speech at the probable tomb of Cyrus the Great on the occasion of the inauguration of the obscene festivities commemorating the 2500th anniversary of the foundation of the 'Iranian Empire'; the speech culminated in the words, 'Sleep happily, Cyrus, for we are awake!' Meanwhile, organised political activity was carried on abroad, by various (mainly newly formed) political groups, and Iranian student unions, most of which were affiliated to the Confederation of Iranian Students. At home, however, all attempts at organising clandestine movements were, until 1970, rapidly suppressed by the SAVAK.

At the same time, General Taimūr Bakhtīyār – the notorious first chief of the SAVAK – had been plotting against the Shah, first in Europe and later in Iraq, where the government had for its own reasons given him refuge. The Shah was genuinely frightened of Bakhtīyār, both because of his ability, and because Bakhtīyār was as ruthless and cruel and as amoral and self-seeking as the Shah himself. Bakhtīyār's main weakness was his past SAVAK career, which made it impossible for him to attract the co-operation of any self-respecting oppositionist person or party. Nevertheless, the Tūdeh Party – more of whose members had been arrested, imprisoned, tortured and killed by Bakhtīyār's SAVAK than was the case with any other political group – had established serious contacts with him, even to the extent of sending a high-level delegation to Baghdad for exploring possible areas of co-operation. But once the matter became public, the party leadership accused Dr Reżā Rādmanish, the party leader, of having personally decided and carried out this plan without the knowledge of the other leaders and party cadres, and therefore dismissed him from his post. In July 1970, however, Bakhtīyār himself was assassinated by a couple of SAVAK infiltrators, and the Shah could heave a sigh of relief.

But not for long; for, a few months later (on 8 February 1971), a Marxist guerrilla group launched a small-scale armed struggle from the village of Sīyāhkal, in the forested Caspian province of Gīlān. This the régime quickly routed, with many of the fighters losing their lives in action, or being summarily executed afterwards; but the movement, which in any case was led by educated young people from Teheran, quickly rectified its fatal strategic mistake in starting a *rural* guerrilla campaign, and switched to *urban* guerrilla tactics, inaugurated with the assassination of General Farsīyū, the Army Prosecutor-General, who had borne the 'legal' responsibility for the killing of their captured comrades, as well as the imprisonment of many political dissidents since 1964. From 1971, this Marxist guerrilla movement, the Fadā'īān-i Khalq, together with its radical Muslim counterpart, the Mujāhidīn-i Khalq, continued in operation – until now, after the revolution, they are both public political parties, although it is very likely that both, and especially the former, still maintain some underground party cells.

Up to the fall of the Shah's régime, members of both these guerrilla groups attacked police stations, isolated gendarmerie posts, notorious SAVAK leaders and personnel, and the like. In retaliation, the agents of injustice attacked them in their hideouts and places of contact, where these were discovered; and gun-battles were fought out in the streets. When they managed to arrest them peacefully, or captured them alive in open confrontation, they subjected them to the vilest, most hideous, gruesome and hair-raising physcial and mental tortures: they flogged and whipped them beyond human endurance; they subjected them to electric shocks, with the electrodes connected to their recta, their genitals and their nipples; they sodomised and raped them to the end; they sodomised and raped their close relatives, even including their six- or seven-year old children, in front of their eyes; they urinated inside their mouths; they roasted them alive such that the air in some of the special interrogation centres permanently smelled of burned human flesh.[4] Meanwhile, the country was arriving at 'the gates of the Great Civilisation', and the likes of Lord Chalfont – in Britain and elsewhere – were busy both praising the Shah's great 'achievements' and defending him, and his pack of wild dogs, against decent individuals and groups: men such as Jean-Paul Sartre and the British MPs Stanley Newens and William Wilson, and organisations such as Amnesty International – all of whom were becoming increasingly nauseated by the Shah and his Iranian and foreign propagandists.

At the same time, there were political activities which used traditional Iranian forms: mosques, funeral services, religious sermons, annual religious festivals and mourning periods all served as spatio-temporal channels for symbolic expressions and manifestations of political dissent. In the month of Muḥarram – in which Imām Ḥusain, his family and his followers had been heroically martyred by an army of Yazīd, the second Ummayid caliph – even the lampposts in the more traditional city districts were wrapped in black material. When in a mosque, or a private house, the audience roared approval of the ceremonial damnation of Yazīd and his men by the officiating preacher, few people, including SAVAK agents, missed the allusions to the Shah and his henchmen, which were in everybody's mind. On the birthday of the twelfth Shīʿite Imām – Hujjat ibn al-Ḥasan al-ʿAskarī; the Redeemer who is always present, but remains invisible until the moment of his advent – the huge banners put out in the streets carried thinly disguised political slogans: 'Oh Redeemer of all humanity, hasten in your advent, for the world is now full of injustice [*ẓulm*]'; 'With the advent of the Lord of the Time; may God Almighty hasten his deliverance; injustice will be completely uprooted in this world'; and so on. In August 1977 I even saw a banner – displayed in Nīyāvarān Street, which leads straight to the Shah's most recent palace – carrying a suitable quotation from Bertrand Russell (together with his name), on the occasion of the Mahdī's birthday.

The régime retaliated by arresting, gaoling, banishing, even killing under torture (as, in 1970, in the case of the religious preacher Saʿīdī) the more active and outspoken religious leaders and their followers. They harassed and persecuted the merchants who paid their religious dues, made additional financial contributions and – sometimes – personally took part in religio-political activities: they closed down their shops, occasionally set fire to parts of the Teheran *bāzār*, refused to renew their victims' business licences, and marked them out for special treatment by different tax departments. Even as late as December 1977, a top-secret official letter quotes large amounts of money received by some religious leaders and spent for political purposes; the document says that the Shah had already been informed of its contents, and had written in his own hand that the Ministry of Finance, and the SAVAK should be notified.[5]

The Revolutionary Process

We have already seen the various ways in which, over the long and the short term, the gunpowder for a major revolt accumulated. Yet, the timing of the explosion, and the form taken by the events leading up to it, depended on the specific factors, forces, tactics and strategies of the two sides, and the social groups and personalities who led the way. As usual, the public manifestation of dissent began in scattered writings, tracts, critical essays and open letters by the intellectual élite, and the wider circle of educated and professional people. As early as 1975, Ali Aṣghar Ḥāj-Sayyed-Javādī, a notable Iranian journalist and essayist, and one-time member of the socialist Third Force Party, addressed a long critical essay on the country's state of affairs to Nuṣratullah Mu'īnīyān, the powerful chief of the Special Bureau. This was the closest that he felt he could possibly go to a direct approach to the Shah himself. The style of the essay would now appear to be cautious and moderate, but the contents were highly critical. In fact the 'cautiousness' of the style itself betrays the atmosphere of total official terror in which it had been written, and 'illegally' published.

By then, it had become a routine practice of the SAVAK to arrest those intellectuals who had become known for their dissident views, and torture them in order to force them to recant their ideas and praise the régime in recorded television 'interviews' arranged by themselves. Among others, this had nearly happened to Dr Manūchehr Hezārkhānī, the famous critic and pathologist, and Ni'mat Mīrzā-zādeh (Āzarm), the outspoken poet, although at the time (i.e. before the oil-revenue explosion), the régime did not yet feel strong enough to go to such lengths in all such cases, and usually limited this tactic to those few educated dissidents whose participation in underground political acitivities could be proved.[6] Dr Ghulām-Ḥusain Sā'idī, the eminent playwright and psychiatrist, arrested in 1974 on no specific charges, managed to dodge the show by a stroke of good fortune;[7] but Reżā Barāhinī, the controversial critic and poet, succeeded in obtaining his release (and, later, departure to USA) only by submitting to this exchange of character assassination for indefinite incarceration. Barāhinī has always been a controversial character, both for political and, especially, for non-political reasons; but it would be unfair to attack him, or any other person, for the mere fact that he was forced to yield to this act of self-denigration. It was against such a terrifying background, however, that Ḥāj-Sayyed-Javādī concluded his first critical essay by saying that it contained *all* his views, and that if any ideas and opinions to the contrary were subsequently expressed or published by him, then everyone should know that these must have been obtained by means of 'insufferable tortures'. He continued to issue similar pamphlets, essays, books and open letters, with suitably growing outspokenness, until the fall of the régime.

Meanwhile, the generalisation of the state of torture and persecution, and the barbarity of the methods and techniques employed, began to attract the attention of international public opinion (although I am not aware of any manifestation of this in the mass media of the socialist countries). The Shah and his apparatus had always (generally successfully) done their best, by propaganda as well as direct and indirect bribery, to maintain a 'good image' abroad, in spite of efforts by the Sartre Committee for the defence of Iranian political prisoners, and of similar activities by a few British and American public personalities. The meticulous and conscientious efforts of Amnesty International and its Iranian department, led by Anne Burley, played a significant role in the very difficult task of collecting reliable information and evidence, and piecing it all together into incontrovertible public statements about the systematic and hideous violation of human rights in Iran.[8]

The Western, especially American, strategy to counteract the attractions of their political-power rivals both in their own sphere and, particularly, in the Third World was thus timely and helpful. The human-rights offensive of the West had two separate, but related, strands of cause and effect. First, it was intended to exploit some of the weakest aspects of life in the Soviet Union and some other socialist countries in order to score substantial propagandist points and – as a part of this – provide general support for political dissidents in those countries. This was the aspect of the human-rights offensive which was supported by all those who wielded and shaped political power and opinion in the West – that is, not only President Carter and Andrew Young, but also Henry Kissinger and Lord Chalfont. Secondly, the image of the Ugly American – who would spend substantial sums of money, supply arms, and even, in the case of Vietnam, enter a long and painful war, all to support some of the vilest, most corrupt and most hated régimes in the world – was at long last being reexamined, in terms of its costs and benefits, in America's corridors of power; and a *realistic* assessment, which was dictated not by selfless altruism but by 'enlightened self-interest', convinced many American policy-makers – other than Henry Kissinger and his likes – that their postwar strategy had been a disastrous failure. These and similar considerations inaugurated the era of human rights, at a time when all other short- and long-term factors were ready for a political confrontation in Iran.

On 13 June 1977, an open letter addressed to the Iranian Prime Minister and signed by forty leading writers, journalists and others demanded official permission for the Iranian Writers' Union – which, since its formation in 1968, had never been officially recognised – to open a centre in Teheran. This was followed by another letter, dated 19 July 1977, signed by an additional fifty-nine members of the Union. Eight days before, a group of prominent advocates had signed a public statement demanding the return of judicial power and status to the law courts, which – as the last bastion of the rule of law had been gradually reduced to pathetic powerlessness and nauseating corruption. Within a few months, various, largely recent political and professional groupings began to appear: the Union of the National Front Parties (later reconstituted as the National Front), led by Karīm Sanjābī; the Freedom Movement of Iran, led by Mehdī Bāzargān; the Radical Movement, led by Raḥmatullah Muqaddam-Marāgheh'ī; Junbish (Movement) led by Ali Aṣghar Ḥāj-Sayyed-Jāvādī; the Iranian Group for the Protection of Human Rights, led by Bāzargān, Sanjābī; Muqaddam, Ḥāj-Sayyed-Jāvādī, and others; the Society of Iranian Lawyers, led by Hedāyatullah Matīne-Daftary; and so on and so forth. Leaflets, open letters and public meetings began to proliferate at a rapid rate.

The régime (which had already declared its intention to 'liberalise'[9] society) responded in various ways: first, in August 1977 it replaced the largely corrupt and bureaucratic Cabinet of Amīr'Abbās Hovaidā with the mainly technocratic government of Jamshīd Āmūezār: many of the new cabinet members were old hands in various (usually non-cabinet) posts; but a number of them enjoyed untarnished reputations with respect to financial corruption or administrative recklessness. This 'change', however, was too little and too late: these were powerless men, and the régime was still His Majesty's own 'Imperial System' – the term that had officially replaced 'constitutional monarchy' as a description of the country's form of government. There is a little-known rumour, worth mentioning without vouching for its veracity, that in the spring of 1977 the Shah had visited Allāhyār Ṣāleh, the old, respected and moderate leader of the second National Front, hoping to persuade him to form a government. If this is true, then it betrays the Shah's usual tactics of wanting to get his chestnuts out of the fire by the use of other people's reputations, until the time came when he could safely dump them in the dustbin of history, and resume his Imperial System. However, the attempt had proved unsuccessful, and, in the meantime, Ali Amīnī – whom the Shah still personally despised – had begun to gather a few younger men around himself, and let it be known that he was ready to assume office.

Secondly, the SAVAK and uniformed police, who could no longer resort to indiscriminate arrests and suchlike methods, changed some of their tactics, and began to attack political meetings and beat up the participants with clubs and sticks, and to select individual leaders and activists for 'retribution'. The official 'political party', the National Resurgence Party, pretended to close ranks, and organised the Imperial Nationalists under the leadership of a fallen politician, 'Abdulmajīd Majīdī, the former powerful Plan Organisation chief. Secret Committees of National Revenge were ostensibly set up to avenge the nation on the traitorous dissidents and intellectuals who – according to the official propaganda – were *agents of American imperialism*! Whether or not such committees truly existed, SAVAK agents carried out their declared terrorist functions. It was in this way that, among many others, the physician Dr Ḥabībullah Paymān, the academic historian Homā Pākdāman (Nāṭiq) and the poet Ni'mat Mīrzā-zādeh were kidnapped and pusillanimously beaten and wounded, by large gangs of official thugs, in isolated parts of Teheran; that bombs were planted in the offices or houses of Mehdī Bāzargān, Karīm Sanjābī, Hedāyatullah Matine-Daftary, 'Abdulkarīm Lāhījī' and others; and that an attempt was made to kidnap Ḥāj-Sayyed-Javādī's fourteen-year-old daughter.[10]

Thirdly, the Shah's agents began a bizarre press campaign against the intellectuals and political leaders, accusing them of being agents of American imperialism: some of them, such as Ali Amīnī, were directly named, though they were given no opportunity to defend themselves; but the idea itself amounted to no less than a general theory, put out by the state, that the whole thing was simply the result of an American plot either to frighten the Shah into accepting imperialist demands (for instance, not to press for oil-price increases), or to overthow him. It would be a mistake to think that this 'theory' was entirely cynical, and that it had been *merely* intended as a propagandist device. It is a historical tragedy of Iranian politics that every major (and minor) political event is attributed to an elaborate design by foreign powers. Indeed, some left-wing Iranians – both inside and outside the country – regarded the movement as an American device to bring Amīnī back into office, though they did not see a contradiction between this 'theory' and their own existing view that the Shah, too, was an *agent* of imperialism. Even if the Shah and his henchmen had had no faith at all in their own theory of an American conspiracy, they must have correctly assessed the psychology of their opposition in choosing their propaganda tactics.

Until the end of 1977, the main initiatives were still in the hands of the modern educated and intellectual groups. This phase of the revolution came to a climax in a series of poetry recitals, attended by large groups of people, in which leading poets recited pieces of their symbolically political works. But within a few weeks this intellectual momentum was lost, and the movement's leadership increasingly passed to religious leaders and communities. The régime itself unconsciously played a decisive role in bringing about this change of leadership, as we shall see in a moment.

Space does not permit us to discuss in detail all the revolutionary events that led up to fall of the Shah's régime. Three events which proved to be major turning-points are, however, worth emphasising: the first was the publication of an article, written under a pseudonym, in the daily newspaper *Iṭṭilā'āt* that mounted a dastardly attack on the person of Āyatullah Khomainī, the exiled *Marja'al-taqlīd*, to the point of accusing him of 'black [i.e. British!] imperialism'.[11] This was the Shah's personal response to the Āyatullah's written and spoken edicts calling for the overthrow of the Shah's régime. Up to that moment, although religious leaders and groups had been active in the movement, and religious occasions had been used by all the participants for political demonstrations, the initiative was still in the hands of the divided and badly organised conventional political groups and forces. The attack on the Āyatullah led to large street demonstrations in the holy city of Qum, and on 9 January 1978 the demonstrators were fired on by the police, leaving many dead and wounded. This merely made people all the readier to sacrifice themselves in the struggle. The other *Marāji'* – and, especially, the Senior *Marja'*, Āyatullah Sayyed Kāẓim Sharī'atmadārī, responded by condemning the killings and demanding the prosecution of those responsible. Sharī'atmadarī, a highly intelligent, tactful and respected senior religious leader, concluded his first statement with the following verse from the Qur'ān: 'Those who commit injustice will learn where they will be returning to'.[12] Once the Shah had granted permission to shoot at the crowds, events escalated rapidly: to observe the traditional fortieth day of the massacre of Qum, Sharī'atmadarī had advised his religious followers in Tabrīz to go on strike, and attend memorial services in mosques; but he had instructed them to refrain from all street demonstrations, so that the régime would have no pretext for another massacre. But the SAVAK – probably without the Shah's prior knowledge – sent busloads of men to the city to reinforce its existing *agents provocateurs* and provoke another bloodshed. They fulfilled their mission, and an even greater massacre resulted. Gradually, street demonstrations all over the country became a part of daily life – and death. The most audacious provocation yet was when, on 10 May 1978, a group of commando crack-troops, led by their supreme commander, General Khusrudād, landed in Qum, raided Sharī'atmadārī's house in his absence, emptied bullets into doors, windows and walls, and deliberately shot and killed two or three entirely innocent theological scholars who had refused to shout 'long live the Shah'.[13]

The second major turning-point was the burning on 19 August 1978 of the Cinema Rex in Iran's oil capital, Ābādān: all the exits had been securely locked, and large amounts of petrol had been used to set fire to the cinema; as a result over 400 men, women and children were roasted alive. The matter has never been investigated – not even since the revolutionary triumph – but the obvious theory was that it was a SAVAK operation, with or without the Shah's prior knowledge. This would be consistent with the régime's more recent propaganda line that the revolutionaries meant to restore black reaction in Iran. There can be no doubt, however, that the people interpreted that cold-blooded mass murder as a SAVAK atrocity, and the whole country rose in revolt. Within a few days, the Light of the Aryans, who had already tried to calm the people down by a few unsuccessful conciliatory gestures, dismissed the Āmūzegār cabinet, and appointed Ja'far Sharīf-Imāmī, the Senate President, to the premiership. Clearly, the old despot had become a prisoner of his own past trickeries: he could not yet see that this was no mere uprising, no simple conspiracy, no passing event, but a total revolution. Sharīf-Imāmī was the man that the Shah had used as a caretaker in 1960; it did not occur to the Shah that the passage of eighteen years had turned this man into a wholly disreputable character; and the task which he was given was in no way comparable to what either of them had experienced in the past.

Sharīf-Imāmī claimed to have suddenly become a completely new man, a firm believer in constitutional monarchy, free elections, and freedom of speech and the press. The press was in fact freed; the pathetic *Majlis* deputies, only a few of whom had begun to speak out in the previous months, began to think of their uncertain prospects; but the demonstrations did not cease. On the contrary, a people who had hitherto not existed as social beings came out in massive numbers to vent their feelings. On 4 September 1978 a massive and well-organised demonstration and street prayers were held in Teheran – on the occasion of the great Islamic Festival of *Fiṭr* – which must have both frightened and angered the Shah and his 'loyal' servants in the army, especially when on the following day hundreds of thousands of people took part in an organised street demonstration shouting 'Say death to the Shah!' On Friday 8 September, the same crowd gathered in Zhāleh Square, and it was mowed down with tanks and sub-machine guns. This was probably the greatest single massacre of the Iranian people in the twentieth century. The night before martial law had been declared, and General Ovaisī, the martial-law administrator of the bloody massacres of June 1963, had been given a free hand. Yet, it is very likely that most of the people who went to Zhāleh Square on that fateful day were unaware of the declaration of martial law and the banning of all public demonstrations. This was the third major blunder of the régime from which it was never to recover.

All this time, it was Āyatullah Khomaīni alone who, from his place of exile in the holy city of Najaf (in Iraq), was calling for the complete overthrow of the Shah and his régime. He was far from the only political leader who wanted to get rid of the Shah; in fact, there can have been very few, if any, of the revolutionary leaders and forces who had any desire to keep the Shah on his throne for his own sake. But, from his place of exile, the Āyatullah had the unique advantage among them all of being able to express this popular demand in no uncertain terms, and – apart from that – he realised that the establishment of his own, traditionalist Islamic state would not be possible without the complete overthrow of the Shah and of the system of constitutional monarchy itself.[14] That is why a few political leaders – some of them Muslim believers and practitioners themselves – began to worry about what would happen after the revolution if there were no orderly transfer of power (with or without the Shah) to the revolutionary forces. Having been convinced that it was the influential person of Khomainī alone who stood against all forms of a negotiated settlement short of unconditional surrender, the Shah and his men decided to force the Āyatullah to return to Iran and face the 'realities' of the situation. They brought diplomatic pressures on the Iraqi government to restrict Khomainī's activities to the point that he would have to leave that country. Khomainī then tried to go to Kuwait, but the Kuwaiti authorities, also under pressures from the Iranian government, refused to give him leave of entry. It was at this point, in October 1978, that Khomainī responded to the call of his followers in the West, centred in Paris, to take the unlikely and unexpected decision to fly to Paris. Once in Paris, he became the focus of attention of the Western press and media, the object of pilgrimage for thousands of Iranians in Europe, America and Iran itself, and the undisputed leader of the revolution.

The psycho-political atmosphere of the period between October 1978 and February 1979, when the Shah's régime finally toppled, is highly instructive, both of the course of events in the Iranian Revolution, and of mass political movements in general. The *mass* of ordinary Iranian people were prepared to follow Khomainī's lead alone, because they regarded the Shah as the very symbol of all they were fighting against, Khomainī as the very symbol of their total rejection of the Shah, and religion – although not a traditionalist Islamic state, of which they knew very little – as the binding force and the obvious channel for the war against the Shah's pseudo-modernist despotism. The experienced political leaders of the opposition – and some religious leaders, such as Āyatullah Sharī'atmadārī – shared many of the ordinary people's sentiments and beliefs, but, in different degrees, were worried (a) that the wholly uncompromising stance of Khomainī would result in an army backlash (possibly encouraged by America), and (b) that the revolutionary triumph under the leadership of Khomainī and those of his followers who wanted to establish a traditionalist Islamic state, would result in something other than they were hoping to achieve. However, they were rendered helpless and impotent for the following reasons: first, the mass of the people were behind Khomainī and his call for the overthrow of the Shah; secondly, the bulk of the left-wing groups and parties, intellectuals, and educated people at large each for their own different reasons regarded any attempt at a negotiated settlement as a betrayal of the revolution: in such an event, one can image the 'ideological analyses' which would have described the 'betrayal of the revolution' as the work of 'the national bourgeoisie and its compromising tactics, which are typical of its class characteristics'; thirdly, there was no one among the more experienced political leaders who would have the courage, the ability, and the potential popular appeal – for example, one such as Dr Muṣaddiq – to rise above the situation and try to compete with Khomainī.

The position of many intellectual and educated younger politicians and activists – most of them left-wing, of various descriptions – was also typical: they had originally refused to believe that there was a revolution, because – given the general slogans and forms of the uprising – their ill-adapted and misapplied theoretical frameworks could not fit the reality into any of their rigid boxes. Hence, it simply could not be true, or at best, was merely some sort of 'revolutionary movement', until such time as its forms and slogans acquired the 'right' characteristics. Later, when the reality persisted, they had to revise their 'analyses' and identify Khomainī and the *mass* of his followers with 'the petty bourgeoisie', and the conventional politicians with 'the national bourgeoisie', which was about to make a deal with the Shah through the intervention of American imperialism – although they did not quite explain why, given their own theoretical boxes, 'the *national* bourgeoisie' should co-operate with imperialism. Consequently, although they were privately critical of Khomainī's ideological attitude, they would do nothing to help 'the national bourgeoisie' at the expense of 'the historically more progressive petty bourgeoisie'. A researcher into the norms of both scientific and ideological *practice* – of the psychology of professional academics, as well as of left-wing intellectuals – would be generally struck by the powerful influence and uncritical application of existing frameworks, forms and passions in shaping their views about specific issues and events. This is what, in the sphere of scientific knowledge, Thomas Kuhn has approvingly described as normal science. It is the paradigm of all paradigms against which the Galileos, the Voltaires and the Marxes of human history in their own times revolted. The great Persian classical poet and mystic Mawlavī (Rūmī) was right in saying that 'It takes time for blood to turn into milk.'

The Shah, who still wanted to preserve more than he possibly could, was finally forced to settle for what a month earlier he would have regarded as wholly unacceptable: the appointment of a government headed by a conventional opposition leader, and a member of Muṣaddiq's government. Dr Karīm Sanjābī, the leader of the new (and relatively weak) National Front, agreed to act, on the condition that he would reach a settlement with Khomainī first. Allāhyār Ṣāleḥ, the aged former leader of the second National Front, and Muhammad Surūrī, the equally aged former President of the Supreme Court, had already declined the offer. Sanjābī flew to Paris, and after visiting Khomainī, issued a public statement saying that there could be no settlement with 'the illegal monarchical régime'. In this way he felt he was leaving the door ajar for a settlement within the broader framework of the existing constitution once the Shah had agreed to leave the country, and possibly abdicate.[15] But the Shah would not be drawn, and instead appointed a military government – headed by General Azhārī, the army chief of staff – most of whose cabinet members were, however, civilian. The army chiefs, as well as the Shah's loyal civilian advisers, were clearly divided between the hard and soft-liners. General Ovaisī, the chief martial-law administrator, symbolised the military 'hawks', and he was nearly appointed Prime Minister instead of the 'dovish' Azhārī. The pattern had become typical of the attitude of the Shah's party since the massacre of 8 September: a group of his military and civilian advisers were counselling caution and compromise, while others were insisting on tougher action.

The situation was of course tough enough: each day, hundreds of unarmed people were being killed and wounded by the army in towns and cities all over the country, and any escalation would have involved indiscriminate attacks on whole residential districts by tanks and possibly aircrafts – in Teheran, Qum, Mashhad, Isfahan, Tabriz and Qazvīn, in particular. If this 'final solution' was never applied, it was because (a) there was a real danger of insubordination, even mutiny, by the army rank-and-file; (b) some of the Shah's well-wishing advisers would have been alienated; (c) even the Light of the Aryans had by then realised that this would result in no lasting solution for the survival of his dynasty; and (d) the world had been watching the whole affair with increasing disgust for the régime and admiration for the selfless heroism of the Iranian people. These were the reasons why the régime blew hot and cold, fired on the demonstrators and, at the same time, begged them to stay home and believe that things were going to change radically in their favour. For example, on 11 December 1978, when, in defiance of martial law, the revolutionaries planned mass demonstrations for the tenth day of the holy month of Muḥarram (the day of the martyrdom of Imām Ḥusain and his people), the régime first responded by threatening what would have been a complete bloodbath, for in Teheran alone 2 million men, women and children participated in the march. But at the eleventh hour a compromise was reached, and the march was officially permitted, so long as it did not pass through no-go areas reaching up to the Shah's palace in the northern suburbs of Teheran.

In despair, the Shah turned to Dr Ghulām-Ḥusain Ṣadīqī, Muṣaddiq's Minister of the Interior and a highly respected political figure and sociology professor, who for twenty-five years had been an object of special hatred for His Majesty. Ṣadīqī was a relatively strong personality with no worldly ambitions who – mainly because of his unhappy experience in 1960–3, when, as one of the very few men of substance in the leadership of the second National Front, he had had to put up with the pathetic tactics and strategies of that political organisation – had not publicly participated in recent revolutionary activities. However, no sooner had he begun to explore the possibility of breaking the deadlock than his efforts were repudiated and condemned by various political groups and activists: the new National Front issued a statement declaring that Ṣadīqī was not one of its members, and deploring his move; others did the same, even to the point of wrongly claiming that Ṣadīqī had not been involved in the politics of the opposition since 1953![16] Āyatullah Khomainī alone maintained public silence over the news. In fact, it is rumoured that he personally sent a message to Dr Sanjābī, the National Front leader, saying that Dr Ṣadīqī was a patriotic personality and should be given a chance before his actions were judged. According to this account, Sanjābī never received the message, because the intermediary had decided not to deliver it in time. Given this hysterical mood, Ṣadīqī had no choice but to insist that the Shah should leave the country immediately after his assumption of premiership. The Shah refused, and Ṣadīqī wisely withdrew from the arena.

The final act of the great drama was played by the ill-fated government of Dr Shāpūr Bakhtīyār, whom in a number of private meetings Queen Faraḥ had already sounded out. Earlier, the Shah himself had tried to talk General Firaidūn Jam (a reputable former chief-of-staff) into taking on the task, but the latter had declined the Shah's bid after he had refused to give up the active supreme command of the armed forces. Bakhtīyār is a man of courage and practical ability, with a lot of political ambition but little popular appeal; besides, his daring personality usually has the better of his practical wisdom. Son of Sandār Fāteḥ a Bakhtīyārī chieftain and leader of the *Mashrūṭeh* Revolution, brought up and educated in France since his early youth, a leader of the second National Front who bears a large share of responsibility for the failure of that movement, and a man ill at ease with Iranian religious culture and tradition, he was both the only conventional opposition leader who would be ready to isolate himself from the torrent of popular emotion, and the one who was least suited to the impossible role which he had assumed.

Up till then, American and British political and diplomatic opinion was divided over the whole question. Clearly, foreign powers of all kinds – each according to its power and position – were not merely watching the events; just as clearly (even though popular mythologies may have it otherwise) none of them was involved in a grand conspiracy, properly understood the events, or took a well-defined course of action at any point in the proceedings. They all had to cover themselves for the possible triumph of *either* side in the revolution; they all had to try and ensure that the outcome, whatever it might be, would not be grossly against their local and global interests. The position of the Americans was more precarious than was that of the rest: Carter and his men were prepared to go to some lengths in order not to take sides; Kissinger and his type demanded support for the Shah; the Shah himself was applying pressure both through the normal channels and through his personal friends and propagandists in America, Britain and the Federal Republic of Germany; the friends and political clients of America, especially in the Arab Middle East, were making it clear to the American government that the Iranian situation was a test of its commitments. That is why Carter and the British Foreign Secretary, David Owen, would one day express support and sympathy for the Shah, and, a few days later, Carter and Callaghan would say that the matter was entirely an internal Iranian affair. However, when matters came to a head and a definite position had to be adopted, having satisfied themselves that there could be no reasonable solution with the Shah, and there would be no serious danger to their local strategic position (including the supply of oil) even if Khomainī himself took over the realm (and, in this connection, personal contacts, such as the visit to Khomainī in Paris by the former American Attorney-General, Ramsay Clark, must have been important), they decided to exert public and private pressure on the Shah to leave the country, and hope that Bakhtīyār would succeed in riding the storm. Bakhtīyār himself must be given credit for his role in forcing the Shah at long last to take the decision to go. The Shah and his wife finally left Iran on 18 January 1979.

It was too late. The army general staff was divided; there were growing signs of insubordination in the army and, especially, airforce; the continuing general strike, including the all-important stoppage of the oil workers, showed no sign of breaking; the masses of the people now wanted Khomainī and none other; the anxious conventional political leaders, and intellectuals, had left themselves no independent initiative. Alarmed at the prospect that Bakhtīyār might manage to consolidate his position now that the Shah had finally departed, Khomainī refused to talk to Bakhtīyār as long as he was Prime Minister, declared that he would appoint an alternative government, and decided to lose no time in returning to Teheran. This was delayed for a few days, because of disagreements among Bakhtīyār and the generals about whether or not it should be permitted, but in the end they realised that they had no real choice in the matter.

Khomainī arrived in Teheran on 26 January (exactly sixteen years after the Shah's 'referendum' for his White Revolution) to a tumultous welcome which must be unique in living memory. On arrival, he appointed to the premiership Mehdī Bāzargān, leader of the Freedom Movement, a practising Muslim, and a former associate of Dr Muṣaddiq. If it was in Bakhtīyār's power to do so, he then made an eventful mistake in not handing over to Bāzargān without delay. The public demonstrations and military violence continued, though at a reduced scale, while Bakhtīyār went on declaring that he would not yield before normalisation, to be immediately followed by general elections for a constituent assembly. While the demonstrators chanted the slogan 'Bāzargān, Prime Minister of Iran', Bāzargān himself acted with care and caution: he did not appoint a cabinet; he, and similar politicians, were in constant touch with Bakhtīyār in an attempt to solve the impasse; and, as a face-saving formula, both he and Bakhtīyār – even though they used different words – described Bāzargān's position as that of the leader of a 'shadow', 'alternative' government.

As the airforce officers and men became more and more vocally involved in favour of the revolutionaries – some of them even participating in an officially permitted public demonstration in full uniform – the army hard-liners, and especially the twin professional Imperial and Immortal corps, hand-picked and raised merely for the protection of His Majesty's person and position, became more and more restless and agitated. It was an appropriate epitaph on the lack of political leadership all round that an 'accident' should seal the inevitable outcome of the situation: on 5 February 1979, a group of soldiers from the Immortal Corps took it upon themselves to teach a hard lesson of loyalty to those airforce officers and men who, in their Teheran barracks, were watching, with roars of approval, a television documentary on the triumphant arrival of Āyatullah Khomainī and his entourage. But, when the punitive force of the Shah's own soldiers arrived, the airmen took up positions and began to fight the zealots. The news of an attempted 'army coup' spread rapidly, and the people, led by the guerrilla groups (who until then had wisely refrained from a general armed insurrection) went to the airmen's help, and attacked the Shah's soldiers from the rear. Communication lines broke down, and the feeble efforts of the top leadership of both sides failed to control the situation. Finally, on 11 February the generals agreed to hand over power to Bāzargān, and declare the army neutral by ordering all the troops back to their barracks. Typically, however, this surrender, too, was too late.

The guerrilla groups, and other people who were now armed with light weapons, refused to lay down their arms, even after the Voice of the Revolution had come on the air through the radio and television networks. In particular, they attacked the barracks of the Imperial and Immortal corps in the northern suburbs of Teheran, who, in their total confusion and bewilderment, surrendered with little or no resistance. The inglorious collapse of His Majesty's mighty imperial army, together with its sleek generals, its Chieftain tanks, its Phantom jets, its rockets and missiles, and so forth, was the final monument to the failure of petrolic pseudo-modernist despotism.

Within twenty-four hours, however, the Voice of the Revolution became the Voice of the *Islamic* Revolution, much to the disenchantment of the intellectuals and educated masses, and their political parties. Two months later, a plebiscite was held for the declaration of an Islamic republic, without sufficient time for public discussion, or official permission to all revolutionary forces to use the mass media for presenting their views. At the time of writing, elections are being held for a *selective* constituent assembly, which has been boycotted by many political parties – the Muslim People's Republican Party, the National Front, and the National Democratic Front, to name but a few – in order to produce the final draft of an already-written new constitution, for submission to another general plebiscite. The indications are that, if successful, the resulting constituent assembly will reduce the broader framework of an Islamic republic to a narrow constitution for a traditionalist Islamic state. It appears that the Iranian people have been condemned to act as the guinea-pigs for zealous social experimentation – one day, by despotic pseudo-modernists, and, another day, by authoritarian traditionalists; and that the hope that a genuine Iranian synthesis of worthy traditional and modern values and techniques might break this truly vicious circle has again been thwarted.

NOTES

1. "Iqtarabat al-sā'a wa 'in shaqq al-qamar.'
2. 'Dhahaba min quṣūrihim' ilā qubūrihim' – a line in Arabic composed and sung by a blind Iranian funeral reciter at the turn of this century.
3. On one such occasion, reported (for the first time) by the daily press in July 1977, the agents of injustice beat a householder to death in an attempt to evict him from his house.
4. For further details see Amnesty International's *Briefing Paper on Iran*, Nov 1976.
5. The document, a letter from the Ministry of Foreign Affairs to the Ministry of Finance, mentions very large sums paid by well-to-do merchants to lower-rank religious leaders, who had transferred part of the funds to a Shī'ite religious base in Lebanon. This was discovered and published in the Iranian press after the revolution. In another document (*Sepīd-u-Sīyah*, no. 1110, 9 June 1979), addressed by SAVAK headquarters to the SAVAK head office in Kirmānshāh, in March 1976, the case of a lesser religious leader of that city is extensively discussed, and the local SAVAK is ordered not only to tape all his conversations, censor his letters, and collect other evidence against him, but also to pressurise influential people with whom he was in contact to abandon him, try to weaken the financial position of those who paid him dues (the use of taxes, rates, and so on, is specifically mentioned), and spread rumours that he was himself a SAVAK agent. Another revealing document is a letter from the Deputy Minister of Culture and Arts to an Iranian film director in April 1974 (*Jumbish*, 6 Dec 1978). In this the film director is severely censured for making films which 'have a religious theme', is reminded of His Majesty's orders to prevent the production of such films at all costs, is promised 'material and moral' fortune if he is prepared to make ordinary feature films, and is threatened with dire consequences, including the withdrawal of his foreign wife's residence permit, if he refuses to co-operate.
6. For example, such was the case of Kurūsh Lāshā'ī, who was arrested sometime after his clandestine return to Iran from Geneva (probably *via* China). He had already been active in Kurdistan before his arrest. The television 'interview' was held in late 1972.
7. After subjecting him to torture and threatening him with thirteen years of imprisonment, they forced him to give an 'interview' attacking the Iraqi régime. But, before they managed to televise the show, the Shah suddenly made his deal with the Iraqis in Algiers, and rendered the show useless. Sā'idī had already been released, and no amount of further pressure would make him repeat it. Before his final arrest, he had several times been beaten up savagely by SAVAK agents in the streets of Teheran.
8. See Amnesty International, *Briefing Paper on Iran*, 1976. A detailed article on torture in Iran also appeared in *Index on Censorship*, Feb 1976. The reproduction of parts of this in the *New York Times* had a significant effect in the wider political circles of America.
9. The Persian euphemism used for this was *fażāy-i bāz*, or 'open space'; but it was the society that had been closed: the space had always been open!
10. All these events, and many more, are recorded in numerous opposition publications and statements of the time, most of which have been reproduced in the bulletins of the Committee for the Defence and Promotion of Human Rights in Iran, nos 1–16, 1977–9.
11. See 'Aḥmad Rashīdī Muṭlaq', *Irān va Isti'mār-i Suikh u Syīah* [Iran, and Red and Black Imperialism], *Iṭṭilā'āt*, 7 Jan 1978, p. 7.
12. 'Wa saya' lamulladhīna ẓalimū 'ayy-i munqalibin yanqalibūn' (*Sūrat al-Shu'arā*',

277). See the full text in the bulletin of the Committee for the Defence and Promotion of Human Rights in Iran, 21 Jan 1978.

13. In his address to a group of religious leaders and faithful the next day, the Āyatullah himself referred to two deaths, but a number of public statements by various protesting groups mentioned three. See further ibid., June 1978.
14. The fact that other leading figures in the revolution could not openly call for the overthrow of the Shah himself, and, apart from that, were keen to preserve the democratic heritage of the *Mashrūṭeh* Revolution, is nowhere more clearly documented than in an interview of the International Channel of the French radio network with Āyatullah Sharī'atmadārī. When he was asked to comment on the view that Khomainī had adopted 'firmer positions' (*vis-à-vis* the Shah) than he had, he said that their positions were 'ultimately the same', 'but our particular situations inside the country, and his being abroad, have made the conditions tactically different'. When asked to express his general attitude and programme he replied, 'We have said many times that we emphatically demand the application of the true constitution . . . of 1906, which had been achieved under the leadership of the progressive Shī'ite leaders and at the expense of the blood of the martyrs of the road to freedom. . . .' See the full (Persian) text of the interview, ibid., Oct 1978.
15. There has been a lot of talk (especially, though not exclusively, since the collapse of the Shah's régime, and the resulting discovery by many of what should have been perfectly obvious to them earlier about the views and methods of the pan-Islamic group) about whether or not Sanjābī should have acted as he did. It would be a mistake to think that Sanjābī (or anyone else) could have been successful in the face of total opposition by Khomainī. Sunjābī's tactical mistake was to appear to be *taking orders* from Khomainī, rather than negotiating with him as a leading politician in his own right. He could at least have obtained certain paper guarantees for the future, and, even failing that, he could have returned to Teheran, declined the Shah's offer, and issued a full public statement of all of his conditions for accepting office (which would have been declined by the Shah), rather than issuing a short general slogan, dictated by Khomainī, in Paris. Compare the fact that two weeks later Bāzargān, a veteran *Muslim* politician without an offer of premiership from the Shah, visited Khomainī in Paris, but, although he was asked, he effectively refused to issue a similar statement in those conditions, by hurrying back to Teheran.
16. Sanjābī wrote him a public letter in which, in no uncertain terms, he told him not to 'obliterate your entire reputation', and threatened that the National Front would firmly oppose his government. Furūhar, the Front's Secretary, issued a statement saying that Ṣadīqī was not a Front member, which betrayed a concern to forestall possible charges of 'guilt by (past) association'. The Iranian playright Ghulām-Ḥusain Sā'idī, then in London, claimed in an article in *Irānshahr* (published in London, 22 Dec 1978) that Ṣadīqī had had *no* involvement in politics since the 1953 coup (thus overlooking his years of imprisonment as well as his active role in the leadership of the second National Front). Perhaps by then Sanjābī had become a 'representative of the petty bourgeoisie', while Ṣadīqī was still a 'representative of the national bourgeoisie'!

18 Results and Prospects: Whither Iran?

The Nature of the Revolution

The People's Revolution was fought against despotism and pseudo-modernism, much in the same way as the earlier, *Mashrūṭeh,* revolution had been fought against despotism and traditionalism. Therefore, it was a revolt of all the urban social classes and groups and political tendencies against the Shah, his army, his machinery of terror, and the hard-core of his privileged bureaucratic henchmen. It would be familiar and fashionable, but unoriginal and incorrect, to regard it as yet another French Revolution, in which for the time being the radical petty bourgeoisie, 'the Jacobins', have gained the upper hand, just as it should by now be clear that *Mashrūṭeh* was not a bourgeois revolution. In any case, how many bourgeois revolutions can there be in a given society? The Iranian society is *not* classless; but the total domination of all social classes by the powerful and functional state led to the revolt of most of them against it, with the acquiescence of the rest: the Shah and his henchmen simply had no social base on which to depend in their hour of despair.

All the revolutionary forces and tendencies fought against pseudo-modernist despotism and its consequences – official lawlessness, political persecution, social injustice, economic mismanagement, financial corruption, bureaucratic arrogance, and so on and so forth – within the overall religious framework, which, as in the *Mashrūṭeh* Revolution, provided the main formal channels for action, and the cultural and historical context for a united revolutionary front. The claim that the great majority of the revolutionary masses – let alone their leadership – were consciously fighting for a novel concept of Pan-Islamic ideology is completely false. They followed Khomainī both against the Shah and for the restoration of their various rights and freedoms, including respect for their more deep-rooted and, therefore, worthwhile cultural and religious beliefs, because Khomainī had become the symbol of their total revolt. But they did not follow him for the establishment of an obscure, ahistorical and untraditional Pan-Islamic socio-political system, the implications of which are even at present not fully known.

In a lecture on the meaning and implications of the (Pan-) Islamic state, a lesser light among Khomainī's entourage had said, in a Paris meeting in

November 1978, that Islamic rule meant the rule of God through his representative on earth: there would be no question of elections and dismissals in this case, for, if God's representative violated his rules he would be 'automatically dismissed'.[1] In his obvious unawarness of the simple rules of state administration, or (otherwise) in his deliberate oversight of such important questions, Dr Muhammad Ṣādiqī did not propose any social mechanism whereby this 'automatic' appointment and dismissal of God's emissary on earth could be understood by lesser mortals. But, even more important than that, this entirely novel idea (*bid'a*) reveals the extent to which – in spite of its occasional claims – the Pan-Islamic faction is untraditional, unfundamentalist and radically revisionist as judged by the basic tenets and traditions both of Shī'ite and of Sunni Islam.

According to the orthodox, Sunni, tradition, prophets alone, the last of whom is the prophet of Islam, Muhammad ibn 'Abdullah, are directly chosen or 'appointed' by the Will of God; and those who succeeded him – particularly the first four caliphs (the Khulafa'al-Rāshidūn) – were the *Prophet's*, not *God*'s, successors for running the affairs of the community of the faithful (*al-umma)*. The Shī'ite view of the succession, the *Imamate*, is radically different from this, in so far as it regards the right of succession as having been predetermined by God himself for Imām Ali and his descendants. Thus, according to the Twelver Shī'ite faith – which is adhered to by most Iranians – the Twelfth Imām first went into hiding (the *Ghaibat-i ṣughrā*) and then disappeared from sight (the *Ghaibat-i kubrā*); and, although he is omnipresent in time and space, he will reappear as the Mahdī, the Redeemer, at a time and place unknown and unknowable by any of his followers: at all times, and in all places, although invisible to the ordinary eye, he alone is the Lord of the Time (*Ṣāhib al-zamān*) and the Guardian of the Age (*Walī al-aṣr*).

Now, if the Pan-Islamic faction genuinely believes in the above basic doctrines of the Twelver Shī'ite faith, it would follow that Dr Ṣādiqī's novel idea is both baseless and heretical: for, without being the Mahdī himself, one can neither claim to have been appointed by God to rule over the faithful, nor (in that capacity) be answerable to God alone. In any case, according to the beliefs of *all* Muslims, God's emissaries are all innocent and omniscient, and there can be no question of their 'dismissal' once they have been chosen. With the disappearance of the Twelfth Imām, (i.e. the *Ghaibat-i kubrā*), the leadership of the faithful among the Twelver Shī'ite sect evolved into a decentralised system whereby an ordinary human being could, through learning and faith, become *mujtahid* (i.e. doctor of religious law, qualified to interpret the Qur'ān and the traditions), and a few of these would rise to the position of *Marja' al-taqlīd*, or Source of Supreme Guidance to the faithful. None of these religious leaders are appointed by God, or the Twelfth Imām, but all of them may regard themselves as the Imām's 'deputies' (or *Nawwab al-Imām*), without any guarantee whatsoever that they, or their beliefs and practices, enjoy his approval.

One should perhaps not be too hard on Dr Ṣādiqī's naïve and heretical religious beliefs – even though he claims to be a devout practitioner of the Shī'ite faith – when an Isfahani *mujtahid*, Āyatullah Khādemī, has put forward similar views as recently as July 1979. The Āyatullah quotes the Qurānic verse, 'The rule is God's alone (*'Innal-hukma 'ila Allāh'*), to argue that the new Islamic constitution should not be democratic, for the people have no right to interfere in God's Will.[2] Apparently the Āyatullah does not realise that (a) as a *general* statement the Qurānic Verse must be perfectly true according to *any* (including the Pan-Islamic) religious doctrine which regards God as omnipotent, omniscient, omnipresent, and so on; and (b) that, within the Twelver Shī'ite faith, it could be further interpreted to support the principle of *Imamate*, and the right of succession of Imām Ali and his descendants, ending with the Twelfth Imām. In other words, the very verse which is thus quoted in support of a heretical view may be turned against the Pan-Islamics themselves: if it is true that the rule is God's alone, then how can anyone, or any body of people, claim the exclusive right to rule, unless, of course, they further claim to be the Twelfth Imām himself? That is also why the title of Imām, given to Khomainī by his entourage and accepted by him, is not without religious and social significance. In its original Arabic, the word *imām* merely means 'leader'. In its original Sunni Islamic usage it is given to the first four caliphs, who are held to have combined the power of worldly administration with the authority of moral and spiritual guidance. In their later practice, the Sunni sect reserved the title only for learned religious leaders and philosophers such as Imām Abū Ḥanifa (Nu'amān ibn Thābit) and Imām Muhammad Ghazzāli. However, in the theory and practice of the Shī'ite sect the title is exclusively reserved for the Twelve Shī'ite Imāms, *and none other*. So far, there has been no clear explanation for the bestowal of this title on Khomainī: in verbal conversations, his followers emphasise the original Arabic meaning of the word, 'leader', without apparently realising that, in the context of the history and tradition of Shī'ism, this is no a longer a simple *word*, but a *theological term and concept*; for, if it were merely intended to mean 'leader' and nothing else, why not use the well-worn Persian words *rahbar*, *pīshvā*, and the like? Or, to make the point in a different way, would they likewise approve of the use of this word 'Imām' as a title for various other religious, social and political leaders in Iran? Such is the inconsistency, in terms both of theory and of tradition, of the views of the so-called 'fundamentalist' Pan-Islamic faction of the People's Revolution.

However, the real nature of the People's Revolution – as opposed to the propagandist claims of its Pan-Islamic faction – may be best understood by a historico-analytical comparison between this and the previous (*Mashrūṭeh*) revolution. On the face of it, the two revolutions were very different in 'ideological' aspirations. This, indeed, is what the Pan-Islamic faction has been both directly and indirectly claiming, to the extent that it has openly tried to rehabilitate, and even raise to the status of martyrdom, Shaikh Fażlullah

Nūrī, a leading *mujtahid* of the time, who was executed by the *Mashrūṭeh* revolutionaries (with the full knowledge *and* approval of most other religious leaders) in 1909, for his active support of Muhammad Ali Shah's despotism in the name of *Mashrū'eh*, or the rule of religious doctrine, and his full involvement in Muhammad Ali's persecution, imprisonment, torture and killing of revolutionary leaders and activists, many of whom had been religious leaders and preachers themselves.[3]

We have already seen that the People's Revolution of 1977–9 was a perfect replica of the *Mashrūṭeh* Revolution in so far as it enjoyed the support of all the urban social classes and political forces and tendencies which were independent from, and opposed to, the despotic state's apparatus and total power. It may further be argued that the ideological framework of the People's Revolution is also perfectly *analogous with*, although not *identical to*, that of the *Mashrūṭeh* Revolution. The latter had been fought, first and foremost, against traditional despotism, which was both at odds with modern political ideas and economic aspirations and contrary to the strict interpretation of the Shī'ite theory of state; and it was led by religious leaders, traditional merchants, and modern intellectual and educated elites. The reason for the movement's ideological domination by these groups, especially after its triumph, was precisely due to the attractiveness of European political views and economic achievements, which – rather naïvely – the majority of the revolutionaries regarded as infallible instruments for the abolition of traditional despotism, and the attainment of rapid social and economic progress. Reżā Shah's pseudo-modernist despotism destroyed a lot of these illusions, and led to the formation of the following ideas and tendencies: the left-wing pseudo-modernism of the Tūdeh Party, which was contemptuous of *all* Iranian social, cultural and religious traditions, as remnants of backwardness and reaction; the 'Iranianism' of the Popular Movement – including its left, even Marxist, wing – led and symbolised by Muṣaddiq, which combined a love of independence and progress with a rational and realistic, not nationalist and romantic, consciousness of the significance of Iranian history, and its cultural norms and values; and the conservative traditionalist tendency, led by landlords and many religious leaders, of differing views, who were in favour of a stabilisation of the post-war *status quo* into an authoritarian, though not despotic, monarchy, in which they themselves would play the largest role. On the fringes of these broad ideological groupings, stood the Shah's as yet unrevealed pseudo-modernist despotic aspirations (together with the Pan-Iranian nationalist, even racist, bands of younger educated zealots), and an insignificant group of Pan-Islamic romantics with unformulated views about the establishment of an Islamic state.

The turn of events finally led to the 1953 *coup d'état*, which was conceived and executed by a coalition of the Shah and the conservative traditionalist forces, aided by technical and material support from the American CIA. The lanlords *as a class*, and the religious leadership *on the whole* were both directly and indirectly involved in the coup, and, especially, in the stabilisation of the régime which it established: in particular, the prominent religious leaders in Qum, Teheran and elsewhere did not raise the faintest protest against it, and even commissioned common preachers, such as Falsafī, to defend it openly and on all occasions; they said nothing about the violence against Muṣaddiq and the masses of his followers; they maintained total silence when large numbers of dedicated and idealistic members of the Tūdeh Party rank and file, and its military network, were imprisoned, tortured and killed, against the laws of the land.

But, perhaps most significant of all, they did not say a single word when the small group of Pan-Islamic zealots, the Fadā'īan-i Islam, were arrested, after an unsuccessful attempt of only *one* of them on the life of Prime Minister Ḥusain 'Alā (their conservative friend, who escaped the attempt with a minor head injury), were secretly 'tried', and were massacred by firing squad. Not even Sayyed Abulqāsim Kāshānī, the most radical of the prominent conservative religious leaders, who had been known to be in some sympathy with the group, made any move before or after this act of perfect official lawlessness; and certainly there was no objection from Sayyed Muhammad Behbahānī and Mirza 'Abdullah Chelsutūni (the powerful and conservative religious leaders of Teheran), or the religious leadership in Qum (see Chs 9 and 10, above).

It was only after the 'resignation' of Ḥusain 'Alā, the old-school conservative politician, and the appointment of Dr Iqbāl in his place, that the conservative traditionalists gradually began to become uneasy about the increasing concentration of power in the hands of the Shah, and his military–bureaucratic apparatus, together with its incipient pseudo-modernist social implications. That is why in 1960, as we saw in Chapter 15 above, Āyatullah Burūjirdī, the only *Marja'al-taqlīd* in the country (though there were others resident in the holy cities of Iraq), who had hitherto refrained from any public interference in matters of the state, issued a *fatvā* (or religious edict) against the marginal tenancy-reform bill which the Shah and Iqbāl had managed to pass through the Iranian parliament, basically for American consumption. Yet, when Amīnī and his group, forced on the Shah by the country's circumstances, as well as their American supporters, sought to carry out a land-distribution programme, the Shah at first closed ranks with his old conservative and traditionalist allies, at least as a tactical measure by which to outmanoeuvre Amīnī. However, once he had realised the risks of failure which this tactic involved, he decided to turn an unexpected somersault and became a White Revolutionary himself. It was at this point that his conservative and traditionalist allies – landlords, as well as conservative religious and political leaders – turned against him. Those thousands of people who were massacred during the revolt of June 1963 were not fighting against distribution of land, or, for that matter, women's suffrage. But the control of their leadership had fallen into the hands of conservative religious leaders, partly because of the helplessness and incapacity of the second National Front leadership, partly because of the undoubted influence of the overall religious framework, and partly because of the financial and communal power of landlords and the religious community.

The Shah eventually managed to silence the landlords as a class, at first by granting major concessions in the Second Stage of the land reform, and, later, by turning many of them into his earliest and most privileged social clientele, through the agency of the increasing oil revenues. But the rift with the religious leadership was quite another matter: they *all* insisted on the retention of their social and economic autonomy from the state, which was contrary to His Majesty's arrogant despotism. The conservatives among them were opposed to any social reform, and the tolerance of *any* modern norms and values, both at the political, and at the social level; and the more enlightened and radical among them were not obscurantists and reactionaries, but – in line with the people at large – were nauseated by the Shah's claim to possession of all power, knowledge, wisdom, and so forth, which involved the wanton destruction of all historical and religious values and traditons, and the forceful superimpositon of his pseudo-modernism in the name of economic development. Therefore, any genuine settlement between the Shah and the religious community as a whole (as well as the entire democratic opposition) would have been the very antithesis of petrolic pseudo-modernist despotism, symbolised by the Shah himself. Meanwhile, conservative religious leaders who had once been disappointed with Muṣaddiq for not taking orders from them, and later cheated by the Shah, their old ally, of their share of power and influence, reached the conclusion that this time they should impose their own direct rule. Such are the social and political origins of the modern Pan-Islamic faction of the revolution, whose claim to have originated from the earlier small group of the Fadā'īān-i Islam (not that this in itself bestows any special honour) has no basis in historical truth.

The People's Revolution was, in the same way as the *Mashrūṭeh* Revolution, fought in the first place against a corrupt, lawless and despotic régime, within an overall religious framework, with the difference that, whereas the old, Qajar despotism had been identified with traditionalism, reaction and backwardness, the new (petrolic), Pahlavi despotism was unmistakably entangled with an extreme form of pseudo-modernism. In the *Mashrūṭeh* Revolution the people struggled both against despotism and for modernisation and progress. In the People's Revolution, they fought both against despotism and for the restoration of their social and cultural identity (i.e. against mindless pseudo-modernism). The hopes of genuine progress against the background of traditionalist despotism had given the upper hand in the *Mashrūṭeh* Revolution to the modern educated leaders, although they, too, had acted within the overall religious framework of that movement. The disillusionment with Pahlavi pseudo-modernism gave the upper hand in the People's Revolution to the religious leadership, although the modern educated and intellectual leaders of this revolution also acted within the broad religious framework in which the struggle was conducted. In the *Mashrūṭeh* Revolution, the people and most of their religious and political leaders pushed aside *Mashrū'eh*, because of its identification with the Qajar *traditionalist* despotism. In the revolution of 1977–9, the people, and most of their religious and political leaders, rejected attempts at a negotiated constitutionalist settlement (which could even have excluded the Shah himself) because of their disillusionment with the Pahlavi *pseudo-modernist* despotism.

The *Mashrūṭeh* Revolution finally led to the restoration of despotism, at least partly because of the zealousness with which its hopes and aspirations for social and economic progress degenerated into a purely formalistic urge – by the pseudo-modernist Right as well as Left – for abandoning the whole of Iran's history in a fruitless emulation of European ideas and techniques. The People's Revolution of 1977–9 now threatens to degenerate into a purely formalistic urge for abandoning the whole of Iran's history to the haphazard whims of the Pan-Islamic zealots. The degeneration of the *Mashrūṭeh* Revolution led from dictatorship to despotism and, with a brief interruption, back to dictatorship, followed by despotism. The Pan-Islamic faction of the recent revolution has already taken significant steps towards the establishment of a dictatorial régime, which – if allowed to succeed – will end up in a new despotism. Neither result was *intended* by those who fought in these two revolutions; and Pan-Islamic despotism would fail as surely as its pseudo-modernist counterpart. Long-term stability and progress can only be achieved by the choice of an *Iranian* social and economic system, which would successfully combine relevant lessons, values and techniques from its own experience – its own history – with suitable ideas and methods adapted from other peoples, including those of European origin, of the Middle and Far East, and of Africa.

The Rise of the Pan-Islamic Dictatorship, March 1978–August 1979

Amid the romantic euphoria that accompanied the retreat of the Bakhtīyār government and the collapse of the army, it was inevitable that Āyatullah Khomainī and the Pan-Islamic faction, which enjoys his blessing, would become the sole inheritors of state power. The Bāzargān cabinet consisted of a few older and middle-aged politicians and activists from his own Freedom Movement, the new National Front, and the Mardum-i Iran (People of Iran) Party, and a number of holders of key posts appointed directly by Khomainī himself: in particular, Dr Ibrāhīm Yazdī, Ṣādiq Quṭbzādeh and Dr 'Abbas Amīr-Intiẓām were appointed by Khomainī as deputy premiers for Revolutionary Affairs, Radio and Television, and Public Relations, respectively. In the first couple of weeks, it looked as if power would be largely in the hands of this cabinet, with occasional, perhaps private, counsel by the

Āyatullah himself. Yet, it soon became clear that even this exclusive cabinet, whose members had had the approval of Khomainī himself, was no more than a helpless puppet, shadowed by a secret Revolutionary Council – made up predominantly of religious leaders and preachers – which would wield the real power.

A large number of former ministers, generals, SAVAK agents, state officials and prominent businessmen during the Shah's régime – including Amīr 'Abbās Hovaidā, Prime Minister between 1964 and 1977, General Ni'matullah Naṣīrī, the notorious SAVAK chief, as well as a few others who had been previously arrested by the Shah and, later, Bakhtīyār – were put on trial in Revolutionary Islamic courts. The judges of these courts still remain unknown, although Shaikh Ṣādiq Khalkhālī has personally admitted being the president of the main Islamic Court in Teheran. From the beginning, the conduct of these courts became a subject of controversy, both in Iran and abroad, for a variety of reasons. First, the judges were unknown; the accused were not allowed to be defended by counsel; the indictments were summary; the charges – typically, 'spreading corruption in the world', waging war against God, his Prophet and the Imām (it is not clear whether this refers to the Twelfth Imām or to Khomainī) – were obscure, in that they referred to no *objective* legal, social or moral criteria; the trials themselves were swift and summary; and there was no provision for appeal. Secondly, the trials, and their sentences, tended to become selective and partial, reflecting personal and factional settlement of past accounts, rather than judicial prosecution and punishment for major crimes: for example, Dr 'Āmeli Teherānī, a former *Majlis* deputy, and cabinet minister only in the last two months of the former régime, was executed for entirely unknown 'crimes'; Senator 'Allāmeh Vahīdī was likewise 'tried' and killed for the 'crime' of having been the official supervisor of the Teheran Mosque and *madriseh* of Sepahsālār under the former régime; airforce general Nādir Jahānbānī was condemned and executed on no specific charges – the daily newspaper *Iṭṭilā'āt* simply referred to him as 'the blue-eyed Iranian general', and mentioned that he owned four horses, whose stable was allegedly furnished with fitted carpets; Parvīz Nīkkhāh, the former star of the Imperial Palace 'conspiracy' trials, who had later joined the régime and become a high official of the state television, was also killed, but a few days later it was unofficially leaked out that his execution had been due to the court's mistake in believing that he had been the writer of the anti-Khomainī article in January 1978! These are just a few of the well-known cases in Teheran alone. It will probably never be known how many truly innocent people lost their lives through private vengeance in provincial towns and cities.

Yet the most serious objection to these trials was the fact that they prevented the full story of the former régime's atrocities and corruption from being told in public and put on record. It is likely that the Pan-Islamic faction was worried lest a few of the prominent defendants would reveal the past cooperation of some prominent (dead or living) religious leaders with the Shah in the 1953 coup, and his post-coup régime. A public trial of at least some of these individuals – for example, the SAVAK chief Naṣīrī, who had been privy to the coup-makers in 1953 – would have blown the lid off the *whole* story since the 1953 coup; and this, for reasons which we have seen already, was not in the interests of the Pan-Islamic faction, whose differences with the Shah dated back only to 1963. It is not surprising that in these past few months the Pan-Islamic leaders, including Khomainī himself, have not lost a single opportunity of downgrading Muṣaddiq and the Popular Movement, even to the extent of saying, in the words of Khomainī, 'They say he nationalised [Iranian] oil. So what? We did not want oil, we did not want independence, we wanted Islam.'

From the very early days, the radio and television networks, now entitled the Voice and Face of the Islamic Revolution, were quickly turned into the voice and face of the Pan-Islamic faction alone – that is, exclusive instruments of state propaganda. This was difficult enough to take for all those other political intellectual and professional groups – including not only the independent Marxist – Leninist Fadā'īān-i Khalq, but even the Muslim Mujāhidīn-i Khalq (both former guerrilla groups) – who had fought in the revolution. However, this state monopoly of radio and television was quickly followed by a concerted campaign against independent newspapers and magazines – for instance, the *Āyandigān* and *Paighām-i Imrūz* dailies, and the *Tehrān-i Muṣavvar* and *Āhangar* weeklies – as well as political newspapers such as *Āzādī* ('Freedom'), the official weekly paper of the National Democratic Front. At the time of writing, twenty-two independent journals have been banned by the Pan-Islamic régime.

The revolutionary and post-revolutionary era saw a proliferation of many political parties and groups: the Radical Movement group, led by Muqaddam Marāgheh'ī, plus the Junbish group, led by Ḥāj-Sayyed-Javādī, and other groups had already been in existence for some time. However, a number of more extensive political groupings and regroupings emerged soon after the revolution: the Islamic Republican Party (led by Sayyed Muhammad Bihishtī), a coalition of the Pan-Islamic forces, together with its extremist wing, the new Fadā'īān-i Islam, which is led by Khalkhālī; the Muslim People's Republican Party, which enjoys the good-will of the Senior *Marja'al-taqlid*, Āyatullah Sharī 'atmadārī, and has a firm base in Azerbijan; the National Democratic Front (NDF), made up of a number of past and newly formed groupings, such as the People's Liberation Front of Iran and the Union of the Left group, but whose main base is probably the reorganised Socialist League, which was once led by Khalīl Malekī. It was originally hoped that the NDF would be much more comprehensive in its coverage, and, in particular, include the two former guerrilla groups. However, for a variety of reasons, these two groups did not join the NDF, although they publicly acclaimed its formation and promised co-operation with it. Only the Tūdeh Party, with its leaders back from east European countries to lead a much reduced and less popular organisation than formerly, had its application to join the NDF turned down.

Early in April 1979 a plebiscite, wrongly described as a referendum, was held for the formal abolition of the existing constitution, and declaration of an Islamic republic. The official claim of 99 per cent support from *the whole of the Iranian electorate* must be taken with a pinch of salt, on elementary principles of statistics; but there can be no doubt that it was given overwhelming popular support. Many political groups and parties had been bitterly complaining that (a) the plebiscite was being unnecessarily rushed, without sufficient time being allowed for discussion and airing of views; (b) in any case, the Pan-Islamic faction alone had had the use of the radio and television networks to present its interpretation of the meaning and implications of an Islamic republic; and (c) the subject of the plebiscite had been undemocratically formulated such that all those who would vote against it could be branded as being pro-Shah, anti-Islamic, or both. As a result, the NDF and the Fādā'īan-i Khalq boycotted the election, and some other political parties, such as the Mujāhidīn-i Khalq, took part in it with reluctance.

The increasingly evident powerlessness of the Bāzargān cabinet, and its domination by Khomainī's nominees, Yazdī and Quṭbzādeh, finally led to the resignation and public protest of Dr Karīm Sanjābī, leader of the new National Front and Foreign Minister, and, later, the quiet departure of Dr Mubash-shirī, another prominent National Front member, who had been Minister of Justice without an effective department. But Dārīyūsh Furūhar, the one-time pro-Muṣaddiq Pan-Iranist leader, stayed on in the cabinet, thereby alienating his group from the National Front, to which it had been affiliated. The Pan-Islamics had already caused a public confrontation with Āyatullah Tāliqānī.

The Pan-Islamists began their 'social reorganisation' by trying to force women to wear the *chādur*, the traditional Iranian 'veil'. This, in fact, is the best example of how the spirit and the methods of the new zealots are perfectly analogous with those of the pseudo-modernist despots, even though they are directed towards totally opposite goals. However, the Iranian women and their various organisations reacted quickly and courageously by holding public meetings, staging demonstrations, and so on. They were attacked by organised thugs and knife-pullers – reminiscent of the types who had been paid to participate in the 1953 coup – and many of them were injured. Yet, sooner rather than later, the zealots beat a retreat and withdrew their 'edict'. Nevertheless, 'unofficial' tauntings, showers of abuse and obscenity, and even mob attacks – all in the name of Islam and morality – have continued to threaten those women who may find themselves in relatively isolated public places.

The régime's military and security arms have been varied, and are becoming relatively specialised in application. The army provides its main source of power in dealing with major regional and ethnic insurgencies. The newly formed Revolutionary Guards make up a paramilitary force which is used in major urban security operations as well as in less important regional tasks. The Khomainī committees, later renamed the Imām's committees (again it is not clear whether the reference is to the Twelfth Imām or to Khomainī), are arbitrary groups with powers of administration and arrests far beyond those of the government departments. They have been involved in the arrest and flogging of many people suspected of drinking alchoholic beverages, petty theft, sexual offences (including youths trying to approach girls), and so forth. In the provinces, there is wholesale arbitrary arrest and assault on people according to the whims of the local preachers leading such committees: for example, there are unofficial reports that fingers have been cut off for attempted petty robbery. In any case, women have been officially executed for prostitution, and there is a total prohibition on the production, sale and consumption (in private) of alchoholic drinks. As a result, a flourishing black market for these drinks has developed, in which highly expensive (and, sometime, poisonous) intoxicating liquids are sold at astronomic prices.

None of these self-righteous and misguided 'policies' is due to the organised chaos which undoubtedly exists everywhere in the country. In one of his earlier speeches, Khomainī himself had declared that, if a few hands were cut off, and a number of people publicly flogged, there would be a complete end to theft, immorality, and so on.[4] At present, the bathing of men and women in the same pool, or off the same beach, is totally banned, on pain of beatings and arrest. Only recently, an all-Armenian swimming pool in Teheran, with official permission for mixed bathing on account of religious freedom for the Christian community, was attacked by a group of thugs, and all the swimmers were subjected to savage beatings by the organised Pan-Islamic mob.

Ethnic and regional minorities of Iran have been a main source of difficulty for the régime: in particular, the Iranian Kurds, Arabs and Turcomans, who have suffered decades of persecution, harassment, extreme economic poverty and total cultural deprivation, had understandably expected to be given a fair hearing on account of their past grievances, and to obtain a basic improvement in their status. In addition, given the fact that these communities (together with the Iranian Baluchis in the south-east) make up the bulk of the Iranian *Sunni* Muslims, they may have been anxious about the attitude of the Pan-Islamic faction, which claims to adhere to Shī'ite Islam. Early clashes between these communities and the new régime were followed by mutual accusations of wanton provocation. What is certain is that the régime's immediate response in all such cases – by accusing the minorities of being 'anti-revolutionary', 'pro-communist', 'pro-American', 'pro-Zionist', and so on – has been both unconciliatory and indicative of a basic lack of sympathy for the grievances of these highly exploited Iranian people.

The combination of all the events, attitudes, methods and 'policies' of the Pan-Islamic faction led to the alienation of most political parties and groups – including the Mujāhidīn-i Khalq, the Muslim People's Republican Party, and the National Front – from the Pan-Islamists, and even Bāzargān's provisional cabinet. In fact, among the larger political parties, it was the Tūdeh Party alone whose leaders – true to their tradition – supported the régime and most of its 'policies'. It can be safely said that their recent inclusion among the political parties incurring the wrath of Khomainī and his men has been earned against their own wishes and despite their sincere loyalty towards the régime.

From the beginning, a major bone of contention has been the nature and content of the new constitution, about which all kinds of conflicting official 'views' have been put out. At any rate, all the various organs of the régime had let it be known that the draft constitution was democratic, would be open to changes by a fully elected constituent assembly, and would later be submitted to a plebiscite in one piece. But, in June 1979, the Pan-Islamists suddenly began to talk about an *appointed* Council of Experts in place of an elected constituent assembly. This was evidence of their warranted fears that they themselves might no longer dominate an elected assembly, through loss of popular support in the country. The decision was denounced by the main political parties, as well as Āyatullah Sharī'atmādārī. The Pan-Islamists partially retreated by deciding on a *select* Council of Experts, of seventy-five members in all, to be elected for the whole of the country. There was simply no justification for this selective procedure for drafting the country's most important single document, which would exclude many millions of people, especially in areas where the Pan-Islamic faction lacks support, from having a say in their future destiny. Consequently, many political parties, including the Muslim People's Republican Party, the NDF and the National Front, boycotted the whole of the shambles.

At the time of writing, with the Council of Experts ostensibly in session, matters have come to a head with the banning of the Kurdish Democratic Party and the independent journals; the warrants issued for the arrest of Hedāyatullah Matīne-Daftary, a leading member of the NDF and Deputy President of the (all-) Iranian Bar Association; the military confrontation in Kurdistan; and so on. The Kurds are familiarly accused of 'anti-revolutionism', 'pro-Zionism', and the like; Matīne-Daftary is held responsible for the large number of casualties of an unprovoked attack by an organised mob of Pan-Islamic zealots on a peaceful protest demonstration held by the NDF; independent newspapers are regarded as enemies of Islam, the 'Imām', and so forth. In a series of recent speeches, Khomainī has declared himself commander-in-chief of the army, and has regretted the fact that the Pan-Islamists did not massacre leading revolutionary politicians and activists, and 'break the pens' of writers, journalists and intellectuals, in the early days. All these people he has described as 'not human beings, but animals'.[5]

It now looks as if a democratic settlement and stabilisation of the social and political situation in Iran is no longer possible. The Pan-Islamic faction has forced an open confrontation with most other political forces and their parties, which the latter had desperately tried to avoid. This is clear evidence that the Pan-Islamists are frightened of losing the democratic contest to others, because of their own lack of appropriate ideas, administrative capacity and the necessary flexibility for governing the country. It follows that the Pan-Islamic rule cannot last for long in its present form: it will either have to retreat and conclude a genuine compromise with the democratic groups; or consolidate its position with a view to the formation of a petrolic Pan-Islamic despotism; or lose both popularity and power to other political forces. The first possibility is unlikely, because of the experience of the past few months; the second possibility is also unlikely, because, however they may wish it, the Pan-Islamists do not possess the necessary political ability; and the last possibility is more likely, although not inevitable: a lot will depend on the conduct of the other political parties, their tactics and strategies, their sense of realism, and the degree of genuine co-operation between them.

The reader may not be surprised to learn that, among all Iranian political tendencies, the most popular theory now circulating with regard to past events and future prospects identifies the role of foreign powers – and especially America – as the primary determinant: the Pan-Islamists accuse their opponents of being agents of Zionism, American imperialism, and the Soviet Union; their opponents also believe that the Pan-Islamic leaders are agents of American imperialism! History will doubtless prove both views to be mistaken.[6] There is no doubt, as has been repeatedly affirmed throughout this book, that foreign powers, including America, are not standing idly by, and that they will do their best to safeguard their local and global interests as far as they possibly can, although they too have made many mistakes in the past and may do the same in the future. There are two fundamentally different ways of judging the role of foreign powers, in Iran and elsewhere, even on the basis of the same factual information: one is to believe that, at any given moment, governments or their political opponents are no more than agents of America or wherever, receiving their 'orders' from their masters and/or taking their decisions with their counsel and approval – this, in general, is a complete myth, although these powers have their own individual agents everywhere; the other view is that the indigenous governments and their opponents are primarily agents of their own ideas, ambitions, interests and socio-economic base, which they try to promote through tactics and strategies that include their attitude towards, and relations with, various foreign interests.

For this reason, a realistic view of the role of foreign powers in domestic political games can be taken by *either* party anywhere, without necessarily turning them into foreign agents and puppets, or mortgaging to various imperialists the country's political independence and economic riches. The Nicaraguan revolutionaries were not agents of America. But, as a result of realistic, wise, as well as independent and sovereign, conduct, they forced the Americans to accept the fact that it would be against their own interests to continue to support Somoza. Admittedly, this analysis is not so readily reducible to simple slogans which would move emotional crowds to loud cheers. Loud cheers are, however, useful only as long as the cheering crowd is being led, *not* followed, by the political leaders – whatever the movement. It is one thing to use political slogans, simple concepts and ideas, in order to communicate with the masses of the people in ways which they can readily understand; but it is something very different for their leadership itself to know no better than those simple categories – to become a victim of its own propaganda. One would hope, although with few illusions, that in the Iranian school of political theory and experience this lesson will at last be learnt. But, of course, old habits – including habits of thought – die hard.

A Longer View for the Iranian Political Economy

The Iranian political economy is in need of a basic reconstruction which is absolutely vital for its long-term peace, stability and progress, regardless of the political party, tendency, creed or ideology which may happen to hold the reins of power. Any dogmatic experimentation, the uncritical application of a total abstract framework, imported or concocted, is doomed to failure, and that includes the pseudo-modernisms of both Right and Left, and the pseudo-traditionalism of Pan-Islamists and their likes. What the country cannot afford is the superimposition of the ill-conceived beliefs of any bunch of frustrated zealots who may, consciously or unconsciously, believe that the main problem for success is the maintenance, or seizure, of political power alone. Likewise, an entirely *ad hoc* approach to the country's problems would not be commensurate with the enormous, and complex, difficulties which the political economy confronts. What is needed is a combination of a broader vision with objective realism, of general theories modified by past and present experiences, in order to put the country back on its feet within a socially acceptable framework.

It is true that the present rulers of the country, including their powerless executive cabinet, could not have achieved a great deal in the past six months. But what is significant is that their *attitudes, methods and decisions*, have already revealed that, neither in terms of ideas nor with regard to administrative ability are they able to face up to the tasks which require urgent, efficient and productive application. Up to now, most of their decisions have betrayed a combination of dogmatic idealism and practical inability, which are normally two sides of the same coin. The country is in political and administrative chaos; the heads of government and provincial departments, of state industries, banks, corporations and other services, are still appointed in the ultra-centralist style of Darius I's administrative system; the economy is in a complete shambles, with a third of the whole labour force (and a half of the urban labour force) unemployed, the rate of inflation (especially food prices) soaring, aggregate demand deficient, the rate of home production significantly below capacity, agriculture and the peasantry in a plight, the modern educated groups leaving the country as fast as they can obtain foreign visas, and the oil revenues still pouring in as the only instrument which keeps the show going.

The recent nationalisation of private banks, insurance companies and a few, mainly heavy, industrial concerns cannot even be regarded as propagandist window-dressing: many of these firms were heavily indebted to the state, in some cases even beyond the total value of their assets; many of their owners, or main shareholders – who had already escaped the country before the final collapse – were corrupt financiers and intermediaries of the Shah, his family or his state machine; and, in any case, a mere transfer of ownership, or replacement of one boss by another, would earn the economy absolutely nothing in terms of output and employment. This is not intended as an argument against the extension of public ownership wherever appropriate, if only because many of the 'nationalised' firms had been already mortgaged to large state loans. Rather, it is meant to emphasise the point that what the country requires is not superficial manoeuvres, but substantial politiconomic decisions.

In the realm of political as well as economic management, the country is in urgent need of a comprehensive democratisation of the administrative and productive processes. This would imply a strategy for the decentralisation of management and decision-making, both geographically and bureaucratically. Iran is still a country in which even the governors of small towns in distant places are virtually sent from Teheran, or a major provincial capital, by direct appointment, and the manager of a small branch bank in a rural township is, likewise, virtually appointed by the bank chairman in Teheran; and this goes for all other institutions, including education, finance, and so forth. It is also a country in which, down to the present day, the directors and managers of state firms and enterprises – be they banks, insurance companies, steel plants, or whatever – are appointed by the cabinet, and/or other powers that be, without consultation with the permanent staff of those concerns. Furthermore, the hierarchy of power and decision-making, not only in government departments but even in these 'public' business concerns, resembles a Victorian military chain of command, rather than a civilian framework for the production of goods and services. Like the people of the country at large, the 'civil servants' and other state employees enjoy little freedom and, therefore, accept no responsibility. Consequently, there is little motivation or sense of commitment and duty; and the public, in whose name all these 'services' are rendered, receives the same treatment from the petty bureaucrats as they themselves receive from their own bosses. It is a long and involved story, a full discussion of which would demand a separate treatise. But, perhaps these brief references will suffice for all those who care to see the problem.

It follows that, in an attempt to solve some of these problems, two major, and complementary, sets of decisions must be taken and implemented. First, there must be a decentralisation of the administrative system across the whole country. This would entail (a) a remapping of the country's administrative regions – which, in their present form, were intended to serve the stranglehold of the centre over the regions – so that they have socio-culturally meaningful, or 'natural', boundaries, and the cultural homogeneity and identity of the various Iranian communities may be brought out rather than submerged; (b) a gradual, but earnest, democratisation of provincial governments with the strategic aim of making these regional governments fully representative some time in the near future; and (c) a separate arrangement, involving measures of home rule, for ethnic Iranian communities, including the Arabs, the Kurds, the Turcomans, the Baluchis, and others, each according to their different needs, requirements and aspirations. Clearly, these are no more than the basic heads of a programme which would require substantial consultation and negotiation before being given effect, if its application is to be beneficial to the whole of the country and its people.

Secondly, there must be a democratisation of the hierarchy of the state, its executive departments and its business enterprises. This would involve: (a) the formulation of a new, and workable, civil-service code aimed at the creation of a permanent civil service up to, and including, the highest ranks immediately below the cabinet ministers, their *political* deputies, and under-secretaries; (b) a real change in the status of civil servants from the age-old 'lackeys of the state' (*nawkarān-i dawlat*), to responsible servants of the people with commensurate rights and obligations, which, among other things, would require a genuine delegation of power, responsibility and dignity to the various ranks; (c) a similar democratisation of, and delegation of responsibility to, the central-government offices in provincial towns and cities, together with a conscious attempt at ensuring that most of the officials are appointed from among the local people themselves; (d) the grant of a large amount of managerial independence to state firms, plants and corporations, with even greater measures for the participation of their senior and junior employees in the administrative and production processes.

The two sets of major democratisation strategies described above would ensure the long-term integrity of the whole country, the democratic participation of all the people in their own local affairs, an efficient system of central-government administration, a productive use of public industries and services, a greater regional balance in terms of income and status, a much weaker motivation for the concentration of the country's capital and human resources in Teheran and a few other major cities, a much greater sense of commitment, responsibility and 'job satisfaction' among all public employees, and a much smaller sense of public frustration either with a soulless bureaucracy or with an impersonal machine monopolising all power in the centre of the country.

The short-term economic measures for the promotion of production and employment are so obvious that they are not worth a brief discussion, even in spite of the apparent incapacity of the country's present rulers to grasp and implement them, instead of the economically feeble, socially destructive and politically corrupt policy of direct and indirect hand-outs of the oil revenues to those people, employed or unemployed, who are expected to provide mass audiences for the country's rulers, or attack the peaceful demonstrations of their critics. What is of much more significance is a longer-term politiconomic strategy for the country's economic and social progress. However, in case the following facts, together with their politiconomic significance, have not yet become obvious, it should be pointed out that (a) more than a third of Iran's national income is earned from the sale of oil products, and received *directly by the state*; (b) the country's other energy and mineral resources, especially gas and copper, which are actually not insignificant, and potentially enormous, *are also owned entirely by the state*; (c) nearly all the modern large-scale industries of various kinds, the means of transport and communications, as well as banking, insurance and other concerns, *are likewise wholly or mainly owned by the state*; (d) there are still a sizeable number of rural properties, farms and agri-businesses *which, too, are owned by the state*; (e) over 90 per cent of the proceeds of the country's exports *are received by the state*; (f) and the 'private' sector as a whole – i.e. the peasant smallholders, shareholders in farm corporations, rural handicrafts industries, private wholesalers, retailers, urban artisans, private workshops, small industrial and service firms, and so on – claim less than 20 per cent of the national income, and even less of the country's total assets. *It should therefore be clear that – unlike in nineteenth-century England, and similar societies then and now – the primary politiconomic question is not so much a problem of private* versus *public ownership as a question of what economic strategies should be pursued, and democratisation policies implemented, in order to achieve long-term progress, and enable the masses of the people both to participate in running, and to enjoy the fruits of, what they are already supposed to own collectively.*

The country's basic long-term politiconomic requirements are, very briefly, as follows: (a) the creation of an alternative export sector which would reduce the economy's dependence on oil as well as other mineral exports; (b) the promotion and diversification of domestic output in order to reduce the country's dependence on imports of consumer goods, intermediate products, and capital machinery, in that order; (c) a sustained growth rate of the national income and living standards which would be consistent with the country's politiconomic capacity to absorb, without leading to the creation of major economic or sociological bottlenecks and frictions; (d) a direct and indirect redistribution of income, education, health and other social goods to the poorer sectors of the economy, regions of the country and classes of the community.

An earnest desire to achieve the above basic goals would include the following main strategies: (a) investment in many of the local, labour-intensive industries, and attempts at their renovation and modernisation on the basis of existing techniques and skills, and investment in basic consumer products, both old and new, which are objects of consumption by the masses – including not only textiles, home appliances and suchlike goods, but also education and health services, housing and so forth, *for the masses*; (b) a complete redistribution of land among the peasantry with the provision of financial, technical and other extension services in an unbureaucratic fashion, including schemes for co-operation in production and/or distribution suitable to different regions and crops, and long-term channels and facilities for the movement into other productive activities, including rural industrial production, of surplus agricultural labour – for instance, the children of peasant households who, if they stayed on the household farm, would be the cause of its division into uneconomic units of production (it is perhaps worth emphasising that this general approach to the reorganisation of Iranian agriculture need not result in the creation of 'rural capitalism', because (i) the emphasis would be on the use of household labour, rather than the employment of landless wage-labour, (ii) we are talking about *52 per cent* of the population, who, at present, claim *less than 10 per cent* of the national income and, (iii) even the Soviet collectivisation of agriculture was dictated neither by irrelevant romanticism, nor by an 'ideological' urge to emulate the past experiences of other countries, but by the strategic objective of capital accumulation for rapid industrialisation, and it is probably clear that Iran is in no need of squeezing a much poorer peasantry than its former Soviet counterpart in order to acquire a surplus for investment in urban industry); (c) investment in industries in which the country can reasonably compete in the regional (Middle Eastern), as well as the world, market; (d) rational and realistic attempts at the extension of the country's heavy industrial and engineering base, using a selective and discriminatory approach that would avoid acute shortages of skilled labour and the production of expensive and inefficient products with few customers; (e) conscious attempts to develop the country's existing technology and skills either independently or, if this is not possible, with the help of appropriate modern technology developed in advanced countries (taking care to avoid the wholesale and indiscriminate superimposition, as opposed to careful application and adaptation, of imported technology); (f) the creation of regional and provincial economic balance and complementarities, by a suitable diversification of industrial location across the land; (g) investment in *universal* free education and health facilities (including the provision of adequate sewerage, and the like), to promote literacy, numeracy and the maximum freedom from disease; (h) an appropriate use of various general and local taxes for the prevention of socially damaging high consumption by favoured minorities, and unreasonable accumulation of personal wealth.

The above suggestions make up no more than a basic outline; nor do they promise the attainment of the millennium. They are merely intended to serve as guidelines for the kind of attitudes, methods and strategies that are essential if any real progress is to be made in that direction. Indeed, the object of all the facts, arguments, analyses and theories presented in this book is simply to suggest a framework within which a combination of reason and reality may finally jolt the Iranian political economy out of its past unhappiness, and afford to a people who have periodically been ready to offer so much of their blood a reasonable return for their priceless sacrifices. What remains must be left to the judgement of history, and those who care to take the relevant lessons from it. For, as the apposite Persian verse has it,

> The tale of our good and our evil will be writ,
> For history has a book, a pad, a page.

NOTES

1. See the abstract (in Persian) of Dr Sādiqī's lecture in the Maison de l'Italie, Cité Université, Paris, 4 Nov 1978.
2. See his interview with *Parkhāsh* (weekly newspaper), 25 July 1979. A comparison of the wording of Khādemī's argument with Sādiqī's abstract cited above gives the impression that they are based on a single original source. Āyatullah Khomainī has himself written a book entitled *Vilāyat-i Faqīh* ('Government by the Theologian'), but this is now difficult to find, and I have not managed to consult a copy. But both he and members of his entourage have repeatedly contrasted 'the rule of God over the people' to 'the rule of the people over the people' (i.e. democracy). The crucial questions that remain unanswered is *how* God manifests his rule over the people, and *how* any one can claim to represent that rule, assuming that the mere seizure of worldly power, and its maintenance by the use of weapons (made in non-Islamic countries), is not a sufficient proof of such a mission. More than six centuries ago, the Iranian chronicler Ḥamdullah Mustawfī, who was a Sunni Muslim, pointed to this issue by saying that the Umayyids' claim to Islamic rule was based on their political – military power and nothing else (see his *Tārīkh-i Guzīdeh*). The problem is much wider than the present issue: for example, on seizing power, a certain political party claiming to 'represent' workers and peasants could set up a 'workers' state' and exclude all others (including the workers themselves) from genuine participation in the processes of political decision-making, because workers-as-a-whole, *as an abstract concept*, could nowhere be found to confirm or refute the party's claim to be representing the proletariat.
3. See Ch. 4, above.
4. 'If the hands of four thieves are cut off in public, [robbery] would come to an end. If four people guilty of prostitution were subjected to whipping, prostitution would disappear from society . . . .' See *Āyandigān* (daily newspaper) 3 July 1979.
5. The blanket term 'Pan-Islamic faction' is intended to cover all the various Islamic tendencies which have been using Khomainī as a symbol of their claim to power. However, the faction consists of many different, sometimes conflicting, tendencies, as well as individuals competing for power. At present, the only factor which binds them together is their collective attempt to exclude all the other political tendencies, including senior Shī'ite leaders such as Sharī'atmadārī, whose views are in fact much more consistent with the traditional theory and practice of Shī'ism. The currently dominant group within the faction is the secret organisation *Amal*, which is apparently concerned more with the establishment of its own Islamic state in Iran than with seriously participating in a global Pan-Islamic movement.

6. In a speech to his followers in Paris (delivered on 24 December 1978 and published for circulation), Āyatullah Khomainī said, 'Many of the [political] parties which have appeared in Iran since the beginnings of *Mashrūteh* have, so far as one can tell, been founded – without their followers' knowledge – by the hands of others [i.e. foreigners]. I think it is probable that in the powerful countries of the time, for example Britain, they set up parties in order to deceive the backward countries which they wanted to use. . . . Of course, a civilised country must have parties; we too must have parties. But the parties which have so far appeared in our country are such that they spend all their time fighting one another. I think that, in Iran, parties were first created in this way. Now, they have acquired other forms. One even observes that these parties treat each other like enemies, and oppose each other. I think it probable that a hand from outside [the country] is involved' (*Matn-i Sukhnrānī-yi Qā'id-i Buzurg-i Islām, Imām Khomainī, Madda Ẓillihu*). If modern educated and progressive Iranians find these views unacceptable, then it would be only fair for them to reflect on some of their own cherished ideas, which, though they may appear to be a little more subtle and wrapped in 'ideological' jargon, betray a basically similar political vision.

Index